Archaeology & Cu Resource Management

MW00811209

Contributors

Pat Barker
Nevada State Museum and Department of Anthropology,
University of Nevada, Reno

Sarah T. Bridges
US Department of Agriculture, Natural Resources Conservation Service

Susan M. Chandler
Alpine Archaeological Consultants, Inc., Montrose, Colorado

David Colin Crass
Georgia State Historic Preservation Office

Hester A. Davis
Arkansas Archaeological Survey and Department of Anthropology,
University of Arkansas, Fayetteville

T. J. Ferguson
Anthropological Research, LLC, Tucson, Arizona, and School of Anthropology,
University of Arizona

Julia A. King
Department of Anthropology, St. Mary's College of Maryland

William D. Lipe
Department of Anthropology, Washington State University

Douglas P. Mackey, Jr.
New York State Office of Parks, Recreation, and Historic Preservation

Lynne Sebastian
SRI Foundation, Rio Rancho, New Mexico

Archaeology & Cultural Resource Management

Visions for the Future

Edited by Lynne Sebastian and William D. Lipe

SAR
PRESS

School for Advanced Research Press
Santa Fe

School for Advanced Research Press

Post Office Box 2188
Santa Fe, New Mexico 87504-2188
www.sarpress.sarweb.org

Managing Editor: Lisa Pacheco
Manuscript Editor: Jane Kepp
Designer and Production Manager: Cynthia Dyer
Proofreader: Kate Whelan
Indexer: Catherine Fox
Printer: Cushing-Malloy, Inc.

Library of Congress Cataloging-in-Publication Data:

Archaeology & cultural resource management : visions for the future / edited by Lynne Sebastian
and William D. Lipe. — 1st ed.
    p. cm. — (Advanced seminar series / School for Advanced Research)
    Includes bibliographical references and index.
    ISBN 978-1-934691-16-8 (alk. paper)
    1. Archaeology—United States—Forecasting. 2. Archaeology—Government policy—United States.
    3. Archaeology—Social aspects—United States. 4. Cultural property—Protection—United States.
    5. Historic sites—Conservation and restoration—United States. 6. United States—Antiquities—
Collection and preservation. 7. United States—Cultural policy. I. Sebastian, Lynne.
II. Lipe, William D. III. Title: Archaeology and cultural resource management.
    E159.5.A675 2009
    930.1—dc22
                        2009035654

Cover illustration: Excavation in progress at LA 25860, Sandoval County, New Mexico.
Photo © Office of Contract Archeology, University of New Mexico. Used with permission.

To Charles R. McGimsey III—the "other" CRM,
in gratitude for his support and advice
and for his decades of leadership in the field of
cultural resource management.
Every place we went, we found his footprints.

Contents

Figures

Tables

Acronyms

ACHP	Advisory Council on Historic Preservation
ACRA	American Cultural Resources Association
ARPA	Archeological Resources Protection Act (1979)
CRM	Cultural resource management
NAGPRA	Native American Graves Protection and Repatriation Act (1990)
NCHRP	National Cooperative Highway Research Program
NEPA	National Environmental Policy Act (1969)
NHL	National historic landmark
NHPA	National Historic Preservation Act (1966)
NRHP	National Register of Historic Places ("the register")
RPA	An archaeologist who is registered with the Register of Professional Archaeologists ("the Register")
SAA	Society for American Archaeology
SHA	Society for Historical Archaeology
SHPO	State historic preservation officer
THPO	Tribal historic preservation officer

Foreword

Charles R. McGimsey III

This book addresses some of the still unresolved problems in cultural resource management (CRM) archaeology that were raised by participants in a series of seminars held in 1974 at a Virginia retreat called Airlie House. Even more, it concentrates on others that have arisen since that time. Volumes such as this often can be evaluated on the basis of questions they call to our attention, as well as those they help to resolve. Such is the case here. I would like to discuss, briefly, some of the questions brought to mind when I read these stimulating chapters.

Hester Davis establishes beyond a reasonable doubt that archaeologists are a retrospective lot, almost as fond of analyzing their own discipline as they are of analyzing earlier cultures. She lists a number of such studies made in the time between the Airlie House conference and the one resulting in this volume. I know of no follow-up analysis of these studies. Because they were conducted by some of the best minds in the business, I think it would behoove us to get someone to do such an analysis, reviewing which ideas have been developed repeatedly but not pursued, and why; which have been pursued and what the outcomes were; and so forth. Such an in-depth review might be revealing. Dave Crass, for example, provides in his chapter an interesting study along these lines, looking at the recommendations made in the Airlie House report with regard to communications.

Sarah Bridges presents a helpful review of the various codes of ethics published by individual archaeological societies. But to me, the most interesting section of her chapter is the one in which she elaborates on Chip Colwell-Chanthaphonh and T. J. Ferguson's work, bringing out how essential it is to establish trust among all the entities involved in CRM archaeology. She cites several examples that illustrate this, and at least half the other chapters touch on its importance. I can also testify to this from my experience in

Arkansas. When the Arkansas Archeological Survey was being established, the various educational institutions at which the Survey archaeologists would be based wanted an agency designated that would be responsible for evaluating the Survey's performance. Having worked closely with the Arkansas Archeological Society for years while getting the state legislature to establish the Survey, we knew that the Society could be relied upon to support good archaeology. Therefore, we took the unusual step of proposing that the enabling legislation direct the Society, representing the state's avocational archaeologists, to provide the public with an annual evaluation of the performance of the professional archaeologists working for the Survey. The successful operation of such an overview program—and it has been very successful—obviously requires trust and mutual respect between the professional and the avocational archaeologists in the state.

I found Bill Lipe's chapter 3 on management particularly stimulating and illuminating. We had all discussed management as applied to archaeological resources, even before the Airlie House seminar crystallized the concept, but until now no one has dealt satisfactorily with exactly what archaeological management encompasses. Some have maintained that there is no such thing as resource management by archaeologists, arguing that management is conducted only by those who own or control the land. They forget that decisions are (or should be) based on information, and only if that information is adequate and properly used in decision-making is there any hope that a decision will be appropriate. In short, the archaeologist's information is an essential and integral part of the decision. And so is the archaeologist. Lipe spells out in abundant detail precisely what this information can and should be, thereby performing an invaluable service. Indeed, it is difficult to believe that it was not provided sooner.

Lipe also correctly points out the vital role played by what he calls "investigator-initiated research"—that is, research carried out by people often labeled with the more restricted term *academics*. But for some reason it has not been pointed out that these investigators are working with the same restricted database as are all other archaeologists. The time is long past—and indeed never actually existed—when, from a management perspective, archaeology conducted under contract is any different from that carried out by academic investigators. We must strip ourselves of the delusion that academic investigators, when making decisions affecting the resource base, are managing that resource to a lesser extent than are contract archaeologists. In fact, academic investigators have an unlimited choice of problem and area and a much greater ethical responsibility to achieve the best possible management results from the resource base because of their freedom to choose both problem and place. The discipline cannot afford, for example, to have an investigator choose to excavate the sandbox in the yard at an eighteenth-century house site, the last of its kind in the state, because a test revealed the possible presence of a large number of exotic toys—the investigator's favorite subject since childhood—while the house site itself is destroyed by vandals. Neither can we afford to have a contract archaeologist arbitrarily decide to use the available funds to completely excavate the living room and a corner of the kitchen when it is possible to use the funds to sample the entire house.

I use these examples to emphasize an essential point. Although a case can be made that archaeologists are still sufficiently ignorant of the total database that a skilled manipulator can justify to himself digging almost anywhere, it is time we acknowledge that the eternal limitations of time, money, and personnel require that all field research, by whomever it is conducted, be designed in accordance with the best possible management plan.

I have frequently stated that there is no such thing as private archaeology. I hope the arguments presented here and throughout the rest of this volume demonstrate, too, that there should be no such thing as a "private archaeologist." Archaeologists must at all times endeavor to derive maximum public benefit from their research.

In her chapter 5, Lynne Sebastian criticizes reliance on the criterion of eligibility for nomination to the National Register of Historic Places as the sole mechanism for determining which sites will be given further attention and which will be ignored in complying with Section 106 of the National Historic Preservation Act. As a substitute, she suggests establishing criteria based on significance as viewed in the context of a broad-based regional summary, although she does not develop in detail the exact mechanisms to be used in developing this transition.

This brings me to a final point. The discipline of archaeology has progressed beyond having to create new laws or change existing ones. The "significance approach" Sebastian recommends would require changing National Park Service guidelines, but the other changes recommended in this book can be accomplished by modifying the actions or attitudes of archaeologists themselves. We do not need to change laws in order to develop adequate guidelines for the description of collections being curated. It takes a change in attitude by archaeologists to implement trust;

it cannot be legislated. In short, the discipline itself bears almost total responsibility for achieving the operational changes necessary to improve the future of CRM archaeology.

Even in cases in which outside entities would have to make the needed changes—for example, in the National Park Service guidelines just mentioned—this can best be achieved through intense peer pressure by all archaeologists. What is most needed now is for the discipline of archaeology to become a unified force of acknowledged professionals. Once that is achieved, archaeologists as a group will be in a position to exert peer pressure on individual archaeologists to perform always in a professional manner. Such unity will also enable archaeologists to exhibit the united front that is so essential if the profession is to successfully confront other entities and get them to modify their ways appropriately. To achieve this unified front, it is necessary only for individual archaeologists to join the relevant societies (primarily the Society for American Archaeology, the Society for Historical Archaeology, the Archaeological Institute of America, and the American Cultural Resources Association) and, if qualified, register with the Register of Professional Archaeologists. Only when we enable these organizations to speak with the force of all of us can they bring about the changes now needed to improve our discipline. It can be done. It must be done.

Archaeology & Cultural Resource Management

1

The Future of CRM Archaeology

Lynne Sebastian

Sometimes the idea behind a book grows slowly through the accretion of experiences and thoughts over a long period. At other times, the idea of the book crystallizes in a single moment. This book is of the latter sort, and the idea arose from an assignment I was given for a symposium in honor of Bill Lipe at the 2002 Society for American Archaeology (SAA) meetings in Denver. The organizers asked me to speak about the influence of Bill's 1974 paper "A Conservation Model for American Archaeology" on the subsequent direction of archaeology in the field of cultural resource management (CRM).

In my chapter in the book that grew out of that symposium (Matson and Kohler 2006), I noted: "Reading the article again, I was immediately struck by the congruence between Lipe's vision for the future, as described in the article, and current historic preservation practice. I was also struck by the continuity between many of the problems that Lipe identified in 1974 and the problems that still vex us in CRM archaeology today" (Sebastian 2006:109). While preparing the chapter, I also realized that "the kind of broad-scale, long-range vision that Lipe articulated in this article is extremely rare in CRM archaeology today. We have become so bogged down in the regulations and guidance and standards, in the business and the practice of CRM, that we fail to pause periodically and ask critical questions: Are we where we want to be, where we need to be in CRM archaeology? What are the major directions we should take as a discipline? What are the problems we will need to solve over the next 30 years?" (Sebastian 2006:124–125).

I formed, at that moment, a plan for bringing together a set of colleagues with great depth and variety of experience in the field of CRM archaeology, locking them up somewhere beautiful, feeding them great food, and coaxing from them a vision for the future of our profession.

This is not, of course, to imply that no one else is thinking about visions for the future. In one of a number of recent examples, one of the contributors to this book, Julia King, with William Lees, organized and subsequently published an excellent forum discussion among colleagues in historical archaeology (Lees and King 2007). This discussion asked whether the public was getting its money's worth from CRM and what could be done to improve the cost–benefit ratio. Despite such examples, it seems to me that the "broad scale, question everything, and think big" style of introspection that characterized the early years of CRM archaeology has become exceedingly rare and needs to be revived.

Without question, it would be valuable to identify needed changes and develop a vision for the future of cultural resource management in general, but in this book we have chosen to focus on archaeology rather than try to tackle the whole field at once. The problems and issues faced by those who deal with the built environment are very different from the problems and issues encountered in dealing with the archaeological record, and both differ from the problems and issues surrounding traditional cultural places or cultural landscapes.

ARCHAEOLOGY AND PUBLIC POLICY: A NEW VISION FOR THE FUTURE

With Bill Lipe serving as my co-organizer, I was fortunate to secure support from the School of American Research (SAR; now renamed the School for Advanced Research on the Human Experience) for an advanced seminar titled "Archaeology and Public Policy: A Vision for the Future," which was held in July 2007. SAR not only met the "beautiful place and great food" criteria admirably but also gave us the luxury of spending an entire week discussing and pondering a topic about which all the participants felt passionate. In addition, we had the honor of being chosen as the first Douglas W. Schwartz Advanced Seminar in Anthropological Archaeology. This biennial seminar series celebrates Doug Schwartz's 34 years of service to SAR. Even better, from our perspective, our selection as a Schwartz Seminar meant that Doug sat in on many of our discussions and gave us the benefit of his broad and always thoughtful perspective on our deliberations.

My approach to inviting the other eight seminar participants was to select people who had a great deal of practical experience with compliance and cultural resource management archaeology, either in agencies or as consultants, or both. I wanted people who had strong ideas and were willing to let go of "how we've always done it" and think about "how it should be." I wanted people who could write and people with whom I could be locked up in the SAR seminar house in Santa Fe for a week without contemplating either homicide or suicide.

Beyond that, I took a simple, Noah-like approach: two federal agency archaeologists, two state historic preservation office archaeologists, two CRM business owners, and Bill Lipe and Hester Davis to serve as CRM archaeology elders and provide both "institutional memory" and new perspectives. I also wanted someone with experience in tribal CRM programs and tribal issues, and a balance between easterners and westerners. The practice and realities of CRM archaeology are very different in the American West, with its arid environment and vast tracts of public land, and the East, with its heavy vegetation, dense population, and largely private land tenure.

When our "ark" was populated, we worked together to identify a set of basic topics to be addressed at the seminar. Each participant not only provided thoughts on critical issues but also queried his or her network of colleagues for additional suggestions. Eventually we settled on the following:

- Significance, information potential, and eligibility—how can we do a better job of evaluating the significance of archaeological sites?
- Mitigation, excavation, and research—how can we learn more for the money being expended?
- Preserving sites, conserving sites, and learning about the past—where is the balance?
- Managing the past—what are the appropriate roles of agencies, reviewers, consultants, professional organizations, and tribes and other descendant communities?
- Disseminating what we have learned—who controls the data? How do we deal with the gray literature? How do we maximize public access and benefits?

After everyone had carved out his or her seminar topic, we found that we had done a surprisingly thorough job of covering these organizing concepts and several other important issues as well. With only 10 people and strict page limits on our book, we could not possibly cover everything, and indeed the book was not intended to be the encyclopedia of CRM archaeology. We all chose to cover what we knew best and felt most strongly about. Two important topics that we ultimately chose not to address were the curation crisis and the issue of how to prepare students for career paths in CRM, as opposed to academic, archaeology. Although these are critical issues for the future of CRM archaeology, they are so broad and complex that they would easily fill whole volumes. Fortunately, both topics are also being addressed in a variety of other venues.[1]

In addition, as one of our reviewers pointed out, we have not focused heavily on technology. Fieldwork, analysis, planning, and information management and dissemination have all benefited enormously from technological advances over the past 20 years. Some of the most intractable problems in CRM archaeology—access to the gray literature, for example—may finally become manageable through the miracles of digital technology. As generally seems to be the case, however, these modern miracles generate their own sets of problems. For example, with more and more archaeological data being collected, manipulated, and stored in digital form only, how do we ensure that these data remain readable and accessible over the long term?[2]

The topics we chose to cover, which represent the basic processes and decisions of CRM archaeology, have received less broad-scale scrutiny within the profession than have the issues of curation and education. The bureaucratization of CRM archaeology has become so entrenched that many practitioners not only find it difficult to examine the process critically and envision substantive change but even feel threatened by the very ideas of critique and change. Federal agencies have periodically sponsored efforts to reimagine or reinvent the compliance process, but these efforts tend to focus on details and try to retrofit and readapt existing components of the process. They rarely or never question the viability of those components in the context of the process as a whole. My instruction to the seminar group was that the deck chairs on our ark did not require rearranging; our job was to apply critical evaluation and creativity to the larger issues of how and why we do archaeology in the public sector.

We gave our seminar the working title "Archaeology and Public Policy: A Vision for the Future" because we wanted to emphasize the publicly funded nature of CRM and the critical need to maximize both the public benefits and the professional quality of CRM archaeology. By most estimates, as much as 90 percent of the archaeology done in the United States today is carried out in the field of cultural resource management. The impact of this work on the archaeological record, the archaeological profession, and the heritage of the American people would be difficult to overemphasize. CRM archaeology affects a wide range of federally funded or authorized developments. It influences the way we educate our students, work with indigenous people, and curate field records and artifacts. It has yielded an enormous wealth of data on which many recent advances in our understanding of North American archaeology depend. This is "public" archaeology in the clearest sense of the word: it is done because of federal law and policy, and it is funded directly or indirectly by the public.

PUBLIC POLICY AND THE LEGISLATIVE UNDERPINNINGS OF CRM ARCHAEOLOGY

Everything we do in CRM archaeology is based on and should be (but often is not) informed by the laws that mandate consideration and protection of the nation's heritage. Too often we become mired in the minutia of "compliance" with the law and lose sight of the central issue of "intent." Why are we doing this in the first place?

The Antiquities Act of 1906, the first historic preservation law in this country, established the principle that the federal government has a legitimate interest in protecting archaeological sites on public land from unauthorized excavation. The Antiquities Act established federal control over the archaeological record on public land and had an enormous effect on subsequent developments in historic preservation law in the United States. It did not, however, establish an explicit federal policy with regard to preservation or state why preservation matters.

The first national policy statement about the value of the country's historic heritage appeared in statute nearly 75 years ago in the Historic Sites Act of 1935. This law, which institutionalized within the National Park Service many of the New Deal programs pertaining to history and archaeology, begins with a simple declaration: "It is hereby declared that it is a national policy to preserve for public use historic sites, buildings, and objects of national significance for the inspiration and benefit of the people of the United States." Every historic preservation law enacted since then has begun at the same place: preservation of the national heritage in the public interest. The Historic Sites Act goes on to establish programs and procedures that appear repeatedly in subsequent laws: surveys of historic and archaeological sites, buildings, and objects; determinations about which of these are of value for commemorating or illustrating the

7

history of the United States; historical and archaeological research and investigations; restoration and rehabilitation of heritage sites; collection and maintenance of data about historic and prehistoric sites; and dissemination of this information to the public.

In the 1960s and early 1970s, the United States Congress passed a variety of landmark laws designed to achieve some balance between the need for infrastructure and development in this country and the desire of the American people to see more consideration given to protecting their natural and cultural heritage. The first of these laws to address cultural resources was the Reservoir Salvage Act of 1960, which explicitly referenced the purpose statement of the Historic Sites Act as the reason for its enactment. As the name implies, the act required collection and preservation of historical and archaeological data and materials that would otherwise be destroyed by federally supported dam and reservoir construction.

In 1974 the Reservoir Salvage Act was amended to cover all federal or federally approved ground-disturbing activities and was retitled the Archaeological and Historic Preservation Act (colloquially referred to as the Moss-Bennett Act, after its congressional sponsors). The expanded law made it clear that federal agencies have a responsibility to determine the effects of their projects on archaeological and historical sites and are authorized to spend funds to mitigate, or lessen the severity of, those effects through data recovery. Like the Reservoir Salvage Act, Moss-Bennett specifically references the purpose statement of the Historic Sites Act, noting that the goal of preserving historic and prehistoric sites and the information that can be derived from them is to provide inspiration and benefit for the people of the United States.

Of all the conservation-focused laws of the 1960s and early 1970s, the National Historic Preservation Act and the National Environmental Policy Act have had the broadest influence on federal agency planning and decision-making.[3] The statements of federal policy and congressional intent in these statutes should be the guiding principles for policy decisions about archaeological resource management, but some people making such decisions, and even more of those who provide the data and recommendations on which such decisions are based, appear to have lost sight of that intent.

The National Historic Preservation Act (NHPA), which became law in 1966, resulted from a grassroots effort organized by the National Trust for Historic Preservation and other preservationists, operating under the imprimatur of the United States Conference of Mayors (Glass 1990). The first section of the statute lays out, clearly and eloquently, the intent of Congress in passing the law:

The Congress finds and declares that—

(1) the spirit and direction of the Nation are founded upon and reflected in its historic heritage;

(2) the historical and cultural foundations of the Nation should be preserved as a living part of our community life and development in order to give a sense of orientation to the American people;

(3) historic properties significant to the Nation's heritage are being lost or substantially altered, often inadvertently, with increasing frequency;

(4) the preservation of this irreplaceable heritage is in the public interest so that its vital legacy of cultural, educational, esthetic, inspirational, economic, and energy benefits will be maintained and enriched for future generations of Americans.

The second section of the law establishes the federal government's policy concerning preservation of the nation's heritage:

It shall be the policy of the Federal Government, in cooperation with other nations and in partnership with the States, local governments, Indian tribes, and private organization and individuals to—

(1) use measures, including financial and technical assistance, to foster conditions under which our modern society and our prehistoric and historic resources can exist in productive harmony and fulfill the social, economic, and other requirements of present and future generations;

(2) provide leadership in the preservation of the prehistoric and historic resources of the United States and of the international community of nations and in the administration of the national preservation program in partnership with States, Indian tribes, Native Hawaiians, and local governments;

(3) administer federally owned, administered, or controlled prehistoric and historic resources in a spirit of stewardship for the inspiration and benefit of present and future generations.

The proponents of the legislation that became the NHPA wanted Congress to do two things: to exhort federal agencies to be better stewards of historic places under their control and to require agencies to determine how their actions will affect historic properties and to take those effects into account in planning. Congress addressed these goals in Sections 110 and 106 of the law, respectively.

In Section 106, federal agencies are enjoined to take into account the effects of their undertakings on historic properties and to provide the Advisory Council on Historic Preservation (ACHP) with an opportunity to comment on those effects. The agencies do this by identifying historic and prehistoric places that may be affected, evaluating their eligibility for the National Register of Historic Places, determining how the eligible properties will be affected, and formulating measures to avoid, minimize, or mitigate any effects that diminish their historical integrity.

Section 110 of the law requires that federal agencies assume responsibility for the preservation of historic properties under their ownership or control and establish programs to identify, evaluate, and protect such properties. This section also requires that an agency's preservation program and planning activities be carried out in consultation with state and local governments and Indian tribes, as well as the public.

The principles underlying these and all sections of the NHPA are public benefit and balance, or "productive harmony," as the law terms it, between government-sanctioned or government-sponsored development and preservation of the nation's prehistoric and historic heritage. The ACHP's regulation implementing Section 106 (36 CFR Part 800) reiterates this concept: "The section 106 process seeks to accommodate historic preservation concerns with the needs of Federal undertakings through consultation" (§800.1[a]).

The National Environmental Policy Act (NEPA), signed into law in 1969, also established a policy to guide the actions of federal agencies. Section 101(a) says:

> The Congress, recognizing the profound impact of man's activity on the interrelations of all components of the natural environment,…declares that it is the continuing policy of the Federal Government, in cooperation with State and local governments, and other concerned public and private organizations, to use all practicable means and measures, including financial and technical assistance, in a manner calculated to foster and promote the general welfare, to create and maintain conditions under which man and nature can exist in productive harmony, and fulfill the social, economic, and other requirements of present and future generations of Americans.

In Section 101(b), NEPA establishes the goals to be met by this policy, among them the following:

> In order to carry out the policy set forth in this Act, it is the continuing responsibility of the Federal Government to use all practicable means, consistent with other essential considerations of national policy, to improve and coordinate Federal plans, functions, programs, and resources to the end that the Nation may...fulfill the responsibilities of each generation as trustee of the environment for succeeding generations...preserve important historic, cultural, and natural aspects of our national heritage, and maintain, wherever possible, an environment which supports diversity, and variety of individual choice.

NEPA and Section 106 of the NHPA create processes for informed federal agency decision-making. The shared language and concepts in the introductory sections of the two laws are a clear indication that both are intended to result in public policy decisions that yield tangible public benefits and reflect a balance between preservation and development.

THE RISE OF CRM ARCHAEOLOGY

Although archaeologists had carried out both large- and small-scale efforts to "salvage" archaeological data threatened by development activities since the Great Depression and the passage of the Historic Sites Act in 1935, those efforts had generally been ad hoc and almost always constituted crisis management rather than actual management of historic and prehistoric resources. The Reservoir Salvage Act began the movement toward routine, legally mandated consideration of the effects of federal projects on the archaeological record. With the passage of the NHPA and NEPA and the 1974 expansion of the Reservoir Salvage Act into the Archeological and Historic Preservation Act, the profession and the practice of archaeology in the United States changed profoundly over a short period of time. Suddenly, archaeology, which had been largely a pursuit for scholars and avocational enthusiasts, both of whom engaged in occasional bursts of data-gathering barely ahead of the bulldozers, became an integral part of land-use planning and federal agency decision-making.

In response to the burgeoning field of federally mandated archaeology, the archaeological profession engaged in serious debate and discussion about what the goals of CRM should be and how best to accomplish those goals in the interest of archaeological excellence and good public policy. Mainstream journals such as *The Kiva* (Lipe 1974) and *Science* (Davis 1972) and major scholarly publishing houses such as Academic Press (Schiffer and Gumerman 1977) published important works on the theory, methods, and ethics of legally mandated, publicly funded archaeology. In 1974 the SAA organized and the National Park Service funded a series of six week-long seminars at Airlie House in Virginia. The resulting publication (McGimsey and Davis 1977) established a vision and direction that guided the practice of archaeology within the field of CRM for many years.

As the ACHP, the National Park Service, and other federal agencies developed regulations and guidance documents in the 1970s and 1980s, the practice of CRM archaeology became increasingly standardized, and the directions taken by the field became the purview of federal and state bureaucracies rather than of the archaeological profession. With rare exceptions (for example, King 2002), post-1970s publishing in CRM archaeology was focused not on evaluating and redesigning current practice but on creating "how-to" manuals (Neumann and Sanford 2001) and introductory texts (King 1998) that, unfortunately, often served to reinforce the status quo. The loss of an intellectual focus on method and theory in CRM archaeology and the absence of a discipline-wide debate over how best to do archaeology in the public arena and for the public benefit contributed substantially to the schism between academic and public-sector archaeologists that developed in the 1980s and continues today. The SAA sponsored a series of regional conferences in the mid-1980s that attempted to foster discussion of standards and quality control (Irwin-Williams and Fowler 1986), but the effort received little notice in the profession. Likewise, in the 1990s the SAA and the Society of Professional Archaeologists, in partnership with the National Park Service, co-sponsored a series of working group conferences, "Renewing Our National Archaeological Program," as Hester Davis describes in chapter 2, this volume. This initiative led to the development of some additional guidance for the Section 106 process, but like the initiative reported by Irwin-Williams and Fowler (1986), it did not lead to widespread debate or substantive change.

A VISION FOR THE FUTURE

It has now been more than 30 years, counting from the Airlie House seminars, and more than 20, counting from the efforts reported by Irwin-Williams and Fowler, since archaeologists as a profession instituted a broad examination of how archaeology is done in a CRM context and a debate over how to do it better. Instead of continuing and building on these efforts, we have allowed ourselves to fall into a bureaucratically imposed set of standard operating procedures that cost large amounts of money (some estimates run as high as $300 million to $400 million a year) and that often work against our ability to produce either good archaeology or good public policy.

Given the nonrenewable nature of the archaeological record and the substantial sums of public money being expended to manage that record, it is essential that our approach to archaeological resource management be both good archaeology and good public policy. Some of the fundamental questions being asked by people in our profession and by policy makers about publicly funded archaeology these days are the following:

- Is the public getting its money's worth from CRM archaeology?
- Are the dollars spent on managing archaeological sites necessary, and are they being spent where they will have the greatest return?
- Are the procedures used to evaluate the significance of archaeological sites really successful at distinguishing the "important" sites from those that are unimportant?
- Are the dollars being spent on the mitigation of effects to archaeological sites yielding a proportionate increase in our understanding of life in the past and serving to inform, inspire, and engage the public?

Many archaeologists who work day-to-day with the theory, practice, and regulatory praxis of CRM recognize that "business as usual" CRM archaeology is contributing both impetus and ammunition to those who would weaken protections for archaeological sites. The widespread interest in archaeology among the American people should provide us with a strong source of support for retaining and even strengthening the legal protections for archaeological sites. Instead, we have too often forfeited the public's support because we have failed as a profession to focus on major issues and broad insights about the past and to share what we have learned about these important issues with the public in an accessible and engaging manner.

Exponential increases in the rate of suburban and rural development are putting more and more of the irreplaceable archaeological record at risk. At the same time, considerable political pressure is being brought to bear to weaken legal protections for historical, cultural, and natural aspects of the environment. In recent years, for example, both administrative and legislative initiatives have targeted aspects of historic preservation law and practice that are essential to appropriate management and conservation of archaeological resources.

Although the pro-development, anti-regulatory political climate of recent years, with its emphasis on short-cutting review processes and limiting environmental protections, seems to be changing somewhat, economic pressures and new, high-impact developments such as solar energy will continue pushing archaeologists and resource managers to reexamine their standard operating procedures. Our goal in writing this book is to get ahead of the coming changes and bring the debate about the appropriate conduct of public-sector archaeology back under the intellectual guidance of the archaeological profession.

Our contributions to this debate begin, as all good archaeological projects do, with culture history—in this case, the culture history of professional archaeologists. In chapter 2, Hester Davis offers an engaging narrative of the process by which archaeologists organized themselves into an effective, recognized profession able to track, influence, and ultimately manipulate legislation and regulations affecting cultural resources. She also describes archaeologists' efforts to adjust, as a profession, to a whole new way of doing archaeology that was created by the very laws they helped to form.

In chapter 3, Bill Lipe reminds us that although we say "public benefit" when we speak of the importance of giving good value for the money spent on archaeology in this country, there is a multiplicity of "publics" with interests in what we do. He argues for a "values-based" approach to archaeological resource management, one that considers what resource values sites may have and how those values can be realized as public benefits. The archaeological resource values he discusses are preservation, research, cultural heritage, education, aesthetics, and economics.

The authors of the next three chapters examine specific aspects of the historic preservation compliance process: identifying historic properties, evaluating the significance of archaeological properties, and mitigating the adverse effects of federally funded or authorized projects on archaeological sites. Pat Barker, in his aptly titled chapter 4, "The Process Made Me Do It," advocates an approach to archaeological resource management that is regional in scope and focused on outcome rather than process. He argues that decisions about identifying and managing archaeological resources should begin with land-use planning and should be carried out, to the maximum extent possible, on a programmatic rather than a case-by-case basis.

My chapter 5 is focused on deciding which archaeological sites are "important" enough to be considered in federal planning. I contend that we archaeologists have (wrongly) come to believe that eligibility for the National Register of Historic Places is the only basis for making these decisions. I argue that we should instead embrace a more comprehensive approach to archaeological significance and use it as the basis for managing the archaeological record—an approach that would yield both better archaeology and better public policy.

Susan Chandler, in chapter 6, looks at the issue of mitigation of adverse effects on archaeological sites. She examines a variety of measures for avoiding, minimizing, and mitigating effects on archaeological sites that have been used to supplement, augment, or replace standard data recovery through excavation. Noting that approaches that "achieve broader public involvement with archaeology can lead to increased appreciation of the past and a greater willingness to expend public funds in the pursuit of preservation goals," she provides detailed descriptions of the advantages and problems of several important alternative mitigation projects.

In chapter 7, Julia King addresses access to archaeological information—specifically, collections data and the "gray literature," or limited-distribution reports of surveys and excavations. She also addresses the potential for generating usable syntheses of information about the archaeological record from a variety of sources. As she notes, although digital technologies are an important part of the solution to these issues, digital technologies come with their own problems—cost, long-term viability, and obsolescence, for example.

T. J. Ferguson, in chapter 8, takes up one of the most pervasive and sensitive topics in American archaeology today: the involvement of Native Americans and other descendant communities. He describes five modes of interaction between archaeologists and descendant communities—colonial control, resistance, participation, collaboration, and indigenous control—that affect all aspects of the conduct and outcome of CRM archaeology. Although the participation mode meets the basic legal requirements for consultation, Ferguson argues, the collaboration mode yields richer and more culturally sensitive archaeological research. He also notes that the establishment of tribal historic preservation officers, pursuant to the NHPA, moves CRM on Indian land toward indigenous control.

The next two chapters, 9 by Douglas Mackey and 10 by Sarah Bridges, concern the issue of improving the quality of archaeology carried out in a CRM context. Mackey addresses this issue by focusing on archaeological practice. He argues that high-quality research and up-to-date methods and tools are not only central components of good archaeological practice but also essential components of a successful CRM business.

Bridges examines archaeological ethics. She surveys the wide range of ethics standards and principles that have been adopted by archaeological and anthropological organizations and notes the presence of several basic values. She believes that a broader recognition of these shared values would benefit not only the archaeological resource base but also the interests of professional practitioners and various concerned communities and publics.

In the final chapter, 11, it is David Crass's role to bring us back to the reason we are doing all of this in the first place: the public benefit. It does us no good to improve the compliance process and the practice of CRM archaeology if the results of our work never become "a living part of our community life...in order to give a sense of orientation to the American people," in the words of the NHPA. Crass observes that we have made progress in some areas since the Airlie House report described a "crisis in communication," but we have far to go. He offers a series of tactical suggestions that virtually any archaeologist can use to enhance his or her communications, as well as more strategic recommendations for improving our ability to communicate with multiple publics.

It is interesting, in light of the 30 years that have passed since Airlie House, to compare the topics that the organizers of those seminars chose to address with those that we found compelling. Some of the Airlie House topics were at the top of our list as well as theirs—the "Crisis in Communication" is indeed still with us—but the awareness of multiple publics and multiple heritage values, as explored here in Lipe's chapter 3, was still many years in the future. Other Airlie House topics, particularly "Archeology and Native Americans" and "Certification and Accreditation," reflect the very beginnings of archaeologists' efforts to address these issues of concern to the profession. A comparison of those reports with the Ferguson and Bridges chapters (8 and 10, respectively) gives an encouraging sense that perhaps we have made progress in at least some areas over the intervening years.

The Airlie House seminars "Law in Archeology," "Cultural Resource Management," and "Preparation and Evaluation of Archeological Reports" remind us that the intractable bureaucratic process that Baker (4) and Chandler (6) and I (5) wrestle with in our chapters has not, despite its fossilized state, actually been around since the Pleistocene. In the mid-1970s archaeologists were faced with new legal mandates and a virtual absence of regulations and guidance about how to carry out those mandates. They responded by getting a group of professional archaeologists together to propose a vision and a process. Thirty years later, we are proposing that archaeologists shake off the psychic constraints of "we've always" and "we never" and "we can't," reexamine the process, and recommit to the vision.

Our organizing principles for both the seminar discussions and our chapters were these: describe what you see as the "ideal" state for the future; identify the obstacles keeping archaeologists from reaching that ideal state; and propose measures to overcome those obstacles. As our brains began to overload in Santa Fe, we decided that it all came down to what we called "SDSS^2," or "stop doing stupid stuff; start doing smart stuff." The more tired we became, the funnier that seemed, but unaccountably, the folks at SAR Press did not view it as a suitable title for this book. Maybe you had to be there. Nevertheless, it is our hope that this book will serve as an impetus for dialogue and debate in American archaeology on how to implement the SDSS^2 philosophy so that in the future, CRM projects and programs will yield both better archaeology and better public policy.

Acknowledgments

I would like to thank my colleagues at the SRI Foundation, especially Executive Director Terry Klein. They not only encouraged me to pursue this project and gave me the benefit of their substantial experience in CRM archaeology but also covered meetings, projects, and workshops for me, thus freeing up my time to put together the seminar and this book. I also thank the seminar participants, many of whom had to use their vacation time in order to come to Santa Fe and all of whom were remarkably forbearing about my endless stream of e-mails labeled "gentle reminder." The work they have produced speaks eloquently to their broad experience and their dedication to our profession. I also thank the three anonymous SAR Press reviewers who diligently read the manuscript and gave us excellent advice. Finally, a word of thanks to Mary McGimsey, whose assistance as an amanuensis made it possible for Bob McGimsey to participate with us in producing this volume.

Notes

1. See Childs 2004 and Sullivan and Childs 2003 for good discussions of the curation issue. For recent discussions of the issues in graduate education, see the special section "Revisiting the Graduate Curriculum: The Professional Face of Archaeology" in the November 2006 issue of the *SAA Archaeological Record* (www.saa.org/Portals/0/SAA/Publications/thesaaarchrec/nov06.pdf) and the special section "A Model Applied Archaeology Curriculum" in the January 2009 *SAA Archaeological Record* (www.saa.org/Portals/0/SAA/Publications/thesaaarchrec/jan09.pdf).

2. This issue, too, is being addressed in a variety of venues. See, for example, the Web sites for two such initiatives, Digital Antiquity (http://tdar.org/confluence/display/DIGITAQ/Home) and Archaeoinfomatics (http://archaeoinformatics.org/).

3. It is not my intent to downplay the important role of narrower statutory provisions such as the Archeological Resources Protection Act and Section 4(f) of the Department of Transportation Act in preserving specific segments of the national heritage. These statutes, however, like the Antiquities Act, establish controls and restrictions but have not, in a general sense, established national policies with regard to heritage.

2

Archaeologists Looked to the Future in the Past

Hester A. Davis

Shakespeare said, "What's past is prologue," which I take to mean that we should pay some attention, as archaeologists, to what we have done in the past in order to influence the future of what is now known as the cultural resource base and its management. In the review that follows, I summarize some of the major events, laws, organizations, and efforts by professional archaeologists over the past 100 years that created and helped shape current cultural resource management archaeology. The items I describe fall generally into a chronology in which archaeologists have worked, first, to get a public policy established (1895–1906) in the form of the Antiquities Act of 1906; second, to organize themselves into an effective, recognized scientific discipline (1920–1945); third, to track, influence, and perhaps even manipulate legislation and regulations affecting cultural resources (1946 to the present); and, fourth, to professionalize the discipline and adjust to a whole new way of doing archaeology because of laws that archaeologists themselves helped to manipulate (1968 to the present).

THE ANTIQUITIES ACT OF 1906

Before the end of the nineteenth century, some leaders of the Archaeological Institute of America (AIA, established 1876) and archaeologists working at the Smithsonian Institution's Bureau of Ethnology raised a hue and cry over the looting and destruction of some of the large prehistoric pueblos in the American Southwest. At that time, only a few scientists were employed as archaeologists in the well-established universities and museums in the northeast, and even fewer in the Southwest. One of the latter was Edgar Lee Hewett, the first archaeologist to become directly embroiled in the politics by which the Antiquities Act of 1906 was created. He actually wrote the final version of the act (Harmon, McManamon, and Pitcaithley 2006; Thompson 2000).

Although battlefields and buildings had been preserved before 1906, largely by private organizations and even individuals, the Antiquities Act, in order to recognize the place of historic sites in the country's past, established public policy that is still the foundation upon which the United States builds its federal historic preservation program. The act proclaims that the federal government holds responsibility for recognizing and protecting historic and prehistoric sites on land it owns or controls. President Theodore Roosevelt signed the bill and soon thereafter designated several national monuments, an authority given to the president in the act.

Between 1906 and 1920, archaeological activity was largely carried out by individuals, often trained in disciplines such as history or geology and usually sponsored by eastern museums. The greatest activity, however, was the continuation of indiscriminant digging throughout the country, done for personal gain. Something needed to be done.

THE COMMITTEE ON STATE ARCHAEOLOGICAL SURVEYS

In 1920 the Division of Anthropology and Psychology of the National Research Council created the Committee on State Archaeological Surveys (O'Brien and Lyman 2001:3). Clark Wissler, an ethnologist working at the American Museum of Natural History, was named chair. Describing the committee's expected function, he wrote: "A committee was appointed to encourage and assist the several States in the organization of State archaeological surveys similar to the surveys conducted by the States of Ohio, New York, and Wisconsin. The plan contemplates the coordination of all the agencies within those States, enlisting the cooperation of local students and interested citizens so that an effective appeal may be made to the various State legislatures for special appropriations for these surveys" (quoted in O'Brien and Lyman 2001:3).

The ultimate effect of this committee's activities and accomplishments on the growth—actually the creation—of the discipline of archaeology was enormous. Until its time, the few professionally trained archaeologists and the scientists and historians working as archaeologists had met and given papers at the annual meetings of the American Anthropological Association (AAA) and the Section H (Anthropology) meetings of the American Association for the Advancement of Science (AAAS). The Committee on State Archaeological Surveys was soon to offer a new set of regional venues for professional communication.

The committee's influence is indicated by its summary report for 1921, which includes statements on activities in 13 states. By 1935 Carl Guthe, of the University of Michigan, who chaired the committee from 1927 to 1937, had a mailing list of 192 correspondents (Griffin 1985:263).

Under Guthe's leadership, the committee organized three "seminars," each with a slightly different focus. The first, the Conference on Midwestern Archaeology, was held in St. Louis in May 1929. Fifty-three people took part, including archaeologists but also chancellors and presidents of universities, government officials, several state archaeologists and geologists, heads of state historical societies, and "three high-profile amateurs— Don F. Dickson of Lewiston, Illinois; Harry J. Lemley of Hope, Arkansas; and Jay L. B. Taylor of Pineville, Missouri" (O'Brien and Lyman 2001:21).

The second meeting was the Conference on Southern Prehistory, held in Birmingham, Alabama, in December 1932. The theme of this meeting was the status of knowledge of the prehistory in the Southeast and the means by which it could best be studied.

The final committee-sponsored gathering was held in Indianapolis in early December 1935 and was attended by 19 archaeologists, linguists, and ethnologists. This conference "was called for the specific purpose of discussing the technical problems relating to the comparative study of the archaeological cultures in the upper Mississippi Valley and Great Lakes region" (O'Brien and Lyman 2001:339).

It seems as if, when archaeologists found the opportunity to talk with others from nearby states who faced similar problems of looting, taxonomy, and classification and to compare actual artifacts, they flung the gates open wide, and everyone rushed in. Guthe himself visited all the state organizations in the Mississippi Valley in 1928, encouraging amateurs and professionals to cooperate and handing out a mimeographed pamphlet on archaeological "method and technique" issued by the National Research Council.

Just before the committee was organizing its three conferences, A. V. Kidder, in 1927, organized the first regional archaeological conference at

Pecos, New Mexico—now an annual event called the Pecos Conference. It produced a classification system for indigenous cultures as they developed in the Southwest, where archaeological field training courses had been held by Bryon Cummings in Arizona beginning in 1919 (Gifford and Morris 1985). Edgar Hewett held field schools in New Mexico in the early 1930s, and Fay-Cooper Cole, at the University of Chicago, introduced a field school in the same period.

Finally, the creation of the Society for American Archaeology (SAA) came as a direct result of the Committee on State Archaeological Surveys' efforts to gather archaeologists to talk about the future directions and needs of the discipline. Guthe brought up the idea of a national organization of American archaeologists at the committee's 1933 annual meeting, and the idea was approved. In December of that year, the committee met again, at the AAA meeting in Columbus, Ohio. Guthe described the committee's meeting there: "A group of archaeologists gathered in a hotel room to kick the idea around a bit. It was on this occasion that Paul Titterington, another [amateur] friend of archaeology, strongly advocated a national organization composed of professional and amateur archaeologists. The upshot was the adoption of an informal program of action which I, as chairman of the Committee, agreed to help carry out in 1934" (Guthe 1967:437).

Guthe (1967:437) mailed the plan for the suggested national society to almost 300 people, asking for comments and criticisms. The responses were enthusiastic. A constitution and by-laws were drawn up, and a slate of officers was chosen. The organizational meeting took place in Pittsburgh, and Guthe's plan was adopted. The SAA held its first annual meeting in 1935.

By 1937 most of the committee's functions—publications and meetings, in particular—had been taken over by the SAA, and the National Research Council discharged the Committee on State Archaeological Surveys. In addition to publishing the quarterly *American Antiquity*, the SAA's by-laws (article VII, section 3) provided that the society publish the mimeographed *Notebook*. Many of the brief articles that appeared in this short-lived publication in 1939 and 1940 seem to have been aimed at the amateur members.

The Committee on State Archaeological Surveys fared poorly in its efforts to educate the general public, particularly looters and landowners. By 1930 any effort to do so, which the committee members felt should be led by individual states, was doomed by the coming Great Depression, during which the Ohio and Mississippi river valleys experienced heavy destruction of prehistoric cemeteries and mounds as desperately poor people dug for artifacts to sell in order to feed their families.

THE HISTORIC SITES ACT, 1935

Passage of the Historic Sites Act in 1935 seems to have slipped by the archaeologists of the time. The Committee on State Archaeological Surveys certainly was not involved in its development and passage, which took place under the leadership of the National Park Service (NPS). Section 2 of the Historic Sites Act directs NPS, among other things, to "make a survey of historic and archaeologic [sic] sites, buildings, and objects for the purpose of determining which possess exceptional value as commemorating or illustrating the history of the United States." With this charge, the National Park Service was designated the lead federal agency in historic preservation.

Meanwhile, something else was happening that changed archaeology and the careers of a good many people who were studying in the expanding graduate archaeology programs. As Guthe remembered, it happened at the same meeting in Columbus, just after Christmas 1933, at which the question of forming a national archaeological organization was debated:

> It was during an afternoon session...in a small lecture room of the Ohio State Museum—the attendance that year was meager because of the depression—that [Fay-Cooper] Cole, then President of the Association (AAA), interrupted the proceedings to announce the receipt of a telegram from Major [William S.] Webb [of the University of Kentucky]....It was a sensational call for help in finding reasonably competent supervisors to direct the work of some 1,200 laborers who would start archaeological excavations in the Tennessee Valley on the Monday following New Year's Day, 1934. (Guthe 1967:436)

That the administrators of Roosevelt's New Deal thought archaeological fieldwork would be a great way to put large numbers of people to work had been known since the beginning of 1933. The Tennessee Valley Authority had recently been created and was intent upon building reservoirs to provide water and electricity to large areas in the south-central United States. The Federal Emergency Relief Administration was also created in 1933, soon adopting another guise as the Civil Works Administration (CWA) and finally becoming the Works Progress Administration (WPA) in 1935. With no known prompting by archaeologists, the CWA asked the Smithsonian Institution to furnish archaeologists to take charge of field projects in places where the climate was mild and there was an abundance of unemployed laborers. The result was that many graduate students with meager field experience—much less any experience supervising 100 or more people digging complicated, stratified sites—found themselves doing just that throughout the Southeast and for a scattering of projects in other parts of the country (Fagette 1996; Haag 1985; Lyon 1996).

THE BASIC NEEDS COMMITTEE

Complaints began to spread about the "chaos" in some of the WPA projects: inexperienced supervisors, no standards for record-keeping, and collections accumulating without proper curation (Jennings 1986). The complaints reached the bureaucrats in the WPA, who asked the National Research Council to appoint a committee to study the basic needs of American archaeology. Carl Guthe was, at this time (1939), chair of the council's Division of Anthropology and Psychology, and presumably he appointed the seven committee members. By the end of the year, they had issued a document titled, not surprisingly, "The Basic Needs of American Archaeology" (Guthe 1939). The basic needs they discussed were essentially those about which the WPA archaeologists had complained.

The members of the Basic Needs Committee seem not to have considered any follow-through after their statement was prepared and distributed, possibly because World War II was almost upon them. The committee continued to exist until 1945 (Wendorf and Thompson 2002:319), but the WPA projects were closed down in 1942, as was almost all other archaeological field research in the country.

A group of archaeologists working at the Smithsonian during the war learned through newspaper accounts that the US Army Corps of Engineers and the Bureau of Reclamation had plans for building many large reservoirs, 108 of them in the Missouri River basin alone (Brew 1962:14). By 1944 Fred Johnson, an archaeologist working in Washington, DC, for the navy and assisting Julian Steward at the Smithsonian's Bureau of American Ethnography (Wendorf and Thompson 2002:319), met with other archaeologists working in federal agencies and came to the conclusion that the WPA work and the 1935 Historic Sites Act could and should be recognized for what they were—a real commitment by the federal government to the preservation of historic and archaeological sites. He and his colleagues asked the SAA to establish a planning committee to consider how to salvage the thousands of sites that would be destroyed in the construction of the proposed impoundment projects and eventually by inundation. The three-person committee was appointed in July 1944, with Johnson as chair.

THE COMMITTEE FOR THE RECOVERY OF
ARCHAEOLOGICAL REMAINS (CRAR)

The result of the SAA Planning Committee's deliberations was the creation in 1945 of the Committee for the Recovery of Archaeological Remains (CRAR). This committee took over the work of both the Basic Needs Committee and the SAA Planning Committee. Fred Johnson later described it:

> In 1945 the Committee for the Recovery of Archaeological Remains was created almost out of thin air. Sponsorship by the American Anthropological Association, the Society for American Archaeology, and the American Council of Learned Societies was arranged, and endorsement by the Learned Councils in Washington was also secured. The Committee was left free to act as conditions dictated and as the members' consciences permitted.... The objectives of the Committee were to advise and assist the government agencies so that there would be organized a program which would salvage archaeological values in river basins to be developed by the Federal government. Its purpose—to see that the program was administered so that the results met the highest standards and were achieved as efficiently as possible. (Johnson 1961:1)

By the fall of 1945, a memorandum of understanding was signed, with some prodding by CRAR, in which the Bureau of American Ethnography (BAE) agreed to contribute the scientific leadership, and the National Park Service, the bureaucratic and financial administration (Congress appropriated funds for the program to NPS, which passed them on to the Smithsonian). The Smithsonian then created the River Basin Surveys (SI-RBS) within the BAE, with several centers around the country. Agreements followed between NPS and the Corps of Engineers and the Bureau of Reclamation, the two principal agencies involved in building dams and creating recreation areas around the reservoirs. Each of the latter agencies transferred funds to NPS for the first year of the program, which were then transferred to the Smithsonian. The next year, the Bureau of the Budget ruled that funds for this program had to come out of the NPS appropriation (Wendorf and Thompson 2002:324). Much of CRAR's time for the next few decades was devoted to lobbying for an adequate appropriation to NPS. It was sometimes successful and sometimes not.

In the early 1950s, two other crises developed. First, gas and oil companies began to build pipelines, and "huge trenching machines began cutting ditches through hundreds of miles of countryside" (Brew 1962:18). Second, President Dwight Eisenhower announced his "fifty-six billion dollar road program" (Brew 1962:19), in which the planned interstate highways would also slice through thousands of miles of terrain—and archaeological sites. Jesse Nusbaum, consulting archaeologist to the Department of the Interior, convinced the El Paso Natural Gas Company to fund an archaeological survey of its pipelines in New Mexico and hired Fred Wendorf to supervise the program (Wendorf 1962). Wendorf talked other gas and oil companies into doing the same. The Federal Aid Highway Act of 1956 specifically required archaeological salvage on highways (McGimsey 2004:175). Wendorf brokered the creation in New Mexico of the first federal highway archaeological activity (Wendorf 1957). Eventually, section 4(f) of the Department of Transportation Act of 1966 contained relatively strong language indicating that a transportation program that would damage cultural resources would be approved only if "there is no prudent and feasible alternative to using...land of an historic site of national, State, or local significance" (National Park Service 2002:99). One result of all of this was that in 1957 Wendorf was invited to participate in CRAR meetings representing highway salvage archaeology.

CRAR met at least once a year with representatives of the federal agencies involved in the national preservation program to receive updates from them on work and problems with funding. Although the whole program was somewhat stabilized by the passage of the Reservoir Salvage Act in 1960, it still took tireless vigilance on the part of CRAR members to try to ensure adequate funding. Few though they were, CRAR members also produced pamphlets, wrote articles for popular and scientific magazines and journals, and organized at least four symposia at the SAA annual meetings about the River Basin Salvage program (Corbett 1961; Roberts 1961).

By the early 1970s, however, many of the reservoirs had filled, and the work of the River Basin Salvage program was being scaled back. "Events had swept beyond the CRAR, which worked well when federal archaeology was in its infancy but became increasingly irrelevant as the federal bureaucracy grew. While the profession needed to continue to prod the government, CRAR was no longer the most effective mechanism for doing so" (Wendorf and Thompson 2002:327). Indeed, by the early 1970s the SAA was taking the leadership role in looking after archaeology's future. CRAR faded away in 1976.

In one sense, the legacy of this small but effective committee was the rescue of an incredible amount of information that surely would have been lost underwater without the committee's vision and persistence. But its activity in dealing with agencies and Congress was not well known among archaeologists, so the profession as a whole learned few lessons from what the committee did or what it accomplished.

THE PROFESSION'S EFFORTS TO TAKE CONTROL OF ITS FUTURE, 1968 TO THE PRESENT

In retrospect, the 1970s were exceedingly busy years for archaeologists in general and for the SAA in particular. For the first time, most archaeologists, excluding only some academic and museum archaeologists, became involved in trying to keep up with the changes brought about by legislation and the ensuing regulations.

Archaeology might have changed abruptly in 1966 with the passage of the National Historic Preservation Act (NHPA), but archaeologists were not yet keeping track of what Congress was considering. It was the leaders of the National Trust for Historic Preservation, largely historians and architectural historians, who drafted and saw the bill through Congress (Mulloy 1976). The National Environmental Policy Act of 1969 had not been on archaeologists' radar, either (McGimsey 2004:9). It took a couple of years, while agencies and archaeologists awaited the regulations that would tell everyone how to comply with these two new laws, before archaeologists sprang into action.

In 1968 the Arkansas Archeological Survey sponsored three meetings attended by most of the archaeologists working in the Mississippi River valley below St. Louis. The Survey had discovered that the Soil Conservation Service (SCS, now the Natural Resources Conservation Service) was leveling vast acreage in eastern Arkansas and southeastern Missouri by pushing down low natural levees created by the Mississippi River over several thousand years. On these low rises sat a majority of the area's Archaic and early Woodland sites. To the participants in the meetings, which were held in Greenville, Mississippi, Popular Bluff, Missouri, and East St. Louis, Illinois, it was immediately obvious that this leveling was going on throughout the whole valley. John Corbett, senior archaeologist at NPS, attended these meetings and took the problem to the SCS officials in Washington. That meeting revealed that SCS had concluded that because it owned no land but instead worked with individual farmers, providing only technical assistance, it was not subject to the 1966 National Historic Preservation Act— and besides, it was not authorized by its organic act to spend any money on archaeology.

This decision by SCS was a tough nut to crack at this early stage in the development of the new law. Discussions with Corbett ended in a "eureka moment" for Charles R. McGimsey III, director of the Arkansas Archeological Survey, and Carl Chapman, director of archaeological programs at the University of Missouri, when one of the three men said, in all innocence, "Why don't we just get a law passed giving all federal agencies authority to spend their own money for doing archaeology required by the law?" McGimsey approached Arkansas's senior senator, J. William Fulbright, for advice. Fulbright believed legislation an appropriate action but cautioned that it would probably take six years—three Congressional sessions—to achieve success, and indeed it did. By the middle of 1969, McGimsey and Chapman had drafted a bill and taken it and their story to members of the congressional committees that would consider it. They also found a senator and a representative willing to sponsor the bill in their respective houses. As a result, archaeologists will forever remember the names of Senator Frank Moss of Utah and Representative Charles Bennett of Florida. The law is still often referred to as the Moss-Bennett Act rather than by its more bureaucratic name, the Archaeological and Historic Preservation Act of 1974.

For this discussion, the most significant section of the bill provided that all federal agencies were authorized to spend their own program money to do whatever was required to consider the effects of their programs on archaeological resources, as called for by the NHPA and NEPA.

Gaining the attention, much less the support, of the whole profession for the proposed legislation was the job of the SAA's Committee on Public Archaeology (COPA). Created in 1966, by 1969 COPA consisted of one person from each state, in addition to the chair (Hester Davis at the time). Through this network, information flowed from the chair to archaeologists and from them to the public. For six years, COPA was the clearinghouse for information as the draft bill went through revisions, and it advised supporters about how to influence Congress. McGimsey, Chapman, and Davis also produced a leaflet, "Stewards of the Past" (1970), aimed at landowners. COPA handled the distribution of the leaflet through its network; about 60,000 copies were printed and distributed by archaeologists across the country. McGimsey (1973) wrote a booklet, published by the SAA, titled *Archaeology and Archaeology Resources*, aimed at federal agencies and landowners, and the SAA handled the distribution of about 20,000 copies. Three other publications helped spread the word about the destruction of sites during the period when Congress was considering the draft bill: *Archaeology* magazine published an illustrated article, "Is There a Future for the Past? (Davis 1971); McGimsey's book *Public Archeology* (1972) suggested that all archaeology was public archaeology; and *Science* magazine published a short article (Davis 1972) titled "The Crisis in American Archeology," which indicated that the laws were in place, but not the funds, to allow consideration of potential harm to significant evidence of the country's past.

The result of this grassroots effort to get the bill passed did more than change the world of archaeology—it changed the career choices of all budding archaeologists. Equally significant, the six-year effort had politicized both individual archaeologists and their professional organizations.

THE AIRLIE HOUSE SEMINARS, 1974

In 1974 Charles McGimsey became president of the SAA. He was particularly concerned that the profession be prepared for what could be some major changes when the Moss-Bennett bill became law. In May 1973 the Arkansas Archeological Survey sponsored a meeting in Fayetteville that was attended by area archaeologists and representatives of the federal agencies most concerned with the pending legislation. A similar regional meeting was held in Farmington, New Mexico, in January 1974, followed by a larger meeting in mid-April of that year in Denver. The Denver meeting carried much more force than the first two because its proceedings were published before the end of that year (Lipe and Lindsay 1974) and because its attendees knew that the bill had passed both houses of Congress and was on President Richard Nixon's desk for his signature (he signed it in mid-May).

Meanwhile, McGimsey had proposed to the SAA executive board that it sponsor "Six Seminars on the Future Direction of Archaeology," which the National Park Service agreed to fund. The seminars took place in the summer of 1974, two at a time, at a convention center retreat in rural Virginia known as Airlie House (McGimsey 2004:101–105). The six topics covered were "A Consideration of Law in Archaeology," "Cultural Resource Management," "Guidelines for the Preparation and Evaluation of Archaeological Reports," "The Crisis in Communication," "Archaeology and Native Americans," and "Certification and Accreditation."

The publication resulting from these seminars (McGimsey and Davis 1977) contains much that still seems relevant today. The seminars on cultural resource management and Native Americans are perhaps the most dated. Only the seminar on certification and accreditation offered specific recommendations for action. The published report was written immediately after the seminars and stands as a historical document, but the editors' preface to the certification seminar provides details on actions that had taken place on this topic between the late summer of 1974 and January

1976, when the Society of Professional Archaeologists (now the Register of Professional Archaeologists) was created as an independent entity, separate from the SAA.

The seminar on communication reviewed what was being done at the time to get information about the results of research to archaeologists and the general public and then gave suggestions for what could be done in the future. The SAA's Committee on Public Archaeology became the Committee on Public Education, which has concentrated largely on providing information to and making contact with K–12 teachers.

SIX BUSY YEARS, 1974 TO 1980

William Lipe's article "A Conservation Model for American Archaeology" was published in 1974. It provided the inspiration for the formation of the American Society for Conservation Archaeology (ASCA) during an evening session in the hotel bar at the 1974 cultural resource meeting in Denver. ASCA was to be a clearinghouse for information about cultural resource management and about the changes taking place in all aspects of archaeology, taking over the function of COPA.

By the end of 1974, archaeologists began to tackle the foreseen changes, and federal agencies began to hire their own archaeologists. Southwestern archaeologists held annual meetings with representatives of federal agencies. In May 1975 "115 people met at the University of Massachusetts–Boston for a two-day conference to assess the state's manpower and resources for meeting provisions of the federal and state antiquities legislation, and to discuss the course of cultural resource management in Massachusetts" (*ASCA Newsletter* 2[2]:12). The public, professional organizations, individual archaeologists, and federal agencies made comments on NPS's draft regulations for the Moss-Bennett legislation.

In 1978 President Jimmy Carter created the Heritage Conservation and Recreation Service as a new agency in the Department of the Interior. The Office of Archaeology and Historic Preservation was moved out of the National Park Service "into a non-land-managing context, placing it with the old Bureau of Outdoor Recreation (BOR) and the yet to be authorized Natural Resources program; its name was changed to the Interagency Archaeological Services" (Corbyn 1980).

Meanwhile, during this time when archaeologists were so active, various federal actions brought some much needed guidance. In 1971 Nixon signed Executive Order 11593, which directed federal agencies to inventory their land to identify properties that would qualify for listing on the National Register of Historic Places. In 1973 the Advisory Council on

Historic Preservation (created by the NHPA) issued "Procedures for the Protection of Historic and Cultural Properties" (36 CFR Part 800), giving federal agencies and archaeologists some guidance for conducting reviews of proposed, legally required archaeological projects and for compliance with the NHPA's Section 106 (King, Hickman, and Berg 1977:37).

In May 1976 the Advisory Council on Historic Preservation appointed a Task Force on Archaeology Policy because archaeologists' needs for and approach to complying with the regulations were different from those of historians and architects. Five archaeologists were appointed to the task force, and deliberations over the next few years included a conference of invited archaeologists held in September 1978 in Taos, New Mexico, to discuss the task force's charge and concerns. The task force's report to the council listed 11 problems and 8 recommendations for dealing with them (ACHP 1979). The recommendations dealt with inventory, evaluation, mitigation, the federal-state relationship, compliance, antiquities legislation, late discovery, and curation—all topics that continue to be discussed today. The report included an appendix by Fred Wendorf summarizing the deliberations of the Taos meeting.

Also in May 1976, a symposium was held in St. Louis, "Regional Centers in Archaeology: Prospects and Problems" (Marquardt 1977), which dealt especially with the problem of curation of the massive collections already being generated. In 1977 and again in 1978, Interagency Archaeological Services sponsored two workshops at Texas Tech University that considered the new roles as managers and contractors that archaeologists were facing (Mayer-Oakes and Portnoy 1979; Portnoy 1978).

During this period, COPA and the government affairs committees of the various professional organizations commented on many matters. An important issue was a proposed amendment to the NHPA to require that sites being evaluated for Section 106 compliance need only be *eligible* for the National Register, not already officially listed on it. This amendment passed in 1976.

After several years of conflicting court decisions, meetings, changes, and testimony before congressional committees, the Archaeological Resources Protection Act (ARPA) of 1979 was passed (Fowler and Malinky 2005). This new act tightened the definitions found in the Antiquities Act of 1906, providing a new permitting process and much heavier sanctions for violations. In 1980 there came more important amendments to the NHPA, upon which the SAA, SHA, and many other organizations had been working hard for several years. The most important addition was Section 110, which emphasized the responsibilities of federal agencies with regard to historic property management, in essence, making law of Executive Order 11593, signed by Nixon in 1971.

The greatest change that took place between 1976 and 1980, however, was the response to the expected demand for more archaeologists to meet the needs of federal agencies, states, counties, and municipalities that were responding to the federal program. This demand was met largely by the many individuals who formed for-profit companies that could contract directly with federal agencies or with businesses working under federal licenses or permits (Doelle and Phillips 2005; Roberts, Ahlstrom, and Roth 2004). Some archaeologists went to work for environmental and engineering firms that were already working on the environmental impact statements required by NEPA but needed archaeologists for NHPA responsibilities. Some archaeologists took jobs in the environmental divisions of federal agencies. Several university departments of anthropology created contract archaeology arms, although they found it difficult to compete with businesses because they relied on students and faculty who were unavailable for full-time work during the school year.

More important, a good many universities began offering courses in cultural resource management (CRM) or in historic preservation. A few institutions even created master's degree emphases on CRM, but most of these programs have since ceased to exist. In some cases, CRM information was (and is) mainstreamed into other courses in archaeology. Articles in journals and newsletters on problems encountered in this new world of archaeology surged, as did published comments on the problem of establishing the significance of sites in order to ensure their eligibility for nomination to the National Register. Archaeologists increasingly debated what constituted appropriate survey techniques in different environments (King 1977). The ever-present worry over how to "mitigate the adverse effect" of a federal project's damage to a site addressed the question of how much digging was sufficient and how much money was enough or too little (Schiffer and Gumerman 1977; see also General Accounting Office 1981, 1985, 1987).

SHAKEDOWN TIME, 1980 TO 2000

A legislative and financial crisis occurred in 1981. When President Ronald Reagan submitted to Congress his budget for the fiscal year beginning October 1, 1981, he requested that the total budget for the federal historical preservation program be zeroed out. The resulting clamor from agencies, institutions, the National Trust for Historic Preservation, historical societies, state governors, the general public, and all archaeological organizations led Congress to include the funding in the budget it approved. The new administration, however, abolished Carter's Heritage Conservation and Recreation Service, and the preservation programs returned to the National Park Service.

In addition, the lengthy recession of the 1970s and early 1980s meant that many federal agencies had to cut projects and scale back their planning. Consequently, less environmental and cultural resource work was needed. This put many small archaeological contracting firms out of business. To help, the Small Business Administration issued a ruling that federal agencies had to reserve 10 percent of their compliance contracts for small businesses. This was good for the small archaeological firms, but it meant that several surviving university contracting programs shut down. By the end of the 1980s, firms with business know-how were surviving, those without business savvy had evaporated, and the relatively fierce competition for contracts had begun to level out.

The profession still had concerns about the quality of fieldwork and reports and about the curation of the growing mass of information and artifacts. There was much anguish that agencies were employing master's degree graduates who had little or no knowledge of the laws and regulations, of the way bureaucracies worked, or of how to evaluate a report and its recommendations. People were going into the field and making eligibility decisions about sites in areas of the country where they had no previous experience—they did not know what they were looking for, much less how to establish its significance.

The efforts of the Advisory Council on Historic Preservation's Task Force on Archaeology Policy to make recommendations about the problems it perceived brought out the considerable inconsistency among the agencies funding archaeology, in terms of their requirements for work. In addition, there were inconsistencies in the guidance given by each state historic preservation office about how work was to be done.

One SAA response to these problems was to sponsor a series of regional conferences on cultural resource management, starting in late 1984. Cynthia Irwin-Williams and Don D. Fowler, who were in charge of organizing the conferences, wrote an "open letter" to SAA members: "[Since the Airlie House seminars]new political contexts, the development and implementation of the RP3 [Resource Protection Planning Process] by the National Park Service, new federal procedures, and the perception of 'knots' in the compliance process have made it necessary to review and rethink many issues discussed in the Airlie House report, as well as a number of new issues. Further, it has become clear that many issues and problems can be most fruitfully addressed on a regional basis" (Irwin-Williams and Fowler 1984:1).

The charge to each of the regional conferences was to discuss and prepare a report on the following topics: "Purpose of the Regional Conference," "Status of the Regional Data Base," "The Conduct of Cultural Resource Management in the Regional Context: Standards and Guidelines," and "Relation of SAA Regional Conference to State/Federal Guidelines." Although the SAA published a final summary report on all nine conferences (Irwin-Williams and Fowler 1986), how much influence or follow-through any of these reports had on the conduct of archaeology in the regions is unknown.

After several years of efforts and compromise, Congress passed the Abandoned Shipwreck Act in 1986. The Society for Historic Archaeology, the Council on Underwater Archaeology, and the National Park Service led the fray to try to control some of the most egregious of the looting of Spanish galleons for their gold. The act essentially defined abandoned shipwrecks within the limits of national boundaries as coming under the existing historic preservation laws, and it provided for states to prepare guidelines that would balance competing interests such as those of sport divers, salvagers, and archaeologists.

Another sea change for archaeologists began in the early 1970s as Native Americans made known their distress over the fact that archaeologists were digging up their ancestors, studying the bones, and then putting them in boxes on shelves in curation facilities. In 1979, when the Archeological Resources Protection Act was passed, its Section 4(c) required that descendant tribes be notified if a permit request for excavation on public or Indian land might harm religious or culturally significant sites. Nationally, there began a series of meetings between Native American leaders, archaeologists, anthropologists, museum curators, and lawyers concerning the excavation of prehistoric graves and the relationship of archaeologists to the descendants of the people whose remains they were digging up. Several cases in the 1980s drew the interest of the public and Congress to this relationship. One example, which galvanized the attention of Senator Daniel Inouye, was a proposal to build a resort hotel on top of a Native Hawaiian cemetery. Again after several years of meetings, negotiations, changes, and work with congressional committees by archaeologists, bioarchaeologists, museum curators, and Native Americans, the Native American Graves Protection and Repatriation Act (NAGPRA) was passed in 1990.

NAGPRA, perhaps more than any other law, has changed the way archaeologists do their work in the United States, particularly when they work on federal or Indian reservation land or under federal contract or permit (Ferguson 1996). Consultation with the appropriate, federally recognized tribes is required before excavation begins if burials are known or suspected to be present. If they are discovered during excavation, work must stop until consultation takes place concerning the treatment of the skeletons and any associated artifacts. In addition, institutions that receive any federal money must inventory all their human remains and known grave goods, sacred objects, and objects of cultural patrimony and provide the descendant group with a copy of the inventory. The Native American group can then claim these items for repatriation. Some archaeologists raised a hue and cry because, if the tribes wished to rebury the remains and artifacts, large portions of the information needed to interpret the past would become unavailable for archaeologists to study. In the years since the bill passed, the protests have largely faded away, and NAGPRA relationships have proved to be beneficial to both Native Americans and archaeologists in many cases (see Ferguson, chapter 8, this volume).

Starting in the late 1980s, the SAA Government Affairs Committee and Loretta Neumann, the SAA's political consultant, initiated the Save the Past for the Future project. As part of this project, a "working conference" was held in May 1989 at the Fort Burgwin Research Center in Taos, New Mexico. According to the final report on the conference (Society for American Archaeology 1990:9), it brought together more than "70 national experts in a variety of related fields—archaeologists, law enforcement experts, social scientists, agency managers, politicians, and citizens concerned with the problem of archaeological looting and vandalism." The resulting publication described the three break-out working sessions ("Understanding the Problem," "Preventing the Problem," and "Combating the Problem") and summarized the major findings as follows: "Information must reach the public; education and training must be improved; laws must be strengthened; protection efforts must be increased; agencies must improve coordination; more research is needed; [and] alternatives must be provided" (Society for American Archaeology 1990:8–9). The summary also listed eight actions that had already taken place between the time of the meeting and the publication of the report. For example, the SAA had promoted add-on funding of $500,000 in the 1990 congressional appropriation for NPS's law enforcement efforts on park land.

This conference successfully stimulated some people to return to their work fired up to make things happen. The same can be said for the "Save the Past for the Future II" meeting, held in Breckenridge, Colorado, in

1994 and attended by 171 committed people. This time, the participants included prosecutors, educators, and people from tribal programs, federal agency law enforcement, state governments, and academia. NAGPRA had by now been passed, and considerably more experience had been gained with prosecutions under the Archaeological Resources Protection Act. As in the Taos meeting, the attendees were divided into three work groups to deal with the topics of education, integrated resource management, and law enforcement, respectively. Bill Lipe's summary report on the whole conference (1994) appeared within a month of the meeting. His personal observations were that this was a group of intense and committed people who "were going to have to recruit and inspire an army of recruits" and that there were overlapping solutions among the three discussion groups, indicating that priorities should be set (Lipe 1994:4).

One of the outcomes of this meeting was yet another workshop organized by the SAA Committee on Public Education's Task Force on Curriculum. This relatively small conference was held at Wakulla Springs State Park in Florida early in 1998, and its discussion was concentrated on the need for more appropriate curriculums in higher education, at both the bachelor's and graduate levels. The conference produced two results: the publication *Teaching Archaeology in the Twenty-first Century* (Bender and Smith 2000) and the development at Indiana University of a Web site describing MATRIX (Making Archaeology Teaching Relevant in the XXI Century, www.indiana.edu/~arch/saa/matrix/homepage.html). With the aid of a National Science Foundation grant and the sponsorship of the SAA, a group of academics and others developed information, ideas, and course material for use by college and university professors in the United States who taught undergraduate archaeology.

ETHICS IN ARCHAEOLOGY

Meanwhile, the Society of Professional Archaeologists (SOPA) sponsored a symposium at the 1989 SAA annual meeting titled "Ethics in Professional Archaeology." SOPA had, by that time, more than 10 years of experience with its code of ethics and grievance procedure. The papers from the session were published by SOPA as Special Publication 1 (Woodall 1990). The SAA's "Four Statements for Archaeology," which dealt with ethical issues (Champe et al. 1961), was seriously in need of updating and expansion, given the pressures under which archaeologists were working in the 1990s. A Committee on Ethics in Archaeology was appointed, and in 1993 it convened a meeting in Reno, Nevada, "to begin the important process of updating and recasting SAA's policy statement on archaeological ethics" (Lynott and Wylie 1995:5). This group developed six broadly defined draft principles of archaeological ethics, which were presented in the form of position papers in a public forum at the SAA annual meeting in 1994. The SAA quickly published the revised position papers and the principles (Lynott and Wylie 1995; see also the second, revised edition [2000] and Bridges, chapter 10, this volume).

In 1996 the American Cultural Resources Association (ACRA) was born. Its full membership is made up entirely of private firms that contract to do cultural resource management (Doelle and Phillips 2005), and it accepts associate members whose interests coincide with those of private contractors. It is a trade organization that holds annual meetings in which common problems are discussed in workshops and small discussion groups; no scholarly papers are read. Its officers have been extremely active in keeping up with what Congress is doing relative to the federal historic preservation program. They provide an additional and knowledgeable voice in working with other archaeological organizations and with agencies. Furthermore, many students learn about CRM through employment in these private firms. Many ACRA members consider their companies experienced in most aspects of cultural resource management, and they now refer to the private company business as an "industry."

RENEWING THE NATIONAL ARCHAEOLOGICAL PROGRAM

In 1995 the SAA created yet another task force to contemplate "Renewing American Archaeology." The task force organized a forum at the SAA annual meeting that year to begin presenting its deliberations to a wider audience for comment. In early 1996 the task force held a small conference at Arizona State University, in Tempe, sponsored by the SAA and SOPA, with support from NPS. This "renewing" conference "was intended to be an initial step in focusing debate and discussion on current problems and their solutions" (Lipe and Redman 1996:15).

The group focused on five issues, recognizing "that the scope of discussions had to be limited if anything was to be achieved" (Lipe and Redman 1996:15). The five issues were these: improving the implementation of the National Historic Preservation Act; increasing professional knowledge and expertise at all levels of archaeological resource management; making better use of existing information in decision-making about archaeological resources; improving the dissemination of information from publicly mandated archaeology; and recognizing multiple interests in archaeology and archaeological resources. For each of these five issues, the group made several recommendations about how to achieve some success. Lipe and Redman's report was designed to spread the word that these areas of concern were being considered. Comments were solicited from the profession in general and particularly from other archaeological organizations that might be able to commit to tackling some of the recommended actions.

In February 1997 the task force held a second meeting in Tempe to "develop an implementation plan for some or all of the recommendations" put together at the first conference (Lipe's report on this second meeting was posted on the SAA Web site, www.saa.org/Society/Ethics/renew.html). Principles were stated for the five issues, and recommended actions were suggested. In 1999 Frank McManamon, consulting archaeologist for the Department of the Interior and chief archaeologist and program manager for the NPS Archaeology Program, agreed to serve as chair of the task force. He called another small meeting in October to prioritize the recommended actions and assign work to appropriate individuals, organizations, and agencies.

Since 2000, when the final report of the Task Force on Renewing American Archaeology was placed on the SAA Web site (www.saa.org/Government/renew.html), some of the recommended actions have been taken, and others are still being deliberated by various archaeological organizations. The issues identified by this task force are broad, involving what are considered to be national issues and needs for improvement in the national archaeological program. McManamon wrote to me in an e-mail on January 1, 2007: "It probably isn't necessary to spend a lot of time redefining what the needs are; more energy should be devoted to coming up with ideas for addressing them."

LESSONS LEARNED

After more than 100 years of history as a profession—of forming archaeological and preservation organizations, struggling to get legislation passed, and then adapting to the results of that legislation—what have we archaeologists learned that can help us better manage and conserve the nation's cultural and historical resources? Here are the lessons I believe we have learned to our greatest benefit:

- We can effect change if we—individuals and organizations—work together, giving a consistent message to Congress, regulators, and agencies about changes we think are needed.
- Preservation organizations must give some priority to keeping track of what is going on in Congress. Several organizations have done this,

creating government affairs committees or the equivalent and hiring consultants to help guide the actions and contacts needed.

- Vigilance is imperative. Laws can be amended with little notice; provisions affecting historic preservation can be added unnoticed to bills in Congress on non-preservation-related issues. Someone must keep watch. This is done most effectively through partnerships among all the preservation constituencies.

- Democracies work best through compromise and negotiation. We must be willing to accept less than perfect laws and regulations, identify where realistic improvements can be made, and then work together to achieve acceptable changes.

- It is best to prioritize goals and then focus on those needing immediate attention. Archaeologists learned this from the Renewing American Archaeology conferences, which dealt with five very general issues. The task force then broke down each issue into work assignments, but follow-through and results have been hard to achieve. We must be realistic in our implementation.

- Public education works. A crisis arose during the 109th Congress (2005–2006) when amendments to the National Historic Preservation Act were proposed, amendments that might have weakened the ability to consider and protect cultural resources of all kinds in the Section 106 process. Members of the House and Senate were bombarded with e-mails and letters from individuals and groups expressing dismay, even indignation, at the suggested changes. The amendments got no further than committee consideration, and luckily for archaeologists, their sponsor was not re-elected to his House seat.

- Individuals can be most effective by developing personal relationships with those who are affecting the resources—congressional staff, agency managers, city planning commissions, developers (and their national organizations), mining companies, cell phone tower builders, and others in development industries who are going to need the services of archaeologists. Special attention should be given to members of local preservation organizations, as well as to organizations of amateur archaeologists, historians, and architectural historians. These may well be people with much local influence. They will feel incensed if, for example, the town planning commission suggests moving a historic house to widen a road or approves a nine-story condominium with retail stores and restaurants on a street in a historic district, as happened in my hometown (we beat them). While we are cultivating these relationships, we can be sure to make these people aware that the historic house sits on a historic archaeological site. For archaeologists, as for others, working with such grassroots organizations is public education at its finest.

- Any "vision for the future" needs to take into account what has worked and what has not worked in the past. I have mentioned some of the actions with which I am most familiar. The political scene is changing as I write (November 2008). People's attitudes may change; the laws and regulations may change. Archaeology is changing.

And last, something that has *not* been learned. Cultural resource management is now considered a separate career path for people who have academic training in archaeology. But the archaeology being taught in universities has not adjusted to this change. The skills and knowledge needed by archaeologists working under contract with agencies or private clients who require archaeological expertise are generally not taught in academic programs in most universities. Academia has yet to adjust to reality. This is not true, however, in the study of history and architecture. The field of public history was born from a need to train students of history in the areas of specialization created by the National Historic Preservation Act. There are now separate departments of public history in American universities, and there are specializations within architecture devoted to architectural history and historic architecture. Many more jobs are available in these fields than in academia. Anthropology departments have not been flexible, and increasing numbers of students are graduating with master's degree specialization in archaeology but without acquaintance with the laws or proposal-writing, much less with how to advise bureaucrats and federal agencies in the management of the resources for which they are responsible. Academic archaeologists have not learned this lesson—yet.

3

Archaeological Values and Resource Management

William D. Lipe

A resource is something that is valued because it is or can be useful: "something that lies ready for use or can be drawn upon for aid" (King 2002:5). The starting point for thinking about how to manage archaeological sites as cultural resources is to consider what resource values these sites might have and how management can enable these values to be realized as public benefits. Archaeological resource values include preservation, research, cultural heritage, education, aesthetics, and economics. These are not hard-and-fast categories with impermeable boundaries; there is much fuzzy overlap among them, and different analysts might come up with somewhat different concepts (see, for example, discussions in Mathers, Darvill, and Little 2005). I refer to "values" rather than "significance" because I think that the first term is more general and encompasses the second and because in the United States the term *significance* tends to be defined by federal historic preservation policies and regulations (ACHP 2008; but also see Bruier and Mathers 1996). The National Register of Historic Places criteria that form the basis for assessing significance explicitly address research, heritage, and aesthetic values and can be interpreted to include educational value, so I do not intend to imply that my more general terminology is in opposition to these criteria.

What does value-based archaeological resource management imply in terms of what we might actually do? At the most basic level, it implies that the starting point for management is to consider a variety of resource values when making choices about which sites to protect and how to manage them. It also implies that management programs should proactively take steps to ensure that public benefits are "delivered"—that is, to see that the public can in some way access the values that archaeological sites can provide and for which they presumably are being managed (Lipe 1984, 2000a; Little 2002, 2007a). Such access can be direct, as when researchers, culturally related groups, or lay people study or visit sites, or it can be indirect, as in dissemination of articles, images, accounts, and interpretations based on the archaeological record.

My frame of reference for thinking about values-based management for public benefits is derived substantially from my experience with federally administered public land in the western United States. Consequently, many of my comments are focused on that context for archaeological resource management. However, many of the issues faced by federal cultural resource managers apply in other settings as well.

In what follows, I begin with a general discussion of archaeological resource value and the role of authenticity. Next is a brief section on the contexts in which archaeological resource values are formed and accessed. In the main part of the chapter, I consider in more detail each of the six values already noted, with some comments on how current management approaches might be improved to better ensure that these values can be realized as public benefits. I draw examples largely from US public land contexts. Archaeological resource management requires numerous actors, including firms or individual consultants working under contract. In the US federal system, however, it is agency managers who are responsible for developing and maintaining programs for managing the archaeological resources controlled or affected by their agencies, including implementing sections 106 and 110 of the National Historic Preservation Act. Consequently, I often refer to "managers" as the primary agents in archaeological resource management while recognizing and in fact advocating that multiple other stakeholders need to be involved in these efforts as well.

The historic preservation movement grew up around the idea that preserving historic properties can ensure that their values remain publicly accessible over a long-term future. In fact, preservation, in and of itself, may be value enough for many people, much as establishing wilderness areas is supported by many who do not intend to visit, do research, or otherwise make direct use of such areas. In a larger perspective, however, in-place preservation of archaeological sites is generally a passive value—permitting but not ensuring the achievement of social benefits.

Preservation is thus an indispensable element in the archaeological resource manager's tool kit, but it is not the only element required for a resource management program to be successful.

A comprehensive (and idealized) archaeological resource management program requires (1) identifying sites; (2) assessing them in a frame of reference that considers both their intrinsic characteristics and their resource values as established within particular, historically developed social contexts; (3) responding to the potentially destructive effects of economic development by proactive planning and by selecting sites for preservation or for study, if they are to be destroyed; (4) taking active steps to promote preservation of the archaeological resource base in general and over the long term; (5) ensuring that records and collections resulting from the preceding steps are adequately curated; and (6) providing ways in which at least some segments of society can directly or indirectly access the resource values that were the reason for managing the sites in the first place. Because archaeological resource managers are not the sole arbiters of what constitutes value, they must maintain some type of two-way interaction with the segments of society most engaged in establishing and accessing these values. Effective implementation of the Section 106 process can contribute to achieving some of these goals but does not in itself constitute a comprehensive resource management program.

WHERE DO ARCHAEOLOGICAL RESOURCE VALUES COME FROM?

Resource value is not an inherent characteristic of archaeological sites, at least not in the same sense that site size or age or the distribution of artifacts and sediments is inherent. Assignment of value depends on particular socially and historically developed contexts or frames of reference (Darvill 2005; Lipe 1984:2). Assigning resource value also requires taking into account the particular intrinsic characteristics of the property in question, and ordinarily it depends on some confidence in the property's authenticity. Thus, a Puebloan archaeological site may be considered significant because it represents what scholars have decided is a particular architectural style from a particular time period. The site must have physical characteristics that represent this style and must date to the appropriate period. Further research may show that the characteristics of, say, the site's masonry do not conform to the assigned style, so the evaluation may change. Thus, recognition of value depends both on a culturally constructed context and on the specific characteristics of the property itself.

The dependence of archaeological resource value on context means that the value assigned to a particular site or artifact is not immutable. To suggest another example, an archaeological site might be judged to have low research potential when viewed from the intellectual context of classic American processual archaeology but to have high research potential for postmodern interpretation and middling research potential for building a culture-historical sequence. The site will have been discovered in one sense as a physical entity, but its research value will be "discovered" only in another sense, that is, by inferring what one or more communities of scholars might see as its potential for productive research. Likewise, a descendant community might view the site as valuable because it represents important aspects of the group's history and social identity.

Since the 1960s, American archaeological research has shifted from a primary focus on individual sites "typical" of a particular period and culture to a focus on populations of sites in a locality or region. In this view, the research value of individual sites is largely as data points documenting variation within the population. This approach may lead to a lack of fit between the site-by-site evaluations typically made in compliance with federal historic preservation laws and the way researchers conceive of research value. Concepts of heritage value have also expanded to include, in some instances, historic cultural landscapes in addition to individual sites. Historic preservation policy and procedures are changing—though not always comfortably—to accommodate these shifts in archaeological resource values.

The question of authenticity is also an important one (see discussions in Lipe 1984, 2002). Since at least the emergence of modern *Homo sapiens* and quite possibly before, humans have used their physical environment as a kind of mnemonic database. This happened when people began to name and thus culturally appropriate features of the natural environment, and the process "took off" when cultural features and modifications began to be added to the landscape, thus greatly expanding the repositories for cultural memories. Archaeological sites generated by past societies remain as tangible, physically authentic links between cultural memories as understood in the present and the lives and cultures of the individuals and groups who left those sites in the past. Establishing authenticity is also essential if researchers are to claim that inferences made from study of a particular site pertain to the period and the sociocultural contexts being investigated.

A determination of authenticity is of course a present-day judgment, but one constrained by the characteristics of the site in question, as well as by socially endorsed standards used to infer or test authenticity. The important point is that authenticity—the demonstration or belief that a property has survived from some time in the past to the present day—has the power to provide both evidential and evocative connections between past and present. Such tangible connections to the past complement those based on historical accounts transmitted orally or through surviving documents. Authenticity thus contributes to all six types of resource value discussed here.

In the US cultural resource management (CRM) context, "integrity" is a key concept used in evaluating sites. However, what constitutes adequate physical integrity is highly relative to the kind of value being imputed. The archaeological record typically does not satisfy the "Pompeii premise" (Schiffer 1985, 1987) but results from numerous formation processes, some of which continue to be active. For example, data from sites that have been plowed, looted, or even substantially destroyed may be adequate for a variety of research questions. This is not to say that disturbance of archaeological deposits is unimportant—it may preclude some ways of accessing resource value. But again, assessment of "integrity" depends on what is proposed to be done with the resource, as well as on the degree of disturbance.

THE SOCIAL CONTEXT OF ARCHAEOLOGICAL RESOURCE MANAGEMENT

Those entrusted with the job of protecting and managing cultural resources must take into account how conceptions of archaeological value are formed in society; how well (and whether) these conceptions are represented by the laws, regulations, and policies that guide their work; which values and sites are important to which stakeholder groups; and how the interests of such groups in accessing various resource values can be met within the structure of existing law and policy. Sites from any given period are by definition nonrenewable resources, so there must also be a concern for providing public access to resource values in ways that do not remove or substantially erode the characteristics that made the properties worthy of management in the first place.

Government archaeological resource managers can use public laws and regulations as tools in pursuing values-based management, but these tools do not create the social contexts in which resource values are established and enjoyed. Hence, effective resource management often requires communication and cooperation with individuals, institutions, and groups from various communities. Such communities may be diffuse—for example, persons with a general interest in archaeology and history. In order to provide benefits to this type of community, the manager's interactions will most likely be with educators, writers, and other "interpreters" who bring information and insights about archaeology to a larger public. Also, managers interact with tribes, businesses, researchers, environmental groups, and other well-defined entities that have specific interests and concerns related to specific archaeological sites or land areas that contain sites.

Effective archaeological resource management thus recognizes that the resource values associated with archaeological sites and artifacts are largely defined by various stakeholder groups (see, for example, Ferguson, chaapter 8, this volume; Mathers, Darvill, and Little 2005; Smith 2006). And effective management recognizes that it must have as a goal some type of public benefit, which in turn requires considering how this benefit might at least potentially be delivered. The publics this benefit from access to archaeological resource values are also stakeholders, although they are not necessarily the same as the stakeholder groups involved in defining the values. For example, traditional Native American communities may assign heritage meanings and value to particular sites. Members of the general public might be interested in learning about these traditional meanings and values, yet descendant communities might see satisfying this broader interest as intrusive or as destructive to their heritage. Resource managers, researchers, and archaeological interpreters must be sensitive to the possibility of such conflicts (see chapters 8 and 10, by Ferguson and Bridges, respectively, this volume).

Resource managers will be most effective if they recognize the stakeholder role and respect the agendas of the various communities that define and make use of resource values. In addition, however, they are responsible for encouraging and in some cases demanding that the stakeholder groups recognize the multiple values at play, as well as the need for long-term protection and management of the archaeological properties in question. This may require mediating conflicting demands made by various populations of resource users. Most often it is the demands of economic development that need to be balanced against other values, but in some cases there may be conflicts among research, heritage, educational, and aesthetic values. The complex demands of archaeological resource management thus require the manager to adopt a broad, multidimensional view of the contexts within which archaeological properties acquire resource value and through which various publics attempt to benefit from those values.

There are numerous discussions of types of archaeological resource value in the literature (for example, Briuer and Mathers 1996; King 1998; King, Hickman, and Berg 1977; Lipe 1984; Little 2002; Mathers, Darvill, and Little 2005; Smith 2006). The brief review that follows is intended to highlight several ways in which archaeological sites can be used as resources to produce information or experiences seen as meaningful by one or more communities within American society.

PRESERVATION VALUE

Site preservation is in one sense a passive means directed toward the end of actively providing research, heritage, and other value-based public benefits. In another sense, preservation can stand as a value and benefit in and of itself; it demonstrably is seen this way by substantial numbers of people. And although those people may have a background awareness that sites can be useful for research, public education, heritage, and so forth, it is preservation that is their concrete, immediate interest. Organizations such as the Archaeological Conservancy and the National Trust for Historic Preservation have effectively responded to this generalized interest in preservation.

Volunteers can find an engagement with preservation personally rewarding and often can influence attitudes in their communities in favor of protecting sites from looting and vandalism. For example, in many Bureau of Land Management (BLM) public land units, people eagerly volunteer to become "site stewards" (BLM 2007a). Although law enforcement is an essential component of site protection, it would be counterproductive and in any case economically impossible to have large numbers of enforcement-qualified rangers patrolling the many thousands of sites on public land. Site stewards can help by reporting damage or other problems at sites. More important, they can serve as ambassadors for archaeology and site preservation through contacts with other public land users, as well as friends and neighbors in their communities. In southwestern Colorado, the area with which I am most familiar, the BLM's 164,000-acre Canyons of the Ancients National Monument (CANM) currently has more than 50 enrolled site stewards. In the same area, the Anasazi Heritage Center (AHC, jointly administered with CANM) received more than 13,500 hours of volunteer help in 2006. And the AHC-CANM has partnerships with numerous local and regional groups for activities ranging from trail-building and maintenance to research (Lipe 2006a). Several other public land agencies offer the US Forest Service's Passport in Time program (www.passportintime.com), which engages volunteers in cultural resource service projects. The National Park Service has its VIP (Volunteers in Parks) program, which may include cultural resource preservation projects (www.nps.gov/volunteer).

Mobilization of volunteers requires a substantial commitment of staff time from the land-managing unit. This may happen because some especially committed persons just "find the time" to do the necessary outreach and coordination with volunteers and groups. For such efforts to succeed consistently and continue to expand, however, they need to be built in to staff job descriptions, and the people filling those positions must have the training needed to make them most effective. Engaging more volunteers in preservation-oriented work has a number of benefits, both for the citizens who become involved and for the missions of the public land agencies.

Only a fraction of the archaeological sites representing a particular period will have survived the winnowing of time, and those surviving are continually at risk from the forces of nature and from economic development projects. In the United States, regulations stemming from Section 106 of the National Historic Preservation Act establish widely used procedures designed to identify and take into account the cultural resource values of historic properties when federal undertakings are planned that might affect such properties. This process typically leads to identifying some sites as eligible for in-place preservation, insofar as that is feasible. Subsequently, some of these may be recommended for intensive recording or excavation before destruction. In some cases, preservation may ultimately be ineffective because of the cumulative effects of multiple projects. In this volume, Barker, Sebastian, and Chandler (chapters 4, 5, and 6, respectively) all discuss aspects of the Section 106 process and suggest improvements that take into account both the character of the archaeological record and the goal of providing societal benefits from archaeological resource management programs.

RESEARCH VALUE

Archaeologists and specialists from other disciplines have developed formal methodologies for making inferences about the human past based on systematic studies of the physical traces and remains preserved in the "archaeological record." These methodologies emphasize standard ways of gathering and analyzing empirical evidence to support conclusions. For the recent part of the historical continuum, documentary research may complement evidence gained from studying material remains. Archaeologists and other scholars also are increasingly attempting to analyze oral traditions as another complementary source of evidence. Conversely, some Native American scholars have begun to use oral histories and traditions as starting points for a critique of standard archaeological and historical scholarship (for example, Echo-Hawk 2000; Ferguson, chapter 8, this volume). And "indigenous archaeology" (for example, Watkins 2000) attempts to develop archaeological research methodologies based on integrating indigenous intellectual traditions of inquiry with those stemming from Western academia.

The primary contribution to society of formal research is accounts of the past based on methods of data collection, analysis, and inference that have been established within communities of researchers. The methods and results ordinarily are subject to critical comment within and across related disciplines. This criticism, reactions to it, and the continual flow of new data, ideas, and accounts give the results of formal research a dynamic, ever-changing quality. Formal research depends of course on socially constructed frames of reference that incorporate both explicit and implicit value judgments about what is important to study and what is a credible interpretation of the evidence. Although the "culture of archaeological scholarship" to a substantial extent crosses national and cultural boundaries, it tends to be associated with socially dominant groups and with intellectual traditions generally identified as "Western." Interpretive bias stemming from the sociology and history of archaeology cannot be eliminated, but the hope is that reliance on empirical evidence and the contentious and critical nature of the discourse (including critiques based on indigenous intellectual traditions) will correct or at least make transparent some of the biases that threaten sound conclusions.

Archaeological researchers form a community or set of communities that seek and receive benefits from access to the archaeological record. The inferences about the past that researchers produce are the principal source of broader public understandings of archaeologically based history and of the practice of archaeology. The large number of books, magazine articles, television productions, lectures, classes, museum exhibits, and Web sites devoted to disseminating the findings of archaeological research testify to the broad public interest in this type of inquiry and its results. The highly technical, contentious, and ever-changing qualities of formal research can be frustrating to those attempting to access its results from outside the research disciplines. These qualities also pose a challenge for writers and other interpreters who attempt to provide various lay publics with access to research results. However, the dynamism of research constantly provides such interpreters with new evidence and ideas. And clearly, over the past century, formal archaeological research has resulted in great increases in reliable knowledge about the human past and has continuously invigorated public interest in and understanding of that past.

Archaeological research often requires altering some aspects of the in-place archaeological record, and it thus may have an effect on site preservation. One reaction is the development of "conservation archaeology" (Lipe 1974, 2000a). There, the goal of on-site investigation is to obtain a large amount of relevant information while physically altering only small portions of the archaeological record. This approach has become the norm in US archaeological fieldwork. Over the past several decades, adherence to a "conservation ethic" has been made easier by the development of sophisticated sampling methods, more intensive ways of investigating the in-place archaeological record (including use of remote sensing), and new and more productive methods of analyzing the artifacts and specimens. The rapidly rising costs of fieldwork, laboratory analysis, and curation have reinforced a conservative approach to excavation. Archaeological excavation remains the primary way to obtain certain kinds of evidence, but as it is conducted today, it makes a distinctly minor impact on the in-situ archaeological record relative to the effects of economic development, natural erosion, looting, and vandalism.

I think that there are three ways in which greater public benefits can be realized from the research values of archaeological sites that are subject to federal CRM actions: better dissemination of the results of CRM archaeology, encouragement of complementary investigator-initiated research, and better communication between researchers and interpreters.

Disseminating the Results of CRM Archaeology

Many of the technically best and most substantively informative archaeological studies currently being done in North America are those done in a CRM context. The thousands of studies done every year under these auspices produce thousands of reports. For projects that involve testing and excavation, these are often lengthy and extremely detailed, and they frequently include multidisciplinary contributions. Yet, the most significant results of much of this work often remain effectively hidden from other archaeological researchers, let alone from the general public. King (chapter 7, this volume) effectively reviews the problem and a range of possible solutions (see also chapters 6, 9, and 11 by Chandler, Mackey, and Crass, respectively, this volume; Lees and King 2007; Little 2007a). Most solutions involve allocating a small fraction of the funds currently spent on "compliance archaeology" not only to the broader dissemination of the detailed technical reports already required by contract but also to the production of topical and regional data syntheses of the type, for example, produced in Colorado in the late 1990s (see discussion in King, chapter 7, this volume). The only practical way to disseminate large technical reports is by posting them on the Internet; fortunately, this is also the least expensive way. Topical and regional syntheses can also be disseminated by this means, although their smaller size makes traditional monographic publication feasible as well.

In my opinion, it would be desirable and cost-effective (in the sense of yielding public benefits) for major projects to be required to produce one or more articles suitable for publication as scholarly articles or book chapters. If accepted, such publications would feed into the well-developed system of journals and presses that not only scholars but also educators, media specialists, and other interpreters rely on to find out "what's happening" in archaeology. For example, the findings of the Dolores Archaeological Project that have made their way into the general Southwestern archaeological literature are largely those that were published in journal articles or book chapters after this multi-million-dollar project was completed (Lipe 2000b). These publications, however, were the results of individual initiatives, and few received any funding from the project itself. Such article-length works can be included in the final report(s) of major CRM projects "for the record," but many are likely to be accepted for publication as well and therefore to be disseminated through the long-established scholarly publication systems that have developed to serve all research fields and ensure timely access to new research results.

It would also be productive for federal agencies having CRM responsibilities to build in more consultation with relevant portions of the archaeological research community at the beginning stages of major projects (see, for example, suggestions in Judge 2006). By "research community" I mean to include both CRM and academic archaeologists who are knowledgeable about the topic or area to be investigated. Archaeological research values are established within this larger community; advance consultation would help agency resource managers develop or select research designs that address significant problems in technically appropriate ways. This would in turn promote sharing of information generated by the projects and, ultimately, wider dissemination of these results (see chapters 6, 7, and 9 by Chandler, King, and Mackey, respectively, this volume).

Contributions from Investigator-Initiated Research

By "investigator-initiated research" I mean studies done outside the CRM system to address particular research problems. Ordinarily, such studies are done by researchers from universities, museums, or research centers, and they frequently involve grant funds awarded after peer review of research proposals. This approach to research characterizes American science in general and is responsible for some of its dynamism (Lipe 1978). In most areas, and especially on public land, investigator-initiated research will remain infrequent relative to CRM investigations, but it can deliver significant public benefits, not the least because it is done in social and intellectual frameworks that promote publication. In many cases, such research can complement CRM-based research by focusing on areas or kinds of sites unlikely to be subject to intensive CRM surveys or "mitigation" studies. Public land managers are in a position to encourage such complementary research efforts by engaging in discussions with both academic and CRM researchers and by developing cooperative agreements with problem-oriented investigators.

Most public land resource managers attempt to accommodate well-justified applications for problem-oriented research permits under the Archaeological Resources Protection Act (ARPA). However, it is my impression that some managers take the position that research that physically alters the archaeological record should be undertaken only in the service of "mitigating" loss due to development projects or to recover data from sites that have been seriously damaged by looting. This position implies that obtaining new information about the past through problem-oriented excavation can never be a better reason for intruding on the archaeological record than, say, building a road, a power line, or a parking lot. This view seems an unfortunate interpretation both of a conservation ethic and of the social responsibilities inherent in the notion of cultural resource management (Lipe 2000a, 2001). This minority of cases in which proposals for problem-oriented excavations are given little consideration seems to me to result from seeing Section 106 compliance as discharging the agency's total responsibility in the cultural resource arena. ARPA, however, clearly treats investigator-initiated research as a legitimate use of archaeological sites on federal land, and this kind of research can often help agencies meet their obligations under Section 110 of the NHPA.

A recurring problem with investigator-initiated research is the lack of incentives, and often funding, for production of the kinds of detailed technical reports that regularly issue from CRM-based projects. Granting agencies and the academic community need to accept responsibility for reporting in some detail the archaeological contexts and analyses that support published conclusions. Again, the Internet can reduce the costs of making such technical reports available, but academic researchers (and administrators) also need to assign more importance to such reports and hence improve the incentives for their production. Resource managers can also specify a reporting requirement as a condition of granting an ARPA permit.

Improving Communication between Researchers and Interpreters

By "interpreters" I mean K–12 teachers, college and university faculty, journalists, visual media writers and producers, museum exhibitors, tour leaders, park rangers, backcountry guides, and others who rely on research results as they communicate with the members of various publics about archaeology. Some researchers also write for the public, lead tours, and so forth, and thus also serve as interpreters. Interpretation is not a one-way street—rather, it gives members of "the public" access to experiences, ideas, and information that they use in constructing their own understandings of the past. And many of the people who seek a better understanding of archaeology will do so through books and other media rather than through actual visits to archaeological sites.

As the review by Crass (chapter 11, this volume) demonstrates, the intermediary role of interpreter is a vital one in enabling various publics to gain something of educational value from archaeological research. In the United States and elsewhere, interpreters are increasingly attempting to include traditional cultural heritage perspectives, as well as those derived from application of formal research methodologies (which may increasingly be based on collaboration between archaeologists and representatives of indigenous communities, as Ferguson discusses in chapter 8).

I second the plea by Crass for archaeologists and archaeological resource managers to recognize the need to link journalists, video producers, and other interpreters with the most knowledgeable researchers from both the CRM and academic communities. They must also make every effort to ensure that interpreters understand and respect the interests of groups with related cultural heritage interests. And it is essential for archaeologists and resource managers to educate interpreters about the fragility of the archaeological record and about its legal protections so that the resulting public products do not end up encouraging inadvertent damage or looting.

CULTURAL HERITAGE VALUE

Artifacts and historic properties have great power to symbolize and represent the past, at least in part because they provide a physical, tangible link between past and present (Lipe 1984:4–6). This linkage and its symbolic and evocative effectiveness depend, however, on a context in which something is known about the past that is being represented and also about the object or property that serves as a link to that past. This knowledge can come from formal archaeological or historical research, or it can come from traditional sources such as oral traditions or documentary accounts that record traditional knowledge.

Some authors have emphasized the political character of cultural heritage as a way of asserting claims to particular visions of identity, at scales ranging from the family to the nation. Heritage, although typically based in traditional practice and beliefs, continues to be created and negotiated in the service of present-day interests. Lowenthal (1996) contrasted heritage with history, emphasizing the association of the former with identity politics and the latter with critical examination of various types of evidence. As noted earlier, however, formal research disciplines have also developed in particular historical, social, and cultural contexts; archaeological interpretations based on formal research often have significant political implications (Smith 2004).

Skeates recognized two common uses of the term *heritage* as applied to archaeological remains: "first, as the material culture of past societies that survives in the present; and second, as the process through which the material culture of past societies is re-evaluated and re-used in the present" (Skeates 2000:9–10). He noted that governmental agencies tend to use the more descriptive definition, even though the choices they make regarding what to preserve and what interpretations to make inevitably privilege particular views of group and national history and identity.

Smith (2004, 2006) focused on heritage as an ongoing process that might or might not incorporate historic properties but that depends on the use of ideas about the past to construct group identities. She was concerned with the way "the idea of heritage is used to construct, reconstruct, and negotiate a range of identities and social and cultural values and meanings in the present. Heritage is a multilayered performance—be this a performance of visiting, managing, interpretation or conservation—that embodies acts of remembrance and commemoration while negotiating and constructing a sense of place, belonging, and understanding in the present" (Smith 2006:3). She developed a thorough critique of what she called "the authorized heritage discourse" (Smith 2006:11–43) and illustrated her critique with examples of alternative approaches to heritage-building taken by indigenous groups, as well as with a study of how visitors to particular social history museums "critically and actively utilize these places as cultural and social tools in remembering and memory making that underwrite a self-conscious sense of class and regional identity" (Smith 2006:196). She argued that the authorized heritage discourse generally treats visitors to historic sites as passive receptacles for "education" provided by authorized interpreters. It fails to recognize the active way in which visitors use these experiences to create their own cognitive and emotional understandings (Smith 2006:66–74).

As Ferguson's review (chapter 8, this volume) demonstrates, increased legal and regulatory requirements in the United States for consultation with Indian tribes and other groups culturally related to historic properties (including archaeological sites) have resulted in "opening up the system" to a greater diversity of readings regarding which properties should be considered for preservation, which values should be emphasized in management, and which groups and individuals should be involved in decision-making and interpretation. The growth of large tribal CRM programs has contributed to this process (for example, Ferguson, chapter 8, this volume; Stapp and Burney 2002; Watkins 2000), as has more systematic treatment of "traditional cultural properties" (for example, King 2003).

These developments require cultural resource managers to accommodate a greater diversity of views and interests than in the past; to do otherwise would be to continue to ignore and marginalize groups that have undoubted historical and traditional connections with many of the sites being managed. Increased democratization of the "heritage process" on occasion leads to conflicts as received notions of "who owns the past" are challenged by new voices and as oral traditions are arrayed against accounts based on formal research (as in the battle over disposition of the Kennewick skeleton in Washington state [Owsley and Jantz 2001; Stapp and Longenecker 1999]). Ferguson (chapter 8, this volume) discusses how similar remains were handled in a more collaborative way at On Your Knees Cave in Alaska, where Tlingit people were enlisted as research participants from the outset.

Difficult questions may arise when different groups such as researchers, preservationists, and descendant communities disagree on whether intrusive research should be permitted, whether general public visitation to a historic property is acceptable, whether site stabilization is appropriate, and whether the adverse effects of a proposed development can in fact be mitigated and if so, how. For example, the "preferred alternatives" of the Draft Resource Management Plan for Canyons of the Ancients National Monument states that "standing wall features would be thoroughly documented, then allowed to deteriorate through natural erosive forces, except at sites developed for public use" (BLM 2007b:287). This provision responds to recommendations received during tribal consultations but seems likely to be questioned by individuals or groups concerned with historic preservation, aesthetic values, or the local economic potential of increased backcountry visitation. Multiple-use land-managing agencies such as the BLM have long histories of having to make management decisions in the face of conflicting views among stakeholder groups.

In response to the increased prominence of cultural heritage claims and traditional histories in both identity politics and formal scholarship, we are beginning to see museum exhibits and popular accounts that "tell multiple stories" from traditional cultural perspectives, as well as from those of researchers. Public interest in traditional histories and indigenous views of archaeological sites extends well beyond the members of particular heritage communities. There also are opportunities for exploring similarities and differences in the assumptions and perspectives underlying archaeological and Native American interpretations of the archaeological record (for example, Tessie Naranjo 1995; Tito Naranjo 1999). Ferguson (chapter 8, this volume) makes a number of cogent observations and recommendations regarding ways in which the articulation and in some cases the integration of research, educational, and heritage interests can be pursued in projects involving Native American archaeological sites.

My sense is that the ability of tribes and individual Native Americans to participate fully in collaborative work with archaeologists is often limited by time and funding constraints, particularly on the Native American side. Archaeologists engaged in such collaborations may be able to justify this kind of work as part of their paid employment, but this is often not the case for Native American participants. As a practical matter, we need to find ways to diminish and eventually remove that financial obstacle.

AESTHETIC VALUE

Humans very likely have species-specific preferences for particular combinations of form, texture, color, materials, and settings that contribute to the appreciation of a historic property for its aesthetic qualities. We also seem to have a fondness for novelty in that things "curious" catch the eye. Broadly speaking, the aesthetic value of archaeological materials thus runs the gamut from a fleeting interest in "curios" and "relics" to powerful aesthetic responses across multiple cultural contexts. Any innate preferences are always to some extent conditioned by culturally based standards and preferences. Some historic properties preserve characteristics that give clues to the aesthetic standards and preferences from the period in which the properties were created and thus can serve as representatives of past styles and modes of construction. People observing historic buildings and archaeological sites today will also evaluate them in terms of current standards and preferences, which may change over time (think of the late-twentieth-century reemergence of an appreciation for late-nineteenth- to early-twentieth-century architecture).

A visitor's positive response to the aesthetic qualities of an archaeological site may emotionally amplify the experience of making some kind of tangible contact with a valued past. Such responses might also make the visitor more receptive to whatever heritage- or research-related messages are on offer at the site. Aesthetic, or at least visual, concerns may lead some site managers to adopt dubious reconstructions of ancient sites or to "tidy up" the visual scene to the point of misrepresenting the site's original social and cultural context. In such cases, an imposed aesthetic may unintentionally or intentionally communicate that present-day worldviews and values are timeless and in some sense inevitable.

Aesthetic appreciation of sites can sometimes be gained without intruding on the fabric of the historic property itself. Many sites offer visitors the opportunity to experience aesthetic values by "just looking," and visitor management devices such as trails can often be constructed with little or no intrusion on the site's physical fabric. However, archaeological sites commonly are repositories of removable artifacts that some people value primarily for their aesthetic or at least "curio" qualities. Undocumented excavation focused on acquiring visually pleasing objects for the digger's private collection or for the antiquities market almost always compromises archaeological research values, and it may damage heritage, educational, and economic values as well. The majority of the artifacts from North American archaeological sites that make their way into the antiquities market come from looted Native American graves. Not surprisingly, Native Americans see this as one more way in which the dominant society perpetuates historical patterns of disrespect for and marginalization of their communities and their heritage.

Although aesthetic appeal may be a primary motivation for artifact collectors, in many cases there is also a contribution from historic interest, rarity, and the appeal of authenticity. Regardless of the precise mix of motivations, possessing beautiful and rare archaeological artifacts is seen as a benefit by the collector, who may in some cases be willing to make that benefit more public by showing the objects to friends and associates or by loaning or selling these for display in a gallery or museum. Most archaeologists oppose this type of public benefit because the market created by collecting supports looting, which works against translating most of the other types of archaeological value into public benefits. Bridges (chapter 10, this volume) discusses some of the ethical issues that archaeologists face if they do attempt to find common ground with those who excavate sites and possess artifacts outside the "public trust" assumptions (Knudson 1991) held by nearly all archaeologists and resource managers.

This is not the place to review the increasingly abundant literature on the damage to research, heritage, aesthetic, and educational values caused by the market in antiquities and the destructive looting of sites that feeds the market (for example, Atwood 2004; Brodie et al. 2006; Renfrew 2000). From the standpoint of archaeological resource management on US public land, much is yet to be understood about the motivations, demographics, and modus operandi of unauthorized diggers and collectors. Assuming that their motivations are primarily economic is likely to be off the mark in many and perhaps most cases (Goddard 2008a). Some research has been undertaken on these issues (for example, Ahlstrom et al. 1992; Colwell-Chanthaphonh 2004; Goddard 2007, 2008a, 2008b; Nickens, Larralde, and Tucker 1981), but much more remains to be done. This kind of "ethnoarchaeology" is important in order to assist in law enforcement but even more so to help design educational messages and alternative opportunities for contact with archaeology that may forestall looting.

EDUCATIONAL VALUE

The educational value of the archaeological record lies in its usefulness to people who wish to learn something about the past. Direct contact with archaeological sites and artifacts helps people visualize some aspects of past human life and experience a sense of personal connection to that past. Indirect contacts with archaeology through various media also clearly have much appeal and contribute to what people know and think about the past. People also bring previous knowledge and ideas to their direct and indirect encounters with archaeology; these preconceptions may or may not result from prior structured "education" about archaeology or history. Their encounters with archaeology may help them construct new perceptions of the past or may simply reinforce their preconceptions.

Not all archaeological sites are equally valuable for giving people a sense of having learned or experienced something about the past, and certainly not all sites provide equally good opportunities for the "show and tell" approach to on-site education. "Undeveloped" backcountry sites may be very effective in helping people reflect on the past and construct their own views of history. A great variety of archaeological sites can be effective in participatory education, which involves people in excavating, recording, or monitoring sites. The number of participants necessarily will be much smaller, however, than at, say, a "developed" site in a national park. Suitability for educational use may be a factor in decisions to preserve and to provide public access to particular sites and places. When archaeological sites are selected for direct educational use, cultural resource managers are obligated to develop ways of accommodating visitors without sacrificing the sites and without letting development and visitation compromise the values that are the focus of the educational experience.

"Archaeological education," whether directed toward K–12 classrooms or toward society more generally, has emerged as a professional specialty in American archaeology, in part because of the effective efforts of the Society for American Archaeology's Public Education Committee since its formation in 1989. A number of "how-to" books, media resources, Web sites, and curricula are now available for use by K–12 teachers and cultural resource managers (for example, Bender and Smith 2000; Davis 2001; Davis and Connolly 2000; Project Archaeology 2007; Smardz and Smith 2000). Resources that place more focus on historic buildings and sites include the National Register's "Teaching with Historic Places" lesson plans (National Register of Historic Places 2007). In addition, there are increasing numbers of academic and general treatments of the theory, method, and practice of public education in archaeology (for example, Jameson 1997; Little 2002; see also links in the Society for American Archaeology's Web page "Archaeology for the Public," www.saa.org/publicftp/PUBLIC/home /home.html).

And of course the success of popular magazines such as *Archaeology* and *American Archaeology*, the numerous media treatments of archaeological topics, and the enormous number of Web sites featuring archaeology all testify to a great public interest in thinking and learning about archaeology. The most expansive conception of archaeological education would include general works that cause people to think about regional or even global culture history, such as Jared Diamond's phenomenally successful books *Guns, Germs, and Steel* (1997) and *Collapse* (2005).

Educators in the broad sense, or "interpreters," as I have called them, are in various degrees stakeholders in archaeological resource management. Archaeologists and public land managers need to recognize this role and establish to the extent possible a two-way dialogue with those individuals and groups who make a living bringing archaeological understandings to various publics. For example, educational trip leaders and backcountry guides may have valuable insights into which sites "work best" for public education. And their experience may enable them to provide advice on whether or how to "harden" or develop sites for high-frequency public access and how to subtly establish low-impact access routes at less frequently visited backcountry sites. Likewise, archaeological resource managers must require group leaders and guides to present accurate information about research and heritage and to ensure that the participants in their programs understand the fragility of the archaeological record and the importance of using proper "site etiquette" to protect it from damage.

Much of the work labeled as archaeological education has as one of its

objectives instilling an ethic of respect for and protection of the archaeological record. This assumes that students and adults will be more protective of archaeological sites if they understand how much can be learned
from these through research and how important these are to the cultural
heritage of some groups. Is this the case? Hollowell (2006:86) reported
that "a quantitative study of eighty-four projects conducted in various (non-
US) locations found that projects that included more public outreach
reported higher incidences of looting in the area." She referenced an
unpublished SAA meeting paper (Hollowell and Wilk 1995).

My own experience is that people often do not make the connection
between liking archaeology and needing to protect archaeological sites
from illegal digging or unregulated economic development. Even if they
do understand the connection, they do not necessarily relate it to their
own behavior. That is, some may love visiting archaeological sites and reading about archaeological research but still do not refrain from purchasing
archaeological artifacts. Efforts to make explicit the linkage between
buying artifacts and destroying sites may be seen as heavy-handed "guilt-
tripping" and hence be counterproductive. It seems to me that we need
considerably more research on what approaches might be most effective in
converting an overall interest in archaeology into an aversion to the antiquities market and support for archaeological preservation in general.

Another area in which linkages are weak to the point of nonexistence
is in public perceptions of cultural resource laws and policies. Admittedly,
this is an arcane area sometimes poorly understood by archaeologists and
resource managers themselves. However, these laws and policies are central
to the way archaeological sites are protected and managed in the United
States today, and they facilitate field research and the preservation of cultural heritage sites. My impression is that the majority of the people who
visit archaeological sites on public land or who read about archaeological
research and cultural heritage preservation in the United States are unaware
of the dependence of these activities on federal cultural resource law and
policy. There seems to be a much wider public awareness of federal laws
and policies that affect wildlife and the natural environment than of those
governing cultural resources. Threats to cultural resource law and policy do
not readily result in opposition from those who otherwise care for archaeology. We need more discussion and research about how public interest in
archaeology can be expanded to include the legal and regulatory structure
that underpins federal archaeological resource management. The suggestions offered by Crass (chapter 11, this volume) for interacting effectively
with the media about archaeological research can perhaps be extrapolated
to this area as well.

ECONOMIC VALUE

Preserving and managing archaeological sites always involves comparing the economic costs of doing so with both the monetary and the nonmonetary benefits. Some sites may have positive economic values in that they can serve as attractions that draw crowds and support the development of tourism. Most sites have little or no direct visual appeal to visitors, even though they may be extremely valuable for research or cultural heritage and hence have the potential to contribute indirectly to public understanding and appreciation of archaeology. When archaeological sites are "in the way of" development, they are usually viewed by the developers and often by large segments of the local populace as having negative economic value—that is, protecting them will increase the project's costs without increasing its monetary benefit. It takes law, regulation, public opinion, or all three to weigh in on the side of nonmonetary archaeological values.

For archaeological sites that have appeal as tourist attractions, the lure of the aesthetic and the authentic enhances direct public engagement with archaeological values. These situations also create opportunities for marketing books, videos, classes, tours, and other media that can enable visitors to understand the site in broader contexts. In some cases, "cultural tourism" may allow visitors to interact with individuals or groups having a cultural heritage connection to the site(s). Archaeological tourism can make, and in many cases has made, a significant contribution to public appreciation of archaeology and cultural heritage and to public support for archaeological resource management. The articles collected by Rowan and Baram (2004) review the extensive literature on many aspects of "marketing heritage." Among the "downside" issues are physical destruction of structures and properties due to unwise overuse or overdevelopment, the creation of false or "hyped" histories and heritages, the promotion of looting at unprotected sites, and the overwhelming of local societies and traditional beliefs and lifeways through the effects of cultural tourism. The papers assembled by Derry and Malloy (2003) discuss the effects of both archaeological research and archaeological tourism on local communities, particularly those in the third world.

Besides providing opportunities for tourism, archaeology often has less obvious economic benefits. In some areas, the CRM profession, museums, colleges or universities, and independent research and educational organizations (such as Crow Canyon Archaeological Center in southwestern Colorado) are significant sources of local employment. People often move to areas that offer a variety of interesting things to do; this is especially true for retired and semiretired people. In many parts of the US West, these amenities may include opportunities to visit developed or backcountry archaeological sites, to be a site steward or volunteer, or to participate in a local archaeological society. Archaeological employment and opportunities for engagement outside the standard "tourism" category should be taken into account in totaling up the economic benefits of archaeological resources.

SUMMARY AND CONCLUSIONS

"Management" is not a goal in and of itself but requires answering the question, "Management for what ends?" Archaeological resource management is justified to the extent that it benefits various communities and, ultimately, society as a whole. These benefits can be viewed as access to one or more of the values associated with archaeological remains. The principal types of resource value discussed here are research, cultural heritage, aesthetic, educational, and economic. Many people also adhere to a generalized preservation value that implicitly recognizes but does not explicitly call upon the other values. Legal and policy frameworks guide and constrain the way resource managers seek to provide access to these benefits; the policies and procedures generated by these legal frameworks provide means to achieve the larger ends of delivering societal benefits. Much of the discussion in this book is about whether and how the laws, policies, and procedures that guide archaeological resource management can be made to work more efficiently and effectively in service of that larger goal.

Archaeological resource values are socially constructed in contexts that include but usually are not strongly influenced by the public employees and institutions officially charged with management responsibilities. Resource values are not intrinsic characteristics of archaeological sites, but the historical authenticity and physical characteristics of the sites affect the assignment of resource value.

The actual use of archaeological sites as resources may involve direct contacts between people and the sites. Such use often does not result in attrition of the physical characteristics of the sites, but modest intrusions on their physical fabric (as in site stabilization and visitor access measures, as well as some types of research) may be justified through a kind of "cost-benefit" analysis. Larger numbers of people may benefit indirectly from archaeological values—for example, through articles, videos, images, and lectures that are ultimately based on contact with the archaeological record.

Archaeological resource managers can leverage their effectiveness by collaborating and forming partnerships with a variety of outside groups and organizations that recognize various values in archaeological sites and have stakes in the way sites are managed. To be optimally effective, managers must understand and be responsive to the resource value definitions and interests held by various groups and communities, as well as by the "general public."

Rather than think about interested parties as lying "outside" a public agency's well-bounded CRM program, resource managers need to think of themselves and their programs as being "inside" larger social contexts within which people establish and seek to benefit from the resource values of the sites being managed. The manager's responsibility is to design and carry out a program that delivers benefits to various publics while mediating conflicts over use and access and protecting the sites from unjustified attrition.

Many of the problems with US archaeological resource management that are discussed in this book (see especially chapters 4, 5, 6, and 9 by Barker, Sebastian, Chandler, and Mackey, respectively) seem to me to stem from a conflation of means (processes for complying with laws and regulations) with ends (achieving the broad public benefits intended by the laws and regulations). Problems also stem from insufficient recognition that resource values and hence public benefits are defined in social contexts that extend well beyond the regulatory frameworks and cultures of the agencies charged with managing resources on behalf of the public(s). Disciplinary specialists employed in CRM efforts may also take a too narrow view of the goals and social context of their work.

If producing greater public benefits for the time and money spent on archaeological resource management requires changes in current regulations, practices, and job descriptions, then such changes must garner public support and must be based on analyses that are sound in both a theoretical and a practical sense. I hope that this chapter and this book contribute to a productive rethinking of US archaeological resource management ends, means, and practices. This country's archaeological resources are important to a large and diverse set of publics that, collectively, far outnumber those of us who call ourselves archaeologists or archaeological resource managers. In exchange for public support, our responsibility is to provide benefits to those publics in ways that optimize the use of nonrenewable archaeological resources over the long-term future.

4

The Process Made Me Do It

Or, Would a Reasonably Intelligent Person Agree that CRM Is Reasonably Intelligent?

Pat Barker

Potential damage to archaeological resources (a subset of cultural resources) from land-use undertakings on federally managed land or from federally permitted or funded undertakings on nonfederal land is managed under Section 106 of the National Historic Preservation Act (NHPA). In its plain language, Section 106 requires that federal agencies take into account the effects of their undertakings on cultural resources and afford the president's Advisory Council on Historic Preservation (ACHP) and the state historic preservation officer (SHPO) an opportunity to comment on these undertakings before they are implemented. Since the NHPA became law in 1966, implementing Section 106 has evolved through rule-making, congressional amendment, and judicial decisions into an exceedingly complex, costly, time-consuming, and often frustrating bureaucratic process.

Because the NHPA is a process law, the emphasis over the past 40 years has been on creating a legally defensible process, which might or might not include any resource protection or historic preservation. In addition, the way in which the NHPA is usually applied has led to an overemphasis on single-site archaeology at the expense of more regional approaches to historic preservation (see Sebastian, chapter 5, this volume). Finally, the demand for a defensible process focused on managing single sites has created a misplaced emphasis on mitigation by gerrymandering undertakings to avoid sites rather than on treatment to develop refined understandings of the past and a concomitantly more efficient and reasonable approach to archaeological resource management (Lipe, chapter 3, and Chandler, chapter 6, this volume).

Managers, preservationists, and land users become involved in federal cultural resource management (CRM) archaeology because they want the government to do things that require compliance with federal heritage policy, usually Section 106 of the NHPA. They learn that Section 106 compliance focuses on piecemeal management of individual sites affected by individual undertakings in a three-phase process: identifying cultural resources, evaluating their significance, and treating potential effects to them. In this chapter, I focus on identification, with some discussion of evaluating and treating those resources. In chapter 5, Sebastian focuses on evaluation with some reference to identification and treatment, and in chapter 6, Chandler discusses treatment with some reference to identification and evaluation.

Even in the best circumstances, Section 106 compliance can take months to complete at a cost of $50 to $100 an acre. In many cases, it takes much longer and costs much more. Each phase requires written reports, mandated review windows, agency decisions, and SHPO consultation and may require additional consultation with the ACHP or the keeper of the National Register of Historic Places (NRHP). The standard piecemeal approach to Section 106 compliance is essentially reactive and unpredictable. Land managers and CRM archaeologists cannot predict what resources will be found in the identification phase, which of them will be significant upon evaluation, and how damage will be treated. This means that land managers cannot give prospective land users a reasonable time and cost estimate for Section 106 compliance and users cannot reasonably plan and implement their undertakings.

No wonder reasonable nonprofessionals involved in the Section 106 process find it confusing, frustrating, incomprehensible, and unduly bureaucratic. In short, developers, land managers, archaeologists, and other reasonably intelligent people find the Section 106 process to be increasingly unreasonable and in need of serious revision or elimination.

If CRM is to become more predictable, then CRM archaeologists could (should?) refocus management on regional approaches to Section 106 compliance and on the outcome of the effort rather than the process by which the outcome is reached. Regional approaches work better in the American West, where large tracts are managed by single agencies.

However, in the East all levels of government have some sort of planning process that incorporates cultural resources and can benefit from regionalized justifications for planning decisions. The best regional approaches focus on large-scale historic or prehistoric settlement and subsistence patterns to predict resource distribution and significance and are not tied to modern political boundaries. Regional approaches extending beyond modern political boundaries should not be more expensive or time-consuming to produce and can be used by many different polities (see www.mnmodel.dot.state.mn.us/ for a good example from the Minnesota Department of Transportation).

Refocusing on regional approaches can be done in any or all of three ways: (1) redo the ways in which resources are identified by moving from a single-site focus to a regional planning perspective; (2) redo the way in which we determine significance by abandoning the National Register criteria and bureaucracy and moving toward a concept of significance based on refining our understanding of the past and interpreting it to the public (Sebastian, chapter 5, this volume); and (3) redo the way in which we structure treatment to stop avoiding significant resources on a piecemeal basis and focus more on outcomes that further our knowledge of the past. As I discuss in detail later, the way to create a more reasonable and truly defensible approach to CRM is through regional planning modeling as a basis for the rational inclusion of archaeological resource considerations in general resource management and land-use planning.

The planning approach I advocate here should be considered in the context of issues embedded in the fabric of the NHPA and of the evolution of the Section 106 process in reaction to those issues. The fundamental issue is that the NHPA is a process law. A second issue, derived from the first, is an undue emphasis on avoiding different types of errors by archaeologists, managers, and undertaking proponents.

DEFENSIBILITY IN PROCESS LAW IMPLEMENTATION

At the most fundamental level, there are two types of laws dealing with environmental or heritage issues. Some laws, like the Endangered Species Act, mandate a specific outcome, so agency obligations are fulfilled when the mandated outcome is reached, regardless of the process used. Other laws, like the National Environmental Policy Act and the National Historic Preservation Act, mandate a process for arriving at an outcome, so agency obligations are fulfilled when the process is completed, regardless of the outcome.

In implementing process law, activity generally evolves toward legal defensibility and not toward specific outcomes such as historic preservation. CRM archaeologists practice defensive process management aimed at an administrative record that will withstand public and judiciary review but the outcome of which may not actually preserve anything. Defensibility is important; the problem is that archaeologists defend against one type of error, the false negative, and developers and land managers defend against another, the false positive.

Most archaeologists and some other participants focused on resource preservation are concerned primarily with avoiding false negatives—that is, determining that no significant resources exist within the "area of potential effects" (APE) of an undertaking and then being proved wrong. They tend to think it better to be conservative and err on the side of resource protection by always acting as if significant resources will be found within the APE of every undertaking. This kind of error avoidance reinforces the managing of each undertaking and each site without regard for larger issues. It can lead to repeated inventories of places where there are no archaeological resources and repeated excavations at identical sites in identical contexts. Instead, we need to focus on sampling regional site populations, which involves planning models and regional planning.

In contrast, developers, managers, and legislators—perhaps overfocused on avoiding impediments to development—tend to be more concerned about false positives, or the determination that insignificant resources are significant. They assume that preservationists are overconservative (susceptible to false positive errors) and continually ask them when enough is enough. Development expediters want to know why archaeologists keep recording the same information about the same sites in the same places. Our answers are rarely convincing.

When nonprofessionals question what we do, we confront them first with the arcana of the profession by invoking our special knowledge: "They just look like rocks to you, but to a postmodern lithics edgeware topologist [insert your favorite obscure specialty], they are highly significant and need to be studied to document gender hermeneutics [insert your favorite topic] in prehistory." When that does not work, we try blaming the process: "I know this sounds crazy, but because of the process in place, I have no choice but to make this recommendation. If you want me to challenge the system, it will cost money and delay your project. Wouldn't it be better just to go along now?" If all else fails, we invoke the dreaded hierarchical dragon: "I'm with you on this, but I know that the higher-ups [insert state, district, or regional office, SHPO, keeper, or ACHP, as needed] will disagree. We can ask, if you insist, but it will cost money and delay your project. Wouldn't it be better just to go along now and save us the pain of fighting this later?"

With an emphasis on process and not outcome and with critics mystified by arcana, the archaeologist's safest professional call tends to be conservative. Our peers rarely take us to task for requiring inventory surveys or calling marginal resources eligible, whereas they usually treat us as if we have gone over to the dark side when we recommend no inventory or noneligibility. We know that the documentation needed to support determinations of noneligibility or no inventory far exceeds that for a conservative determination. In the short run, the negative political and social effects of a false positive appear to be less detrimental than those of a false negative. Over the long run, however, this bias leads to indefensible political positions and agitation to amend or eliminate the NHPA.

Over time, avoiding false negatives produces an extremely conservative process in which actions tend to be based on past bureaucratic successes rather than on a view toward future understandings of the past. The problem is that focusing on process rather than outcome makes it difficult to avoid either type of error, and over the past 40 years, the process has not been self-correcting. Alternative regional approaches, based on probabilistic modeling, can be self-correcting in ways that identify and reduce both types of errors and move us toward outcomes rather than process.

PROBLEMS WITH IMPLEMENTING SECTION 106

The plain language of the NHPA notwithstanding, over the years, through agency policy, judicial review, public participation, and archaeological practice, each state has developed a phased-consensus approach to compliance with Section 106. The phases are (1) identify resources through archival research and field inventory; (2) evaluate the significance of the resources by applying the eligibility criteria of the National Register of Historic Places; and (3) treat significant resources to reduce or eliminate damage. Each phase suffers from the general problems noted earlier, as well as unique ones.

Identification

CRM archaeology grew out of the salvage archaeology that developed after World War II and continued until the NHPA was implemented after 1966 (Davis 1972:268–269; McGimsey 2004:9, 16–18). Salvage archaeologists heroically concentrated on being "in front of the bulldozers," saving any information they could before a site was plowed under (Murtagh 2006:134–135). In most salvage situations, resources were located during development activities and had to be quickly salvaged to minimize delays to the development work (Davis 1972:268–269). What better example than the cover art on Bob McGimsey's personal perspective, *CRM on CRM*, showing a young McGimsey scraping a grader cut with a trowel while a competing grader scrapes away the site beside him (McGimsey 2004; see Davis 1972 for other good examples).

When Section 106 and the National Register criteria were codified, most archaeologists were seeking stratified sites from which to build cultural chronologies and not attempting to discover distributional patterns (Thomas 1988:167–169). It did not matter how sites were found, so long as they produced good dates (Binford 1972:148). With the rise of regional archaeological approaches in the 1970s, the way sites were found became, and remains, a major focus of archaeological theory, and research-design-driven archaeology became the norm (Kohler 1988:26–33). Research designs for identifying sites became part of academic archaeology but not generally of CRM archaeology.

One legacy of salvage archaeology is that many archaeologists deemphasize the planning of the identification phase and generally do not create research designs for inventories. Instead, there tends to be an explicitly or implicitly negotiated standard operating procedure (SOP) among CRM practitioners that allows identification to proceed immediately, so long as the SOP is followed. Normally, without involving regulators or land managers, a developer contracts with a CRM firm, and it implements its version of the identification SOP. The first contact with regulators and land managers comes when the draft inventory report lands on the regulator or land manager's doorstep, along with another frantic request for expedited processing in order to meet the developer's deadlines. This means that there is no time to assess the need for inventory or to develop alternative approaches to it.

Evaluation

After identification, the next phase in the Section 106 process is to evaluate resources for eligibility for inclusion on the National Register of Historic Places. During evaluation, resources that occur naturally as a continuous, variable population are sorted into two arbitrary categories: significant resources, which are eligible, and trivial resources, which are ineligible. Significant resources are the subject of the treatment phase of the process, and trivial resources are not. In effect, determining significance determines the fate of the resource.

In practice, many CRM archaeologists determine significance by applying consensus rules of thumb to individual sites, rather than by applying explicit research designs to site populations. For example, sites that have depth are considered significant, but surface sites are not; sites with diagnostic artifacts are significant, but those without are not; lithic scatters are significant, but tin can scatters are not; and rock art is significant, and so forth. We all have our lists. This approach tends to become set in stone without any self-correcting mechanism. As with identification, expediting the process for each undertaking outweighs building a self-correcting global process. Redirecting our efforts toward evaluation based on site populations in regional context could help alleviate this problem.

Treatment

The treatment phase is the one most coveted by archaeologists and most familiar to land managers and the public. Everyone knows that archaeologists dig sites and find the past in them. And finally the process lets them dig. The problem is that we go about testing and mitigation in convoluted ways that evolved in an environment focused on process and not on outcome. We identify sites as eligible because of their ability to answer scientific research questions, and a reasonable person would think that we then mitigate damage to them by recovering the data and answering questions. Alas, this is not what we do.

Processual Section 106 compliance has created a schizophrenic federal CRM program in which research design usually becomes a meaningless exercise in boilerplate production. One myth is that each and every effect to each and every historic property must be mitigated. Another is that data recovery on sites or portions of sites not directly threatened is unethical because it unnecessarily damages sites that could be avoided. A third myth is that avoidance, no matter how unlikely in reality, is the preferred treatment approach. The avoidance myth has been reinforced because the regulations and guidance implementing the 1992 NHPA amendments are interpreted as establishing the new concept that mitigation through data recovery is by definition an adverse effect on tribal heritage values that can be resolved only by avoiding data recovery (36 CFR 800.5[a][2], www.achp.gov/apply.html).

This means that we simultaneously find sites eligible because of their research information potential and mitigate effects to them by not recovering the information. Treatment plans increasingly call for dealing with information loss by avoidance, by formal nomination of sites to the NRHP, or by other actions that recover no information. Without new information, we cannot advance our understanding of the past. In turn, this limits our ability to inform the public about their past by limiting the information available for developing interpretive opportunities—books, videos, brochures, signs, kiosks, and so forth. In many contexts, avoidance is indeed preferable, but in others it is not (see www.achp.gov/archguide/current-issues-achp-archaeology-guidance). For example, in closely spaced development areas such as oil and gas fields with numerous small operators, sites are avoided for each undertaking but tend to be lost through cumulative damage. More important, without data recovery and analysis, it is difficult to refine our approach to CRM in ways that reduce effort and frustration without compromising the resource. Moving toward regional planning based on modeling is one way to make avoidance more effective and reasonable.

STATE-BASED HISTORIC PRESERVATION PLANNING

The National Park Service, the SHPOs, and federal agencies have attempted to resolve these problems through state-based historic preservation planning. This kind of planning begins with some sort of state historic preservation plan and associated "historic contexts"—explicit definitions of how resources are determined to be eligible (see Hardesty and Little 2000:13–16; Sebastian, chapter 5, this volume). These plans were invented by the National Park Service (King 1998:233–240) and subsequently mandated in NHPA revisions. Nevada's experience with this planning approach illustrates the issues involved.

The first Nevada State Historic Preservation Plan was developed in 1978. It was focused on architectural resources and historic themes and did not address archaeological issues (Becker 1986:8). The SHPO then formed a team and developed the needed archaeological context (Becker 1986:8). Two years later, at a conference assessing CRM in the Great Basin (Aikens 1986), Becker noted reasons why agencies and contractors were not using the plan: "The research questions for each unit are vague and general …[and] often it is difficult to judge whether sites discovered during surveys have the potential to answer key research questions" (Becker 1986:10).

In January 1990, the Bureau of Land Management (BLM) in Nevada and the Nevada SHPO tried, with limited success, to correct these problems. As it played out, each firm or agency unit developed a set of proven research designs or contexts because these were reliably acceptable to regulators and land managers. This meant that the operational problems with the plans and with the practice of CRM archaeology could be ignored—or at most, constantly lamented—and archaeologists were forced to soldier onward, reluctantly if gallantly, salvaging sites in the face of enormous development pressures.

During the same period, however, archaeologists were developing regional approaches to understanding settlement and subsistence systems based on empirical stochastic modeling that could (and should) be used to rationalize the practice of CRM archaeology (see Ebert 2001; Sullivan 2001, 2008).

REINTRODUCING RATIONALITY

One good method of reintroducing rationality into the Section 106 process and increasing its efficiency and predictability is to make the process less reactive and more proactive. The best way to do this is to step back from piecemeal processing of an endless stream of high-priority undertakings (salvage archaeology) and toward deliberate cultural resource management by incorporating archaeological resources into land management planning before the stream starts to flow. Planning models derived from probabilistic locational models of past land use make this possible in deliberate and defensible ways.

Just before and immediately after World War II, cultural ecology became an enduring research paradigm in Americanist archaeology (Bettinger 1991:48–51; Kohler 1988:26). In the Great Basin, argued Steward (1938), for example, local ecological parameters limited the range of variation in cultural adaptations in predictable causal pathways (Trigger 1989:289–291). In the early 1970s, modeling became more empirical and less anecdotal with the development of site-catchment analysis (Bettinger 1991:66–70). In this approach, explicit rational economic decision criteria were introduced to define the relationships between local environmental parameters and archaeological sites (Kohler 1988:31). Then, in the late 1970s, archaeologists in the Great Basin (Bettinger 1991:70–73), the Southwest (Plog and Hill 1971), and other regions demonstrated statistical associations between site types and environmental variables that allowed the creation of predictive locational models (Kohler 1988:30–33). Finally, by the 1990s, locational modeling included middle-range theory (Bettinger 1991:61–77) and various optimal foraging strategies to rationalize resource use decision-making (Bettinger 1991:83–110; Kelly 1995:73–110; and see www.srifoundation .org/library.html for eastern military examples).

Concurrent with these developments, computer technology evolved to the point that large databases and geographical information systems (GIS) enabled land managers to map resource sensitivity in ways that facilitated regional land-use planning. Sebastian, Van West, and Altschul (2005:35–47) provided a concise summary of modeling and its uses in archaeology and CRM.

Since the late 1990s, BLM Nevada has been developing resource planning models of the archaeological record and using them to develop cultural resource management plans or cultural resource components of multiresource land-use plans (for specific examples, see Drews, Ingbar, and Branigan 2004; Drews et al. 2004; Zeanah et al. 2004).

Cultural Resource Planning Models in Nevada
As outlined by Ingbar and colleagues (2001), formulating a model and an associated management plan entails several steps (fig. 4.1) that are best illustrated by an example. The northern Railroad Valley is a major oil and gas interest area in Nevada. In the 1990s, BLM oil and gas leases were offered and purchased with a general warning about Section 106 compliance but without specific stipulations for cultural resource conflicts. With no better information available, oil and gas operators relied on anecdotal information about archaeology problems in planning their leasing and exploration activities (Ingbar et al. 2001). Before a model and a cultural resource management plan (CRMP) for Railroad Valley were developed, operators had no reasonable ability to anticipate cultural resource conflicts before the lease and faced unpredictable high costs and significant delays from Section 106 compliance.

On the cultural resource side, resources could be better managed if specific stipulations could be placed on leases before sale and if operators could alter their bids accordingly. The BLM could significantly improve operations in Railroad Valley by limiting oil and gas leasing in areas with significant resources. Finally, with more formalized information, BLM and the SHPO could agree on plans to minimize or eliminate inventories in low-probability areas and to maximize inventories in high-probability areas or where there was insufficient information to determine inventory needs.

In 1997 the BLM Nevada state office contracted a planning model and regional CRMP for the northern Railroad Valley. The Railroad Valley study area includes all or parts of 22 townships—approximately 530,000 acres, or roughly 825 square miles (Ingbar et al. 2001). The archaeological record for the study area was derived from more than 450 CRM inventories (fig. 4.2) that recorded 1,358 archaeological sites and isolates (Zeanah et al. 2004:1). With this information in hand, the contractor developed a habitat-based model of the study area (fig. 4.3).

The planning model was derived by applying optimal foraging theory to information from previous studies in the western Great Basin. The contractor developed the initial model without reference to the Railroad Valley archaeological record so that the existing archaeological data set

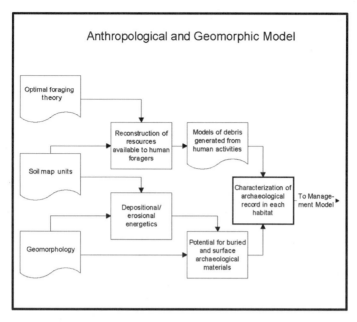

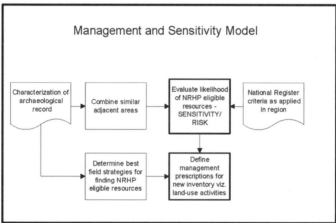

FIGURE 4.1

The process for producing planning models. Reproduced by permission from Ingbar et al. 2001.

could be used to test and refine the model (Ingbar et al. 2001). The model was adjusted to reflect changes through time (Zeanah et al. 2004:61–76), with cross-references to habitat types. The result, using all relevant data, was a model of the past 10,000 years of land use in Railroad Valley (Zeanah et al. 2004:iii).

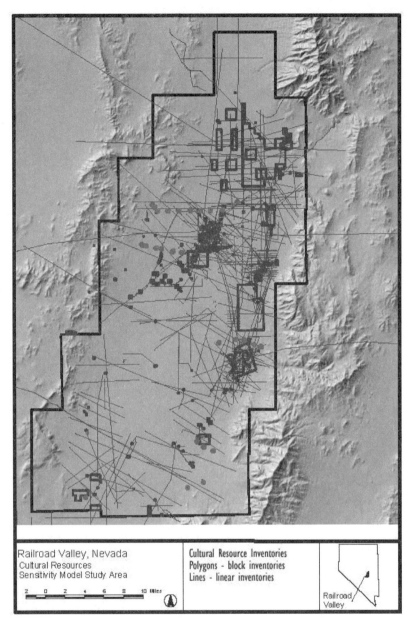

FIGURE 4.2

Inventory coverage in the Railroad Valley, Nevada, study area. Reproduced by permission from Ingbar et al. 2001.

It is important to note that optimal foraging theory or any other decision criterion will bias the model in specific ways (Mehrer and Wescott

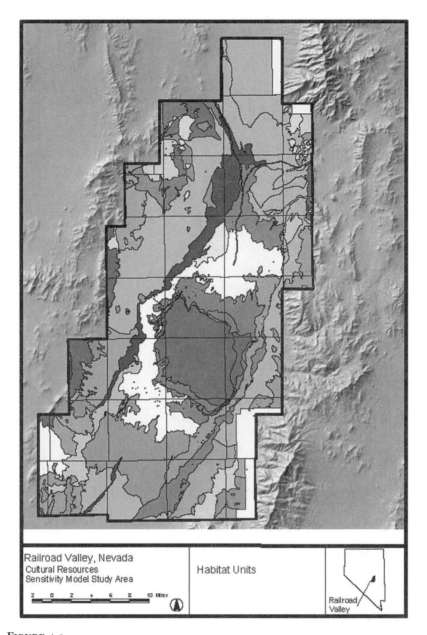

FIGURE 4.3

The habitat-based model of the Railroad Valley study area. Reproduced by permission from Ingbar et al. 2001.

2006). Simple correlation modeling probably introduces the least theoretical bias, but it suffers from a lack of self-correcting mechanisms (Mehrer

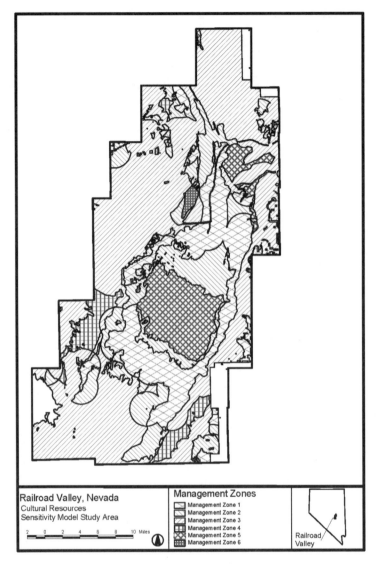

FIGURE 4.4

Management zones in the Railroad Valley study area. Reproduced by permission from Ingbar et al. 2001.

and Wescott 2006). Also, models need not be limited by modern political boundaries—a major issue in regional approaches in the East. In modeling, habitat boundaries are important, and political ones are not. Political boundaries become important when developing CRMPs, but plans can be based on regional models that cross political boundaries.

TABLE 4.1
Railroad Valley Management Units

Mgmt. Unit	Inventory Type	Transect Interval	Special Considerations	Monitoring Requirements	Site Density (ha/site)	NRHP Site Density (ha/site)
Zone 1	Systematic	30 m	Dunes, tool-stone sources, water sources, cutbanks, zone margins	All blading and trenching	14	128
Zone 2	Systematic	30 m	Dunes, tool-stone sources, water sources, cutbanks, zone margins	All blading and trenching	12	319
Zone 3	Systematic	45 m, perpendicular to contour	Dunes, tool-stone sources, water sources, cutbanks, zone margins	Case by case	17	649
Zone 4	Intuitive	Case by case	Dunes, tool-stone sources, water sources, cutbanks, zone margins	Case by case	23	N/A
Zone 5	None	N/A	N/A	Case by case	52	N/A
Special mgmt. units	Per data-recovery plan	Per data-recovery plan	Per data-recovery plan	Per data-recovery plan	Varies	Varies

Source: Ingbar et al. 2001.

In the Nevada case, the initial planning model was tested with half the available archaeological record for Railroad Valley. This was done by independently classifying the sites recorded in the valley in the same way they were conceptualized in the model and then comparing this known distribution with the model's predictions (Zeanah et al. 2004:122–130). After being tested and refined, the model successfully predicted the density and content of 94 percent to 97 percent of the known sites in Railroad Valley (Zeanah et al. 2004:131–150). Further, because the model's success was highly correlated with National Register eligibility, it became useful as a planning tool (Zeanah et al. 2004:151–168).

The complex mosaic of habitat types was reduced to six management zones (fig. 4.4) with relatively uniform sensitivity and buried site potential (Ingbar et al. 2001:7–8). The five zones were then used as the basis for a CRMP that defined inventory intensity for each zone. The results are shown in table 4.1. With the model as justification, the BLM, with SHPO concurrence, implemented the CRMP in 1999.

The immediate effect of implementing the CRMP was the exclusion

PAT BARKER

TABLE 4.2

Estimated Cost Savings for Railroad Valley Inventories, at $35 per Acre

Mgmt. Zone	Acres	Prior Cost ($)	Current Cost ($)	% Change	Reason
1	88,401	3,094,035	3,094,035	0	No change
2	92,954	3,253,390	3,253,390	0	No change
3	272,996	9,554,860	6,369,907	−33	Increased sample transect interval to 45m
4	20,909	731,815	182,954	−75	Intuitive inventory strategy
5	49,493	1,732,255	0	−100	No inventory required
6	2,427	84,945	84,945	0	No change
Net	527,180	18,451,300	12,985,230	−30	

Source: Ingbar et al. 2001.

of 12,423 acres from further inventory, reduced inventory intensity on another 294,239 acres, and increased inventory on a further 220,510 acres (Zeanah et al. 2004:i–ii). In addition, the boundaries of three special management areas were decreased to reflect actual resource–habitat relationships. Although the long-term results of the CRMP remain to be seen, table 4.2 shows an estimated overall 30 percent reduction in inventory costs from implementing the model (Ingbar et al. 2001:7–8).

Cultural Resource Planning Models in New Mexico

Following the success of the Nevada model, the US Department of Energy contracted to use planning models to identify more effective cultural resource management practices in the Powder River basin, Wyoming, and in southeastern New Mexico (Ingbar et al. 2005:6). The models developed were similar in design and application to those in Nevada, and I do not describe them in detail here. The results of modeling in Wyoming and New Mexico, however, are worth some consideration.

Ingbar and colleagues (2005:6) noted that the volume of CRM work in these areas was "truly stunning," with more than 10,000 inventories and 16,000 sites recorded in the Powder River basin and more than 21,000 inventories and 8,000 sites in southeastern New Mexico. Unfortunately, they also observed a significant amount of overlap, redundancy, and inefficiency in these inventories.

For example, between 1997 and 2002 in the Loco Hills, New Mexico, study area, 5,196 CRM inventories were conducted (fig. 4.5), covering

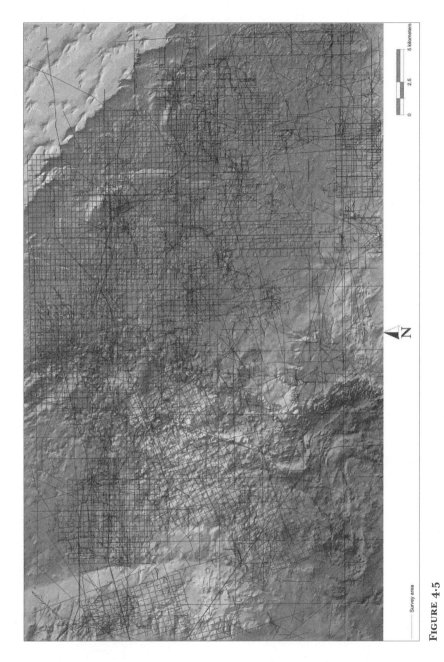

FIGURE 4.5
Surveys conducted in the Loco Hills, New Mexico, study area, 1997–2002. Reproduced by permission from Sebastian et al. 2005:69.

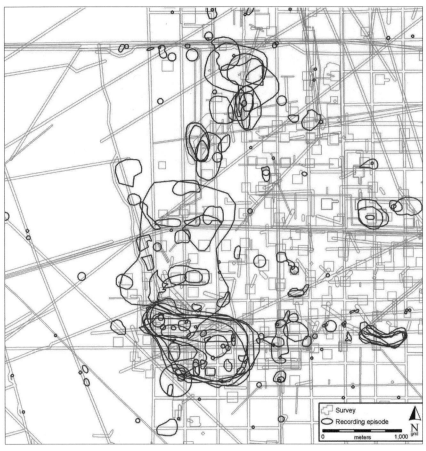

FIGURE 4.6

Inventory and recording episodes in part of the Loco Hills study area. Reproduced by permission from Sebastian et al. 2005:56.

75,223 acres (117.5 sections) (Altschul et al. 2005:54–55). The inventories recorded 1,625 archaeological sites. These appear to be respectable numbers, suggesting that about 25 percent of the area had been surveyed. This coverage, however, was more apparent than real (Altschul et al. 2005:75–76). Of the 1,625 sites, 508 (31 percent) had been recorded more than once, and of the 75,223 acres, at least 12,348 (16 percent) had been inventoried more that once (fig. 4.6). At $100 an acre, this meant that more than $1.2 million had been spent on unnecessary inventory.

Cultural resource planning models have been used to manage the identification phase of the Section 106 process with some success (for

82

extended examples, see Ingbar et al. 2005; Zeanah et al. 2004). Yet, as Altschul and colleagues noted:

> BLM still has difficulty making this determination [eligibility] with any confidence, even with all the survey data from Loco Hills.... BLM must err on the side of calling too many sites eligible. Projects are delayed, redesigned, moved, and moved again to avoid sites that may or may not...yield important information. In part...the absence of regional research designs or historic contexts means that property types eligible for the National Register have not been defined. (Altschul et al. 2005:74–75)

The use of planning models in providing an empirical, rational basis for CRM decisions can be expanded beyond justifying inventory intensity to include more comprehensive planning approaches.

COMPREHENSIVE PLANNING

One way to get away from the salvage archaeology mentality and single site–single undertaking archaeology is to limit development and other sources of potential conflict in places where significant resources exist. On a limited scale, this is one of the effects of special designations—national parks, national monuments, historic landmarks, national conservation areas, wilderness areas, and the like—on federal land. Similar designations have been made at other levels of government throughout the country. One problem with these special designations is that they require legislative approval and therefore are rarely made. Another is that resources outside the specially designated areas are deemed insignificant and receive no protection. The main value of such designations is that they protect resources indirectly by limiting what can be done within the boundaries of the specially designated areas.

The route to protecting resources before they are threatened by individual undertakings, without having to pass special legislation, is to appropriately include archaeological resources in land-use planning at all levels of government. This in turn requires a focus on developing and implementing planning models without regard for political boundaries to justify CRM restrictions in general land-use plans.

Land-use planning is most effective for large areas managed by agencies with single-use mandates. It can be less effective in areas managed for multiple uses, regardless of their size. It is also challenging for agencies such as departments of transportation that have undertakings crossing

TABLE 4.3

BLM Planning Use Allocations, Desired Outcomes, and Management Actions

Use Allocation	Desired Outcome	Management Action
Scientific use	Preserved until research potential is realized	Permit appropriate research, including date recovery
Conservation for future use	Preserved until conditions for use are met	Propose protective measures/designations
Traditional use	Long-term preservation	Consult with traditional users; determine limitations
Public use	Long-term preservation; on-site interpretation	Determine permitted use; on-site interpretation
Experimental use	Protected until used	Determine nature of experiment
Discharged from management	No use after recordation; not preserved	No use after recordation; not preserved

Source: BLM 2005.

multiple jurisdictions with varying degrees of conformity among their land-use plans. But even in these cases, inserting CRM elements into general land-use plans and cooperative agreements for multiple jurisdiction undertakings that are based on regional models is a reasonable approach to CRM.

Because my experience is with the BLM, I use its planning approach as an example, although most levels of government have some sort of land-use planning system that could be used to better manage the archaeological resources in their jurisdictions (King 1998:233) in ways analogous to those available in the BLM system. In BLM land-use planning, management decisions identify uses or allocations that are allowable, restricted, or prohibited in order to facilitate commodity uses or protect resource values (BLM 2005:13). In the BLM system, resources can be allocated to one of six uses (table 4.3), each of which is associated with a different set of management actions (BLM 2004:31–35, 2005:Appendix C, 9).

Archaeological resources were included in early BLM land-use plans through Section 106 compliance discussions and sometimes by special designations for critical archaeological resource areas. As GIS capabilities improved, regional approaches became possible. The primary value of GIS-based locational modeling in CRM is that it results in statistically defensible spatial models. These models rationalize regional land-use recommendations in ways that are meaningful to other resource specialists, land managers, developers, and the public. If GIS-based locational models are developed and used to support cultural resource elements of agency land-use planning, the result is the kind of regional cultural resource planning models that are being developed in Nevada, the Southwest, and elsewhere.

Through regional planning models, we have the tools to develop usable cultural resource sensitivity maps and make them available to land-use planners and project proponents (Sebastian, Ingbar, and Cushman 2005:175). These maps in turn constitute an empirical basis for defensible land-use decisions, at all levels of government, in which an area may be excluded from development or in which development actions may be controlled before specific developments or undertakings are considered. Undertaking-focused management would still be needed in areas where development is allowed. But if significant classes of resources are identified in plans and if management actions or use restrictions are specified, then everyone is aware of the restrictions before beginning to plan development activities. Resource protection is built in to the basic structure of land-use plans.

At any level of government, when archaeological resources are given the appropriate consideration during planning, other uses can be managed to accommodate those resources before encountering them while considering a specific development or undertaking. When the basic geography of land use has been determined in a land-use plan, planning models can be further used to rationalize CRM in areas where other uses are allowed and where cultural resource conflicts may affect the location, timing, or method of development or the use of other resources in the planning area (BLM 2005:Appendix C, 8).

Evaluation

The BLM planning process is one reasonable alternative to simple binary NRHP eligibility determinations as a measure of the significance of archaeological resources. Sebastian (chapter 5, this volume) discusses others. In the BLM approach, categories of resources and threats to them are managed for each resource type's potential use (BLM 2005:Appendix C, 9) and not to preserve some ascribed condition such as eligibility for the NRHP. This approach is also advantageous because it can be derived directly from cultural resource planning models that determine sensitivity on the basis of the nature and usefulness of archaeological resources. Finally, a use allocation system can include explicit decisions about treatment when land managers are dealing with subsequent developments or undertakings. In effect, at all levels of government or agency planning, managing by use allocations based on models and associated resource management plans simplifies the compliance process so that the key data needed are the number and types of resources in an area of potential effects. After this is ascertained, treatment based on predetermined management actions associated with use categories can be implemented without extra review.

Treatment

Contingent treatment planning means developing treatment plans by using automated databases, planning models, and decisions already incorporated into regional plans to associate treatment options with resource types before considering individual development projects or undertakings. These options can be implemented after the identification and evaluation phases have defined the array of resources in the area of potential effects. With contingent treatment planning, an agency or a local government can outline how to use regional approaches to cultural resource identification, evaluation, and treatment, which make CRM more rational and truly defensible. Each action taken during treatment is contingent upon the results of previous activities. Because it is grounded in previous regional analyses that transcend local political boundaries, contingent planning allows creative approaches to resources that are rare or highly valuable in a region. It encourages innovative approaches to treatment based on regional needs and the use of site samples rather than every eligible site.

RECOMMENDATIONS FOR REGIONAL APPROACHES

On the basis of this analysis of the problems with cultural resource management as currently practiced and the arguments for improving it, I offer the following recommendations for making the practice of cultural resource management more rational, understandable, and predictable for everyone involved.

First, use existing automated databases of regional cultural resources to generate appropriately scaled resource sensitivity maps, ideally based on probabilistic modeling, to identify areas of high and low sensitivity. These maps should transcend local political boundaries. With appropriate obfuscation of site locations, provide these maps to all parties involved in CRM: agencies, proponents, archaeologists, the general public, tribes, interest groups, and so forth. Such maps will inform all parties of the potential for resource conflicts and, when linked to maps showing likely development patterns, could reduce people's surprise and frustration at encountering unexpected resources during the land-use approval process. These maps could also be used to better integrate CRM in regional land-use planning. Agencies with greater financial resources could develop regional models and share them with other agencies and governments in the region. Maps could be used to develop interagency or intergovernmental cooperative agreements for CRM across political boundaries.

Second, regionalize CRM by moving beyond simple one site–one undertaking approaches to managing damage to archaeological resources through land-use plans, at all levels of government, that are in place before any development or undertaking that might create a resource conflict is considered. At any level of government, the land-use plan is where the most basic decisions are made—decisions about where and how land uses will be managed. If these basic decisions are made without appropriate consideration of archaeological resources, then CRM managers are forced to continue using unsystematic, historically derived, and flawed compliance processes. In the federal system and at most state and local levels of land-use planning, the regional approach can be especially effective in dealing with discretionary land uses.

Third, regionalize CRM by using regional land-use planning to develop management actions to minimize the conflict between archaeological resources and land uses before considering any particular proposed land use. This will allow everyone to consider CRM actions in a reasonable and timely way during the general resource management planning. It ameliorates the challenge of making CRM decisions while being pressured to avoid impeding a pending land use. It also brings standard practices to the start of the process rather than to its end. Prospective land users will know what to expect when they contemplate a land-use application. This knowledge allows better planning and should minimize the surprise and outrage people sometimes feel when use limitations to manage archaeological resources emerge later in the process.

Fourth, recognize that all approaches to CRM are subject to both false positive and false negative errors and take steps to minimize them rather than identify errors but continue to make them. Ideally, managers can strike a balance between the two types of errors so that the very real problems posed by managing one type but not the other are minimized. The best way to do this is through adaptive management that facilitates self-correction and improvement. In CRM, this means a self-corrective process for resolving conflicts between protection of archaeological resources and other land uses. Regional planning models, based on regularly updated automated databases, are amenable to adaptive management and can be updated to identify changes in understandings of the past. Regional planning models also keep everyone focused on dealing with regional site distribution patterns and on managing to minimize damage to types of sites and not on managing individual sites considered in a vacuum. At all levels of government, planning models based on managing types of resources, deployed in an adaptive management process, are also the best way to identify and manage cumulative effects that are not apparent when people are focused on one-on-one compliance activities.

Fifth and last, keep our understanding of the past current and make it available for adaptive management. This involves abandoning the long-standing policy of avoiding sites at all cost and, through regional planning, allowing systematic data recovery projects that actually answer questions and advance our understanding of the past.

As we come to understand the past, resource sensitivity will change, as will the values of particular types of resources and their uses and importance in CRM. With increased understanding, questions will be answered and innovative approaches will emerge. Data with which to answer questions that are the focus of intensive research can be included in routine resource recordation during identification activities. Treatment efforts can be allocated to dealing with new issues.

In the American West, obsidian hydration and sourcing data are good examples of this approach to refining research questions. CRM archaeologists routinely regard gathering such data as a part of data recovery. Some sites are considered significant simply because they contain obsidian to be sourced and hydrated during mitigation. However, it would be both more efficient and much cheaper in the long run if obsidian was gathered during identification and routinely sourced and hydrated. If this was done, we could avoid identifying otherwise insignificant sites as significant simply to justify gathering obsidian. Similar situations exist in the East, and with regard to historic resources everywhere, this could be handled by more front-loading of data collection before evaluation and by less reliance on inappropriate eligibility determinations simply to get basic analytical data.

The same "front-loading" approach to data-gathering that has been taken in collecting obsidian projectile points during initial resource identification could be used for other materials, such as ceramics, surface hearths, and environmental samples, or for routine site descriptors, such as depth, stratification, and patterning. If protocols for routinely gathering such materials were developed in advance, independently of any particular undertaking, then spurious and often unanswerable open-ended questions could be dropped from research designs and treatment plans. The end result would be research designs and treatment plans that are focused on answerable questions and whose adequacy can therefore be judged.

We do not have to begin each project as if we know nothing about the past, limiting ourselves to basic, open-ended questions. We can instead ask and answer interesting questions about the past and once again appear reasonable to reasonable people. In this way, we can refine our approach to understanding the past and allow it to evolve over time.

CONCLUSION

At all levels of government, cultural resource planning models should complement existing CRM processes. The main value of cultural resource planning models is that they provide an empirical and defensible way to justify land-use restrictions in general land-use plans. These models resolve resource conflicts on a regional basis and can be used by any agency or at any level of government to resolve conflicts within its jurisdiction. Individual undertakings in areas open to other land uses could still be subject to CRM, but the adverse effects of the current process and its historically derived irrationalities could be minimized.

These irrationalities—process over outcome, single site–single undertaking focus, error mismanagement, and binary significance determinations—are now so entrenched in CRM policy and practice that their effects cannot easily be ameliorated (Sebastian, Ingbar, and Cushman 2005:173–174). The best way to redress the current imbalance between process and outcome and to ensure that natural resources can be developed and used without undue destruction of archaeological resources is to follow regional CRM founded in appropriate land-use planning. With a focus on cultural resource uses (outcomes) and not on assessing their conformity to set, idealized, abstract, and culture-bound values (process), CRM becomes more rational and palatable to managers, politicians, and developers at all levels of government.

This is not to say that the Section 106 or any other CRM process can or should be circumvented through appropriate land-use planning. Instead, the most efficient way to ensure that the focus of CRM remains on resource management and protection is to take archaeological resources out of the salvage archaeology arena and put them into comprehensive regional planning systems used at all levels of government to develop and implement better land-use plans.

As long as CRM is limited to dealing with the immediate, repetitive confrontation between high-value archaeological resources and the processing of high-priority, time-sensitive developments, making CRM more responsive to larger societal or political concerns will be limited either to the fruitless quest for more funding to hire more staff to process more undertakings or to continual attempts to eliminate or eviscerate CRM in the political arena.

Developers and managers could anticipate conflicts with archaeological resources and design undertakings accordingly if regional plans curtailed or eliminated development in high-value cultural resource concentrations and allowed it in areas with low cultural resource values. This could be done after the use and management of cultural resources are specified before opening areas to development. In this context, the compliance process could be a valuable tool for managing residual resource conflicts in ways that foster the public's understanding and appreciation of the past.

5

Deciding What Matters

Archaeology, Eligibility, and Significance

Lynne Sebastian

In chapter 1, I summarized the public policy goals for preserving the national heritage that Congress established in the National Historic Preservation Act (NHPA) and other laws. In this chapter, I focus on a problem area in cultural resource management (CRM) archaeology as it is practiced today, one that limits our ability to achieve those goals. The mechanism we use for deciding which archaeological sites are important profoundly affects the management of the archaeological record and on the public benefits derived from publicly funded archaeology.

In examining this issue, I address three questions: What kinds of places did the framers of these laws have in mind as worthy of protection or consideration? How have these ideas been applied to the nation's archaeological record? And given the public policy goals articulated in the laws, how can we better evaluate and manage the archaeological record to meet those goals over the long term?

WHAT DO THE LAWS DEFINE AS PLACES THAT MATTER?

Sections 106 and 110 of the NHPA specifically focus on management of and effects on "historic properties," which means any "prehistoric or historic district, site, building, structure, or object included in, or eligible for inclusion on the National Register of Historic Places" (§301[5]).

The National Environmental Policy Act (NEPA), in Section 101(b)(4), speaks of "important" historic and cultural aspects of the nation's heritage but does not define these terms. The implementing regulation from the Council on Environmental Quality, however, requires that agencies consider both effects on properties listed on or eligible for the National Register and actions that "may cause loss or destruction of significant scientific, cultural, or historical resources" (40 CFR 1508.27[b]8). The NEPA regulation, therefore, recognizes historical and cultural significance beyond the specific requirements of the National Register.

The Archeological Resources Protection Act (ARPA) applies only to "archeological resources," defined as "material remains of past human life or activities, which are of archaeological interest" and are found on public or Indian land. The law exempts materials less than 100 years old but covers all other sites that meet these requirements. A 1996 executive order, number 13007, "Indian Sacred Sites on Federal Land," is also relevant. Although it does not specifically address archaeological sites, it defines a "sacred site" as "any specific, discrete, narrowly delineated location on Federal land that is identified by an Indian tribe, or Indian individual determined to be an appropriately authoritative representative of an Indian religion, as sacred by virtue of its established religious significance to, or ceremonial use by, an Indian religion." Clearly, some archaeological sites meet these criteria.

In the early 1970s, CRM archaeology was still driven largely by a "salvage" mentality (see Davis, chapter 2, this volume), although the passage of NEPA in 1969 provided new opportunities for the inclusion of archaeology in planning for and assessing the impacts of federal projects on the environment. In sharp contrast to the "Section 106–centric" focus of today's CRM archaeology, Lipe's conservation model paper (1974) did not mention Section 106 or the NHPA, nor did the Airlie House report (McGimsey and Davis 1977) and other seminal publications of the time devote much attention to it. This is not surprising; initially, the NHPA and Section 106 were specific to places listed on the National Register of Historic Places (NHRP). Because few archaeological sites were listed and because most of the listed ones were so substantial that federal agencies were unlikely to plow through them, archaeologists saw little benefit in Section 106.

This began to change after 1971, when President Richard Nixon's Executive Order 11593 required that federal agencies consider the effects of their actions on properties *eligible* for listing on the National Register, as well as on listed properties. Because of this executive order, which was subsequently incorporated into the NHPA by amendment in 1976, federal agencies began identifying and evaluating historic properties, including archaeological sites, that *might* be eligible for the National Register, not just examining effects on known, registered properties. As a result, Section 106 became archaeologists' preferred tool for ensuring that effects of federal projects on the archaeological record were considered, the CRM archaeology industry was launched, and NEPA as a tool for archaeological resource management was largely left in the dust being generated by all those Section 106–driven shaker screens.

One of the unforeseen consequences of the stampede of archaeologists from the planning and NEPA camp to the Section 106 compliance camp was a near total focus in CRM archaeology on the National Register of Historic Places criteria as the yardstick for measuring the preservation value or worthiness of archaeological sites. Whereas NEPA, ARPA, and mandates such as Executive Order 13007 recognize a broad range of scientific, educational, and cultural values for archaeological sites, the NHPA is specific to archaeological sites that meet the standard for "historic properties"—places listed on or eligible for listing on the NRHP. This standard has become the basis for virtually all decision-making in archaeological resource management.

SIGNIFICANCE, INFORMATION, AND ELIGIBILITY

The NRHP was originally designed largely for historic buildings. It has been retrofitted for archaeological sites and other kinds of historic places, but the resulting fit has not always been a comfortable one. Although the register recognizes archaeological sites as having other values—their significance to descendant communities, for example—most sites, unless they have architectural significance or a specific association with an event or a person, are evaluated under eligibility criterion D—that is, as places that have yielded or are likely to yield "information important in prehistory or history" (36 CFR 60.4).

According to National Register Bulletin 15, the guidance document on applying the eligibility criteria, "important" information is information that has "a significant bearing on a research design that addresses such areas as: 1) current data gaps or alternative theories that challenge existing ones or 2) priority areas identified under a State or Federal agency management plan" (National Park Service 1990:21).

The problem inherent in operationalizing this concept of "important" information is that it is incompatible with both the nature of the archaeological record and the constantly changing theory, methods, and technology of archaeological research. There is no important or unimportant information in archaeology; there is just information. Every isolated artifact, every tiny site, every enormous site contains pieces of the total record of the past. Some sites contain many pieces, others very few. But no pieces are intrinsically important and others not; they are all pieces of the same thing.

Envision a library. It holds huge, thick books and tiny, thin books, books about famous people and infamous people, books about World War II and the origins of the universe and tying fishing flies and sustainable agriculture and the Fellowship of the Ring and the Russian revolution and a curious little monkey named George. No one book, large or small, is intrinsically more important than another; each is part of the record of human thought and experience. If you go to the library in search of a recipe for chicken picatta, then *The Joy of Cooking* is a far more important book than *War and Peace*. If you are seeking solace for your soul, a slender volume by Emily Dickinson might be far more important than the 34-volume collected works of Sir Winston Churchill.

The NRHP evaluation process for criterion D, however, requires that you adopt the chicken picatta approach: your definition of important depends on what you are looking for at the moment. Important information, Bulletin 15 tells us, must "have a significant bearing on...such areas as *current* data gaps or alternative theories that challenge *existing* ones" (emphasis added).

This is where the library analogy breaks down. If we go to the library looking for Emily Dickinson, we do not then decide that Sir Winston is unimportant and throw out his collected works. Rather, we assume that someday we might want to know about Fortress Britain and read those stirring words, "We shall fight on the beaches, we shall fight in the fields and in the streets, we shall fight in the hills; we shall never surrender." We leave Churchill's 34 volumes in place to await the day when they become "important" in the sense that we need the information they contain.

The NRHP's emphasis on current research interests and data gaps runs afoul of archaeology's fourth dimension—time. The data gaps and theoretical issues of today are soon replaced as a result of the theoretical shifts, technological innovations, and methodological advances of tomorrow. If we manage archaeological sites according to their NRHP eligibility—that is, by the importance of the information they contain relative to today's interests and technology—then the sites that do not make the cut do not stay in the library for future reference; they are lost forever.

Two categories of sites make the NRHP definition of "important" especially problematic. The first category comprises sites that we would classify

94

today as having nothing to contribute to current research questions. Maybe they really do not have anything to contribute. Or maybe we just do not yet know how to access or use the information they contain. I am haunted by a photograph of the Hyde Exploring Expedition's 1896 field camp in Chaco Canyon. In the photo, a big cook stove stands against the back wall of Pueblo Bonito, soot from the flue streaking and staining the whole four stories of the standing wall above it. And where did that soot come from? As they pulled thousand-year-old pieces of wood out of the collapsed rooms in Pueblo Bonito, the expedition members burned them for firewood. Well, of course they did. Decades before the advent of tree-ring dating and dendroclimatological analyses, what else would they have done with all that beautifully seasoned wood in a nearly treeless environment? The information contained in those wooden beams was unimportant to the data gaps and theoretical issues of the 1890s. And surely that is the case with some archaeological sites that we say, today, have no potential to yield "important" information.

The second problematic category is archaeological sites that clearly have the potential to yield information but whose information would be judged largely redundant, given current questions and techniques. These are sites that archaeologists have already studied intensively and from which they have learned much. Additional data recovery at such sites yields diminishing returns; they contain lots of information, but we do not know how to learn anything new from them. Yet.

Let me consider another library analogy. If one were to go to a medical library today, one would find scores, hundreds, maybe thousands of books and articles on polio and smallpox, many fewer books on AIDS/HIV, and very few on bird flu or SARS. Yet, the last are of the greatest current research interest. What if the library were to run out of space? The polio and smallpox books would be considered far less important than the others. We have learned all we need to learn about those diseases, researchers might rationalize. We have defeated them with vaccines, and there is no need to study them any more. Those books can be discarded to make room for the currently important research books.

But what if someday, when those of us with telltale circular scars on our shoulders have all taken our immunity and gone to the grave, it turns out that the smallpox virus was simply regrouping? What if a new and more virulent strain emerges and begins sweeping through the world's population? Suddenly, the information in those discarded books becomes extremely important, but they are lost forever.

Questions change, theoretical issues change, methods and available technologies change, yet using NRHP eligibility as our sole measure of the value of an archaeological site requires us to make live-or-die decisions for these places on the basis of the questions and data gaps and technology of the fleeting "now." There has to be a better way to evaluate the significance of archaeological sites and manage them for future "nows" as well.

Under the current approach, the only choice we have is "eligible" or "not eligible." This results in many sites being classified as eligible when in fact we have no idea how to go about finding out "important" information or sometimes *any* information from them. We do this because the alternative, not eligible, is a death sentence and we all recognize at some visceral level that letting these "library books" slip away unread is a terrible approach to managing the past.

However, calling all these sites eligible leads to many mitigation dollars being spent to gather extremely limited or endlessly redundant data, which are then used to reach trivial or redundant conclusions. I am not making this up: I once reviewed a research design that literally proposed to "test the hypothesis" that "Feature A extends to the other side of the road." And, surprise, it did. Other questions and answers that were once extremely important have pretty well been resolved by now. We *know* that they ate corn; we do not need to keep finding that out again and again. But in some archaeological excavation reports these days, that is probably the most exciting thing the writers have to say about the past. This, we should all recognize, is a terrible approach to public policy.

Agency managers and many historic preservation professionals speak of "the archaeology problem," a strongly held belief that the public is not getting its money's worth from CRM archaeology. And in many cases they are right. One reason for the archaeology problem is that "cultural resource management" has become equated with "Section 106" and management of the country's rich, irreplaceable archaeological record has been reduced to the single consideration of narrowly defined NRHP eligibility.

In addition to other problems, this narrow focus makes it difficult to consider values of archaeological sites beyond their "information potential." Many Native Americans, for example, ascribe religious and cultural significance to archaeological sites that they view as ancestral (see Ferguson, chapter 8, this volume). In an attempt to reflect these "other than information potential" values, they often request that sites be considered eligible for the NRHP under criterion A, for their association with important events in the history of the tribe, or under criterion B, for their association with the ancestors of the modern tribal members. But these NRHP criteria require that specific, important associations be demonstrated between the property and an event or between the property and a person whose contribution to history is known and appropriately documented. Unless physical evidence or oral traditions exist about the association of a pre-European contact archaeological site with specific events or persons in the past, it is usually impossible to make a successful argument for eligibility under criterion A or B, and there is no other NRHP mechanism for recognizing the traditional values associated with archaeological sites.

If we want to get our money's worth, acknowledge the broad range of values embodied in the archaeological heritage (see Lipe, chapter 3, this volume), and achieve "productive harmony" between development and preservation, then we need a new evaluation and management approach. We need an approach that focuses mitigation dollars on sites that can really tell us important things about the past during the current "now" while enabling us to manage the whole archaeological record for future "nows."

I suggest that the basis for such an approach is a focus on the broader *significance* of archaeological sites—a term that encompasses not just eligibility for the NRHP, not just the current "importance" of information that might be recovered from the site, but also long-term research potential and other values. The concept of significance has been discussed and debated in American archaeology since the 1970s (see Briuer and Mathers 1996 for a summary of this debate) and is increasingly a subject of discussion in the archaeological literature internationally (for example, Mathers, Darvill, and Little 2005). In the following sections, I offer some ideas about how we might define the significance of archaeological sites, how we might evaluate the significance of currently known sites, and how a focus on significance, rather than just eligibility, might play out in the basic tasks of federal agency management of the archaeological record.

ARCHAEOLOGICAL SIGNIFICANCE

How, then, do we think about an archaeological site's significance, taking into account both current research importance (eligibility), as required by Section 106, and the need to address the broader issue of "loss or destruction of significant scientific, cultural, or historical resources" under NEPA? How do we incorporate into significance evaluations the traditional cultural values ascribed to archaeological sites by descendant communities? And most important, how do we develop a cultural resource management approach based on archaeological significance—the long-term, nonrenewable value of all archaeological information—rather than on the ephemeral quality of eligibility?

If we restrict our evaluation of the significance of archaeological sites to eligibility, then we have to focus on current data gaps and theoretical perspectives. The NRHP and the publication *Archeology and Historic Preservation: The Secretary of the Interior's Standards and Guidelines* (US Department of the Interior 1983) require us to do this by using developed "historic contexts," that is, discussions of important research issues grouped by place, time, and theme. Historic contexts, it is argued, enable us to define important information and thus identify NRHP-eligible archaeological sites. Virtually every discussion about making better eligibility decisions for archaeological sites, whether in publications or in workshops and symposia, concludes that what is needed are more and better historic contexts.

In practice, however, it appears that relatively few people who are actually making decisions about the eligibility of archaeological sites in a CRM context use the formally developed historic contexts that already exist. Recently, the SRI Foundation, a nonprofit historic preservation organization, conducted a survey of transportation agency staff, state historic preservation office personnel, and CRM consultants to determine how they go about making recommendations about NRHP eligibility. (This survey, funded by the National Cooperative Highway Research Program of the Transportation Research Board, is available at www.trb.org/trbnet/Project Display .asp?ProjectID=1305.) The survey found that what most people actually do is evaluate the physical characteristics and the morphology (the form, likely content, and structure) of the site and make a decision based on those attributes. Is the site largely intact, or is it eroded or looted? Is it mostly buried, or exposed on the surface? How many artifacts are visible? What kinds? Is there evidence of features? Structures? Are there temporal diagnostics?

This approach is not surprising when we think about what actually happens when archaeologists excavate an archaeological site. It does not matter what the "historic context" is. We collect a relatively fixed set of specimens and samples and record similar observational data from all archaeological sites. We collect artifacts, pollen samples, flotation samples, chronometric samples, ethnobotanical samples, perishables, faunal materials, human remains, and grave goods; we record features and structures, as well as the provenience information for all the collected materials, in the form of maps, plans, notes, photos, drawings, and so forth. Some sites yield all these categories of artifacts, samples, and observations, and others, only a few. On the basis of previous experience, archaeologists estimate the likelihood that a site will yield various categories of archaeological data by looking at its physical characteristics. It does not matter whether the site's historic context is "Pueblo II field houses of the San Juan Basin" or "Early

Woodland camps in the Piedmont" or "Cahokia and the American Bottom during the Moorehead phase."

Consequently, when we assess a site's significance or overall potential to yield particular kinds of information about the past, we need to know three things:

- How likely is it that the site will yield artifacts, features, structures, pollen samples, flotation samples, chronometric samples, ethnobotanical samples, perishables, faunal materials, or human remains and grave goods?
- How intact is the site? That is, to what extent are the artifacts, features, and other items in the site in their original context and spatial relationships?
- How rare or common are sites like this one?

Each of these questions is important in determining the nature and scale of questions that can be addressed through excavation of the site, but none of them results in a "pass-fail" outcome.

In order to answer these questions, we need to have the best possible understanding of the relationship between the surface signature of the site as identified during archaeological survey and the likely contents and condition of the site. And that understanding is based not on historic contexts comprising place, theme, and time but on synthesis of previous investigations. If we want to do a better job of assessing the significance of archaeological sites, then what we need is not more formally developed "historic context" documents but more syntheses of existing survey and excavation data (see King, chapter 7, this volume), including assessments of the relationship between surface signature and subsurface contents and between geomorphic setting and site integrity.

Physical characteristics of an archaeological site can be used—and are used every day—to predict the nature of the archaeological information that could be gained through excavation and other forms of investigation at the site. Some of these characteristics have to do with the morphology of the site itself: numbers, distributions, and densities of artifacts, for example; site size; presence (though not absence) of temporal diagnostics; indications of structures or features; presence of ash, charcoal, or other evidence of burning; indications of buried cultural materials.

Other useful predictors of information content are aspects of the site's setting and environment: geomorphic age of the surface on which the site is located, for example; whether the site is in an erosional, stable, or depositional setting; the extent of postdepositional disturbance by natural or cultural forces; the natural resources available in the site vicinity. Mechanisms also exist for assessing other values associated with sites: functional categories, types of features, and sensitive physiographic settings, for example; use of published ethnographic studies and recorded oral traditions; interviews and consultation.

I propose that we develop a systematic way of doing what agencies, state historic preservation officers, and consulting archaeologists do every day—place sites in categories on the basis of their physical characteristics. But in this case, the categories would not be pass or fail, eligible or not eligible. Instead, they would be dynamic, changing as our knowledge of the past and our technologies change, flexible enough to incorporate values other than information potential, and comprehensive enough to structure long-term management of the archaeological record.

To make this proposal more concrete, let me imagine, as an example, that a federal land-managing agency decides to classify its archaeological resources according to the following significance categories:

- Category 1: sites likely to contribute significantly to current research questions and theoretical issues
- Category 2: sites likely to yield substantial information about the past but whose current research potential has been largely exhausted by previous excavation of similar sites
- Category 3: sites whose information potential cannot be tapped with current research approaches and archaeological methods
- Category 4: sites whose information potential appears to have been exhausted by the act of recording their location and characterizing their contents
- Category 5: sites with high traditional cultural values as identified by descendant communities or other sources

Known sites could be assigned to the significance categories by applying a set of simple rules. The input variables might include survey information about the archaeological characteristics of the site, geomorphological studies or modeling, and probability models based on the resource potential of the site's setting. Synthesized information from excavation projects in the general vicinity would be used to estimate the relationship between surface archaeological manifestations and subsurface deposits, as well as likely preservation of pollen, macrobotanical remains, and other materials in the

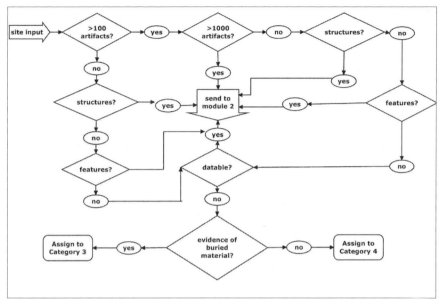

FIGURE 5.1

Sample algorithm for sorting sites into significance categories: the first sorting module.

site deposits. The rules for assigning sites to categories could also incorporate data about the ubiquity or rarity of sites of this type or time period, as
well as information from ethnographic studies and community consultation about cultural values.

Figures 5.1 and 5.2 provide examples of simple rules that would allow
one to begin assigning sites to my hypothetical significance categories. For
databases containing large numbers of known but unevaluated sites (a
common occurrence among federal agencies, in which "flag and avoid" has
been the compliance strategy for years), assignment to categories could be
accomplished mechanically through a set of simple algorithms like those
graphically displayed in the diagrams. I want to emphasize that the categories and rules I provide as examples are simply heuristic devices
intended to make the abstract notion of assigning sites to significance categories easier to visualize. The specific management categories used by a
federal agency would depend on the agency's mission and management
objectives and opportunities. Actual rules for assigning sites to categories
would depend on the nature of the environment and the archaeological
record. (For a more detailed discussion and developed example of this
approach to modeling significance of archaeological sites, see Cushman

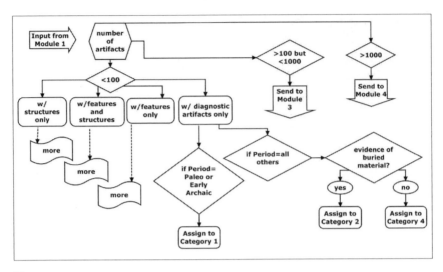

FIGURE 5.2

Sample algorithm for sorting sites into significance categories: first steps in the second sorting module.

and Sebastian 2008.) A full-scale effort to develop a significance model to be used in planning and compliance is under way at the time of this writing through a partnership of the SRI Foundation, Panamerican Consultants, Inc., and Fort Benning, Georgia.

The effectiveness and accuracy of the classification scheme would of course have to be tested through targeted data recovery, but because the treatment approach proposed in the following pages includes preservation and continued management of samples from *all* significance categories, misclassifications would be less problematic than misclassifications under the current "eligible–not eligible" approach, in which all the "not eligibles" may be destroyed without data recovery. In addition, the rules of the classification scheme, the assumptions on which they are based, and the actual classification of known sites would need to be reconsidered and revised periodically as additional data recovery and synthesis take place and as current questions are answered and data gaps filled. These periodic revisions, which would be a standard part of land-use planning for land-managing agencies (see Barker, chapter 4, this volume), would also take into account new knowledge, theories, and research interests and reflect new techniques and technologies for extracting information from the archaeological record.

MANAGING FOR SIGNIFICANCE

A shift from eligibility-based to significance-based management of archaeological sites would affect nearly every aspect of federal cultural resource management. The approach advocated here would enable federal agencies to do the following:

- Manage information about archaeological sites under their jurisdiction or more easily affected by their actions.
- Do a more effective job of long-range planning and of meeting stewardship responsibilities under Section 110 of the NHPA.
- Focus mitigation dollars on sites with the greatest research payoff.
- Deal programmatically rather than case by case with the effects of their undertakings on historic properties as provided in Section 106 of the NHPA.
- Address tribal and descendant community concerns about values of archaeological sites that go beyond their "information potential."
- Address the concerns of review agencies and the archaeological community about sites whose current information potential may be low or enigmatic but which could become critical in the future.

For these and many other reasons, significance-based management could yield both better archaeology and better public policy.

Information Management

Because the assignment of sites to significance categories would be accomplished mechanically—by applying algorithms to computerized data—the large number of unevaluated archaeological sites currently populating agency and state databases could be classified according to the sites' information potential programmatically rather than on a case-by-case basis. Instead of becoming hundreds or thousands of dots on a map, which might or might not require future consideration as historic properties, these sites could be categorized in ways that usefully direct management decision-making. All newly discovered sites could be immediately evaluated and categorized, and all site categories and assignments could be quickly and easily revised to take into account new information or new technology.

Computerized information about site assignments to significance categories could be added as a map layer in existing or newly developed locational predictive models. This would enable managers to predict and display as sensitivity maps the likelihood and densities of sites in different significance categories within the area covered by the model. Whereas current predictive models tend to deal only with the presence or absence of sites—or at best with the presence or absence of broad functional or temporal categories of sites—a model incorporating significance information would provide managers with important additional information for both general and project-specific planning.

Planning

Resource management plans, general management plans, Integrated Cultural Resource Management Plans, and similar documents used by federal agencies to guide future actions are by their very nature focused on long-term, sustainable use of resources under the agency's jurisdiction (see Barker, chapter 4, this volume). The best of such plans reflect an iterative, adaptive management strategy in which problems are assessed, solutions are designed and implemented, results are monitored and evaluated, and adjustments are made to the solutions in a cyclical fashion.

The archaeological component of such long-range plans should be based on a long-term view of archaeological significance, not on short-term values such as "current research issues and data gaps." A significance-based approach to managing archaeological sites would enable a federal agency to broadly characterize the research and other values of archaeological resources within its planning area and identify areas of particular archaeological sensitivity. This information in turn could be used to classify different portions of the planning area for compatible and incompatible uses. Reevaluation of the significance categorization rules and possible reassignment of sites could easily be incorporated into the adaptive management cycles of assessment, evaluation, and adjustment.

Section 110 of the NHPA

A significance-based approach to management could also greatly facilitate better agency compliance with Section 110 of the NHPA. Section 110(a)(2) requires that "each Federal agency shall establish..., in consultation with the Secretary, a preservation program for the identification, evaluation, and nomination to the National Register of Historic Places, and protection of historic properties." This requirement is more commonly honored in the breach than in the observance, for a number of reasons, both good and bad. Many agencies make a desultory attempt to nominate properties to the National Register periodically because the law says that they are supposed to, but the process takes considerable time and money and rarely contributes much additional protection to properties that are already owned or managed by a federal agency. This section of the law was important when only *registered* properties were considered in the Section 106 process. Because eligible and listed properties now receive the same level of consideration in federal planning, the time and money it takes to register properties can usually be more effectively directed toward other preservation-related efforts.

The Section 110 requirements to identify and evaluate (generally interpreted as meaning case-by-case evaluation of eligibility for the National Register) historic properties are unfunded mandates for which agencies have to carve out funds from their already stretched base budgets. Although most agencies recognize the value of proactive, non-project-related surveys, few such surveys are actually carried out, because of the lack of funds.

This brings me to the "protection of historic properties" segment of the Section 110 requirements. If agencies were to shift to a significance-based management approach, they could focus whatever money is available for Section 110 activities on efforts such as the following:

- Developing and refining classification rules and algorithms for assigning known and newly discovered sites to significance categories
- Collecting additional information for sites where the data are insufficient to permit assignment
- Carrying out tribal consultation to identify sites with important traditional cultural values
- Developing distribution and sensitivity maps for sites in different significance categories
- Using the available information to identify high concentrations and representative samples of each significance category to be set aside as reserves for future research and potentially as preserves for sites with high values for qualities other than information potential. This information would then be fed into future iterations of agency resource management plans.

Clearly, an essential component of this approach would be a commitment on the part of the agency to periodically synthesizing new excavation and survey data and incorporating theoretical and methodological advances in archaeology into significance decisions. After each review, the significance category assignment criteria would be reevaluated and potentially adjusted, the representativeness of the sets of reserved sites would be reevaluated and perhaps adjusted, and the significance sensitivity maps would be redone.

NEPA Compliance

One of the most important changes in the Advisory Council on Historic Preservation's 1999 revision of the Section 106 regulation was the requirement that agencies do a better job of integrating Section 106 compliance with the NEPA process. This is important because it is at the early stages in the NEPA process that the greatest number of possibilities for avoiding and minimizing adverse effects to historic properties is available. Completing Section 106 consideration of effects on archaeological properties during the NEPA evaluation can be challenging because of the time and expense required to identify and evaluate archaeological sites when the alternatives include multiple, geographically distinct locations. This issue is often addressed using existing archaeological data that might or might not be commensurate between alternative locations or representative of the actual archaeological remains in the alternatives. Other approaches to combining Section 106 and NEPA compliance depend on sample surveys, which are more likely to be representative and commensurate but can also be expensive and time consuming.

Some federal agencies are turning to locational predictive models as a cost-effective, scientifically valid way to incorporate archaeological considerations into NEPA analysis. These models enable managers to use existing data to project the likely densities of sites within the NEPA study area with a statistically valid degree of confidence.

Locational models, however, project only numbers of sites, although the projections can include variables such as time period and culture category. A significance-based approach to evaluating archaeological sites would expand the effectiveness of archaeological models as analytical tools for NEPA decision-making by allowing managers to project relative impacts on archaeological sites not just in terms of numbers of sites but also in terms of factors such as mitigation costs and avoidance options, yielding a better balance between project needs and historic preservation concerns. Such models could be used at various points in the NEPA process—for example, during scoping, when the needed analyses are determined, or during screening of the conceptual alternatives, when such models could be used to identify the alternatives likely to encounter archaeological "show stoppers." After the alternatives retained for detailed study have been identified, models displaying the number and distribution of sites of different significance categories would provide a scientifically replicable approach to measuring differential impacts in terms of mitigation costs, effects on the archaeological record, and other values.

Section 106 Compliance

Both the law and the regulations for Section 106 explicitly focus on "historic properties," places listed on or eligible for listing on the National Register of Historic Places. The National Register is clear in its definition of what qualifies an archaeological site for listing or eligibility. How, then, could a significance-based approach to management of archaeological sites be incorporated into agencies' compliance with Section 106?

An obvious difference between current Section 106 procedures and procedures using a significance-based approach would lie in the evaluation of previously known sites and of sites recorded during project-specific inventories. Currently, sites that may be affected by a project are evaluated case by case, often through costly and destructive testing, because an argument must be made for whether each site does or does not have the potential to contribute "important" information relative to current research questions and data gaps.

The cost in time and money of testing programs has led, among other things, to decades of "flag and avoid" management, leaving oil fields and military installations, for example, dotted with thousands of unevaluated sites that have cost much money to find and avoid, have contributed virtually nothing to our knowledge of the past, and now constitute a management headache of monumental proportions. Under a significance-based approach, known and newly discovered sites would be assigned to significance categories that would guide avoidance decisions and mitigation strategies for any sites that would be affected by undertakings, as well as guiding long-term management strategies as described earlier.

An even more important change in agency Section 106 procedures would be the adoption of programmatic approaches to resolving adverse effects. Such approaches would focus mitigation dollars on sites with the greatest current potential to yield information, gather targeted information from some other sites, address other research needs, and take into account the importance of preserving sites in all significance categories for future research and other values. Taking the five trial significance categories outlined previously as an example, the general treatment strategy for these categories might be something like this:

- Category 1 sites (those likely to contribute significantly to current research questions and theoretical issues): emphasize data recovery at these sites; reserve a representative sample of them for future research.

- Category 2 sites (those whose current research potential has been largely exhausted by previous data recovery): limited or no data recovery; reserve a representative sample for future research.
- Category 3 sites (those whose information potential cannot be tapped with current research approaches and archaeological methods): reserve a representative sample for future research.
- Category 4 sites (those whose information potential appears to have been exhausted by the act of recording their location and characterizing their contents): broad-scale spatial analysis or no further treatment; periodic reevaluation of category characterization.
- Category 5 sites (those with high traditional cultural values): preserve undisturbed wherever possible.

As part of mitigating the effects of specific projects or of ongoing programs or as part of general management planning, an agency would establish reserves, within which sites would be set aside for future research, and preserves, in which sites with high traditional values would be left undisturbed. There are at least two possible approaches to establishing such reserves and preserves. In one of them, research reserves could be established through proactive, up-front Section 110 programs, with additions to the reserves or replacement of previously reserved sites carried out as part of mitigation for ongoing programs. After these reserves are established, resolution of adverse effects for subsequent individual development projects would focus on the Category 1 and Category 5 sites—the former by conducting data recovery at some or all affected sites and the latter by establishing preserves around the sites if at all possible.

The other approach would be case by case. For each individual undertaking, the agency would do the following:

- Preserve Category 5 sites within the "area of potential effects" (APE) whenever possible.
- Set aside for future research a sample of the affected Category 3 sites, either within the APE or in reserves elsewhere on land under the agency's jurisdiction.
- Set aside for future research a sample of the affected Category 2 sites, either within the APE or in reserves elsewhere on land under the agency's jurisdiction, combined with possible synthesis efforts or narrowly focused data collection on or off site.
- Carry out data recovery at a sample of the Category 1 sites, and set

aside for future research a sample of these sites either within the APE or elsewhere on land under the agency's jurisdiction.

The devil, of course, is in the proverbial details. This approach sounds neat, tidy, and almost doable, as long as we conceive of "an archaeological site" as having a single temporal component and exhibiting a significance value of a single type. As soon as we admit the real-world complications of multiple components and multiple values, the complexity of both sorting and management increases exponentially. Additionally, the approach to mitigation and management I have described would clearly be most readily implemented by land-managing agencies, especially agencies such as the National Park Service and military installations, which exercise the greatest control over the landscape and whose managers are not constrained by a multiple-use mandate. With work and creativity, however, even funding and licensing agencies, such as the Federal Highway Administration and the Federal Energy Regulatory Commission, could make use of many of the ideas explored here. Instead of carrying out data recovery at Category 2 sites, for example, the agency could contribute to the acquisition and banking of Category 2 sites outside the direct impact area, or it could fund syntheses needed to develop new research approaches for sites of this type.

The point is that the current "eligible–not eligible" approach to archaeological resource management leaves us with sites in all significance categories lumped together in the "eligible" box. And if a site is eligible for the National Register under Criterion D, then presumably it should be subject to data recovery before construction begins. So we often end up spending a great amount of money to learn relatively little, because we are digging Category 2 and 3 sites. Under a significance-based approach, data recovery dollars would be focused on Category 1 sites, and sites in the other categories would receive treatments appropriate to their information potential.

For example, in a particular area, perhaps we have diligently floated what amounts to several train-car loads of soil samples collected from a particular kind of burned rock feature without finding any analytically useful macrobotanical remains. Under a significance-based approach, we would stop spending money on collecting, floating, and analyzing such samples and use it instead for something more appropriate to the features' information potential—such as research to determine whether economic plants in the area yielded identifiable phytoliths or to develop techniques to recover and analyze such phytoliths. Maybe the people who lived in this area, too, ate corn, and the organic plant parts are simply not being preserved. Or maybe they ate something else, and we can discover how to find that out.

MAKING IT HAPPEN

By adopting an evaluation and management approach focused on making the most appropriate use of the information potential of every site, we could do better archaeology and achieve better public policy. In order to adopt such an approach, however, we need to make some fundamental changes in our views of historic preservation planning and compliance. The biggest obstacles to adopting a significance-based approach are bureaucratic inertia, fear of litigation or lost employment opportunities, and lack of awareness of the possibilities for creativity and flexibility in compliance with federal preservation laws.

As noted earlier, the fixation on "eligibility" in CRM archaeology is a result of equating cultural resource management with Section 106 compliance and ignoring the other mandates and possibilities. But even in the case of Section 106, a shift to evaluating and managing sites for their significance rather than just their eligibility would require no change in the law or the regulation. The guidance from the National Register, however, would have to undergo a fundamental shift.

The National Register fills two very different roles in the federal historic preservation realm. In the first instance, it is an honor roll—the nation's official list of places found worthy of preservation. In the second instance, it is a planning tool that federal agencies use in managing their preservation programs—including Section 106 compliance. The National Register's position is that the standards for evaluating historic properties are, and should be, identical for both roles of the register. The National Register staff often view consensus determinations of eligibility—agreements between federal agencies and state historic preservation officers that a site will be considered eligible or not eligible for purposes of Section 106—with grave misgivings, and they have good reason to do so, given this "no difference between register listing and Section 106 planning" perspective.

The fact is that there is a great difference between the level of documentation, scrutiny, and evaluation used by the National Register staff to review nominations for listing on the National Register and the level applied by federal agencies and state historic preservation offices to arrive at consensus determinations of eligibility. This is not necessarily a bad thing. A listing on the register has serious implications for tax breaks, grants, and local regulations tied to the listing and for any number of other issues. A consensus determination, in contrast, simply commits a federal agency to considering the effects of its actions on a historic place. It does not mean that the place must be preserved, that mitigation dollars have to be spent on it, that the project must be redesigned, or any other necessary outcome. The agency may decide to do some or all of these things, or it may not. All it is committed to do is to "consider the effects."

What is needed to implement a shift to significance-based management in federal agency Section 106 procedures is a recognition by the National Park Service of the de facto difference between the National Register as honor roll and the National Register as agency planning tool. Also needed is a willingness by all parties to the Section 106 process—agencies, the Advisory Council on Historic Preservation, tribes, state historic preservation offices, and CRM consultants—to work with the National Register to develop guidance for a defensible, well-thought-out "two-track" approach to eligibility, significance, and information that will facilitate better management of the archaeological record and greater public benefit.

The secretary of the interior's *Standards and Guidelines* for archaeology and historic preservation are focused entirely on the "honor roll" aspect of historic preservation, especially as it relates to the use of historic contexts:

> The historic context is the cornerstone of the planning process. The goal of preservation planning is to identify, evaluate, register, and treat the full range of properties representing each historic context, rather than only one or two types of properties. Identification activities are organized to ensure that research and survey activities include properties representing all aspects of the historic context. Evaluation uses the historic context as the framework within which to apply the criteria for evaluation to specific properties or property types. Decisions about treatment of properties are made with the goal of treating the range of properties in the context. (US Department of the Interior 1983:44718)

The *Standards and Guidelines* emphasize repeatedly that this is a document about identifying, evaluating, registering, and treating historic properties and that these activities can be carried out only within the framework of historic contexts. This is probably true for people who are in the business of finding and registering samples of properties representing US history (and prehistory, for that matter). But these standards and guidelines need to be reworked substantially to accommodate more flexible, inclusive, and appropriate measures of significance for purposes of agency decision-making about archaeology under Section 106.

The National Register guidance for archaeology, *Guidelines for Evaluating and Registering Archeological Properties* (National Park Service 2000), is also focused entirely on evaluating sites for listing on the National Register and preparing nomination forms for them. This National Register bulletin at least notes that consensus determination of eligibility for Section 106 purposes *exists*, which is more than most National Register guidance documents do, but it states firmly that "the use of the consensus process does not allow for a lower threshold for significance than the formal Determination of Eligibility or National Register listing procedures" (National Park Service 2000:11). Perhaps a discussion centered on the question "Why not?" would be fruitful. What would be the downside of establishing a clear two-track system for evaluating the eligibility of archaeological sites—one for listing sites on the National Register and one for considering effects to sites as a result of federal agency undertakings? I am not proposing that we take a system that "ain't broke" and fix it; a de facto two-track system already exists, but decisions on the Section 106 track are being made ad hoc. I am proposing that we acknowledge the reality that the two tracks exist and find a way to make Section 106 decisions more consistent, more predictable, better archaeology, and better public policy.

The archaeological properties bulletin also insists that there is no valid way to determine the significance of an archaeological site other than evaluating it within one or more formal historic contexts. Again, this may be true if your goal is to place representative and truly worthy archaeological sites on the honor roll of places in this country worthy of preservation. But if your goal is to figure out what to do about sites that are going under the bulldozer, then your needs are different. You are not picking and choosing from among all the books in the library, trying to put together a "greatest hits" list. You are looking at a whole library about to go up in smoke and trying to figure out how to salvage most effectively the information it contains.

For example, in 2005 the National Park Service's National Historic Landmarks (NHL) program completed an excellent national historic context for Paleoindian sites, titled *Earliest Americans Theme Study for the Eastern United States* (www.nps.gov/nhl/themes/themes-all.htm). This theme study was intended to guide a comparative evaluation of the significance of Paleoindian sites. Are there Paleoindian sites in the United States that would not have sufficient significance to be selected as national historic landmarks? Of course—most of them. Are there Paleoindian sites that would not have sufficient significance and integrity to be listed on the NRHP? Of course—many of them. That is as it should be, and the *Earliest*

Americans Theme Study is an excellent tool for winnowing out the very best sites for NHL designation and NRHP listing.

Are there, however, Paleoindian sites that would *not* be considered eligible for the NRHP in a consensus determination for a Section 106 undertaking? I would argue that few such sites exist, and I believe that this, too, is as it should be. Sites of this age are so rare that any crumb of information we can glean from them is valuable. Should we allow federally funded or authorized projects to destroy any Paleoindian site without gathering those crumbs just because the site would not meet the standards for actual listing on the NRHP? Do we need a developed place-time-theme historic context to answer this question?

I do not in any way mean to say that there is no place for historic contexts in the Section 106 process. For one thing, contexts can be—although they are not always—excellent sources of archaeological syntheses, and as many of the contributors to this book have noted, good syntheses are essential to many of the improvements in CRM archaeology that we are advocating. Additionally, for certain kinds of properties and for certain criteria of eligibility, they are useful and even critical. The results of the National Cooperative Highway Research Program (NCHRP) survey described earlier indicate that historic contexts are considered useful for evaluating properties eligible under NRHP criteria A and C and for historical-period archaeological sites eligible under criterion D. Historic contexts were considered much less useful for properties eligible under criterion B and for pre-European-contact sites eligible under criterion D.

This survey confirmed, however, what many of us in the compliance business already knew: most people do not use formal historic contexts to make eligibility decisions for precontact archaeological sites in the Section 106 process. Why not? For one thing, not many contexts are available, and the possible set of historic contexts just for archaeology is virtually infinite. For New Mexico alone, archaeologists could research and write scores, even hundreds of contexts, from "Apishipa Phase Sites of the Cimarron Drainage" to "Zuni Ancestral Pueblos of West-Central New Mexico," and not come even close to parsing the wealth and variability of the archaeological record.

Even worse, we would spend years and millions of dollars to prepare all those contexts. The current average cost for developing a historic context, according to informal information gathered by the SRI Foundation in conjunction with the NCHRP study described earlier, is more than $100,000. Even if it were possible to fund such an effort (a virtually impossible "if"), what would we do in the meantime? And in the end, how different would the outcome be? When the next federal undertaking came along, I expect that we would still end up making the eligibility decision by asking, "How many artifacts are on the surface? Is there evidence for features? Structures?" and so forth, just as we do now. If the site had morphological characteristics indicating that it might contain data about something, anything, then we would put it in the "eligible" pigeonhole because the only other box we have is the "die horribly" pigeonhole. And when it is in the eligible box, it goes into the data recovery pile, and we dig it up and find out that Feature A extends to the other side of the road and they ate corn.

We need two things in order to do a better job of balancing public policy issues with the critical importance of archaeological sites as windows into the collective human past. First, we need recognition and regularization of the de facto process by which consensus determinations of eligibility are made now. We do not use developed historic contexts. Instead, we use syntheses of the results of previous surveys and excavations—some of them written, but many of them held only in our personal experience—to try to estimate the kinds of archaeological data a site is likely to contain. We know how to do this; we do it every day. And we call many sites "eligible" when we know or suspect that they would not meet the bar set for actual listing on the NRHP. What we need is official acceptance (if not a blessing) of the two-track reality of National Register evaluation—one track for listing, one track for consideration as part of agency planning.

The second thing we need is to shift away from dichotomous thinking. "Call it eligible or watch it be obliterated from the face of the earth" is not a sensible approach to managing the archaeological record. It yields both bad archaeology and bad stewardship and public policy. Instead, we need a significance-based approach to managing the archaeological record that gives us the flexibility to treat sites according to their current and future information potential. Such an approach would allow us to adopt creative and more efficient strategies for resolving adverse effects to archaeological sites while preserving our great archaeological library for future cardholders. Under such an approach, we could focus our expenditure of public money on archaeology to yield the greatest return in knowledge of the past, education, cultural preservation, and other public benefits.

6

Innovative Approaches to Mitigation

Susan M. Chandler

The concept of "mitigating damage resulting from federal undertakings" is derived from the regulations of the National Environmental Protection Act (NEPA), which include provisions for (1) rectifying environmental damage by repairing, rehabilitating, or restoring the affected environment; (2) reducing or eliminating damage over time by preservation and maintenance operations during the life of the "undertaking," or development project; and (3) compensating for the damage by replacing or providing substitute resources or environments (that is, "off-site mitigation"). Like mitigation of damage to natural resources, mitigation of adverse effects to archaeological sites is "generally a compromise between ideal project goals and complete or ideal protection of a variety of environmental resources, with the notion of greatest public good being the decisive principle" (McGimsey and Davis 1977:35). Unlike vegetation or wetlands, however, archaeological sites are finite, irreplaceable resources that cannot simply be restored or replicated upon the completion of a project. The goal of archaeological mitigation, then, is somehow to compensate for the loss of the physical archaeological record and the corresponding loss of part of the national heritage.

The public, if it is aware of the National Historic Protection Act

(NHPA) at all, logically perceives that the act is meant to protect archaeological sites by preserving them. People commonly assume that the discovery of an important archaeological or historic site can be used to stop a
development project. Some even believe that the NHPA can be used as an
excuse for the government to take their property. Archaeologists, however,
know that projects are seldom, if ever, stopped just because an archaeological site happens to be in the way. Yet, many cultural resource management (CRM) archaeologists have the misperception that Section 106
regulations require excavation of significant sites that cannot be avoided.
This view is so pervasive that in 2007 the Professional Archaeologists of
Kansas published a brochure, "Getting the Archaeological Green Light for
Your Projects: A Basic Guide to Complying with Laws Regarding
Archaeological Sites," which told developers that salvage excavations must
be undertaken to mitigate construction damage if an eligible site cannot
be avoided. But even though it is true that a regimented "find it–assess
it–dig it up" approach (King 2002:47) is standard operating procedure for
most CRM projects, this excavation outcome is not a legal requirement.

The standard way of mitigating damage to archaeological sites is
archaeological data recovery, which means a comprehensive program of
archaeological site excavation. Archaeological data recovery includes thorough documentation of stratigraphy and cultural features by means of field
notes, maps, and photographs; collection and analysis of artifacts and ancillary study specimens; research and interpretation to place the results
obtained from the site in a broader context; publication and dissemination
of the results; and curation of project records and artifacts in an approved
repository. Tangible public benefits are attained through the production of
high-quality technical reports, particularly if the reports are accompanied
by shorter versions published in more accessible media such as professional journals, magazines, and books (see King, chapter 7, this volume, on
the challenges of disseminating archaeological data and interpretations).
The problem is that too often there is little public return on the money
spent for archaeology, because the results are restricted to technical
reports with small audiences of agency and other professional archaeologists working in the vicinity. Clients may receive copies of the reports, but
the information is not presented in a way that captures their interest. Also,
archaeologists often fail to apply their results to larger research questions
or to present their research in professional journals or at conferences, even
on a regional level. For these reasons, projects that achieve effective public
outreach are noteworthy (see also Mackey, chapter 9, this volume).

Archaeological data recovery as a mitigation measure also presupposes that the significant values of most archaeological sites are realized when they are subjected to archaeological research. William Lipe (2000a, chapter 3, this volume) has argued, however, that various archaeological resource values—preservation, research, cultural heritage, education, aesthetic, and economic—need to be taken into account when making choices about which sites to protect and how to manage them.

In this chapter, I look first at the standard compliance model, examining problematical aspects of the current process. I then look at the concept of creative mitigation, presenting as case studies examples of several CRM projects that integrated innovative approaches to mitigation. Finally, I look at ways in which we might achieve the goal of "comprehensive mitigation," examining the totality of values associated with archaeological sites and how best to resolve a wide spectrum of effects on those site values.

CURRENT COMPLIANCE

Compliance with Section 106 of the NHPA requires a reasonable, good-faith effort to identify archaeological sites, assess their eligibility for listing on the National Register of Historic Places (NRHP), and resolve potential harm, or "adverse effects," to sites deemed eligible, or "historic properties." According to Advisory Council on Historic Preservation (ACHP) regulations (36 CRF 800.6), "resolution of adverse effects" is to be accomplished through consultation with federal agency personnel to develop and evaluate alternatives or modifications to the undertaking that could "avoid, minimize, or mitigate" the adverse effects.

Assessing Significance

In Section 106 terms, "significant" sites are those that are eligible for listing on the National Register. The NRHP, originally conceived as a way of commemorating particularly important sites in perpetuity, has become the mechanism for making decisions about current site management. All NRHP-eligible sites are treated as if they are equally important, but archaeologists know that they are not.

For archaeological sites, the applicable criterion for NRHP eligibility is generally criterion D, for sites "that have yielded, or may be likely to yield, information important in prehistory or history" (36 CFR 60.4). Because this is a broad and vague criterion, assessments of site significance can be variable. The application of NRHP criteria to archaeological sites is also problematical when it comes to values other than research important to archaeologists, especially in the absence of meaningful consultation with people descended from the original inhabitants or with other interested parties, such as historic preservation or heritage tourism groups. Some archaeologists (for example, King 2002:24, 56–60) have asserted that Section 106 needs to be divorced from the NRHP, and Sebastian (chapter 5, this volume) presents a compelling proposal for making a shift from eligibility-based site management to significance-based management.

Archaeological sites are complex entities that may contain a large variety of artifacts, architectural features, and specimens that can contribute, both individually and as parts of broader patterns, to an understanding of the past. Archaeologists establish criteria for evaluating site significance and priorities regarding site preservation on the basis of current research aims and priorities, which may not provide fully for future research needs or take into account other kinds of site values (Altschul 2005; Lipe 1984). On federal land in the western United States, a large proportion of sites is recommended as NRHP eligible, in part because archaeologists recognize that evaluating a site as not eligible may condemn it to destruction.[1] But NRHP eligibility is a poor measure of a site's research value, and not all NRHP-eligible archaeological sites have equally great research potential (see Sebastian, chapter 5, this volume). This fact is sometimes lost when decisions about site treatment are made. As stated in the Airlie House report (McGimsey and Davis 1977:34), "in making determinations of significance archeologists must be idealists. In making recommendations for programs of investigation based on such determination they must be pragmatists."

Resolving Adverse Effects

The next step in compliance is deciding how to resolve potential damage to archaeological properties. The consulting parties—for example, state and tribal historic preservation officers (SHPOs and THPOs), federal agencies, and clients—reach an agreement about which sites can be avoided, which ones must be preserved, which ones must be excavated, and even how much of a site should be studied.

Effects on archaeological properties can be direct, indirect, cumulative, or all three. A project can affect one site, a group of sites, or an entire archaeological region. CRM managers and consultants generally do a good job of identifying "areas of potential effects" (APEs) for direct damage to sites and assessing what might happen to the archaeological properties within an APE. It is also essential, however, to consider indirect and cumulative damage to sites or groups of sites. Indirect and cumulative effects can be difficult to assess, but they may be of particular concern with respect to site values other than the physical remains themselves.

Avoidance of damage to NRHP-eligible archaeological sites is usually advanced as the preferred option for site treatment. The most common form of archaeological site avoidance is probably project redesign, such as when a pipeline is rerouted around a site or a transmission line structure is moved outside a site boundary. Avoidance is generally effective in the short term, particularly when an archaeological monitor is present during the initial construction to ensure that disturbance does not encroach on the site and to identify discovered cultural features that were not apparent on the site surface. Long-term avoidance of the site can be more problematical, and planning for avoidance needs to take into account the activities that will take place during the operation and maintenance phases of a project. Although sites can at first be relatively easy to avoid through project redesign, avoidance becomes more complicated as an area becomes increasingly developed, especially if a transportation or utility corridor with multiple rights-of-way has been established.

Even assuming that direct damage to an archaeological site can be avoided, indirect damage must also be considered. Sites that have been "avoided" and now lie outside the project footprint may still suffer from short- or long-term indirect damage. An example might be impairment of the historic visual setting for a pioneer trail, vandalism of an adjacent site, or the gradual shaking apart of a masonry wall by vibrations from project construction in the adjacent right-of-way. The issue of collateral damage is a critical one when private land is involved. For instance, it does no good for the Environmental Protection Agency to redesign a sewer project to avoid a site on private land, only to have that parcel become a private housing development (Klein 1994:175). Nor does rerouting a highway around a site provide long-term protection if a fast-food restaurant is later built on top of the site (Kula and Beckerman 2004:1). Unless some active form of preservation is implemented, such as a multiyear preservation easement, the only way damage to an archaeological site can be mitigated is in conjunction with the original undertaking. This is because archaeological sites on private land are not afforded protection under federal preservation laws, unless they are part of a federal undertaking such as a highway project or an interstate gas pipeline.[2]

When site avoidance is infeasible, archaeologists tend automatically to consider archaeological data recovery to be the only remaining option. There is nothing inherently wrong with data recovery as a mitigation alternative; indeed, it often proves to be the best option. In practice, however, excavation may not be the most effective mitigation option.

SUSAN M. CHANDLER

When it comes to selecting sites to be excavated or devising site-specific excavation plans, many consulting and agency archaeologists still operate with an old-fashioned, salvage-archaeology model. Under this model, data recovery efforts are usually restricted to construction zones in which direct harm to or destruction of archaeological sites is planned. This approach generally precludes investigation of large areas at individual sites and often results in investigation of areas of low research potential within sites.

Some archaeologists argue that one of the major benefits of CRM archaeology is that it forces people to study archaeological resources neglected by academic researchers.[3] In traditional academic archaeology, research problems come first, and sites are selected for study on the basis of their ability to answer specific research questions. In contrast, CRM archaeologists choose neither their sites nor their research problems. Instead, they are handed a set of sites and archaeological contexts to which they must match research questions, a budget, and a client's schedule. A great amount of new, unanticipated knowledge about the past has accumulated as a result.

It is expensive to excavate sites, analyze artifacts, process ancillary samples, write reports, and curate artifacts and project materials. Client funds should be spent just as wisely as if the National Science Foundation (NSF) were funding the project. That is, if an archaeologist applying to the NSF for funding would ask, Will the reviewers of the grant proposal be impressed with the research questions being asked? Will they be convinced that the site selected for excavation can provide answers to those questions? Will it be necessary to excavate the entire site or only specific, targeted areas of the site?

Especially on linear projects such as the laying of pipelines, only small portions of sites are excavated within the direct impact zone. As a result, sites are sliced away (or not, if a particular sliver has been determined not to contribute to the site's eligibility), and archaeological data are collected without good context. McGimsey's hypothetical example in his foreword to this volume, in which only part of a house is excavated, is a good illustration of the problem. Advocates for digging only a small portion of a site justify their approach on the grounds that it is irresponsible—perhaps even unethical—to damage archaeological deposits that would otherwise go undamaged. I believe that digging a portion of a site so small that the results cannot be interpreted is itself irresponsible. At a minimum, we need to scrutinize whether the portion of the site outside the right-of-way is truly going to be preserved for the long term.

ALTERNATIVE MITIGATION

Adoption of "alternative" or "creative" mitigation approaches is encouraged by the Advisory Council on Historic Preservation (ACHP), which stresses that "in reaching decisions about appropriate treatment measures, federal agencies should weigh a variety of factors, including significance of the historic property, its value and to whom, and associated costs and project schedules" (ACHP 2007a:29). The council points out that alternatives to data recovery that achieve broader public involvement with archaeology can lead to increased appreciation of the past and a greater willingness to expend public funds in the pursuit of preservation goals. The ACHP lists the following examples of creative mitigation strategies:

- Preserving selected eligible archaeological sites and incorporating them into heritage tourism plans while allowing others to be lost
- Burying sites under fill or incorporating them into the undertaking
- Funding the development of syntheses of existing information about a region or an area instead of, or in addition to, funding data recovery
- Using barriers to route traffic away from eligible archaeological sites
- Funding the development of virtual or Web-based reports or educational media that otherwise would not be produced
- Practicing archaeological "mitigation banking"—the acquisition and preservation of archaeological sites away from the project area in return for doing little or no direct mitigation for sites in the area of potential effects (ACHP 2007a:26)

These ideas are not new. In a 1994 article on alternatives to archaeological data recovery, Joel Klein critically examined avoidance, site banking, site burial, and site stabilization.[4]

These approaches, alone or in conjunction with traditional archaeological data recovery, should be considered appropriate mitigation measures as long as "legal, feasible and practical" (ACHP 2007a:2). From the ACHP perspective, it is good public policy for federal agencies to consider alternative mitigation. The council emphasizes the need to make decisions regarding treatment of archaeological properties through consultation with stakeholders, balancing the significance of the property, the property's value, the constituency to which the property has value, and associated costs and schedules. It points out that projects with public education components may ultimately lead to greater support for archaeology because a general public that appreciates the past may be more willing to spend money on preservation treatments. In addition to assessing the public benefits of mitigation, the ACHP guidance identifies other key issues, such as assessments of benefits to the consulting parties, advancements in knowledge about the past, and preservation and management of archaeological sites in the region. To achieve such benefits, it is necessary to understand what makes the affected archaeological property important. Archaeological sites are most often determined to be significant for their information potential (criterion D of the NRHP), but they can also be important as educational or heritage tourism resources or as traditional or sacred properties.

Mitigation projects often require consulting parties to make decisions about the relative values of archaeological sites. The ACHP guidance suggests asking the following questions: What is the potential of the alternative property to yield important information relative to that of the affected property? Are there significant data gaps that one property can better fill? Does one property have a higher preservation priority because it embodies several kinds of significance and is important to several groups? The ACHP suggests that management or preservation plans be referenced for priority lists of research questions, important information gaps, archaeological sites, and other kinds of relevant information that can provide a context for making site-specific treatment decisions. Such plans may be available from or should be developed by federal agencies, SHPOs and THPOs, Indian tribes, and professional archaeological organizations.

EXAMPLES OF INNOVATIVE MITIGATION PROJECTS

Some mitigation projects that have incorporated approaches other than avoidance or data recovery to resolving adverse effects serve as examples of effective, innovative mitigation. The examples I describe in the following pages also demonstrate the critical importance of trust among the consulting parties when they employ "creative" approaches. I highlight some problems that can be encountered when not all parties are comfortable with departures from the standard compliance model.

Case Study: Pennsylvania

The Pennsylvania Department of Transportation (PennDOT) has gained national attention in the transportation community for its creative mitigation efforts. Under contract to PennDOT, A. D. Marble and Company, Inc., of Conshohocken, Pennsylvania, recently completed two successful alternative mitigation projects.

The Troxell Site (36SN91): S.R. 0522, Section 043,
Bridge Replacement Project

In 1999 and 2000, before replacement of a 1930s concrete bridge over Middle Creek in Franklin Township, Snyder County, Pennsylvania, A. D. Marble and Company performed archaeological investigations that combined cultural resource inventory and testing. The archaeologists documented and tested two prehistoric archaeological sites, both of which were determined to be eligible for the NRHP. Initially, archaeological data recovery was proposed for each site. PennDOT redesigned the project, however, completely avoiding one site and substantially reducing the footprint of potential disturbance through the other, the Troxell Site. According to the project archaeologists, "in the revised situation, the archaeological window on the Troxell Site afforded by the new APE was extremely narrow and was considered unlikely to provide an accurate understanding of the site. Nevertheless, for Section 106 clearance of the project, its effects on this significant resource had to be mitigated to a degree commensurate with the proposed impacts to the site" (Katz and Bailey 2003:1).

PennDOT decided that in lieu of archaeological excavation, funds could be better spent on a broader research study of Native American adaptations in central Pennsylvania. PennDOT and the Pennsylvania Historical and Museum Commission evaluated a number of alternative mitigation plans developed by A. D. Marble and Company and settled on an archaeological and geological study of the locally available Shriver chert in Snyder and adjacent Union counties.

This multifaceted study examined the availability of chert and precontact chert usage. It included field investigations, geological sampling and analysis, replicative studies, and various forms of collections research, including study of artifacts from recorded sites and from local collectors. The project identified 3 previously undocumented chert quarries and 17 other chert outcrops. Samples from 9 chert outcrops and artifacts from six sites were subjected to intensive petrographic, mineralogical, and geochemical analyses to determine which method best distinguished chert sources on regional and local scales. Spatial, temporal, and functional trends in chert use were examined. The results indicated that the chert sources were exploited throughout prehistory, beginning with the study area's Paleoindian inhabitants. The researchers concluded that the Middle Creek area might have been isolated from cultural developments in the Susquehanna River valley between the Late Archaic and Woodland periods (Kula 2007). The successful completion of the project was attributed to close cooperation among the stakeholders, identified as Native Americans, academics, government agencies, preservation groups, CRM professionals, and local collectors and avocational archaeologists (Katz and Bailey 2003:155).

Interstate Fairgrounds Site (36BR210): Athens Bridge Replacement Project

In 1999, A. D. Marble and Company conducted pedestrian archaeological investigations in advance of the proposed Athens Bridge replacement over the North Branch of the Susquehanna River in Athens, Pennsylvania (Lawrence and Weinberg 2003). One of the sites identified during the cultural resource inventory in the project APE was the Interstate Fairgrounds Site (36BR210), which had been seasonally occupied from the Middle Archaic through the contact period. Testing demonstrated that the site was NRHP eligible under criterion D. PennDOT was able to significantly reduce the potential damage to the site by reconfiguring the project to reduce the footprint of disturbance within the site boundary.

At a meeting with PennDOT, the Bureau of Environmental Quality, and the Pennsylvania Historical and Museum Commission, A. D. Marble and Company proposed three options for mitigation of adverse effects, including traditional archaeological data recovery. The project redesign had resulted in what the agencies considered a "sliver take"—that is, only a small portion of the site would be destroyed by the bridge replacement. With that in mind, the consulting parties agreed that the costs of archaeological excavation were likely to outweigh any research benefit gained and alternative measures to resolve the adverse effects to site 36BR210 would be appropriate. The alternative approved was a synthesis and an interpretation of local site information from existing reports, collections, and informants. The study area was defined as the area surrounding the confluence of the Chemung and Susquehanna rivers, which is known as Tioga Point. The approved alternative mitigation had two primary goals: to collect all available information from scattered institutions and individuals to create a unified database of all known, precontact archaeological sites in the Tioga Point study area and to use this database to study precontact settlement patterns in Tioga Point.

Project tasks included examination of private artifact collections, informant interviews, artifact photography, examination of collections at a number of state and local repositories, ground truth reconnaissance, and lectures to avocational archaeological societies in Tioga Point (Lawrence and Weinburg 2003:5). Site documentation was completed for 43 precontact archaeological sites from which collections had been made but for which no site forms had been prepared. Site data for 72 previously documented sites in Pennsylvania and 25 previously documented sites in New York were also reviewed. The project archaeologists were able to refine the locations and boundaries of many of these sites on the basis of local informant information and global positioning system (GPS) mapping, and they created a geographic information system (GIS) database. They gathered additional information about the archaeological contents of these sites and their excavation histories. An inventory of artifact and documentary holdings was made for each site and presented in the report. An electronic version of the report contains an archaeological site database and digital photographs of artifacts. An exhibit was also created for the Tioga Point Museum.

Settlement pattern models for Paleoindian and Early Archaic adaptations, Middle Archaic through Middle Woodland hunter-gatherer adaptations, and Late Woodland agriculturalist adaptations were developed for the 113-square-mile project study area. The observed distribution of documented habitation sites on the Pleistocene and Holocene alluvial terraces in the valley bottom, where more than 95 percent of the known sites are located, was used to model the probable locations of resource procurement sites in the uplands. The settlement model now helps guide management decisions regarding where archaeological surveys may be the most productive in the uplands. Future excavations in the Tioga Point area can be used to test the model and derive a clearer understanding of Native American subsistence and settlement patterns.

Assessment of Results

A. D. Marble's principal investigators for the two projects, John Lawrence and Daniel Bailey, reported being pleased with the results of their alternative mitigation projects (personal communication, 2007). According to them, the projects resulted in the acquisition of a large quantity of meaningful data at a cost that was approximately 40 percent less than the estimated costs of standard archaeological excavation at the two sites. Furthermore, PennDOT's highway construction was able to proceed without delay.

Because the archaeological consultants were unaware of any models for alternative mitigation from similar efforts elsewhere in the United States that they might follow, they felt as if they were working in isolation. They were originally optimistic that the adoption of creative approaches to mitigation would become a trend, but since conducting these projects, they have been presented with no further opportunities. In the past, the Pennsylvania SHPO had been somewhat leery of alternative approaches because no viable examples existed to demonstrate their advantage. Lawrence and Bailey believe that the SHPO's reticence stemmed in part from lack of a thorough understanding of the regional archaeological resource base. Pennsylvania's then most current synthesis of archaeological site data was more than 20 years old, so the SHPO was understandably worried about losing data that might be important. To date, the SHPO still has no updated synthesis, which would greatly assist in making decisions regarding alternative mitigation. Because only small slivers of two sites were to be affected by the PennDOT bridge replacements, forgoing excavations in those instances was palatable to the SHPO.

Among the lessons that Lawrence and Bailey took from these projects was that decisions regarding alternative mitigation must be made on a site-by-site basis. In addition, the archaeologist has to "sell" the approach to the SHPO and the client, and in doing so, it is probably helpful to consider research that the SHPO has identified as a need. They recommend that CRM consultants advocating innovative approaches present a variety of options to the agencies, including traditional archaeological data recovery, and then compare costs and schedules and negotiate. They stress that trust is an important element of creative mitigation. They also emphasize that it is imperative to build flexibility into the project in case research hits a dead end or needs to be expanded, because it is vital to be able to follow a line of research and not be told that the additional work is out of scope.

The agency archaeologists state, "The challenge for PennDOT and our consultants is to find creative and more cost-effective ways of doing things while maintaining the quality of our product. We believe that we will be able to achieve this goal by focusing on outcome rather than on process" (Kula and Beckerman 2004:1). They emphasize that alternative mitigation in lieu of data recovery is not appropriate in all situations. The decision must be made case by case, taking the following factors into consideration:

- A good understanding of the characteristics and information potential of a site. A site in a poorly known area or containing a rare component may not be a good candidate, because any information obtained from it is desirable.
- How much of the site is being affected. If adverse effects to the entire site are expected, then the decision about how to resolve them may be different from the decision made if only a small portion of the site will be damaged.
- The views of other stakeholders, such as Native American tribes, the SHPO, other archaeologists, and the public (Kula 2007).

Case Study: New Mexico

From 1989 to 1994, six independent energy companies drilled more than 3,000 gas wells and constructed more than 400 miles of pipelines in the Fruitland Coal Gas Gathering Systems project area in northwestern New Mexico. Most of the land is managed by the Farmington Field Office of the Bureau of Land Management (BLM). Archaeological site density in this part of northwestern New Mexico is as high as 75 sites per square mile, and the Archaic, ancestral Pueblo, protohistoric and historic Navajo, and historic Hispanic sites represent a broad span of human history.

An unusual approach was taken to the Fruitland Coal Gas Data Recovery Project in that the BLM and the New Mexico SHPO agreed to treat the entire development as a single undertaking. The competing energy companies, the BLM, and the SHPO entered into a single memorandum of agreement (MOA) that, among other things, defined the area of effect and processes for identifying the sites to be part of a data recovery "pool" and for selecting sites to be excavated. A regional research design to be applied to all archaeological data recoveries was prepared for the Fruitland project under contract to the BLM, and a group of professional archaeologists formed the Farmington District Cultural Advisory Group to develop data comparability guidelines for the basic aspects of the data recovery project.

A critical aspect of the Fruitland project MOA was consideration of sites in their entirety, rather than just the portions of sites within pipeline rights-of-way and drill pad locations. This approach was partly a response to the recognition that damage to sites does not stop at the edges of the direct impact area.

While acknowledging that the Fruitland project approach was a consumptive one, in that portions of sites not directly affected by the initial construction were excavated, the BLM archaeologists enumerated several key points with regard to treating entire sites rather than pieces of sites (Copeland and Simons 1995:5): (1) the site is a logical unit of investigation; (2) the excavation of an entire site maximizes data collection at that location; (3) the types of data collected are comparable; (4) observation and identification of intrasite and intersite variability are enhanced; and (5) all archaeological sites are not equally important. Because archaeological research extended beyond the narrow corridors of direct disturbance, the ability to interpret what happened at individual sites and at local and regional levels was much greater than it would have been otherwise.

From the universe of sites that were to be affected, archaeologists selected a sample of sites for excavation. Site selection was based on factors including archaeological data potential (that is, the likelihood that the site contained meaningful artifacts, specimens, features, or structures to answer research questions), the degree of potential effects, and costs. Site selection took place at meetings in which BLM, SHPO, Native American, and industry representatives all participated. More than 500 eligible archaeological sites were included in five separate site selection pools, with more than 125 sites selected for archaeological data recovery at some level. Not all sites were completely excavated, especially the larger ones and those that lay almost entirely outside the right-of-way (Copeland and Simons 1995:9). The energy companies hired multiple cultural resource consulting firms to excavate the sites. Construction delays were avoided either by implementing short-term engineering solutions while data recovery was under way or by excavating just within the right-of-way of a targeted site before pipeline construction and then completing the archaeological data recovery after construction was finished.

Mitigation of adverse effects, however, was not limited to excavation. Because the SHPO was concerned that decisions were being made about which sites to excavate without a broader understanding of the settlement system in the region, the Fruitland project also included some instances in which intensive block inventories were completed in lieu of excavation in order to complement site interpretations based on data recovery. Originally intended to be conducted on a large scale, the cultural resource inventory aspect of the Fruitland project ultimately was restricted to a few selected cases because of the negative response from the local archaeological community to trading inventory for excavation. Other components of the Fruitland project included an annual meeting, known as the Fruitland Conference, which was co-sponsored by the BLM, archaeological contractors, and industry to disseminate project results; a major ethnographic study; and experiments on whether thermal imaging and advanced cesium vapor magnetometer technology could be applied to archaeological research.

Some major contributions to regional archaeology resulted from the Fruitland project research (for example, Hovezak and Sesler 2002; Wilshusen, comp., 1995; Wilshusen, Sesler, and Hovezak 2000). Indeed, Southwestern archaeologists' understanding of the early Navajo and early Pueblo archaeology in the area fundamentally changed because of the unified nature of the Fruitland project research. And although the oil and gas industry was apprehensive about this approach to archaeological mitigation when it was first presented, the project's opponents quickly saw the advantages and became big supporters (Lynne Sebastian, personal communication, 2008).

The BLM archaeologists critiqued the Fruitland project approach in 1995 as follows: "While the project provides for a comprehensive approach to mitigating adverse effects, the process is very complex, time consuming, and difficult to explain to either management or industry" (Copeland and Simons 1995:13). At that time, they noted that it was difficult to get data recovery reports completed in a timely fashion because once the pipe was in the ground, the energy industry (and presumably its archaeological consultants) became focused on building the next pipeline. Twelve years later, when asked for their advice regarding implementation of innovative approaches to mitigation, Dave Simons and Jim Copeland responded that in their opinion, areas in which a large amount of archaeological work had already been done were more amenable to alternative mitigation approaches than were areas of new development. They said that it might take years of effort to get the basics in place so that a regional or landscape-level approach could be taken. They emphasized the importance of building partnerships and of building a rational argument that was in conformance with the laws, with the goal of doing good science that produced meaningful results. It was their perspective that more projects had not implemented innovative approaches when appropriate because the New Mexico SHPO staff preferred to follow a standard compliance process (Jim Copeland, personal communication, 2007; Dave Simons, personal communication, 2007).

Case Study: Utah

The Kern River Pipeline originates in southwestern Wyoming and extends to a point near Bakersfield, California, crossing Utah on a diagonal and passing through a small portion of southern Nevada on its way. The pipeline carries natural gas across state boundaries and therefore is a federal undertaking under the jurisdiction of the Federal Energy Regulatory Commission (FERC). The following project synopsis is for Utah only; alternative mitigation approaches also were incorporated into the treatment plans for Nevada and California (for example, Blair and Winslow 2003).

In Utah, the Kern River Pipeline traverses land managed by the BLM, two national forests, Utah state trust land, and private land. Dames and Moore conducted the archeological inventories and data recovery for the original Kern River Pipeline, in 1991 and 1992. A multivolume draft excavation report was submitted to the agencies in 1994 (Spaulding 1994a, 1994b, 1994c). No final report was ever produced, however, and the results of the large-scale data recovery project never became widely available to the profession or to the public.

SUSAN M. CHANDLER

In 2001 the Kern River Gas Transmission Company (KRGT) hired Alpine Archaeological Consultants, Inc., (Alpine) to inventory the right-of-way for a new pipeline paralleling the original Kern River Pipeline. Many of the sites that had been excavated along the original pipeline route were found to have poor integrity as a result of the original archaeological excavations and subsequent pipeline construction. Despite this, 163 of the 260 sites recorded in Utah were determined to be eligible for the NRHP. A meeting was held in Salt Lake City in early January 2002 to devise a treatment plan for the significant sites. Present at the meeting were archaeologists from the pipeline company, the two consulting firms hired to conduct the mitigation (Alpine and SWCA, Inc.), the BLM state office and field offices, the Dixie National Forest, and the Utah State Historic Preservation Office. The State Institutional Trust Lands archaeologist and the Utah state archaeologist and assistant state archaeologist were invited but did not attend, and FERC deferred to the Utah SHPO and the state and federal land-managing agencies with regard to consultation on the resolution of adverse effects.

The group decided to adopt an approach to archaeological data recovery wherein an entire archaeological site would be considered to be the unit of study, rather than just the portion of a site within the right-of-way. Furthermore, because project sites were so shallow and so much work had already been done in the original Kern River Pipeline corridor, a number of alternatives to data recovery were thought to be more productive than excavating sites in the right-of-way. Decisions were made about which sites held the greatest research potential by means of a numerical ranking scheme that considered each site's potential to provide important data, as well as the amount of previous excavation conducted at the site. In the end, the group decided that controlled excavations should be conducted at a sample of 30 historic and prehistoric archaeological sites in Utah. The BLM and Forest Service archaeologists from southern Utah requested that three off–right-of-way sites potentially subject to indirect damage also be included in the sample because they would provide crucial data that were unavailable from the sites in the pipeline corridor. At least one of these sites was being looted, and the agency archaeologists decided to apply the funds that would have been expended to excavate a site within the pipeline right-of-way to the excavation of this endangered site.

Other tasks incorporated in the Utah treatment plan included the following:

- Archaeological monitoring of all significant archaeological sites in the pipeline corridor during construction and excavation of discovered features.

- Preparation of an administrative history of the project corridor in Utah, including a synthesis of the excavation data for 126 sites excavated by Dames and Moore for the original Kern River Pipeline and a summary of other archaeological research conducted along the pipeline corridor.

- Preparation of a synthesis of prehistoric data from southwestern Utah incorporating previous archaeological research from other CRM projects in the region. The synthesis identified data gaps and provided models of prehistoric adaptations and directions for future research. Its goals were to aid in the development of future research designs in the area and to provide a context for archaeologists making site significance decisions.

- A paleoenvironmental study of the southern Bonneville Basin, including deep coring of dry lakes and other locales, a pack rat midden study, and a geomorphological study. The research was designed to provide an environmental context for understanding Paleoindian adaptations in the Great Basin and to identify resources potentially available to occupants of a Paleoindian site in the project area.

- Refinement of chronological interpretations based on obsidian hydration data.

- Thermoluminescence dating and neutron activation analysis of prehistoric ceramics.

- Historical documentation of significant linear sites (for example, telephone lines, historic canals and ditches, roads, railroads), comprising archival research, photodocumentation, and preparation of National Register nomination forms.

- Preparation of a GIS database and a research context for historic linear features in Salt Lake County.

- Presentation of project results at the 2004 and 2005 annual meetings of the Society for American Archaeology and at the 2005 Great Basin Anthropological Conference, as well as distribution of print and electronic reports to professional colleagues.

- Public dissemination of project results via publication of an interactive CD and a book, *From Hunters to Homesteaders* (Stettler and Seddon 2005), describing the archaeological work in Utah.

The pipeline construction was completed on schedule in 2003, and technical archaeological excavation reports were completed in 2005. Synthetic overview volumes that provided summaries of excavation data and comprehensive research studies by time period were also produced so that the data would be more accessible to other researchers. Project archaeologists incorporated new project data, existing regional archaeological and historical data, and the results of analysis of existing artifact assemblages housed at museums. Because the Utah project reports alone make up 22 individually bound volumes, technical site reports and other project data were also published and distributed in electronic format (Reed, Seddon, and Stettler 2005).

Despite issues of trust and lack of full consensus among the consulting parties, Alpine and SWCA believe that the Kern River project was a success. The pipeline company spent a great amount of money on the project but was able to see tangible results. From the client's perspective, the costs of doing archaeology were not limited to paying the archaeological consultants. The notice to proceed with archaeological data recovery was not issued until the same day the notice to proceed with pipeline construction was issued. The costs of having construction crews sit idle or of moving pipeline construction around archaeological sites would have exceeded the archaeological mitigation costs, and the costs of not getting the project into service on schedule would have been even greater. Innovative approaches helped to avoid conflicts and ensured that money spent on archaeological mitigation actually went toward archaeology rather than toward construction costs. And the results of the research have been widely disseminated.

Site Preservation

Another alternative mitigation strategy is the creation of archaeological preserves. The creation of easements can be an effective mitigation measure—for example, when a developer purchases an easement to provide access to traditional cultural properties by Native Americans. This mitigation strategy is akin to "off-site mitigation" under NEPA, in which preservation of a site outside the APE is substituted for the resources to be destroyed.

As Lipe has so persuasively argued, however, site burial, site banking, and "not digging" approaches to dealing with threats to archaeological resources should be means, not ends. Site preservation is archaeologically justified as a mitigation measure to the extent that learning something by means of archaeological study is postponed into the future. Keeping sites off-limits to research undercuts the basic justifications for protecting those sites in the first place, particularly if the action taken to preserve the sites precludes anyone from ever using archaeology to learn anything from them in the future (Lenihan et al. 1981; Lipe 2000a).

Preservation of archaeological sites must be an active process if it is to be successful. Simply designating a site as one to be conserved for the future is insufficient, and covenant restrictions on land containing archaeological sites do not always guarantee protection. Preservation easements are commonly used to protect historic buildings and can also be used to protect archaeological sites. Some archaeological easements are held by land trusts such as the National Trust for Historic Preservation. Easements also benefit families who want to stay on their land, because many states have tax credits available to individuals or entities that donate preservation easements for archaeological sites.

Jim Walker, the Southwest regional director for the Archaeological Conservancy (TAC), explains that the conservancy prefers full, fee-simple ownership of land over conservation easements for archaeological site protection, because archaeological sites are nonrenewable resources (personal communication, 2007). Unlike resources that can be protected through conservation easements, such as farmland and stands of trees, archaeological sites cannot be reestablished if the terms of the easement are violated. Archaeological preserves established through land donations by developers who chose the mitigation alternative of "avoidance and preservation in place" can be actively managed and protected, in contrast to sites that are avoided but still owned by the developer or other party. Volunteer site stewards patrol preserves owned by TAC. TAC is interested in sites that are truly special and unique. Its board has rejected sites that are difficult to protect, such as rock art panels and lithic scatters.

Another requirement for a TAC archaeological preserve is for TAC to have legal access to the property. When appropriate, TAC has leased some archaeological sites preserved within a housing development back to the homeowner's association as an open-space park, the idea being to integrate the archaeological preserve into the developed community as a useful asset while preserving the site and ensuring its availability for future research. Other examples of this approach include incorporating archaeological sites into golf courses and trail corridors. In some cases, the archaeological site has first been covered with geotextile material and sterile fill to preserve cultural material exposed on the ground surface. The sites are still available for archaeological research by qualified researchers who have an approved research design and who will commit to a timetable for analysis, curation in an approved repository, and publication (Jim Walker, personal communication, 2007).

Developing Educational and Curriculum Materials

Inclusion of a public education component as an element of an archaeological mitigation project can provide funding that would otherwise have been unavailable. For example, two recent pipeline projects in Colorado and Wyoming, the Rockies Express Pipeline and Wyoming Interstate Gas Company's Piceance Basin Lateral, jointly incorporated Project Archaeology into their archaeological mitigation program at the request of the BLM.

Project Archaeology is a national heritage education program for upper elementary through secondary school teachers and their students. The BLM created the program in the early 1990s to develop awareness of the nation's diverse and fragile archaeological sites, to instill a sense of personal responsibility for stewardship of these sites, and to enhance science literacy and cultural understanding through the study of archaeology. Project Archaeology began in Utah as a statewide project to combat the vandalism and looting of archaeological sites and expanded into other western states. Now operating under a partnership between the BLM and Montana State University in Bozeman, Project Archaeology plans to extend its program to all 50 states.

According to its Web site (http://projectarchaeology.org), "Project Archaeology uses archaeological inquiry to foster understanding of past and present cultures; improve social studies and science education; and enhance citizenship education to help preserve our archaeological legacy." Project Archaeology teaches four "enduring understandings": "Understanding the human past is essential for understanding the present and shaping the future; learning about cultures past and present is essential for living in a pluralistic society and world; archaeology is a way to learn about past cultures; [and] stewardship of archaeological resources is everyone's responsibility."

Project Archaeology used funds provided jointly by the two pipeline companies to support teacher participation in field excavations of a prehistoric rockshelter site in northwestern Colorado and to finance the development of curriculum materials. Teachers from rural Colorado schools helped with professional archaeological excavations being conducted by Metcalf Archaeological Consultants, Inc. The Project Archaeology staff, consisting of professional archaeologists and educators, integrated information gleaned from the project to produce classroom resource materials. The resulting documents—*Project Archaeology: Investigating Shelter* and

Investigating a Rockshelter—have been distributed to teachers and their students in northwestern Colorado and southwestern Wyoming. The materials were also intended to form the basis of two workshops for teachers in Denver and Montrose, Colorado, and were to be distributed to teachers throughout the region via the Internet.

Project Archaeology connected with teachers and students in rural areas of the state who would never have been reached otherwise. Teacher evaluations of the program demonstrated the educators' enthusiasm for the project, with teachers planning to use the materials to teach their students about the archaeological sites in their area and the importance of protecting them and learning from them, now and in the future (Tom Roll, Project Archaeology, to Rock Meyer, Rockies Express Pipeline, Jan. 4, 2008).

Other Examples of Innovative Mitigation

The examples I have presented are just a few of the ways in which innovative approaches to archaeological mitigation can be implemented. Other approaches to consider include funding indigenous archaeology projects, such as those discussed by Ferguson (chapter 8, this volume), studies of contemporary theoretical issues, and studies of existing museum collections. Funding for archaeological consultants to prepare journal articles for publication or to hold synthesis seminars resulting in edited books would greatly enhance the public benefits from large data-recovery projects as well because it would make the results of technical reports readily accessible to other archaeologists and the public.

OBSTACLES TO INNOVATIVE MITIGATION

Resistance to innovative mitigation approaches comes from several fronts, including SHPOs who are comfortable doing archaeology in routine fashion with standard approaches; nervous clients who worry that they will be unable to complete their projects on time or that they are being asked to pay for unnecessary work; archaeologists who perceive that changes might threaten their livelihood; and those in the preservation community who are unwilling to look at alternatives to either avoiding or digging every significant site.

Because the past is so incompletely known, archaeologists are fearful of losing important data, the significance of which is not yet identified. The truth is that we cannot save every site; attempting to do so risks public and government backlash. Archaeologists worry—perhaps with good reason—that if clients, politicians, and the public realize that significant archaeological sites can be "sacrificed," then we might be opening the door to letting all sites be destroyed in the interest of the greater corporate and public good (see Lipe 1984).

Caution is certainly warranted. Much of the resistance to considering innovative mitigation approaches stems from a genuine desire to protect irreplaceable archaeological sites that, once destroyed, are gone forever. Because of the nature of the archaeological record, archaeologists have a commitment to their resource distinct from that of lawyers to their clients or engineers to their projects (Wildesen 1984:4). Consulting archaeology differs from these other professional services because, in addition to the professional–client relationship, archaeologists must consider the archaeological record (Raab 1984:57–58). Other scientists do not completely destroy their objects of study, but even the best-designed archaeological mitigation project has the potential to destroy what may be the only example of an element of the past. This applies not only to alternative mitigation strategies but also to traditional archaeological data recovery. An archaeologist who digs a site but then fails to produce a report or make the results of the research accessible to others has effectively destroyed an archaeological site with no public benefit.

Some resistance to creative approaches may also derive from archaeologists being asked to venture into territory in which they have no experience or training (for example, education curriculum and public outreach; see Crass, chapter 11, this volume). It is important to remember that individual archaeologists do not need to perform every task themselves. Just as archaeologists hire specialists to conduct ancillary studies, so professionals who excel at public outreach, such as those involved in Project Archaeology, can be employed to assist mitigation projects in dealing with public education. Similarly, consultants with ties to indigenous communities can be hired to assist in developing mitigation that incorporates indigenous archaeology (see Ferguson, chapter 8, this volume).

SOLUTIONS

Projects that have successfully incorporated innovative approaches into their site treatment plans amply demonstrate the advantages of adopting such tactics. As we move forward, it will serve us well to keep political and economic realities in mind, remembering that the public that ultimately pays for archaeological research deserves to gain some tangible benefits as a result of our efforts.

In order to move forward with comprehensive mitigation, I believe that we must revamp our decision-making. Agency archaeologists and archaeological consultants need to spend more time thinking about how to approach an archaeological project and then much more time and effort talking to each other in the early stages of the project. Clients with fast-track projects, overworked agency archaeologists, and state and tribal historic preservation officers need to be willing to make the time to consult not only with one another but also with other publics who may have interests in the archaeological sites. The examples of innovative mitigation approaches presented here underscore the vital necessity of establishing trust among all parties involved. One recent suggestion is for the American Cultural Resources Association (ACRA) to schedule regular, regional meetings with agency staff in which creative dialogues about the Section 106 process can take place in neutral settings, outside the context of project work (Berkin 2008).

Before innovative approaches to mitigation can even be considered, a foundation must first be built with reasoned and appropriate levels of cultural resource inventory, evaluations of site significance that consider all the kinds of values a site might contain, and comprehensive assessments of effects. A consideration of the public benefits to be gained from mitigation alternatives is also essential. As Joseph Winter (1984:44) pointed out more than 20 years ago, "the scientific method can be used to design the project and to offer alternative approaches, as well as to carry out the project, but it cannot decide which ends should be met and which alternatives should be used, since these are based on economic, political, social, and other reasons grounded in values."

Despite several decades of archaeological research in a CRM setting, we are still struggling to provide frameworks for making decisions about archaeological site mitigation. Archaeologists need to work toward developing overarching research programs so that effort levels for a particular project can be established on the basis of the size and effects of the undertaking (Altschul 2005:205). In an ideal world, management decisions would be made at a regional planning level rather than at site-specific or project-specific levels (see Barker, chapter 4, this volume). Areas of critical sensitivity would simply be off-limits for projects with the potential to disturb archaeological sites, and other projects would be designed to balance site preservation with other resource needs, including development. The BLM's Geographic Area of Development Plan for oil and gas development (BLM Instructional Memorandum no. 2003-152) makes use of this principle on a small scale. Might it be possible to develop a broader vision that transcends agency or even state boundaries? Or barring that, might it be

possible for SHPOs and THPOs to designate groups of advisory archaeologists who are regional experts, who have a larger perspective, and who
could help develop a framework for making choices?[5]

In the meantime, the professional archaeological community should
work to have archaeologists appointed to regional planning committees
such as the Forest Service's and the BLM's resource advisory committees.
When possible, archaeologists need to become involved early in the planning for specific projects (as provided for in NEPA regulations), when an
opportunity still exists to provide meaningful input into decision-making
that takes archaeological resources into consideration in the project design.

Archaeologists should also work with THPOs and tribes to incorporate
their concerns about innovative mitigation approaches, particularly with
regard to archaeological work outside areas of direct effect. Archaeologists
should also be open to including nontraditional mitigation measures that
might be suggested by a tribe in a project treatment plan.

Publishing examples of successful, innovative mitigation approaches in
archaeological journals and showcasing them to clients and agencies will
help to demonstrate the benefit of such approaches and may attract cham-
pions who will promote the widespread adoption of creative mitigation.
For example, the Kern River Gas Transmission Company was awarded the
2006 ACRA Industry Award for "embracing a cultural resources mitigation
program to help public understanding of archaeology, prehistory and history in the Great Basin" (award certificate). Along the same lines, awards
from professional archaeological societies for publication of exemplary
projects —including results from standard excavation projects—might provide incentives for the scholarly dissemination of CRM results.

In summary, archaeologists need to adopt a more comprehensive
approach to archaeological site mitigation that looks at a wide range of
archaeological sites, recognizes that sites have different values to different
publics, and considers all effects on sites and not just immediate threats.
We need to make sure that archaeological research proposed will enhance
knowledge of the past and that the results of our research are widely disseminated to the archaeological profession and the public. At the same
time, we need to be true to the intent of historic preservation legislation
and balance the interests of historic preservation with competing interests.
This can be achieved if we identify mitigation strategies for affected sites
that resolve the adverse effects from the project, have budgets proportional
to the effects, can be completed within a reasonable time frame, and provide benefits to the greater public, which ultimately pays for the archaeo-

logical work through taxes and utility bills. This is the challenge for agency and consulting archaeologists and their clients.

Notes

1. In New Mexico, the Archaeological Resource Management System (ARMS) database shows the following SHPO determinations of NRHP eligibility: 58 percent eligible, 18 percent not eligible, and 23 percent unevaluated (Scott Geister, ARMS, personal communication, 2008). Almost half of all recorded prehistoric and historic sites (62,766 of 133,739, or 47 percent) in the database of the Colorado Office of Archaeology and Historic Preservation (OAHP) are recommended or determined eligible for the NRHP (Mary Sullivan, OAHP, personal communication, 2007). In contrast, 29 percent (17,341 of 59,828) of evaluated sites in Wyoming are NRHP eligible (Mary Hopkins, Wyoming Cultural Records Office, personal communication, 2007).

2. Some states, counties, and municipalities, however, do have historic preservation laws in place.

3. "One of the great things about mitigative archaeology is that it forces us to investigate a lot of sites that we might otherwise not ever look at and thereby creates important potential for serendipitous, unexpected insights that can open new and productive research directions" (Winston Hurst, personal communication, 2007).

4. Despite some drawbacks to these other approaches and a lack of knowledge on the part of archaeologists about effective and appropriate alternative approaches, Klein concluded that archaeologists prefer data recovery because they "like to dig." There are good reasons for this. Excavation provides an abundance of research data that allows archaeologists to publish, obtain peer recognition, and advance professionally. Data recovery is also labor intensive, and Klein (1994:180) argued that many consulting archaeologists "are under considerable pressure to keep small armies of field technicians employed."

5. These kinds of recommendations for regional planning were made in the Airlie House report (McGimsey and Davis 1977:59), which advocated holding regional workshops to develop planning documents that would coordinate activities and facilitate communication among professional archaeologists.

7

The Challenges of Dissemination

Accessing Archaeological Data
and Interpretations

Julia A. King

In 2004, on the eve of the four-hundredth anniversary of the settlement of Jamestown, Virginia, the Omohundro Institute of Early American History and Culture at the College of William and Mary sponsored a conference titled "The Atlantic World and Virginia, 1550–1624." It promised to redefine "the way historians look at the Atlantic world in the era of exploration" (Wilson 2004). The speakers listed in the conference program read like a who's who among Atlantic world scholars: Sir John Elliott, Karen Kupperman, Philip Morgan, Lorena Walsh, and dozens more, including members of Virginia's Indian community. The organizers cast a wide net for participation when it came to approaches for documenting and interpreting the past. Having spent the better part of my career working in the mid-Atlantic region, off I went to Williamsburg, looking forward to a conference that would "redefine an entire field of historical significance" (Whitson 2004). What is more, as one beaming conference participant later commented, the conference showed its stuff "before a large and diverse audience, including a substantial presence by that scarcest of creatures, the general public" (Shields 2005:220).

It was indeed an outstanding conference, and I learned much from my three days in Williamsburg. But I was surprised by archaeologists' lack of participation in this free event, as presenters and as audience members.

Among 71 speakers, only five archaeologists appeared on the conference program, and two of them served as commentators. Of the three presenters, Bill Kelso described the recent excavations at Jamestown, and the other two were coauthors, along with several others, discussing interpretive findings first published in the 1980s and little changed since then. Given all the recent archaeological work focused on the late sixteenth and early seventeenth centuries in Maryland and Virginia beyond Jamestown, much of it undertaken through cultural resource management projects, and given the potential of archaeology for exploring complex issues of culture contact, adaptation, and change, I initially chalked this underrepresentation up to the conference organizers, who, I was convinced, had a distorted view of what archaeology is and how it can contribute to thinking about the past.

After much thought, however, I came to realize that archaeologists bear much, if not the major part, of the responsibility for their absence at events like the Omohundro conference. Despite some 30 years of archaeology in the mid-Atlantic region focused on the early colonial period, much of it at public expense in one form or another, the evidence amassed remains largely inaccessible even to most archaeologists, affecting our ability to develop new interpretations about life at this time. Many of the archaeological sites were excavated by cultural resource consultants, others by archaeologists housed in the region's many museums, and a few sites by archaeologists in the region's universities. The reports from the majority of these projects are almost all limited-distribution photocopies—"gray literature"—typically focused on a single site and characterized by technical jargon. In some cases, especially among the museums and universities, reports have yet to be completed. Collections resulting from these projects are housed in institutions scattered throughout the region, and although most collections are physically accessible, in reality they are only minimally used. Even if a researcher managed to visit the institutions holding the collections, chances are that he or she would find incomplete or altogether missing catalogs and other records.

The organizers of the "Atlantic World and Virginia" conference probably bypassed substantive archaeological involvement because they had little idea that the archaeological work existed.[1] The one presentation at the conference that attempted some form of archaeological synthesis was based on a paper published in 1981. If, after more than 30 years, we archaeologists remain ineffective at using the information we have generated, is it reasonable to expect historians or the interested public to do so? Indeed, despite the effort expended during excavation to document stratigraphic and other contextual information, many, if not most, archaeological collections are organized, perceived, and reported as series or lists of objects rather than as sets of complex relationships that happen to include objects. At this point, archaeology risks becoming less a social science and more an antiquarian exercise, with diminishing relevance to all students of the past, including archaeologists themselves.

In this chapter, I consider the dissemination of archaeological information by exploring three related topics: the challenges of creating access to archaeological data; the challenges of accessing gray literature reports of surveys and excavations; and the challenges of generating usable syntheses. Access to archaeological information (data) and interpretation (findings promised by synthetic or comparative study) is critical—for cultural resource management (CRM) professionals and federal agency decision-makers involved in Section 106 undertakings; for archaeologists in both CRM and the academy who study the larger social and cultural histories and processes represented by archaeological information; and for the public, which wants to know about the nation's rich and complicated human past—all 12,000 to 15,000 years of it—and which also happens to underwrite a good amount of the archaeology undertaken in this country.

Although cultural resource management always includes consideration of archaeological sites in situ, here I focus on archaeological collections—materials removed from archaeological sites, along with their associated records, including gray literature reports.[2] Archaeological collections are rarely, if ever, considered eligible for the National Register of Historic Places (NRHP), although most (but not all) of them derive from sites that are or were NRHP eligible. In theory, data recovery efforts are designed to preserve both horizontal and vertical relationships among strata and other archaeological materials, including artifacts, so that the site can be "reconstructed" in the laboratory. The long-term accessibility of archaeological materials and the information contained in them is critical for the kinds of comparative and synthetic work that will not only inform decision-making by managers but also provide the content for educating the public and for learning more about short- and long-term social and cultural processes.

First, it is important to acknowledge that archaeological materials are products of our own time, created through a modern process by which "things" dug up from the ground are, through excavation and other archaeological practices, reconfigured as historical and scientific "evidence" or "information." Although archaeologists remain committed to understanding how people in the past meaningfully constituted their worlds, we begin this effort by creating categories that would probably make little sense to the people we study. Archaeological excavation—recovering artifacts and other forms of archaeological evidence, including stratigraphic and other contextual information—transforms long-discarded and abandoned "things" into something wholly new. These things and the information they now represent are typically warehoused in a wide range of repositories.

Second, interest in the challenges of disseminating archaeological information and interpretation is not new, nor are the problems involved in doing so. Remarks made in 1982 before the Society for American Archaeology by Ric Davidge, the special assistant to the US assistant secretary for fish, wildlife, and parks, could easily be mistaken for comments delivered last week (King 1982:391–392). Those remarks raised all sorts of by now familiar but still urgent topics and concerns about archaeology, concerns that Davidge attributed to archaeology's "failure to communicate the *ideals* of archaeology and results of work to the very people who have paid for that work." Responsibility for this "failure" should not fall on archaeologists alone, but I think most of us would agree that the problem persists—or appears to persist. Indeed, my colleague Bill Lees and I recently organized and edited a forum for the journal *Historical Archaeology* titled "What Are We Learning through Publicly Funded Historical Archaeology (and Is It Worth the Considerable Expense)?" (Lees and King 2007). Like the special assistant in his speech, we cover much ground in our essay, finding that we (historical) archaeologists "have generally failed to communicate our results to other audiences," a failure resulting in part from a discourse infused with jargon and in part from a focus on method over social, cultural, and historical questions (Lees and King 2007:57–58). If at this point I am beginning to sound a bit like Chicken Little, one might ask, Is the sky really falling? In the following sections, I consider the challenges of disseminating ("communicating") archaeological information and interpretation. Many of the challenges are infrastructural; the way "the system" often works inhibits creative, innovative, and ultimately risky efforts, instead emphasizing process over outcome. Process *is* important, but so are outcomes. Other challenges include limited resources, in terms of both funding and staffing, as well as a lack of skills among professional archaeologists for creating and maintaining accessibility to archaeological data. These skills range from manipulating large data sets to writing for and talking with lay audiences. Nonetheless, archaeologists can point to a number of projects that have successfully disseminated archaeological data and interpretations to diverse audiences, through both traditional and new technologies. In the final section of the chapter, I explore a few of the more successful projects, searching for recommendations to improve efforts to communicate archaeological results and findings, for us and the many publics we serve.

THE CHALLENGES OF CREATING ACCESS TO ARCHAEOLOGICAL DATA

In 2000, staff at the Maryland Archaeological Conservation Laboratory (MAC Lab), the state of Maryland's archaeological collections repository, began the long-term organizing, rehousing, preserving, and—critical to my purposes in this chapter—digitizing of the field and laboratory records associated with each collection in the facility. This work, supported by the National Endowment for the Humanities and ISTEA funds from the Maryland Department of Transportation, has revealed the magnitude of information found in these collections. More than just lists of artifacts, the records contain irreplaceable information about relationships among artifacts and the stratigraphic levels from which they were recovered, information that lies at the heart of archaeology.

Like most archaeological collections nationwide, I suspect, the Maryland materials were not optimally organized, and the MAC Lab staff knew little about the contents of the full collection. And although the state of Maryland had, through its state historic preservation officer (SHPO), dutifully carried these collections for at least a few decades and through three or four moves, only a few archaeologists had ever made use of them. The MAC Lab's goal is to change this, in part by taking advantage of developing technologies that allow for the electronic delivery of information.

Almost immediately, as the scope of the project became clear, MAC Lab staff began imposing limits on their effort, developing a 10-year plan that would, they hoped, result in the preservation and digitization of records (including artifacts, catalogs, and reports) from 34 of the facility's most important collections. These 34 collections—all of them from data recovery projects—represent approximately one-third of the repository's holdings. In other words, after 10 years of concerted effort and greater-than-normal levels of funding, MAC Lab staff estimated that they would process only one-third of their collection—as measured in 2000 and therefore not including collections coming in after that date. And although their colleagues outside the agency unanimously agreed that this was an urgently needed, high-priority project, MAC Lab staff began to wonder, If we build it, will they really come?[3] For years, archaeologists have fantasized, as a profession, about increased accessibility to archaeological information, but would we know what to do with the reality? Would we be like a dog that finally catches the car and then does not know what to do with it?

Maryland, it could be argued, is ahead of the game in collections management and therefore is not the best example for illustrating the challenges we face. The Maryland legislature has consistently supported historic preservation, and Maryland boasts one of the largest state historic preservation offices in the nation, especially given the state's geographical size. But by having the resources to forge ahead, Maryland can serve as a kind of canary in the coal mine to reveal not just the immediate challenges of making archaeological information accessible but also the long-term challenges. Although the state may be able to approach or even set the bar for best practices, areas in which the state's efforts fall short—and they do—can be mined for lessons that will serve archaeologists elsewhere.

As the 10-year period for this project comes to a close, archaeologists and collections managers at the MAC Lab will have digitized more than 200,000 paper and film records, including contextual and formal information on nearly one million artifacts. These digitized materials should eventually be organized in a Web-accessible database that will allow users anywhere in the world to download artifact data and associated field and laboratory documentation. MAC Lab curators hope that this kind of accessibility will dramatically increase the use of Maryland's collections, albeit in electronic format. The nature of this hope has evolved: the curators' initial and perhaps naive belief that the absence of physical or electronic access was the only factor preventing the use of these materials has given way to a growing realization that electronic access (or dissemination) still does not equal intellectual access. It is increasingly clear that many of us lack the requisite computer, statistical, and interpretive skills that would allow us to make full and sophisticated analytical use of these collections. In some ways, this should come as no surprise; although we may have been exposed to and learned these skills, in practice we have either not always used or not always needed them, and when faced with real-world, typically problematic data, we can be stumped.

The Problem of Classification

The effort to organize and digitize the vast array of field and laboratory collections at the MAC Lab has revealed a more immediate and perhaps more insidious problem on both the front and back ends of data collection—that is, a problem with classification. Most archaeologists know that comparing the evidence from just two archaeological sites can be difficult or even impossible, typically because of cataloging variations but just as often because of excavation strategies and methods. In my own research, which is focused on the structure and use of household space in the historic period mid-Atlantic, evidence from long, plowed, surface midden deposits is critical. Yet, rarely do two projects use the same methods. One firm might use 5-by-5-foot units to recover plow zone evidence, and another, 10-by-10-foot units; some work in metric measurements, and others in feet and tenths of feet; some firms use one-quarter-inch screen mesh, and others three-eights-inch mesh; some workers are stratigraphic splitters, and others lumpers; some firms simply strip away the plow zone altogether. These are important deal-making or deal-breaking decisions, and even though more than three decades of research have demonstrated the most reliable and cost-effective methods for recovering evidence about plowed midden deposits (see King 2006), many archaeologists still approach the excavation of a historic domestic site as if this information does not exist or, worse, is irrelevant. When we do talk about excavation methods and the problems posed by varied recovery approaches, many of us respond that rigid excavation standards are not the answer, and it is true that rarely does "one size fit all." These problems are not easily resolved without resorting to "least common denominator" approaches to comparing classifications, or to comparing conclusions and inferences made by various workers rather than comparing raw data.

In archaeology, developing theories to interpret and explain past human behavior has always won the highest status and greatest reward. But if our methods impede our ability to construct detailed analogies and supportable inferences, then of what value, really, are those theories? Methods are not neutral or universal but are intimately connected to interpretation, good and bad. In *The Archaeological Process*, Ian Hodder (1999) attempted to bring closer scrutiny to method and its relationship to interpretation, but it is unclear whether Hodder's work has had any influence on CRM (or, for that matter, academic) archaeology. The methodological differences among data recovery projects that the MAC Lab staff observed for the Maryland records directly affect our ability to move beyond a single-site focus and toward more detailed comparative research—the part of our practice that makes archaeologists anthropologists. This methodological anarchy is especially ironic given the earlier observation by Lees and me that at least in historical archaeology, it is all about the method. So pervasive is this problem of differing methodologies and standards that when Fraser Neiman set out to develop the online database Digital Archaeological Archive of Comparative Slavery (www.daacs.org), he decided that it was simply less expensive to start over and recatalog all the assemblages using a single set of protocols and standards he developed in consultation with students of New World slavery. Even with this level of control, Neiman and his colleagues could not compensate for the wide range of field methods used to recover the data now included in DAACS.

Informed by the debates and discussions in archaeology about classification and typology, Neiman developed an artifact cataloging system for the DAACS project that transcended classification based on the artifact as object, instead focusing on the artifact's attributes. A ceramic fragment is still classified by its type name—for example, "white salt-glazed stoneware" —but the cataloging calls out many more attributes of the fragment that could be obscured by the type name (Aultman et al. 2007). Vessel form, sherd thickness, sherd size, and other attributes that vary within types are recorded in the DAACS cataloging protocols. The protocols serve to standardize data entry, at least with regard to artifacts.

Such information, however, when entered into an electronic database "designed to last for decades at least and meant to be loaded cooperatively with information over time," in the end "poses a real problem" because classifications and terminologies that might have worked at the beginning of the project might not work 5 or 10 years later. The database has become "fossilized," beginning the day it was launched (Madsen 2004:38). Previously unrecorded or even unrecognized attributes, such as paste or glaze composition or glaze thickness, may subsequently be found meaningful but will remain uncollected and perhaps unintegrated. This kind of new information challenges not only electronic databases but also printed or paper ones such as catalog sheets.

The purpose of the DAACS database is to focus on archaeological sites associated with slavery in the Americas. The Maryland archaeological database currently under construction has a different purpose: the dissemination of data from collections covering a far greater time period and including very different societies. Yet a third database, A Comparative Archaeological Study of Colonial Chesapeake Culture (www.chesapeake archaeology.org), was developed for the purpose of making data accessible from seventeenth- and eighteenth-century archaeological sites in Maryland and Virginia. A consortium of researchers representing institutions in the Maryland and Virginia region (Brown et al. 2006) assembled this database by collecting artifact catalogs that were in or could be put into an off-the-shelf Microsoft Access file. Because recataloging was not an option for this project (the kind of recataloging such as that done for DAACS was prohibitively expensive in this case), the structure of the database followed the "least common denominator," and some artifact types had to be combined into higher-order categories, further masking variability. To mitigate some of these problems, individual site databases are also available for downloading.

The larger point is that classification begins with the selection of the sites that are considered appropriate for a particular database, a selection that, in addition to imposing order, has potentially significant effects on research. For example, should collections from planters' dwellings, where enslaved people worked and not a few may have lodged, be included in DAACS? Geography drives the boundaries for the Maryland database, but devising a classification scheme for artifacts spanning 10,000 years is proving unwieldy. Nonetheless, the creation of these three electronic databases has improved access to the information found in the collections they represent, and new interpretations of the past have been generated as a result.

Collections Management versus Research

How collections are organized and made accessible often depends on who is in charge of them. Collections managers tend to organize collections in ways that facilitate long-term preservation. The ability to track objects (including records), maintain environmental controls, and monitor object conditions is paramount for responsible collections management. The way a collection is physically organized for collections management purposes, however, may not be ideal or even relevant for research purposes. Researchers are typically more interested in the relationships among the objects, and although collections managers "maintain" this information as delivered to them in a collection, associational information may remain far less accessible than an individual object or a group of objects.

Despite the issues of classification previously outlined, the digital collection, preservation, and delivery of archaeological information have the potential to shape a rethinking of archaeological collections management, not unlike what geographic information systems (GIS) have done for archaeological site management. Digital technologies are becoming important tools, for example, in the deaccessioning of archaeological materials, providing opportunities to save information about objects that have been discarded or otherwise removed from a collection. These technologies can preserve archaeological information in an electronic form that complements and even enhances paper, film, and artifact conservation records. And digital technologies promise the creation of a wished-for accessibility and use of collections. The forms digital information can take are varied;

to date, archaeologists have experimented with developing and placing online finding aids for research collections, type or reference collections, archaeological reports, and searchable artifact and context databases.

The need for information for research purposes rather than for collections management spurred Neiman's decision to recatalog collections for the DAACS project. Most projects, however, lack the resources to permit such major initiatives. Archaeologists working in southwestern Colorado took a different approach, developing analytical techniques for interrogating databases ostensibly created for management purposes (Ortman, Varien, and Gripp 2007). As a discipline, we are still some way from identifying methods for "excavating" existing collections and assembling the information in them for further research. Still, DAACS and the Colorado initiative provide two important examples for a way forward.

Electronic finding aids are documents posted on the World Wide Web that function the way paper finding aids do: providing a guide to a collection's contents but not necessarily presenting those contents. Because of the complexity and expense of developing and making electronic data both available and secure, many institutions elect to post finding aids online, informing prospective users about a collection's existence and availability. The MAC Lab staff has done this for the collections the institution is digitizing. In this case, users not only learn about available collections but also can request information about a site, including collection catalogs, which can be supplied on CD upon request. Other finding aids that refer to archaeological collections include one on the steamship *Conestoga* and the schooner *Lillie Parsons* (Smith 2007) and one describing collections available through California State Parks (2007).

In the past 10 years, the Web has become a popular space for hosting archaeological type or reference collections (Hoopes 1998; Lange 2004). Electronic ceramic type collections have been developed by California State Parks (www.parks.ca.gov/?page_id=22207), the Florida Museum of Natural History (www.flmnh.ufl.edu/histarch/gallery_types), and the Maryland Archaeological Conservation Laboratory (www.jefpat.org/diagnostic/index .htm). California State Parks has also produced bottle type collections (www.parks.ca.gov/?page_id=22207), and useful projectile point type collections have been developed by Art Gumbus (http://members.aol.com /artgumbus/lithic.html) and the Illinois State Museum (www.museum .state.il.us/ismdepts/anthro/proj_point/). The MAC Lab has recently added a "Small Finds" component to its online typologies. These type collections are especially valuable for CRM professionals, who may seek guidance on local or regional artifact types and chronologies, as well as for members of the public, who use them to identify random finds. I have found electronic type collections to be especially useful for teaching students about artifacts.

THE CHALLENGES OF CREATING ACCESS TO ARCHAEOLOGICAL REPORTS

Many of us would be happy if we could simply organize and make accessible the existing "gray literature"—unpublished or limited-distribution reports that result from archaeological investigation. Although gray literature is most often associated with CRM archaeology, museums and academic institutions produce similar kinds of reports, though perhaps not in the quantity typical of CRM. In 2005 and again in 2007, a forum and a symposium, respectively, concerning the gray literature "problem" were held at the annual meetings of the Society for American Archaeology (Childs 2005; Thomas and Darvill 2007). During the 2005 forum, which included a blue-ribbon panel, presenters described efforts to organize and disseminate gray literature going back to the 1970s and 1980s.[4] Some provided examples of gray literature dissemination at their home institutions and the challenges that emerged from those efforts. The challenges included funding; the sheer volume of materials; the forms the materials took (for example, paper, portable document file [PDF], or other electronic file); determining where responsibility lay for collecting, managing, and making the gray literature accessible, such as at the national, regional, or state level; and establishing standards and ethics for publishing (Childs n.d.). The potential for electronic dissemination of gray literature over the Web, which nearly all the panelists mentioned, raises its own challenges, from the confidentiality of sensitive information such as site locations to the long-term preservation and migration of electronic data. Recommendations included the appointment of a task force on gray literature by the Society for American Archaeology to explore issues raised in the forum in greater detail (Childs 2005).

The 2007 symposium (Thomas and Darvill 2007) took a different but critically related avenue, focusing on "current approaches to the use of results from contract projects, and [opening] a discussion on what more can be done in the future." This symposium involved practitioners from both the United States and the United Kingdom, and although terms used in the two countries differed slightly, their issues were virtually the same—with one important exception. In the United Kingdom, the Archaeology Data Service (www.ads.ahds.ac.uk/) has succeeded in making many gray literature reports and archaeological site databases available via the

Internet and therefore to audiences well beyond archaeologists in that country. US presenters concurred that with improved access to gray literature, archaeologists would be in a much better position to build detailed chronologies and reconstruct past behavior, thereby generating "meaningful research," such as that being undertaken by archaeologists with the Illinois Department of Transportation and the University of Illinois concerning the broader social and political landscape of Cahokia (Pauketat and Emerson 1997).

Perhaps one of the most widely known archaeological management information systems in the United States is the National Archaeological Database (NADB, www.nps.gov/archeology/TOOLS/nadb.htm), administered by the departmental consulting archaeologist at the National Park Service (NPS) and maintained by the Center for Advanced Spatial Technologies at the University of Arkansas. The project is ambitious in its scope and potential, its goal being "to efficiently share archeological information about publicly sponsored investigations[,] thereby helping to eliminate unnecessary redundancy among public agency efforts" (Childs and Kinsey 2004). Developed in the mid-1980s and made publicly available in 1992, NADB consists of three components or modules of information: a bibliographic inventory, NAGPRA information, and spatial information available in the form of maps. For most archaeologists, the bibliographic reports module (NADB-R) offers the greatest utility. The database includes approximately 350,000 reports, and each entry gives a report's title, author, date of completion, and project sponsor. Searchable fields include "work-type," "state," "county," "cultural affiliation," and "material."

NADB is also widely known because in many respects it has failed to live up to its promise. There are significant gaps in the database, largely because it is updated erratically. The last NADB update took place in 2004; before that, it was updated in 1998. Further, a significant number of cultural resource managers, including SHPOs, neglect to supply the National Park Service with information for the database. NPS staff found that in 2002, an astonishing 24 SHPOs reported that "their office personnel [had] never used the [NADB reports module]" and "a few individuals were not aware of its existence." The reasons for this lack of interest? The system is "cumbersome, it often crashes or times out, and no technical service is provided." The system's search apparatus, especially its instructions, appears more cumbersome than it is. In fact, NADB-R provides information on archaeological reports that may be unavailable elsewhere, provided that the material has been submitted. The greatest challenge facing the National Park Service is the lack of sufficient funding to enable its personnel, SHPOs, and personnel from other libraries of gray literature reports to submit correct entries for the database (Childs and Kinsey 2004).

Lynne Sebastian (personal communication, 2008) has observed that NADB is "a top-down system, and these [systems] are usually overwhelmingly difficult to maintain." She believes that a portal system, whereby NPS would provide Internet links to information on reports and other archaeological data maintained by states and tribes, would enable researchers to find what was available in various states or regions and to access those sources more easily. Resources for creating and maintaining such a system, she concludes, would be best expended helping states and tribes upgrade their existing databases and providing a means of linking to those sources of information.

The Society for American Archaeology has not yet created the task force on gray literature recommended by the forum organized by Terry Childs (2005), although SAA's relatively new Digital Data Interest Group (DDIG), which in 2009 included SAA president Dean Snow, is focusing on the electronic delivery of such reports. In 2007 DDIG approached the Advisory Council on Historic Preservation (ACHP) about potential requirements that would encourage or require the electronic production of gray literature in PDF format. There is some confusion, however, about the role the ACHP plays in determining CRM requirements or whether it is the ACHP's place to establish digital standards for gray literature reports—these requirements more typically come from the NPS, the states, and other entities. Nonetheless, ACHP staff agreed to include a discussion of the growing importance of digital information and its preservation and access in the agency's newly developed, Web-accessible guidance (www .achp.gov/archguide).

THE CHALLENGES OF PRODUCING ARCHAEOLOGICAL SYNTHESES

During my tenure as a member of the Advisory Council on Historic Preservation, the issue I heard about more than any other from historic preservationists who were not archaeologists concerned a lack of publicly accessible, professionally presented synthetic studies. Unfairly or not, these colleagues perceived archaeologists as focused entirely too much on the trees at the expense of the forest. These colleagues, many of whom were SHPOs or had served in a state historic preservation office, lamented the large sums of money spent on archaeology coupled with the seeming inability of archaeologists to synthesize this material into some meaningful body of engaging, jargon-free literature that truly revealed "something new." Some saw the cause of the problem as a personality issue peculiar to archaeologists; others saw it as the divide between the academy and CRM, with archaeologists trained for scarce academic jobs filling CRM positions. To these non-archaeology colleagues, the lack of synthesis was clearly an archaeological problem, and the solution had to come from archaeologists.

I agree that far less synthetic or comparative work has been done than we should expect, but a number of outstanding, publicly accessible synthetic studies have been produced that have reshaped our thinking about important social and historical issues. For example, in a study of the Five Points neighborhood in New York City, Rebecca Yamin and her colleagues at John Milner Associates challenged academic and popular notions of the concept of "slums" and revealed the richness and complexity of that neighborhood (Yamin 1997, 2000). Their work serves as a model for urban archaeology and calls into question present-day middle-class attitudes toward and policies regarding economically impoverished urban areas. Yamin wrote about Five Points in archaeological reports and also pieces developed for lay audiences, such as articles for *Archaeology* magazine. She also advised the producers of the film *The Gangs of New York*, although the filmmakers elected to perpetuate romantic stereotypes despite Yamin's findings.

For the scholarly public, a recent study was focused on the historical ecology of Pueblo peoples in the Mesa Verde archaeological region of southwestern Colorado between 600 and 1300 CE (Varien et al. 2007). The researchers used evidence from more than 3,000 habitation sites—the majority of them found in cultural resource databases maintained by government agencies—to examine community formation. They developed new population estimates for the region and documented evidence for both immigration and emigration tied to events in Pueblo history. These findings are being used to interpret change through time in the region, which, interestingly, appears not to be as strongly correlated with climate change as was previously thought, raising implications for the explanation of major demographic changes recorded in the area's archaeology. The researchers found that the "scale of the effective environment that Pueblo people responded to was much larger than our project study area" (Varien et al. 2007:293). These findings and others were based on data sets derived through CRM archaeology, and the researchers have used their experiences to develop methods for querying databases created for management rather than research purposes (Ortman, Varien, and Gripp 2007). A similar project, Coalescent Communities in the Southern Southwest, has used CRM databases to model the population collapse that occurred in the

Hohokam region of southern Arizona between 1300 and 1450 CE (Center for Desert Archaeology 2008; Hill et al. 2004).

An example of a successful synthetic study at the federal level is the product of a collaboration between the US Army Corps of Engineers and the National Park Service. When the Richard B. Russell Dam and Lake in the South Carolina and Georgia piedmont was constructed beginning in the 1970s, cultural resource managers analyzed documents, conducted archaeological investigations, and collected oral histories in an effort to document life in this part of the American Southeast beginning 11,500 years ago. Not only was an important synthetic technical report produced (Anderson and Joseph 1988), but also two "popular" volumes, prepared for a public audience, were published (Kane and Keeton 1993, 1994). In 2000 the popular publications were adapted for posting on the World Wide Web (www.nps.gov/history/seac/beneathweb.htm). Notably, the authors of the popular publications, Sharyn Kane and Richard Keeton, are not archaeologists, but professional writers.

Many synthetic studies have been produced using the resources or involvement of state historic preservation offices. Beginning in the late 1980s, the Virginia Department of Historic Resources (the historic preservation office in that state), along with the Council of Virginia Archaeologists and the Archaeological Society of Virginia, initiated a series of conferences out of which came seven important volumes focused on time periods, from Paleoindian times to the nineteenth century (Reinhart 1996; Reinhart and Hodges 1990, 1991, 1992; Reinhart and Pogue 1993; Sprinkle and Reinhart 1999; Wittkofski and Reinhart 1989). Together, these volumes, which were widely disseminated, serve as a starting point for any archaeology undertaken in the Commonwealth. Similarly, the Colorado Council of Professional Archaeologists has produced a series of synthetic studies, with support from the Colorado Historical Society, which includes the SHPO's office (see Church et al. 2007; Gilmore et al. 2004; Lipe, Varien, and Wilshusen 1999; Martorano et al. 1999; Reed and Metcalf 1999; Zier and Kalasz 1999). For Maryland, a preliminary synthesis of what is known about colonial Chesapeake culture can be found at www.chesapeakearchaeology.org (Brown et al. 2006), and the SHPO has recently dedicated a contractual position to synthesizing archaeological information found in the SHPO's files (J. Rodney Little, personal communication, 2008).

Academic archaeologists have been involved in many of the projects to generate syntheses. Anne-Marie Cantwell and Diana diZerega Wall (2001) assembled CRM information to produce *Unearthing Gotham: The Archaeology of New York City*, which won the New York Society Library's 2002 Book

Award for History and praise from *New Yorker* critic Adam Gopnik. University of Delaware archaeologist Lu Ann De Cunzo (2004) used Delaware SHPO files and gray literature reports to explore what she calls "the cultures of agriculture" and to develop a program for current and future research; the results of De Cunzo's research were published by the University of Tennessee Press. University of California–Berkeley archaeologist Kent G. Lightfoot (2004) synthesized not just archaeological data, much of it generated through CRM, but also oral and documentary history—historical anthropology, really—in order to examine the nature of contact in his part of California and to explain the relationships and political standing of present-day tribes in the region. Lightfoot's well-written book received the Society for Historical Archaeology's James Deetz Award in 2007. Most recently, in 2008, Mark Leone was awarded the James Deetz Award for his engaging synthesis of more than 20 years of archaeology in Annapolis, Maryland (Leone 2005). Leone used the material culture of free and enslaved people to explore relations of power and hierarchy at a time when "freedom" and "liberty" were becoming part of a unique American discourse.

Clearly, usable syntheses have been produced and distributed. These documents appear in technical reports, professional journals, university press publications, regional press publications, and popular archaeology magazines. A growing number, like the products of the Russell Dam and Lake project, are available on the Internet. The Colorado synthesis of historical archaeology (Church et al. 2007) includes a CD, with the document available as a searchable PDF. Some syntheses, such as the books by Cantwell and Wall, Lightfoot, and Leone, are award-winning. And surely, at local and smaller regional levels, synthetic studies have been developed that have been of great interest and value to the relevant communities.

For many other "study areas," however, whether geographical, temporal, or cultural, syntheses have not been generated—or if they have, they have sat on shelves, ignored or otherwise unused. Take the case of Maryland. Although the state of Maryland has shown leadership in the area of collections management, to date no synthetic study has appeared from the state historic preservation office for any part of Maryland's rich and diverse cultural history. How, then, do we get from here to there?

Perhaps the problem should be approached by asking first, as past SAA president Kenneth Ames did (personal communication, 2006), What is synthesis? In an essay on analysis and synthesis, Thomas Ritchey (1991:21) noted that "in general, *analysis* is defined as the procedure by which we break down an intellectual or substantial whole into parts or components.

Synthesis is defined as the opposite procedure: to combine separate elements or components in order to form a coherent whole." Ritchey went on to argue that analysis and synthesis are inextricably intertwined; synthesis is built upon analysis, and analysis requires synthesis to verify its results (1991:21–22). Analysis and synthesis are scientific methods that, used properly, may reveal the world as it is (or, in the case of the past, as it was). With respect to archaeology, the Archaeology Wordsmith, a Web site designed to assist archaeologists with editing and fact-checking (www.archaeologyword smith.com), defines synthesis as a technique involving "the assemblage and analysis of data before interpretation." Synthesis is "also an attempt to pull together a broad range of knowledge about a particular topic or geographical area into a comprehensive document or statement" (Kipfer 2007).

In practice, there are at least three kinds of "synthesis," depending on one's purpose and audience. There are, Bill Lipe observes (personal communication, 2008), "scholarly syntheses designed for other scholars; 'historical contexts' designed to help CRM practitioners make judgments about the significance of historic properties; and popular syntheses directed at the archaeologically literate public." In Maryland, Leone's (2005) book *The Archaeology of Liberty in an American Capital* was published by a university press, and its audience is predominantly a scholarly one. His findings are unlikely to have much effect on the Maryland historic preservation office's ability to more efficiently and productively drive the review and compliance process in the state's capital. And popular syntheses, often presented as booklets, museum exhibits, or guided tours, are typically too general to inform either scholarly or management audiences.

Finally, no matter for whom syntheses are written, they are not and could never be neutral, if simply because the writing of any narrative involves a point of view. For example, in a study of the eighteenth-century backcountry of South Carolina and Georgia, Robert Paulett (2007) found that in virtually everything he read about that period in American history, including archaeological studies, the narrative always took the form of a "frontier story—of one society giving way to the next"—that ended when the "subject [typically the indigenous society] ceases to exist." Paulett credited the long arm of Frederick Jackson Turner with this state of affairs and described his surprising struggle to write beyond or out of this narrative form. Richard Slotkin (1985) recognized the power of the Turnerian thesis to influence not only narratives of American history but also American understandings of culture conflict, such as the Vietnam war, which was often framed using the metaphor of "cowboys and Indians." The power of Turner's thesis is made even clearer by its absence in Joseph Nicolar's

(2007) recently republished account of the Penobscot Indians, *The Life and Traditions of the Red Man*. Nicolar, a Penobscot, first told this story of his people in the late nineteenth century. It unfolds in a way radically different from that of most histories of what is now the state of Maine and is wholly devoid of Turnerian influence. The power of preexisting narratives to shape future understandings is also revealed by Becky Yamin's lack of success, noted earlier, in influencing the making of Martin Scorsese's *The Gangs of New York*.

These observations are not to say that archaeological syntheses are doomed, but simply that although syntheses may promise totality, in reality they are always partial and never complete, often with social and political implications. We already know this: Virginia's series of synthetic studies, for example, are approaching their second decade of existence, and new work exists that will surely test the original findings. But also synthesis is always partial from the point of its creation because, in pulling together "a broad range of knowledge" and incorporating it into a narrative—no matter how turgid and technical that narrative may be—certain elements are included and others excluded through the mechanism of plot. This "plotting" makes meaningful certain behaviors and events and not others of a past we cannot experience or perhaps even fully know; also, a plot always unfolds from a specific point of view (Joyce 2002). Indeed, some archaeologists have argued that a focus on narrative and its mechanisms of plot and point of view can be useful for identifying or exploring avenues of inquiry otherwise missed through technical writing (Gibb 2000; Little 2000).

The creation of usable syntheses, then, requires consideration of several factors, including authors, audiences, and the elements found in any narrative: point of view, structures that create cause-and-effect relationships, and structures that determine which information is meaningful and therefore included in the story (or plot) and which information is excluded. These are factors that, like the effort to create access to archaeological information, deserve discussion at a broad, disciplinary level. At present, the discussion is simply about a "need for synthesis," when it may be more productive to deepen the conversation by discussing forms of synthesis and the sociological and political factors underpinning their creation and use in the profession. For example, Childs's observation (2006) that collections-based research does not enjoy the same standing in the discipline as field research may have relevance, because synthetic studies often involve the use of existing collections. Recent scholarship in library and information science (see Cary 1999) suggests that this difference may be grounded in engendered notions of what constitutes "real archaeology."

Can other trends or practices be identified that might affect the production of synthetic studies, as well as the *kinds* of studies produced? Only by understanding the precise obstacles to synthetic work, some of which are no doubt embedded in the social constitution of archaeological practice, can efforts be made to overcome or remove them.

MOVING TOWARD SOLUTIONS

Although a tendency exists among archaeologists to declare that archaeological collections and other sources and forms of archaeological data are inaccessible, as well as a tendency to declare that syntheses of archaeological information are rare, there are many examples of efforts to disseminate archaeological information and interpretation. Nonetheless, much more remains to be done. Although I am unaware of any study in which someone has attempted to estimate the funds annually expended on archaeology in the United States, most of us would agree that the figures are in the millions—likely the hundreds of millions.[5] For that kind of public investment, should we not have more, and better, products for ourselves and for our multiple publics? Should we not be using these products to improve the way we do business? Of course we should, but how do we get there from here?

These questions are not new—they have been around for decades—and perhaps it would be unreasonable or even dangerous to wish them away. We should always be discussing them. The solutions to the challenges will require the attention not just of CRM consultants but also of archaeologists in all kinds of positions, including the academy, parks, museums, and federal and state land-managing or land-permitting agencies. The professional societies may have the greatest role to play, providing leadership to host the conversation and the forum that brings archaeologists from diverse careers together to approach the challenges in like fashion. In this final section, I look at directions in funding, leadership of the professional associations, digital technologies, and graduate training.

A repeatedly acknowledged challenge is funding. Indeed, few problems of data access and dissemination could not be solved if sufficient public funds were available. For example, Harrison Eiteljorg (2007) blamed a shortage of money for the lack of a digital archiving system, and at least some state historic preservation offices blame a lack of funds for their decisions to opt out of the National Archeological Database. Public funds are limited and are likely to be increasingly so in the near future. If additional monies are to be had, chances are that they will come from a reallocation of existing funds and not from new funds. This is not to say that new public money is unlikely; however, increased public (or governmental) funding depends on the public's willingness to pay for the "public good" of cultural resources (see Navrud and Ready 2002). The taxpaying public has demonstrated that it is indeed willing to support the preservation and management of cultural resources, ranging from the tax benefits of nonprofit status to outright government ownership and management. But the same public does have its limits, and archaeologists have both a responsibility and an obligation to use funds wisely within those limits.[6] Part of the wise use of funds includes both knowing the public's limits and educating the public about the past as learned through archaeology. Not only does this provide a return on the current public investment in archaeology, but it also builds support for future investment, given that a society's willingness to pay can change for the better or for the worse. This support is precisely what Susan Chandler (chapter 6, this volume) argues can be achieved through creative, or wiser, forms of mitigation.

"Creative mitigation" is a hot topic in CRM these days. Everyone recognizes that the system as currently constituted—survey, identify, evaluate, avoid or excavate—has become rote, even as it leads us to unsatisfactory situations such as inaccessible data and reports. Neither Section 106 of the National Historic Preservation Act nor its implementing regulations require this plan of action, but it is a plan that has been followed for so long that it has become very hard to stop. Indeed, Matt Seddon (personal communication 2007), a strong proponent of thinking creatively about the mitigation of adverse effects on historic properties that are archaeological in nature, has pointed out that one manager's "creative mitigation" is another's "unethical practice." Clearly, creative mitigation involves risks, and to sell it simply as a way to save money would be short-sighted. Developing mitigation programs that pay attention to what a community values, as well as what archaeologists value, will involve some work, but it can improve the dissemination of archaeological information and interpretations.

In the meantime, any "new" money specifically to support dissemination will most likely derive from a reallocation of existing money, thereby increasing competition for already scarce funds among cultural resource professionals. If archaeologist Terry Childs (2006) is correct that there is "an attitude in archaeology that fieldwork is much more important than collections care," then funding priority may be assigned to the excavation of sites threatened with destruction. Better to direct maximum funds toward the recovery of data that will be irretrievably lost through land-use change and development, the thinking currently goes, than toward the dissemination of archaeological information that will, theoretically, always be around and therefore available for study and interpretation. The premise upon which this thinking is built is faulty, and shockingly so: nationwide, collections, including artifacts, records, gray literature, and digital files, have been lost or are at considerable risk of loss because of the conditions in which they are held.

Collections awareness is growing, in large part because of the work of Childs, her colleagues, and the professional societies. Having been on the front lines of archaeological collections management from 1996 until 2006, I have seen firsthand the beneficial results of the effort to educate ourselves and our colleagues about the "curation crisis." Yet, the issue at hand in this chapter—dissemination—is a collections issue that has not received the attention it critically deserves. Improved dissemination—from field records and gray literature to the completion and distribution of synthetic studies—requires a reconceptualization of what constitutes the archaeological process, a change that is not only urgently needed but also overdue. The dissemination of archaeological information and interpretations must be valued as much as fieldwork. The end product of any project may still be a gray literature report, but we need more creative and funded avenues for improving access through dissemination.

Some projects require dissemination as part of an educational component; many states, for example, require data recovery projects to turn over collections to public repositories and to include public outreach. In many cases, the outreach has been very successful. This approach does not necessarily require that archaeologists develop expertise in public outreach, although such expertise can only help, not hinder. Museum and other professional educators have expertise with direct outreach, and writers might be hired to produce public products, as was done by the Army Corps of Engineers and NPS for the Russell Dam and Lake project. Nonetheless, as professional archaeologists, we can work to ensure that the results of our projects are available to our colleagues so that new findings on which publicly engaging materials can draw are always being generated. David Crass's observations (chapter 11, this volume) about improving communication with the public and about the growing interest in "public archaeology" reinforce the value of the public as an important audience.

Crass echoes Childs's recommendation (2005) that a task force on gray literature is urgently needed. Whereas Childs suggested that the SAA form such a task force, Crass argues, reasonably and responsibly, that the task force must be larger than the SAA and should include the Society for Historical Archaeology (SHA) and the American Cultural Resources Association (ACRA). Perhaps the National Council of State Historic

Preservation Officers (NCSHPO) and the National Association of Tribal Historic Preservation Officers (NATHPO), the NPS, and the ACHP should be invited to participate in the creation of such a task force. To be sure, there is a risk in creating too large a task force, but in this case I suspect that all proposed organizations are ready and would agree that a problem exists with the dissemination of gray literature as it stands now.

Perhaps some of the best tools at our disposal for disseminating archaeological information are digital technologies. I have cited a number of examples that show not just the promise of these technologies but also some impressive deliverables. Along with the promise, however, come the pitfalls. Now brewing in the field, I suggest, is a "digital crisis" as increasing amounts of archaeological information, from records to images and databases, are created in digital format. This is not a crisis that archaeologists alone face, but in comparison with researchers in other fields and disciplines, at least in the United States, archaeologists have only begun to confront it in any meaningful way. Digital information housed in discontinued formats, for example, is in immediate danger of being lost, as is digital information that has been "abandoned" through its creator's job change or death. Even information housed in up-to-date formats on up-to-date equipment is at risk: discs corrupt and servers crash. Despite all the sophisticated digital technology that exists—and which many of us use—the lack of a discipline-wide conversation about a digital archaeology is perhaps at this time our greatest collections threat. Further, it is not just the creation and preservation of digital data that is of concern (although at this point it is understandable why this should be paramount). Also of concern are the data's accessibility, the expense of digital technologies, and the lack of skills on the part of many archaeologists to put these technologies to maximum use.

Yet, digital technologies will provide an important and perhaps even primary avenue for creating access to archaeological information (Kintigh 2006). Online searchable databases, downloadable data files, reports in digital format, virtual exhibits, and syntheses published on the World Wide Web are key to updating and perhaps even changing current ways of thinking about the archaeological past and disseminating notice of those findings. Web-published products are typically less expensive than paper publications and are much easier to update. The "digital crisis" is going to be the "digital answer" as we rethink the way archaeology is practiced in the United States.

A number of efforts have been initiated to improve the use of digital technologies in archaeology, predominantly through the creation of an archive of some type. The assumption is that archaeologists, from CRM to the academy, are already using digital technologies in their work. It is a fair assumption—image capture, report production, databases, and Web pages are a few of the ways in which archaeological practice has been affected by digital technologies (see Evans 2005; Lock 2003). What most archaeologists conclude is needed is a permanent repository (or repositories) for long-term preservation of and access to this material (Snow et al. 2006). Such a repository could ensure that digital information is maintained, appropriately backed up, and, as necessary, migrated to new platforms over time.

This observation is not new. In the late 1980s, Eiteljorg undertook an early effort to develop such an archive when he created the Archaeological Data Archive Project (ADAP) through the Center for the Study of Architecture (CSA), based in Bryn Mawr, Pennsylvania. The CSA's goals involved "advancing the use of computers, computer technologies, and digital information technologies in the service of architectural history, archaeology, and related disciplines that explore our common heritage" (Eiteljorg 2007). Eiteljorg (2005) attributed the demise of ADAP to one fundamental problem, a lack of funding. He argued that the problem of funding has not gone away and constitutes the greatest challenge to creating an archive.

In 2001 the Alexandria Archive Institute, which is based in California (www.alexandriaarchive.org/index.php), was created as a private, nonprofit organization with the mission of preserving and sharing archaeological and other cultural heritage information. The institute emphasizes the use of ArchaeoML for searching a variety of databases, relating the information, and integrating the findings. At this writing, the institute, which is also developing Open Context as its vehicle for delivering digital information, has mounted a beta version of several searchable data sets. The institute's (and Open Context's) goals are to develop a community of users and to create dialogue about various data sets in an effort to interpret or reinterpret the past.

In 2004 the School for Advanced Research (then the School of American Research) and the University of Virginia received support from the Andrew W. Mellon Foundation to explore the need for a digital archaeology in the United States. In a series of short seminars and other meetings, project directors Richard M. Leventhal and Stephen E. Plog convened a group of archaeologists to articulate the problems, challenges, and promises of a digital archaeology (Plog et al. 2007). Researchers, presidents of the major professional societies, and CRM professionals participated in the meetings, concluding that what was urgently needed in the United States was a "Center for Digital Archaeology." A similar center—the Archaeology Data

Service (http://ads.ahds.ac.uk/)—has been impressively successful in the United Kingdom, focusing on preserving and making accessible an extraordinary array of digital resources for research, learning, and teaching.

Subsequently, a consortium of archaeologists led by Keith Kintigh organized Archaeoinformatics.org, an independent group established "to design, seek funding for, and direct a set of cyberinfrastructure initiatives for archaeology. Archaeoinformatics.org seeks to coordinate..., and develop interoperability of its own projects, with other relevant data-sharing initiatives. It offers to work with professional organizations and federal agencies to promote policies that will foster the development of cyberinfrastructure for archaeology" (www.archaeoinformatics.org/index .html, Mar. 30, 2008). The organization is developing a workable, viable plan following a year-long review of digital initiatives within and outside the field of archaeology.

The major archaeological professional societies, including the SAA, the SHA, and the Archaeological Institute of America (AIA), have various groups or committees that focus on digital issues. Perhaps the most ambitious group is the SAA's newly formed Digital Data Interest Group (DDIG). DDIG's primary purpose is to promote the use of digital technologies among society members, primarily through symposia, forums, and other means of exchange. The SAA's Committee on Museums, Collections, and Curation, charged with promoting "awareness, concern, and support for archaeological collections, associated records and reports" (SAA 2009) and their long-term curation, conceivably includes the preservation of collections in digital formats, a direction in which the committee is now attempting to move.

The SHA currently lacks a committee or an interest group focused on digital issues, but like the SAA, it has a Curation, Conservation, and Collections Management Committee. The SHA is also experimenting with publishing materials on the Web. The AIA, in cooperation with the American Philological Association, established a Joint Task Force on Electronic Publication, which produced a policy statement on electronic publications and scholarly work in digital formats (Archaeological Institute of America 2006) and a final report on electronic publication (American Philological Association 2007). The policy statement encourages the two societies' members, as well as related professionals, to recognize the opportunities the digital dissemination of archaeological information presents for better understanding of the past and to approach peer-reviewed digital publications with the same respect accorded peer-reviewed print publications.

With respect to the use of these kinds of technologies in archaeology, the discipline is in a critical period. The growing interest in and use of digital formats by nearly all archaeologists demands some immediate decision-making to ensure the long-term preservation of and access to digital information. Preservation and access, though related, are different practices with different goals, and decisions made today will likely affect users tomorrow. Given the wide use of digital technologies, it is imperative that these discussions include all archaeologists. Further, social and cultural factors such as ethnicity, gender, and geographical location will, in subtle and not-so-subtle ways, shape the form of a digital archaeology, as they have other disciplines (Cameron and Kenderdine 2007; Spender 1995; Stewart Millar 1998; Travers 1999). The professional societies, through their publications, meetings, and other opportunities for engagement, provide an ideal environment for our discussions. Care must be taken, however, to ensure that these discussions cast a wide net, that all issues are included, and that all archaeologists are represented. The professional societies have an opportunity to avoid what Sebastian (personal communication, 2008) has described as the "top-down" approach of the National Park Service's National Archeological Database, but only through aggressive consultation with their members.

The model of the SAA's Committee on Museums, Collections, and Curation provides a way forward, and it reveals the power of the professional societies to shape archaeological thinking perhaps more than any other force. When this committee was initially handed its charge, curation was considered at a crisis stage in the profession. This committee, along with the SHA's Curation, Conservation, and Collections Management Committee, has succeeded in changing thinking about archaeological curation in the United States, by raising awareness and by providing archaeologists with the information they need in order to move in more responsible directions. The "curation crisis" is far from over, but a significant improvement has been achieved.

The members of all the professional societies, including the SAA, SHA, AIA, ACRA, and Register of Professional Archaeologists, are hindered by the lack of access to and impoverished dissemination of archaeological information. The professional societies, however, have the infrastructure to reach their diverse memberships in a way that other organizations or structures cannot, collaborating on problems and solutions. Together, the professional organizations can also address purposely restricted access to collections, an emerging issue that has not yet been thoroughly considered in the field.

Finally, graduate training has an important role to play in the development of a broad disciplinary ethic concerning the dissemination of archaeological information, the development of skills for moving toward a digital archaeology, and responsibility to the public. Since the mid-1990s, graduate training that includes CRM as integral to the curriculum and a growing interest in what is increasingly called "public archaeology" has provided opportunities to teach the responsibilities archaeologists have to the archaeological record, to their colleagues, and to the public, along with the skills needed to carry out those responsibilities. Still, anecdotal evidence, as well as my own experience as director of the Maryland collections repository until 2006, suggests that even as we have struggled to make the information contained in archaeological collections available, those collections have remained underused.

Will increasingly accessible archaeological data and more syntheses lead to greater cross-disciplinary collaboration? Will the historians of early Virginia think twice about whom they invite to their next conference as a result? What does appear to be happening in the region is a small renaissance in archaeology-based Chesapeake studies, due in no small part to the remarkable access to information provided by the Web site www.chesa peakearchaeology.org (Brown et al. 2006). Archaeological information that has been available in repositories, some for at least 20 years, is now being put to far greater comparative use than ever before. Archaeologists are in charge of these projects, but surely the new findings that are emerging will inform historical scholarship as well.

Acknowledgments

I would like to thank Lynne Sebastian for inviting me to participate in the seminar that led to the development of this chapter. I thank the other seminar participants, including Bill Lipe, for their suggested citations, comments, criticisms, and insights, which greatly improved the first draft. I am also grateful to the many people who responded to my requests for information about the issues explored here, including Ken Ames, Jeff Boyer, Geoff Carver, Henry Cary, Terry Childs, Melissa Diamanti, John M. Joseph, Tom King, Benjamin Nance, Marty Perry, Bob Skiles, and Michael Stewart. Laura Dean, Bill Lees, Barbara Little, J. Rodney Little, and Tom McCulloch generously shared their ideas about and experiences with archaeology undertaken through Section 106 of the National Historic Preservation Act. Dean Snow, president of the Society for American Archaeology, and Lu Ann De Cunzo, then president-elect of the Society for Historical Archaeology, commented on an earlier draft of the chapter. I thank them both for their insights.

The sections in this chapter describing the Maryland Archaeological Conservation Laboratory come from my service as director of that facility from 1996 until 2006. Finally, although I am a member of the Advisory Council on Historic Preservation, the ideas and opinions presented here are solely mine and do not reflect those of the ACHP or any other entity.

Notes

1. Since 2004 several publications have drawn on the archaeological research undertaken in the region (Blanton and King 2004; Graham et al. 2007; Rountree and Turner 2002). Bill Kelso's recently published book on Jamestown (2006) is focused primarily on the archaeology done at Jamestown Island in the past ten years.

2. Long-term preservation and accessibility are critical factors in responsible archaeological collections management, although the goals of each effort may conflict (for example, allowing physical access to collections increases the risk of loss or damage). Acknowledging that discussion of the two must go hand in hand, I nonetheless emphasize accessibility. Long-term collections preservation has been the subject of considerable discussion, and I refer readers to Childs 1995, 2006, and Sullivan and Childs 2003.

3. The Maryland Archaeological Conservation Laboratory is housed within the Maryland Historical Trust, Maryland's state historic preservation office (www.mary landhistoricaltrust.net).

4. Panelists were Jeff Altschul, Andrew Bielakowski, Mary Carroll, Terry Childs (also the organizer), Don Fowler, Eugene Futato, Carol Griffith, Tim Gross, John Hoopes, Fred Limp, and Anne Vawser.

5. These sums are high, but as Marley R. Brown noted at a forum on CRM and archaeology held in 2005 at the annual meeting of the Society for Historical Archaeology in York, England, the cost of producing a new F-22 Raptor amounted to $133 million, a sum that did not include research and development.

6. Precisely what those limits are is unknown, but surely they vary according to a number of factors. This is where the work of cultural economists might be useful to this discussion (see De la Torre 2002; Navrud and Ready 2002; Towse 2003).

8

Improving the Quality of Archaeology in the United States through Consultation and Collaboration with Native Americans and Descendant Communities

T. J. Ferguson

We can improve the quality of archaeology in the United States by developing more effective consultation with the descendants of the past peoples we study and by building upon that consultation to create collaborative research projects. Collaborative research projects enable us to expand the questions we ask, the types of data we analyze, and our ability to interpret the archaeological record—and these are all good for archaeology. The managerial framework necessary to accomplish this is already present in the historic preservation legislation summarized by Sebastian in chapter 1. What we need to do is to make the most of existing opportunities for working with descendant groups and develop long-term working relationships in which we share decisions about how to manage and research archaeological sites. This will enable us to increase the benefits of archaeology for all interested parties, including scientists, descendant groups, and the public.

Consultation in cultural resource management has a dual meaning. First, government-to-government consultation with Indian tribes and other native communities is mandated by historic preservation legislation as part of decision-making by federal agencies. Second, scholarly consultation with indigenous peoples and descendant groups is an essential element of the codes of ethics espoused by our professional organizations. Contemporary codes of ethics, discussed by Bridges in chapter 10, call for all archaeologists to consult the descendants of the past peoples we study about the design, implementation, and publication of research. Beyond consultation, some scholars argue that collaborative projects involving members of descendant communities as active research participants improve archaeology by expanding the intellectual foundation of the discipline. This collaboration provides an extended form of peer review that produces results relevant to a broad public audience.

Identifying descendant communities entails more than simply determining the biological progeny of the people who lived in the sites we study (Borgstede 2002; Singleton and Orser 2003). The historical, cultural, and symbolic associations of descendant communities with sites they consider ancestral must be taken into account, in addition to the biological heritage of individual people. Descendant communities can be local, residing in proximity to ancestral sites, or they may have migrated hundreds or even thousands of kilometers away from the ancient homes of their ancestors. The definition of specific descendant communities is contingent on the interpretation of social and historical contexts, as well as on the self-identification of social groups, and these subjects are sometimes contested. Deciding which social groups form communities that are related in one fashion or another to the past groups we study has political and intellectual consequences that warrant careful consideration.

In much of this chapter, I focus on federally recognized American Indian tribes, but these are not the only descendant communities CRM archaeologists need to pay attention to. There are also state-recognized and unrecognized Indian tribes and other descendant communities, including African American, Hispanic, and Euro-American groups (Cuddy and Leone 2008; McDavid 2002; Medford 2006; Perry, Howson, and Bianco 2006; Shackel and Gadsby 2008). I argue that the specific and limited consultation required by law should be a springboard for sustained scholarly consultation and collaboration that improve the archaeological research conducted for CRM projects.

INCREASING PARTICIPATION OF DESCENDANT GROUPS IN HISTORIC PRESERVATION

In the twentieth century, federal historic preservation in the United States was codified in a series of laws that sought to protect archaeological sites or to recover information from them when they are damaged during the course of development. Historic properties are generally viewed as archaeological or scientific resources belonging to the nation as a whole rather than as heritage resources associated with particular Native American communities. The body of historic preservation legislation, including the Antiquities Act of 1906, the Historic Sites Act of 1935, the National Historic Preservation Act of 1966, the National Environmental Policy Act of 1969, the Archaeological Data Preservation Act of 1974, and the Archaeological Resources Protection Act of 1979, was initially passed with little provision for including Native Americans in the national historic preservation program. Decisions about historic properties were made by agency archaeologists and other experts acting as stewards of the archaeological record, with little input from tribes and other descendant groups. Although several tribes, most notably the Navajo Nation and the Pueblo of Zuni, developed tribal cultural resource management programs in the 1970s and 1980s, decisions about management of historic properties, even those on Indian reservations, were still the domain of the Bureau of Indian Affairs and state historic preservation officers (SHPOs).

Archaeology and cultural resources management in the United States do not exist in a political and social vacuum. Throughout the second half of the twentieth century, Native Americans increasingly asserted the tribal sovereignty recognized by the United States (Wilkins and Lomawaima 2001). This situation eventually led to fundamental changes in the legislative basis and regulatory practices of historic preservation. Today tribes are encouraged to become full partners in historic preservation, and consultation with tribes is explicitly mandated in federal legislation and regulations.

Federal consultation with tribes, in historic preservation as in all other governmental dealings, is a government-to-government activity. This mandate is articulated in Executive Order 13175, issued by President William J. Clinton in 2000, which recognizes that the United States has a unique legal relationship with Indian tribes and acknowledges the right of Indian tribes to self-government and self-determination. In Executive Order 13336, as well as in an executive memorandum issued in 2004, President George W. Bush reaffirmed the federal policy of recognizing the tribal sovereignty established by the Constitution of the United States, treaties, and federal statutes. The federal recognition of tribal sovereignty requiring government-to-government consultation is perceived by tribes to be a fundamental aspect of historic preservation compliance (Versaggi 2006; Welch 2000). Some state agencies, such as the Washington State Department of Transportation (2003), have instituted policies of government-to-government consultation that parallel those of the federal government.

THE NATIVE AMERICAN GRAVES PROTECTION AND REPATRIATION ACT

The Native American Graves Protection and Repatriation Act (NAG-PRA) indelibly changed the way archaeology was practiced in the United States by establishing who owns and controls human remains, funerary objects, sacred objects, and objects of cultural patrimony. NAGPRA requires that museums receiving federal funding prepare inventories of their holdings of human remains and associated funerary objects and summaries of the sacred objects, objects of cultural patrimony, and unassociated funerary objects in their collections. In doing this, museums and federal agencies are required to consult with the appropriate tribes, and this has opened new channels of communication. The repatriation and reburial of a significant number of human remains and funerary objects under NAGPRA represent a potential loss of new scientific data because these items are no longer available for study. However, many of these human remains and funerary objects had sat on museum shelves for decades without study (Rose, Green, and Green 1996), and the documentation of these items created during the preparation of inventories and summaries has provided a substantial body of new information for scholarly use. Some museum curators report that the amount of new information created during documentation, much of it provided by tribal members during consultation, significantly offsets the loss of museum collections (Killion and Molloy 2000). Museums now have more knowledge about the artifacts in their collections than they had previously. Museum implementation of NAGPRA continues as new claims are filed and decisions are made to repatriate human remains and various objects. It is somewhat distressing, however, that whereas virtually all museums in the country are now in compliance with NAGPRA, federal agencies have lagged behind. Many federal agencies have yet to complete the inventories and summaries that were due a decade ago, and these agencies continue to have a mandate for consulting tribes about cultural affiliation as this work proceeds.

As important as NAGPRA is in museums, the real shift in the practice of archaeology comes from the provisions of the law that manage human remains and funerary objects discovered on federal or tribal land after 1990. The ownership of and control over much of these materials are vested with tribes, and this has fundamentally changed the power relationship between Native Americans and archaeologists. NAGPRA agreements with tribes are now needed to govern the way certain aspects of archaeological excavations are conducted on federal and tribal land and to ensure the appropriate disposition of NAGPRA items. Given that federal and tribal land encompasses about one-third of the United States and that most of the archaeological excavations conducted in the United States are now done for CRM projects, the implementation of NAGPRA has substantially affected the way CRM is practiced, especially in the western states. Federal and state agencies now regularly consult with tribal representatives to determine how excavations will be conducted in order to comply with NAGPRA and the National Historic Preservation Act (NHPA), which types of analyses can be conducted on human remains and funerary objects, and the timing and manner of disposition. These decisions structure the research contracts issued to CRM archaeologists.

The negotiations leading to NAGPRA agreements often result in some constraints being placed on archaeological research, most notably proscriptions against destructive analyses of human remains and limitations on the types of allowable documentation. For instance, some NAGPRA agreements prohibit documentation of human remains or funerary objects using photography. Nonetheless, basic documentation of human remains and funerary objects for the purpose of determining cultural affiliation is a fundamental part of most NAGPRA agreements, and this provides valuable information for use in archaeological research. Whether one views the NAGPRA-structured research glass as half empty or half full depends on one's philosophical and political commitment to an equitable and democratic archaeology in which decisions are reached in consultation with descendants and stakeholders. And the fact is that regardless of our personal thoughts about NAGPRA, it is the law of the land, so we have a legal and ethical responsibility to work within its strictures.

Two difficult and unresolved issues involving NAGPRA concern the human remains and associated funerary objects in museum collections whose cultural affiliation cannot be determined and the unclaimed human remains intentionally excavated or inadvertently discovered on federal land after 1990. The extent of this issue is evident in the fact that in July 2009 the National NAGPRA Program reported that 123,483 culturally unidentifiable human remains and 926,670 associated funerary objects were held by 692 museums and federal agencies (National Park Service 2009). Most archaeologists want to retain these remains and funerary objects in museum collections, where they are available for research; most Native Americans would like to see them reburied. The sections of NAGPRA regulations needed to address these issues are still reserved, and 19 years after the passage of the law, these issues have yet to be resolved. Draft regulations on the disposition of culturally unidentifiable human remains in museums were published for public comment in 2007, and the National Park Service

(NPS) received hundreds of comments from individuals, tribes, museums, and scientific organizations. At the time of this writing, it is not known how the NPS will respond to these comments or how long it will be before final regulations are promulgated. Regulations regarding unclaimed remains recovered after 1990 have yet to be drafted.

A related issue concerns how we deal with Paleoindian and Archaic human remains, whose great antiquity means that archaeologists cannot easily ascertain their cultural affiliation with living tribes. Here we have two models. One is the contentious and litigious approach taken in the notorious Kennewick Man case, which has stymied research and engendered substantial hard feelings among scientists and Native Americans (Burke et al. 2008; Watkins 2005). The other model is the more conciliatory approach taken by James Dixon, Timothy Heaton, and their colleagues at On Your Knees Cave in southeastern Alaska, where 10,300-year-old human remains were discovered (Kemp et al. 2007; Sealaska Heritage Institute 2005). There, after Forest Service archaeologist Terry Fifield consulted local Tlingit groups, the Tlingit passed resolutions allowing the excavation to resume and the remains to be studied. The subsequent analysis of these remains and associated archaeological deposits has substantially advanced our knowledge, demonstrating that scientists and Native Americans can work together toward mutual and productive goals of learning more about the past before human remains are reburied. In my opinion, the Alaska model demonstrates that research designed in consultation with Native Americans can yield productive results and build positive alliances between archaeologists and indigenous groups.

The need for tribes to provide consultative input relating to NAGPRA issues on CRM excavations has led many tribal representatives to educate themselves about archaeological method and theory in order to evaluate proposed research. The values of knowledge production need to be balanced with the spiritual danger and cultural harm associated with handling human remains and funerary objects, and this balancing is best accomplished when tribal representatives understand archaeological research. Archaeologists therefore need to articulate in consultation what they hope to learn through scientific studies and the methods needed to attain research goals. Much of the knowledge tribal members gain about archaeology during NAGPRA consultations is transferred and applied in consultation relating to other legislation, most notably consultation associated with the NHPA.

NAGPRA has had unintended positive consequences in that its

requirements for consultation have brought Native Americans and archaeologists into regular and sustained communication, making it possible to form new partnerships and undertake collaborative projects (Goodby 2006; Hughes and Henry 2006). Many archaeologists engaged in the resolution of burial and NAGPRA issues find that it is possible to balance preservation, archaeology, and Native American concerns in a way that benefits all concerned parties (Killion 2008; Simon 2006). Working with NAGPRA is not easy, but it is rewarding when the goals of science are advanced in a manner acceptable to descendants of the people we study.

THE NATIONAL HISTORIC PRESERVATION ACT

The amendment of the National Historic Preservation Act in 1992 includes three key provisions that increase the participation of Native Americans in historic preservation: authorizing tribal historic preservation officers (THPOs) to replace SHPOs in preservation activities on tribal land, increasing the mandate for consultation during Section 106 compliance, and recognizing traditional cultural properties as historic properties potentially eligible for the National Register of Historic Places.

To date, 77 tribes in 23 states have opted to establish THPOs. This represents approximately 14 percent of all the federally recognized tribes in the United States. For these tribes, the replacement of a state official by a tribal official in historic preservation compliance is an important means of maintaining tribal sovereignty (Welch 2000). Having a THPO allows a tribe to participate directly in historic preservation decision-making and to regulate the archaeological research conducted on its reservation. In order to establish a THPO, a tribe must apply to the National Park Service, identifying which SHPO functions it will assume and presenting a tribal historic preservation plan similar to that required for states. As documented by the National Association for Tribal Historic Preservation Offices, funding for THPOs remains relatively static, and as more tribes establish preservation programs, the slice of the funding pie becomes smaller (www.nathpo.org/aboutthpos.htm). The average THPO grant in 1996 was $79,865; by 2005, average funding had been reduced to $48,165. Successful tribal historic preservation offices therefore require financial subsidies from tribal governments to supplement the funding provided by the federal government, and these subsidies demonstrate substantial tribal interest in managing archaeological resources and heritage sites.

When dealing with tribes that have not appointed THPOs, federal agencies still have a responsibility to consult a designated representative of the tribe during review of projects affecting historic properties on Indian land. The tribe is a required signatory on agreement documents and must be asked for concurrence with findings of eligibility and other matters. The only procedural difference between THPO and non-THPO tribes for undertakings on tribal land is whether the SHPO participates in consultation. All tribes therefore have the same power in Section 106 compliance activities regarding their land. Federal agencies must also consult with Indian tribes that attach religious and cultural significance to historic properties on land outside tribal land. Given the long history of forced relocation of tribes in the United States, this means that Native Americans with a cultural interest in archaeological sites can be located hundreds or thousands of kilometers away from a project area. Consultation about historic properties outside Indian reservations is often a regional or national endeavor rather than a local effort.

In the 1992 amendment of the NHPA and in subsequent revisions of the accompanying regulations, consultation with tribes is mandated at specific points in Section 106 compliance (McKeown 1997a; Ruppert 1997). This consultation greatly increases the participation of tribes in decision-making about historic preservation. At its best, consultation seeks to discuss and take into account multiple views concerning the way historic properties should be identified, evaluated, and managed. This type of consultation entails much more than simply providing notification about a project. As the secretary of the interior makes clear in Standards and Guidelines for Federal Agency Historic Preservation Programs Pursuant to the National Historic Preservation Act, consultation for the NHPA is government-to-government and cannot be delegated to nonfederal entities. Federal agencies are charged with soliciting tribal views in a manner sensitive to the needs of tribes, recognizing that consultation can be time consuming and that some information needs to be kept confidential. Litigation has established that consultation for the NHPA must entail more than sending a letter to tribes requesting information (McKeown 1997b; Pueblo of Sandia v. United States, 50 F.3d 856, 10th Cir. 1995).

Importantly, as Francis McManamon (1997) has pointed out, consultation does not necessarily entail obtaining tribal consent. Tribal consent is required only for projects on tribal land. On projects located on federal land, tribal concerns need to be balanced with professional standards, and tribes cannot unilaterally dictate how archaeological excavations and reporting are to be carried out. Nonetheless, effective consultation with tribes often results in changes in project research design. On a recent highway project in Arizona, for instance, the Forest Service archaeologist originally proposed that the archaeological contractor hired to mitigate the adverse effects of construction on historic properties work outside the highway right-of-way in order to investigate entire sites rather than small portions of sites. The Hopi Tribe objected to the destruction of any part of a historic property not directly affected by the project. The Hopi people value ancestral sites as "footprints," physical monuments of their history. When archaeological sites are destroyed, the value of those monuments is greatly diminished. The written reports that mitigate the effects of site destruction for archaeologists are a pale reflection of the physical existence of the monument itself. As a result of consultation, the project research design was revised to include excavation only within the right-of-way. This turned out to be a wise decision because, as in many archaeological projects, more buried archaeological features lay within the right-of-way than originally anticipated and the limited financial resources of the project could be focused entirely on these. Working outside the right-of-way would have meant that archaeological deposits within the right-of-way would not have been fully investigated.

Traditional cultural properties are now formally recognized as historic properties potentially eligible for the National Register of Historic Places. This has increased consultation with Native Americans during Section 106 compliance activities, as well as the participation of native peoples in the research needed to identify and evaluate traditional cultural properties. This participation is essential because the significance of traditional cultural properties derives from their association with the retention and transmission of the traditional cultures of living communities (King 2003; Parker and King 1990). Research of traditional cultural properties is facilitated and made more meaningful when members of traditional communities assist in identifying properties and evaluating their significance in terms of the eligibility criteria of the National Register. This research should not be confused, however, with the government-to-government consultation that needs to take place during the Section 106 compliance review.

In the US Southwest, many tribes now conduct their own surveys to identify and evaluate traditional cultural properties. This research supplements more traditional archaeological surveys and provides the information needed for subsequent consultation with federal agencies and project sponsors. When procedures for managing traditional cultural properties were being developed in the mid-1990s, some regulators were reluctant to require this type of survey because they thought that tribes should already know where their traditional cultural properties were located. Given the highly distributed and restricted structure of knowledge about cultural

FIGURE 8.1

Archaeologists from Desert Archaeology, Inc., confer with Hopi cultural advisors during excavations to mitigate damage from highway construction along US 89 north of Flagstaff, Arizona. Left to right: *Mark Elson, Marilyn Mahle, Yvonne Hoosava, Ronald Humeyestewa, Margaret Takala, Jennie Adams, Beatrice Norton, and Deborah Swartz. Photograph by T. J. Ferguson, August 10, 1998. Courtesy Hopi Cultural Preservation Office.*

sites within many tribes, however, the expectation that a few tribal officials or representatives will know the locations and significance of all cultural sites is naive. A tribe needs to expend considerable effort in locating the appropriate traditional leaders with knowledge about cultural sites in a particular project area. It is often necessary for these traditional leaders to inspect traditional cultural properties in the field in order to ascertain where they are in relation to project boundaries and to evaluate project effects by assessing the environmental and cultural contexts. In my experience, beyond providing the important information needed for consultation, traditional cultural property surveys often locate sites missed in the initial archaeological survey. In addition, some cultural features such as shrines are often recorded by archaeologists as enigmatic rock piles, and tribal research participants in traditional cultural property surveys can provide information that either clarifies the functional attributes of features or generates testable hypotheses about function for investigation during scientific data recovery. During data recovery programs, tribal advisors also provide useful information for interpreting the archaeological record (fig. 8.1).

THE NATIONAL ENVIRONMENTAL POLICY ACT

Since its passage in 1969, the National Environmental Policy Act (NEPA) has required the involvement of the diverse public in the preparation of environmental assessments and environmental impact statements (King 2004). Unlike the NHPA, NEPA has not been amended to explicitly require consultation with tribes. Nonetheless, federal agencies and contractors preparing NEPA documents regularly consult with tribes to define and evaluate NEPA issues. Much of this work is undertaken concurrently with collecting the information needed for compliance with Section 106 of the NHPA. NEPA, however, allows a wider range of tribal concerns to be addressed than does the NHPA's narrow focus on identifying historic properties eligible for the National Register. For instance, some tribes invest considerable value in the preservation of all plants with ethnobotanical significance. In order to be considered a traditional cultural property under the NHPA, a stand of plants has to have been collected for cultural purposes. In contrast, under NEPA the plants themselves are part of the environment that needs to be addressed. Research of environmental resources that do not qualify as historic properties not only produces information useful for managerial consideration but may also yield data useful for archaeological and ethnographic research.

THE ARCHAEOLOGICAL RESOURCES PROTECTION ACT

A provision in the Archaeological Resources Protection Act (ARPA) requires that Indian tribes be notified of possible harm to or destruction of archaeological sites having religious or cultural importance. This includes destruction by authorized excavation or removal of archaeological resources on federal land. Tribal cultural sites are sometimes situated at great distance from the current location of tribal land, so consultation with tribes needs to be conducted at the regional and national levels. If such sites are located on a tribe's land, an ARPA permit cannot be issued without tribal consent, and the permit includes the terms and conditions requested by the tribe. This increases the control that tribes have over archaeological sites on their reservations. The protection of archaeological sites from looting is an issue on which archaeologists and Native Americans share common ground, and the support of tribes in prosecuting ARPA violations is helpful in moving judicial proceedings forward.

STRATEGIES FOR SUCCESSFUL TRIBAL CONSULTATION

Government-to-government consultation for historic preservation constitutes a means, not an end. The goal is to exchange information and views in order to identify and evaluate historic properties and determine how these properties can best be managed. As Darby Stapp and Michael Burney (2002) observed, consultation is the cornerstone of tribal cultural resource management, and views about historic properties are generally best exchanged in face-to-face meetings. Consultation with tribes is routinely conducted by federal agencies in the western United States, where most of the federal and tribal land is located. However, consultation with tribes pursuant to both the NHPA and NAGPRA is also important in the eastern states (Kerber 2006), as well as with descendant communities other than Native Americans throughout the country (Little and Shackel 2007).

Effective consultation is an ongoing process rather than a single event. Given the cultural diversity of tribes, there is no universal, cookbook approach for effective consultation. However, a number of best practices for culturally appropriate and effective tribal consultation have been identified by Stapp and Burney (2002), Joe Watkins (Watkins and Ferguson 2005), the US General Services Administration (2006), and the National Association of Tribal Historic Preservation Officers (Hutt and Lavallee 2005). Analyzing the occasional mistakes that are made during consultation can lead to course correction and better design of future projects (Beckerman 2006). As Watkins points out, tribes need to learn how to negotiate the "white tape" of governmental bureaucracies, and federal agencies need to learn how to negotiate the social complexities of interacting with traditional communities (Watkins and Ferguson 2005). When tribes establish tribal historic preservation offices and assume SHPO responsibilities, they take on responsibilities for engaging in government-to-government consultation with other tribes (Swidler and Cohen 1997). And as in all consultation, one hallmark of "success" is the building of a good relationship between the consulting parties.

SCHOLARLY CONSULTATION ENCOURAGED BY PROFESSIONAL ETHICS

Watkins (2000) referred to the government-to-government consultation mandated by law as "legislated ethics." Every archaeologist, however, also has a professional mandate for scholarly consultation with descendant groups. In the Principles of Archaeological Ethics, the Society for American Archaeology (SAA) states: "Responsible archaeological research, including all levels of professional activity, requires an acknowledgment of public accountability and a commitment to make every reasonable effort, in good faith, to consult actively with affected group(s), with the goal of establishing a working relationship that can be beneficial to all parties involved" (Lynott and Wylie 1995:23–24).

The SAA ethical principle of accountability means that archaeologists can no longer work with impunity; we must discuss all our research activities with the people who are affected by our work (Watkins et al. 1995). Our work has many far-reaching effects on society, so archaeologists need to make every reasonable effort to contact the elected and traditional leaders of the groups whose aboriginal or present-day land is the focus of study. These groups may be Indian tribes or other minority ethnic groups and may also include traditionally associated peoples, religious groups, and people who live or work in our study areas. The goal of scholarly consultation is to involve interested people in our research before, during, and after our fieldwork in order to make our work beneficial for all parties. Working relationships with descendant groups should entail dynamic, continual dialogue rather than static, one-time notification. This type of scholarly consultation is good for our discipline because it advances good public relations and improves our research by allowing descendant groups to identify research questions they find interesting and suggest culturally appropriate ways in which these can be investigated. Not every effort to consult with descendants will lead to greater understanding and lasting working relationships, but many will. The successful efforts provide a foundation of goodwill and positive working relationships that the entire discipline can build on. We need to make consultation and cooperation routine parts of our research in order to develop a truly public archaeology (Watkins 1999).

In defining professional responsibility to the public, the Register of Professional Archaeologists ("the Register") requires registered archaeologists to be sensitive to and respect the legitimate concerns of the people whose culture histories are the subject of research. The Register's Code of Conduct and its Standards of Research Performance do not specify exactly how archaeologists should accomplish this beyond requiring that its members know and comply with applicable federal, state, and local laws and regulations and that they disseminate the results of research with interested persons, as well as colleagues. Although the Register's Code of Conduct is somewhat general, taken in conjunction with the SAA ethical principle for accountability and the federal mandate for government-to-government consultation in historic preservation and NAGPRA activities, it reinforces the need for dialogue with descendant groups.

The World Archaeological Congress (WAC) has established eight principles to abide by and seven rules to adhere to that explicitly define the ethical obligations archaeologists have to indigenous peoples. The principles focus on acknowledging the importance that heritage sites and ancestral human remains have for indigenous groups, asserting that cultural heritage belongs to the indigenous descendants of that heritage. WAC members acknowledge that indigenous peoples have an important relationship with their heritage resources irrespective of legal ownership and that archaeologists should establish equitable partnerships with indigenous peoples whose cultural heritage is being studied. WAC also calls for its members to seek representation of indigenous people in funding and regulatory agencies to ensure that indigenous views are considered in setting research standards, questions, priorities, and goals. As a rule, WAC members agree that before any investigation, they will define the indigenous peoples whose cultural heritage is the subject of study, negotiate with and obtain the informed consent of representatives of those indigenous groups, keep authorized representatives of those groups informed during all stages of investigation, and not remove human remains or objects with special cultural significance without express consent. Furthermore, WAC members agree to present the results of their work with deference and respect to descendant groups and to employ or train indigenous peoples in archaeological techniques and monitoring as part of field projects. As Larry Zimmerman (2000) has pointed out, the WAC code of ethics provides a basis for a covenantal archaeology in which the control of archaeology is shared with or held by indigenous peoples.

The cumulative ethics espoused by the SAA, the Register, and WAC provide a comprehensive directive that archaeologists consult with and seek the involvement of indigenous people and descendant groups in our research. This scholarly obligation for dialogue with descendant groups exists whether or not an archaeologist is employed by a governmental agency with a legal responsibility for government-to-government consultation. Archaeological contractors have an obligation to talk with and involve tribes and descendant groups in their research even if the formal consultation required by law is handled by federal or state agencies. Because much of the government-to-government consultation takes place before the issuance of contracts for archaeological surveys to identify historic properties or archaeological excavations to mitigate the adverse effects of projects, CRM researchers need to discuss their research activities with native peoples and descendant communities after research contracts are awarded. Scholarly consultation has more leeway than government-to-government consultation in integrating traditional leaders and cultural advisors in research activities, in addition to elected tribal officials. Although CRM archaeologists need to respect tribal sovereignty, they can seek out and hire the most interested and qualified tribal members to assist them with project research. This is accomplished most easily in the western United States, where tribes are still in geographical proximity to their ancestral sites.

Many archaeologists refer to all research with Native Americans as consultation. When this type of scholarly consultation occurs, however, it is important not to confuse it with federally mandated, government-to-government consultation. Research to identify traditional cultural properties and other historic properties for Section 106 compliance, even when conducted with Indian tribes, does not constitute the consultation required in the NHPA. Government-to-government consultation addresses a set of required subjects. Research designed to gather information about one of the subjects of consultation and the actual act of consultation between agency and tribal representatives about that gathered information, as it applies to agency decisions within the Section 106 process, are distinct processes. Maintaining research and government-to-government consultation as conceptually distinct processes helps to ensure that the consultation with tribal officials mandated by law actually occurs.

The difference between government-to-government and scholarly consultation also needs to be respected by federal agencies. On a recent CRM project in Arizona, a federal archaeologist sought to control all interaction between Native Americans and archaeologists by forbidding contractors to talk to Indian tribes about research. This violates our ethical charge to consult descendant groups and diminishes the research that is possible on a project. Talking to Native Americans to engage them in archaeological research is not the government-to-government consultation defined in the NHPA and other legislation, and no federal agency should prohibit archaeologists from scholarly dialogue with members of descendant groups.

While engaged in research, contract archaeologists need to respect tribal sovereignty and the mandate for government-to-government consultation. Our desire to facilitate communication and affect management recommendations offered by cultural advisors or tribal research consultants in the field needs to be modulated by bringing those recommendations to the governmental agencies involved in the project. CRM is an instrument of state power that needs to be wielded carefully (Smith 2004).

NATIVE AMERICAN INTERESTS IN ARCHAEOLOGY AND HISTORIC PRESERVATION

As Lipe points out in chapter 3, Native Americans (and other descendant communities) have many interests in archaeology and historic preservation. First and foremost is their desire to protect ancestral sites and the graves of culturally affiliated people (Kuwanwisiwma 2002). Many tribes pass tribal ordinances complementing ARPA to protect sites on their land from unauthorized excavation and removal of cultural property. Many tribes also elect to participate in the research and consultation needed for compliance with historic preservation legislation in order to have direct input into the decisions made about their heritage resources. By identifying and evaluating ancestral sites and traditional cultural properties, tribes make sure that these properties are duly considered in Section 106 compliance activities. Documenting how traditional cultural properties and other tribal heritage resources are eligible for the National Register of Historic Places under criterion A (association with events that have made a significant contribution to the broad patterns of the country's history), as well as criterion D (yielding or likely to yield information important in prehistory or history), increases the opportunities tribes have to consult about the cultural, as well as the scientific, values of properties. Many tribes make a standard recommendation that all adverse effects to their heritage resources should be avoided. This works to ensure that the "no action" alternative on NEPA assessments and impact statements receives due consideration and that project planners involved with Section 106 compliance consider treatment plans that minimize or eliminate damage to cultural resources.

Many tribes are also interested in increasing their control over research protocols and work products so that archaeology in the United States is done in a manner than eliminates or minimizes the potential for cultural and spiritual harm. Decreasing the disturbance of human remains and limiting archaeological excavation to sites threatened with destruction by land modifying projects are two goals many tribes embrace. Some tribes have concerns about the control of intellectual property in the projects they are involved with, both on and off their reservations. These tribes are increasingly negotiating research contracts that assign the ownership of archaeological and ethnographic field notes, photographs, and other records to the tribe. Tribal control of information raises difficult ethical issues. In resolving these issues, tribes should have the same rights as the federal government and private corporations in asserting ownership and control over cultural resource information. When public funds are used to support research with or by tribes, the ownership and control of research results need to be made explicit at the outset of the project so that all parties have a clear understanding of how data and publications will be archived and disseminated. No archaeologist should be forcibly required to adopt a specific tribal view of the past in a research design in order to get a permit to do publicly funded CRM work. At the same time, giving due consideration to tribal views in relation to scientific perspectives opens up exciting research possibilities that archaeologists would be wise to consider.

The ownership of research results is coupled with the responsibility to archive project records to preserve them for future use. With permission of the tribe, these records are made available to scholars for research and publication. Tribes that establish tribal historic preservation offices increase their control over the way cultural resources and historic properties are researched and managed on their reservations. Tribal historic preservation offices also provide focal points for collecting information about the management of tribal resources outside the tribe's land.

The implementation of the NHPA and other historic preservation legislation has created financial benefits for professional archaeologists by providing jobs and business opportunities. Several tribes operate CRM firms in order to reap the financial rewards associated with compliance-driven research (Anyon, Ferguson, and Welch 2000; Begay 1997; Ferguson 2000). In addition to employing tribal members and pumping money into tribal economies, some of these tribal CRM programs provide significant subsidies for the unfunded mandates of tribal historic and cultural preservation programs.

Some tribes participate in archaeological research to ensure that tribal perspectives and concepts are incorporated into the written record created to mitigate site destruction (Kuwanwisiwma 2002). Including tribal perspectives in archaeological reports helps offset the physical loss of ancestral sites. Some of these interpretations entail using traditional cultural knowledge in ethnohistoric research to supplement conventional archaeological interpretations of site features. However, fundamental archaeological research that increases the chronological control over ancestral sites or provides basic information about the plants and animals used by ancient people is also of interest to both tribes and archaeologists.

Hopi research interests, for instance, include humanistic and scientific questions directed toward generating information about the real lives people lived in the ancestral villages and sites studied by archaeologists (Ferguson 1998). Specific research questions of interest to the Hopi include the cultural affinity of archaeological sites, the chronological framework for clan migration traditions, chronological styles and interpretive motifs of petroglyphs and pictographs, the location and procurement of raw materials used in producing ceramic and lithic artifacts, macrobotanical and pollen analysis documenting past cultigens and foodstuffs, genetic analysis of ancient seeds to determine how they relate to contemporary Hopi crops, prehistoric diet, trade and exchange as evidenced by exotic pottery, the chronological development of kiva and domestic architecture, regional scales of land use, the occurrence of violence and warfare, health and disease, past environmental conditions, the social and economic contributions of females, and the integration of clan traditions and ritual information in archaeological research.

Many tribes use NAGPRA to protect their ancestors by repatriating and reburying human remains and funerary objects that have been held in museum collections and by ensuring that graves are not disturbed by new ground-modifying projects. Cultural affiliation, one of the key concepts in NAGPRA, has permeated virtually all archaeological discourse with Native Americans (Adler and Bruning 2008; Welch and Ferguson 2007). Investigation of cultural affiliation provides CRM with a research agenda entailing issues of migration, social identity, and historical linkages between past and present peoples, and these are important issues in contemporary archaeological method and theory (fig. 8.2).

Some tribes participate in CRM research to expand knowledge about their past for the benefit of present and future generations of tribal members and the general public (Dowdall and Parrish 2003). These tribes have a genuine interest in learning more about tribal history and in sharing this information with a broad audience. Tribal interest in archaeology and historic preservation thus serves to further the educational goals of CRM.

NEGOTIATING THE CONTINUUM FROM CONSULTATION TO COLLABORATION

CRM archaeologists face challenges and opportunities in negotiating the continuum from consultation to collaboration. During government-to-government and scholarly consultation, archaeologists are exposed to a full gamut of native attitudes about archaeology (Wylie 1999). Some Native Americans do not think that scientific investigations serve their interests, and they express anger about how archaeologists have treated their cultural remains and their communities in the past. These groups may actively resist archaeological research. Other groups reluctantly agree to archaeological research but insist upon the return of sacred objects and human remains or try to limit their use in museum exhibitions and research. An

FIGURE 8.2

Hopi tribal members (left to right) Marshall Lomayaktewa, Micah Loma'omvaya, and Morgan Saufkie analyze iconography on Salado ceramics at the Arizona State Museum during a cultural affiliation study sponsored by the Hopi Cultural Preservation Office. Photograph by T. J. Ferguson, October 20, 1998. Courtesy Hopi Cultural Preservation Office.

increasing number of tribes want to control access to archaeological sites and information, seeking outcomes that range from complete prohibition of research, to asking that research be conducted with informed consent, to requesting collaboration in research of tribal heritage sites.

In deciding how to respond to the varying positions of consulted tribes, archaeologists should keep in mind the limitations and opportunities

TABLE 8.1

Five Historical Modes of Interaction with Descendant Communities

Colonial Control	Resistance	Participation	Collaboration	Indigenous Control
Goals are set solely by archaeologists.	Goals develop in opposition.	Goals develop independently.	Goals develop jointly.	Goals are set by tribe.
Information is extracted and removed from community.	Information is secreted.	Information is disclosed:	Information flows freely.	Information is proprietary and controlled by tribe.
Descendants involved as laborers.	No stakeholder involvement.	Limited stakeholder involvement.	Full stakeholder involvement.	Archaeologists are employees or consultants of tribe.
Little voice for descendants.	No voice for stakeholders.	Some voice for stakeholders.	Full voice for stakeholders.	Full voice of descendants is privileged.
Acquiescence is enforced by state.	No support is given/obtained.	Support is solicited.	Support is tacit.	Support is authorized by tribe.
Needs of science are optimized.	Needs of others are not considered.	Needs of most parties mostly met.	Needs of all parties are realized.	Needs of tribe are privileged.

entailed in five modes of interaction: colonial control, resistance, participation, collaboration, and indigenous control (Colwell-Chanthaphonh
and Ferguson 2008). These modes affect the ways in which research and
management goals are developed, information is controlled, stakeholders
are involved, and the needs of the various parties are met (table 8.1). The
control over archaeology shifts from archaeologists to indigenous communities as one moves through the different modes of interaction. Historically, several modes of interaction have sometimes operated simultaneously
in different projects or at different stages of the same project.

   The days of colonial archaeology, thankfully, are long gone, although
vestiges of them remain. In the resistance mode, archaeological research is
difficult because descendant groups actively oppose it. Communication
with descendant groups is inhibited, and archaeologists are hard pressed
to fulfill ethical obligations for accountability and consultation with the
parties affected by their work. In the participation mode, archaeologists
often develop research designs independently of descendant groups but
seek their advice and involvement, and stakeholders are kept informed and
offered some voice in research. In the collaborative mode, archaeologists
and descendant groups work together to develop research designs that
address issues important to both groups in a culturally appropriate man-

ner. Descendant groups are fully involved in all aspects of the research, including data collection, analysis, and report preparation. This opens up the discipline of archaeology in exciting new ways by broadening research questions, developing new methods of collecting and analyzing data, and enabling descendant groups to have an active voice in preparing reports and publications. If members of descendant groups are not report authors, they serve as peer reviewers to improve the presentation of information, the efficacy of arguments, and the validity of conclusions. Collaborative projects are effective in realizing the needs of all parties and improving archaeological research. In the indigenous control mode, increasingly common on tribal land, the goals and methods of archaeological research are controlled by indigenous communities. These goals and methods may be similar to those of conventional archaeology or may introduce exciting innovations. Archaeologists working for tribes in the indigenous control mode are simultaneously engaged in collaborative research.

CRM archaeologists have some leeway in deciding which mode of interaction to engage. In the resistance mode, archaeologists can either play an active role in opposing descendant groups or take a more passive role in which they continue the research required for historic preservation in a manner that avoids outright confrontation. Active resistance by archaeologists can lead to contentious litigation that advances a single project but sets back the larger goal of developing long-term collegial relationships with descendant groups. When descendant groups engage in resistance, archaeologists can move the interaction toward participation by offering to inform stakeholders about the results of research and providing them with an opportunity to review project results. When descendant groups elect to be participants in research, this provides a means for developing the personal and professional relationships needed to structure future projects on a collaborative basis.

Collaboration takes time to develop and is always fluid and flexible. A group of co-researchers is formed from archaeologists and members of descendant communities. This creates an opportunity to develop a research design, collect and analyze information, and construct knowledge by drawing upon the cross-cultural experience and understanding of the entire group (Colwell-Chanthaphonh and Ferguson 2008). The researchers in this mode, including members of descendant communities, are not outside the research experience but are a fundamental part of it.

The production of knowledge in the collaborative mode unfolds in ways that stand in marked contrast to the resistance mode. People engaged in resistance link knowledge to positions defined in opposition. For

instance, in the Kennewick Man case, knowledge was structured by a paradigm whereby science stood in opposition to traditional beliefs.
Archaeologists based their arguments solely on scientific ideas, whereas
Native Americans dismissed science and promoted traditional knowledge
(Watkins 2004:72). In the collaborative mode, knowledge is constructed in
a more complex and pluralistic manner, acknowledging the way science
entails mythical elements and the way native "myths" are entwined with scientific knowledge (Cajete 2000; Whiteley 2002). Groups seeking to collaboratively negotiate representations of the past rework scientific concepts
with traditional knowledge to elucidate how various kinds of historical
knowledge all contribute to a holistic view of earlier periods. Theories of
the past using a variety of perspectives are both interesting and advantageous because they are grounded in the experiences of community members rather than being abstract frameworks that operate outside particular
histories and life-worlds (Colwell-Chanthaphonh and Ferguson 2008).

Archaeologists who work collaboratively with Native Americans are
challenged to examine the epistemological basis of their discipline in relation to native knowledge systems. Consequently, cultural relativism and
multidisciplinary approaches are integrated into research programs that
also retain a commitment to collecting and analyzing data using scientific
standards. In this approach, science and traditional knowledge are complementary rather than competitive. It is not necessary to reconcile all conflicts in knowledge in order to create a singular narrative explanation of
the past. Reports are like cut diamonds with different facets of explanation
based on different sources and types of knowledge.

Good examples of collaborative research may be found in Blume 2006,
Dean and Perrelli 2006, Dongoske, Alderderfer, and Doehner 2000,
Dowdall and Parrish 2003, Ferguson 1996, Kerber 2006, Klesert and Downer
1990, Schneider and Altschul 2000, Silliman 2008; Swidler et al. 1997,
Swidler et al. 2000, and Watkins 2000. Common elements in these projects
include archaeologists and descendant groups working together on all
phases of research, from problem definition to collection and analysis of
data, and conferring with each other about research findings (Watkins and
Ferguson 2005).

In collaborative research, the boundaries between archaeology and
ethnography are often blurred, leading to a more anthropological archaeology. Investigation of cultural affiliation and traditional cultural properties in particular requires the use of knowledge derived from traditional
history and cultural practice. Involving native groups in this research is
spurring the development of an indigenous archaeology. This indigenous

archaeology, like ethnobotany, seeks to use native concepts and taxonomies to structure research and native theories to explain the results (for example, Lyons 2003; Webster and Loma'omvaya 2004). Indigenous archaeology is expensive because it requires the same amount of data collection, analysis, and report preparation as conventional archaeology. Although a few pilot projects have demonstrated the efficacy of the approach, it remains for Native American archaeologists speaking indigenous languages to take up this research paradigm and realize its potential.

As increasing numbers of archaeologists come into regular, face-to-face contact with tribal members, either in collaborative projects or in work as tribal employees, a socialization takes place wherein archaeologists come to understand and accommodate Native American values even if they do not personally subscribe to them. This new cross-cultural sensitivity to the cultural values structuring the way CRM research is conducted is profoundly affecting the way archaeologists choose to do archaeology. When native peoples explain in personal terms the harm that certain archaeological practices cause for individuals and communities, few archaeologists do not reevaluate their methods and institute changes in practice. Foremost among these changes are the purpose and methods for excavating burials. As archaeologists find their research constrained in some areas, new research opportunities present themselves in others.

Leigh Kuwanwisiwma (2008) points out that collaboration involves equality, respect, and reciprocity. It is a long-term process in which archaeologists and Native Americans work together as equal partners in research, with a commitment to providing each other with the information and work necessary to attain common goals. The personal and professional relationships entailed in collaborative research transcend specific projects, and Native Americans become long-term colleagues. All parties in collaborative research develop reciprocal social and professional relationships wherein they give freely of their time and resources in order to assist one another with research tasks and other endeavors. Collaboration leads to better research and sustainable working relationships with descendant groups.

A VISION FOR THE FUTURE

As the federal mandate for government-to-government consultation continues, an increasing number of archaeologists working in the CRM context will fulfill the ethical call to confer with and involve the descendants of the past peoples we study. This sustained dialogue will lead to more collaborative projects in which archaeologists and indigenous people work together to research questions of mutual interest. As tribal historic preservation programs demonstrate the social usefulness of careers in archaeology, we will see an increasing number of tribal members becoming professional archaeologists with advanced degrees. Because most archaeology in the United States is now conducted to collect information needed for compliance with historic preservation legislation, most of these indigenous archaeologists will be employed in CRM as regulators or researchers. These trends will increase the social and cultural diversity of our discipline, and this in turn will lead to new intellectual developments in archaeology.

The potential for a truly indigenous archaeology—one that uses native taxonomies and logic to structure research—will eventually be realized. Tribally based CRM companies will take the lead in developing innovative projects in which the funding to mitigate damage to historic properties is used to support indigenous archaeology. Traditional Native American knowledge systems embedded in spatial rather than temporal conceptual frameworks will be used to construct historical knowledge based on geographical referents (Condori 1989; Echo-Hawk 2000). This will produce multiple histories contingent upon native theories of the past. Native speakers of indigenous languages will take the lead in research of their heritage because concepts of time, space, and history are situated in linguistic referents. CRM archaeology, even when done by non-indigenous people, will decolonize itself by advancing research themes that address issues important to indigenous communities, including social memory, storytelling, survival, cultural vitality, historical connections to ancestors, naming, protecting, and sharing heritage (Smith 1999). When fully realized, indigenous archaeologies will take their place alongside conventional archaeologies, and all will contribute in a complementary fashion to the long-established culture of scientific archaeological research.

We will train students preparing for careers in CRM to undertake the complex social negotiations associated with effective consultation and to move from consultation to the development of participatory and collaborative research. In addition to studying the practical and theoretical principles relevant to consultation and collaboration, students will learn the importance of virtues such as patience, honesty, generosity, trust, appreciation for multiple points of view, reciprocity, and commitment to equitable research that maintains high scientific standards. Developing the essential social relationships needed to work with descendant communities takes time, so tribal colleagues will help professors in mentoring students. When their education is complete, students will find employment in CRM companies that support the development of the long-term, reciprocal working relationships with Native Americans and descendant communities that transcend billable hours. This vision is one end of a continuum of archaeological practice. The work of some archaeologists will take this path in the future, and other archaeologists will follow a conventional career trajectory. This diversity in approaches to archaeology will be good for our discipline. CRM archaeology can be touched by and informed by the kind of work described here.

CONCLUSION

The development of CRM in the past 40 years is part of a larger cultural shift occurring in the modes of scientific knowledge production (Gibbons et al. 1994; Heckenberger 2004; Nowotny, Scott, and Gibbons 2001). This shift entails development of transdisciplinary networks and new standards for creating and evaluating knowledge that is produced in the context of application, with greater social accountability and reflexivity. This new mode of knowledge production is associated with heterogeneous organizational structures located outside universities.

CRM archaeologists are located primarily in governmental agencies and private companies. They interact with and answer to diverse groups, including politicians, developers, and descendant groups. Through consultation with descendants, CRM archaeologists are developing collaborative projects that expand the repertoire of research questions investigated, the manner in which research is conducted, and the way this research is evaluated. The production of knowledge takes place in the context of providing the information needed for historic preservation and management of cultural resources. Descendant groups play an active role because of their interest in identifying ancestral sites and traditional cultural properties and the cultural values that make these places significant. The production and meaning of archaeological knowledge are gauged according to multiple epistemological standards. This produces a more inclusive and democratic archaeology that serves the needs of descendant groups, as well as archaeologists. Our discipline benefits from gaining access to new sources of information about the past and new perspectives on the meaning of heritage resources in the present.

Partnership and collaboration with Native Americans are vital to the growth and development of both archaeology and cultural resource management. In addition to studying the things we are interested in, our discipline needs to address issues and questions important to Native Americans and descendant communities. Robert Kelly (2000:101) observed, "Archaeology will become applied anthropology or it will become nothing."

9

Is the Same Old Thing Enough for Twenty-first Century CRM?

Keeping CRM Archaeology Relevant in a New Millennium

Douglas P. Mackey, Jr.

Cultural resource management (CRM) archaeology as a subfield of the larger discipline of archaeology in the United States came into its own in the late 1960s and the 1970s with the passage of significant historic preservation and environmental preservation legislation calling for publicly funded and mandated archaeological research. Rapid expansion of the field followed, and with it came new concerns about how the increasing quantities of data and growing number of archaeologists working in the field would be organized, what the goals of the new publicly funded research would be, and how those goals would be met. Many of these concerns were examined in the Airlie House report (McGimsey and Davis 1977). In the years since that report was published, the field has continued to expand, and public funding for archaeology has continued to increase, as has the number of regulations that call for archaeological research in advance of publicly funded, permitted, or approved projects. In addition to federal legislation, numerous state and local regulations recognize the need to address archaeological resources.

Although most people in CRM archaeology see it as a true profession, making important contributions to modern society, the general public, legislative bodies, and those who pay for archaeological services do not always share this perception. It is disheartening that I often have to explain to members of the public that there are valid reasons for undertaking archaeological research as part of the environmental review process and that despite their views to the contrary, such research can add important knowledge about the past and about how present-day cultures interact with one another and the environment. How the public perceives our work and its results should be of concern to all CRM archaeologists. Because our work is publicly supported, a poor perception of it by the public may lead people to question its value and whether the results are worth the cost. It is incumbent upon CRM archaeologists to ensure that our work is of the highest quality, that it adds something to the public's understanding of the past, and that we reach out to the public in ways that help it perceive the value of our work.

In this chapter, I examine the way both the public and archaeologists perceive the field of CRM archaeology. I also identify potential areas of concern and offer suggestions for ways these perceptions and the issues that underlie them can be addressed in order to keep CRM archaeology in the United States healthy, viable, and relevant as we move deeper into the twenty-first century.

As a discipline, archaeology has gone through a series of methodological and theoretical changes—even paradigm shifts—over the past 100 years. With the introduction of the Antiquities Act of 1906, archaeology gained new status in American society and began to grow as a discipline. Like any other discipline, it has experienced growing pains and matured as new ideas and methods have come to the fore. From culture history to processualism and postprocessualism, theories of how to study the past have evolved, and proponents of those theories have argued with one another, producing stimulating debates and demonstrating the potential for examining the past.

With the advent of the National Historic Preservation Act (NHPA) in 1966 and subsequent legislation, such as its implementing regulations (36 CFR Part 800) and Executive Order 11593 ("Protection and Enhancement of the Cultural Environment," 1971), the cultural resource management industry began to expand rapidly, resulting in an explosion in the need for qualified archaeologists. Initially, the field saw an adaptive radiation of young archaeologists, fresh from their studies and at the heart of the Binfordian wars of the "New Archaeology," eager to test new theories with the mountains of data suddenly available through compliance with the NHPA. Although the field was young, this was an exciting period of growth for CRM archaeology. As the field matured, it became more complacent, and the focus of some practitioners shifted from "What research can this project provide?" to "How do I get my client through this process?" An increase in rules, processes, and lawsuits made this shift inevitable. The unfortunate correlate became the addition of the phrase "as economically as possible."

Over the years, a perception has developed among many professionals with whom I have spoken that fewer established practitioners of CRM archaeology are still interested in the field's exciting scientific research potential. More of them have become accustomed to a routine or formulaic approach that allows them to move from one project to the next with as little disruption to the daily routine as possible. This is clearly evident in many interactions I have had with consulting archaeologists. Some blame this shift on profit motive; others look to the split between CRM and academic archaeology and resulting issues regarding the preparation of new archaeologists. Still others see the standardized or "cookie cutter" approaches to testing strategies required by some state historic preservation offices (SHPOs) as a prime cause of rigidity in the field. Whatever the cause, the perception of CRM archaeologists as professionals worthy of serious consideration by the "outside" world has been affected.

PERCEPTIONS

As background research for this chapter, I sought comments from various segments of the archaeological community regarding people's thoughts about and perceptions of the state of CRM archaeology, the underlying causes of challenging issues, and possible solutions. To gather comments from other CRM practitioners, I queried people on the e-mail lists of regional archaeological groups. To consider the experience of other SHPO archaeological reviewers, I sent a questionnaire through the e-mail lists of the National Council of State Historic Preservation Offices (NCSHPO) and the National Association of State Archaeologists (NASA) (see Appendix). I considered the comments of SHPO reviewers to be important for understanding perceptions because they review the work of a wide range of CRM archaeologists, which allows them to see broad patterns in the types and quality of work being completed. Additionally, SHPO reviewers are in the often unique position of hearing and needing to respond to the perceptions of all the players involved in CRM—archaeologists, state and federal agencies, project sponsors, Native American groups, and the general public.

CRM archaeology is often conducted in compliance with historic preservation laws, not because the project proponent is interested in archaeology or the past but because legislation has identified that archaeological resources are important and should be considered. Every CRM project has a proponent, a person or an agency that is looking to accomplish a project. In some cases, the archaeological investigation is the ultimate goal, as when staff at a national park such as Mesa Verde want to know more about a particular resource that is to be interpreted. For the majority of work undertaken, however, the proponent is an agency or individual who seeks funding, a permit, or approval of an action. A proponent could be the Army Corps of Engineers as it prepares to construct a water control feature along a major river, a limited liability partnership seeking permits for a 200-acre housing development, or an individual who needs an Army Corps permit to build a boat access in his backyard. To these types of applicants, archaeology is often an unwelcome additional cost, creating a less than hospitable environment for the CRM archaeologist.

Many applicants do not see archaeologists as professionals on equal footing with engineers, architects, and environmental scientists. This perception is based not only on the fact that archaeology is not a licensed profession but also, in large part, on the disparity that project proponents see in price estimates for the same archaeological work and the large variation in the quality of work produced. Although similar disparities in cost and quality of work exist in any profession and even in academic archaeological research, it is often easier for the general public to understand the need for and findings of an environmental study than of an archaeological one. As a result, it is difficult for the public to assess the quality of an archaeological study. At this point, it appears that the most dangerous enemy for the future of CRM archaeology may be archaeological professionals themselves. The most difficult obstacles we face are our own apathy, failure to strive for excellence, and failure to help the public understand the value of our work.

The public view of our profession is mixed. On some days, we are seen as experts knowledgeable about the past; on others, we are viewed as nothing more than roadblocks to the successful completion of a project. The Section 106 process and the need for archaeological efforts to find new sites have been attacked politically in the past (Bryne 2005). Although the most recent round of attacks seems to have eased, no one should feel complacent, for the issue is sure to come up again. If we are unable to show the public the relevance of our work and why it has a value greater than the dollars spent on archaeological survey and excavation, then we face the prospect of an uninformed public supporting future attacks on the process and the profession.

Excellent CRM-related research is being conducted across the nation by companies of all sizes, but less inspired, more pedestrian work is being done as well. In general, the perception among reviewers of CRM reports seems to be that consultants produce acceptable "nuts and bolts" field and laboratory work—that is, recording what is excavated, completing forms, photographing features, and so forth—but with a paucity of significant analysis and interpretation of the data gathered. It often seems that the analysis is not really furthering the field of archaeology and that much of the work produced is not being placed in a larger context or integrated with other ongoing and recent work. This situation is one of the factors underlying the biggest threat facing CRM archaeology—the public's perception that our work is costly and results in few or no valid outcomes that have relevance to the larger population.

Another area of concern for both review staff and some members of the public is the integration, or lack thereof, of new approaches, tools, and methods of analysis into CRM investigations. Technological advances over the past three decades have provided a wide array of new tools for archaeological research. Almost any project can benefit from the use of some of these, such as computer-aided drafting and design (CADD) and the contour-plot software Surfer, which have been available for many years, and newer technologies such as global positioning systems (GPS) and geographical information systems (GIS). Even noninvasive technologies that were once seen as experimental and unavailable to everyone, such as ground penetrating radar (GPR), have been shown to be highly effective under the proper conditions and are now widely available at a reasonable cost. Although some CRM firms regularly make excellent use of these technologies, many more have been reluctant or even resistant to updating their methods.

Two major causes seem to underlie both the reluctance to try new approaches and the hesitancy to develop more sophisticated analyses. The first is the initial cost of acquiring the technology, which can be high, and the second is the learning curve, which can be long. The nature of consulting archaeology makes it necessary to keep costs down in order to remain competitive, and many practitioners have expressed the belief that new techniques, such as remote sensing, and new personnel, such as lab specialists, are "too expensive" to use. Others seem to reflect the position of many project sponsors, who question whether public or private funds should even be used for archaeology, let alone to support the use of new or "experimental" methods. Both arguments indicate a lack of understanding of the benefits of such methods for reducing overall project costs in the long term, for better focusing research efforts, and for effecting tremendous time savings.

Another problem of perception facing CRM archaeology today is that many practitioners take a minimalist approach to their work. Often, clients insist that archaeological consultants do the minimum work necessary to pass review. Consultants feel that they must conform to the pressure for minimalism in order to keep the job. A typical rationalization is that the reviewing agency will point out any problems and will often pass any work that meets local guidelines. What holders of this view fail to understand is that wherever guidelines have been set, they identify a necessarily general and minimalist starting point for an array of possible projects. This approach places the burden of ensuring good research on the review agency rather than on the professional archaeologist chosen to conduct the research. Although most review archaeologists attempt to provide useful comments, they are often overworked, understaffed, and rarely expert on any particular topic addressed in the many reports they see. A successful research effort often needs to go above and beyond the minimal guidelines to be worth its cost.

Ultimately, the development of research programs that are cost effective and lead to useful results is the responsibility of the consulting archaeologist, who has intimate knowledge of the project. Economic factors must be one consideration in developing a research program, but they must be balanced with the need for good archaeological research. Under Section 106, an archaeological site is typically considered eligible for the National Register of Historic Places and worthy of data recovery because of its research value— its ability to provide new information about the past. A site cannot "provide information" on its own; only through a well-designed and completed research program can the goals of historic preservation legislation be attained.

The unfortunate theme running through these perceptions is that in many instances, archaeological consultants seem to be more concerned with bottom-line costs than with doing good archaeology. Although this may sound like a condemnation of CRM archaeology, it is important to consider the reasons behind this situation, in addition to simple economic pressures. One of the prime reasons is the very real disconnect between academic and research-oriented archaeologists in university settings and the majority of CRM archaeologists, who work in a business environment. Archaeologists in academic settings have the ability to fully develop specific research topics over a number of years and can take considerable time in developing and testing hypotheses. CRM archaeologists, by the very nature of their work, must be prepared to switch from one research topic to another weekly, if not daily. As the amount of CRM work undertaken has continued to increase, this gap has widened, affecting perceptions of CRM research. A common result of this situation is that some CRM archaeologists have difficulty not only developing significant research questions but also relating the questions to the testing methods employed. The consequence is often an inability to develop data that add something significant to the archaeological record. Although reports on such work provide important raw data, it is often up to the reader to interpret the information and place it in a useful format.

As a corollary to this gap between CRM archaeologists and their academic counterparts, university archaeologists in the United States often seem reluctant to encourage research initiated through CRM. This is not always the case, but the reluctance often comes up in discussions and bears further consideration.

In order to assess the validity of this perception, I contacted faculty members at the four university-based archaeology programs in the State University of New York (SUNY) system. Three of these schools currently have CRM survey programs that provide hands-on training opportunities for their students. I asked faculty members with CRM experience at each school what kinds of support they received from other staff and how the CRM program was viewed within the department (see appendix). At each school with a survey program, the program appeared to generate substantial funding for the university through its contract work, but levels of institutional support for the programs varied. Each of the four schools historically had a CRM survey program, but one had done away with its program completely and at another the program was entirely self-funded, receiving no financial support from the university.

At several of the schools, no antagonism toward the CRM program was manifested, but CRM archaeology was considered a "second-class" or lower-tier profession relative to the academic profession and students were encouraged not to get too involved in it, in order not to be distracted from the real goal of finding employment in academia. One institution offered no undergraduate-level CRM class, although the topic was discussed as part of several, more general classes. At a second institution, a single "public archaeology" class provided an introduction to the topic for both graduate and undergraduate students. At one school, it was noted that colleagues were happy to have the funding opportunities the CRM survey program provided for students, even if CRM was not seen as a long-term career goal. These observations are limited to a small number of schools in one region, so more support for CRM programs may exist in other areas. But discussions with archaeologists from around the country suggest that these conditions are widespread.

Only one school has shown a long-term commitment to a public archaeology–CRM component. For more than two decades, the university at Binghamton has consistently produced graduates who have gone on to successful careers in CRM. Students who pass through this program are encouraged to be research oriented in their work and continue to have a strong research focus as CRM professionals, producing excellent work. Unfortunately, this program seems to be the exception rather than the rule. Greater use of this model for teaching CRM and engaging students in the full process would result in better preparation for a large majority of university graduates who go on to careers in CRM archaeology. I believe that this is an area on which the profession must focus substantial effort to ensure that future generations of CRM archaeologists are well prepared. It is imperative that national organizations such as the Society for American Archaeology, the Society for Historical Archaeology, and the American Anthropological Association accept the reality that the future of archaeological research in the United States lies in CRM. The money spent on CRM archaeology each year overwhelms the efforts of our academic colleagues and has real potential for advancing the field. By acknowledging this and by encouraging academic programs to embrace CRM more fully, identify for students the problems and issues specific to CRM, and provide them with better training in ways to adjust to the needs of CRM, we can greatly enhance the future of archaeology in the United States.

ISSUES TO CONSIDER

It seems clear that CRM archaeology as it is currently practiced does not always attain the lofty goals set in the early years of the discipline. It is time to reconsider what steps need to be taken in order to make it a relevant and successful field in the twenty-first century.

Ethics and Professionalism

Archaeologists have ethical responsibilities to the archaeological record, the public, and their colleagues. The interplay of these ethical considerations among various interested parties has become a complex situation faced by all archaeologists and is worthy of substantial consideration on it own (see Bridges, chapter 10, this volume). Despite this, some basic ethical issues are common to all archaeologists. Among these is the responsibility to "stay informed and knowledgeable about developments in [one's] field or fields of specialization" (RPA 1998).

Archaeology has no oversight authority providing certification, licensing, or other forms of acknowledgment that a practitioner is a recognized professional who produces work meeting acceptable standards. We have only our own commitment to ethical and professional behavior. Unfortunately, experience has shown that not all archaeologists share the same level of ethical concern. This is not to suggest that some in our profession heedlessly commit bad acts, but opinions differ considerably about where the ethical lines should be drawn and what forces should help to determine the placement of the lines—for example, responsibility to the record, responsibility to the client's wishes, and responsibility to inform the client about best practices and legal issues.

Scarre and Scarre (2006:3) provided relevant thoughts on the topic in a recent consideration of the ethics of archaeology: "People who keep their moral hands clean and satisfy the bare requirements of acceptable behavior may be described as minimally ethical agents. In contrast, those who follow a more inspiring view of the ethical life do not merely avoid the bad but energetically pursue the good. These ideas carry over into professional ethics though with an important caveat. Archaeologists should be seeking to realize the highest goods of their profession, whatever these may be."

Each archaeologist needs to ask whether he or she wishes to be considered a "minimally ethical agent" or someone who seeks to realize the "highest good" of the profession. Whether acting as an individual or as a representative of a firm, each archaeologist should realistically consider this question and critically examine his or her own work.

The issue of ethics comes into play in many ways in CRM archaeology. Is it ethical to reduce prices to "stay competitive" to the point that it is questionable whether the archaeological work undertaken is worth the effort? Is it ethical to reduce the level of investigation and research conducted simply to win a contract? Although SHPO staff and other reviewers attempt, through the review of scopes of work and mitigation plans, to ensure that high-quality work is produced, they cannot address the issue of how well the work will be carried out. All too often, a well-developed work scope is turned over to a low-bid contractor for execution, only to yield a disappointing final product or none at all. Although low-bid pricing makes a project applicant happy, the results of the work usually reflect the cut-rate price. As in any business transaction, "you get what you pay for."

Unfortunately, in CRM archaeology there often is no opportunity to revise the work if it is found to be substandard, especially when it comes to mitigation efforts. Many development projects are underway or completed and the site is destroyed long before a final archaeological report is produced. In some cases with federal agency involvement, the agency can take actions to address such situations, as when the Army Corps of Engineers withdraws a permit or withholds funding, suspending a project until the issue has been addressed. Many state and local preservation laws do not provide the same opportunity. For example, under New York's State Environmental Quality Review Act (SEQRA), a municipality, acting as the lead agency, must make a determination about whether a project will negatively affect the environment. Mitigation measures can be developed and agreed to as part of this process, resulting in a finding that "no adverse impact" will take place, on the condition that archaeological work is carried out. Unfortunately, if the condition is not met, it is up to the town to decide how to proceed, and in many cases, the town is reluctant to take action or unsure how to do so.

The issue of balancing cost and competitiveness is often identified as a major reason for not upgrading tools and techniques. Yet, investment in technological advances can result in major cost savings in the long run. For example, the use of advances in mapping technology has become common practice for many firms. The necessary practices of survey and mapping are basic to data collection on every archaeological project. Innovations for collecting data points in the field have involved a progression from optical transits to total stations and laser-based devices, which were widely available by the late 1990s, and GPS systems, which are widely available today. As each of these innovations became available, the time required to collect information in the field and create finished maps was greatly reduced, and so were a project's potential costs. Data processing advances have ranged from the introduction of CADD computer programs nearly 20 years ago to today's GIS systems for producing maps and querying data. Each of these systems has required initial investments in both money and time in order to be used effectively, but in the long run, the true cost savings on every future project has been well worth the investment. Despite this, many consultants continue to spend countless hours hand-producing maps and collecting data in the field using transits or even more primitive techniques (Brunton compass, triangulation with tapes). Although these older methods can be just as accurate as their high-tech counterparts, they are much more labor intensive and thus more costly. If a company truly wants to stay competitive, it is worthwhile to plan for investment in technological advances such as these. Staying current with advances in the field is not only good business. Because CRM is a scientifically based profession, it is also ethically responsible to use the best techniques available.

Related to the issue of balancing cost and competition is the inability of many firms to meet contractual deadlines. Is it ethical to undercut a competitor's price if you will be unable to meet the deadlines of a project? When consultants who are chronically late with reports are asked for explanations, the typical answer is that the volume of work has simply been too heavy and their resources are stretched too thin. These are often the same companies that keep staff levels low, submit low bids on requests for proposals, and have difficulty attracting and retaining advanced-level professional staff. This is a business model designed for failure. Although there is a need for a project sponsor to balance the cost of archaeology within an overall project, that cost is a legitimate expense for a company in the business of development. By advocating for the developer's cost concerns at the expense of good archaeology, some CRM firms do not give their own businesses a chance to succeed and become economically viable. Their solution is to continue to expect archaeologists to work for low wages and for the love of the field. This attitude devalues the profession of archaeology as a whole and is one of the leading factors that keep archaeologists from being viewed on a par with engineers, environmental scientists, and other professionals in the environmental review process. When archaeology becomes established as a legitimate, regulated profession and archaeologists are seen as professionals having value and purpose, developers will stop asking, "Why do we have to do this?" and the general population will be more likely to support archaeological issues.

Each archaeologist has an ethical responsibility to other members of the profession to act professionally and in a manner that helps to advance the field. One of the major obstacles to a perception of CRM archaeology as a legitimate profession by those outside our community is the lack of a license or certification that carries true meaning. Although this issue has been discussed many times and the Register of Professional Archaeologists ("the Register") has been established as a vehicle for resolving it, archaeology still has no true process for establishing that a practitioner has proven his or her ability to complete professional work in a CRM context. We often interact with licensed professionals such as engineers and architects, who must always be vigilant in performance and practice in order to maintain their licenses. Archaeologists have little incentive other than personal pride and satisfaction to strive for excellence in their work.

In the absence of some form of certification or licensing, it is necessary for archaeologists to police their own practices and ethics. The Register has been proposed as a body that can provide some industry self-regulation,

addressing ethical concerns and also guarding against unfounded accusa-
tions of misconduct (Clay 2006). The Register has recently shown that it is
willing to take action in the most egregious of cases (McGimsey, Eisenberg,
and Doershunk 2003). However, not all archaeologists are registered, and
registration is not required in many jurisdictions. Although the Register
will consider any credible grievance against a registered professional
archaeologist (an RPA) and follows a detailed grievance process, historically it has not acknowledged that any action has been taken against an
RPA unless extensive violations of its Code of Conduct and Standards have
been proved. Therefore, it remains up to archaeologists to self-monitor
their practices and ethics. This leaves us open to criticism, often well
deserved.

Further development of the Register program may help to address this
issue. It will be necessary, however, for review agencies to incorporate the
need for RPA registration into their standards. At present, many agencies
do not see the value of this because they are not fully aware of the Register
and the range of actions it can take when a grievance is brought, or the
effectiveness of its actions in addressing problems. It is important for the
Register to become more visible, to publicize all actions it takes, and to be
widely seen as an effective organization before agencies will look to the
RPA designation as a way to ensure quality and ethical work.

The Register may also be able to raise its status among agencies by
developing a program for archaeologists' continuing education and professional development. Unlike many other professionals, CRM archaeologists have no formal system of continuing education to ensure that
practitioners refresh their knowledge and update their skills as new technologies are developed. Development of a continuing education system
would be helpful in establishing CRM archaeology as a profession on a par
with other licensed professions. Although developing such a system and
establishing the collaborative agreements with educational institutions necessary to create successful programs would be major undertakings, they
should be considered for the future. Several existing organizations have
the potential to support such efforts, including the Register of Professional
Archaeologists and the Society for American Archaeology (SAA). These
organizations should be encouraged to make such a system a priority as
part of any attempt to establish a successful certification process.

Adding a continuing education component to the requirements for
RPA certification would help to ensure that RPAs update their skills as
new technologies become available and would provide a way to document
professional development. In the late 1990s, the SAA established a Post

Graduate Education/Professional Development Working Group, which examined the role of continuing education and found the following:

> It is incumbent on the profession to identify and develop opportunities for all professional archaeologists to acquire, maintain, and update their knowledge and skills to keep abreast of changing sociopolitical and technological contexts. To encourage all practicing archaeologists to become lifelong learners, professional societies must encourage through various incentives the participation of their members in continuing education opportunities, such as courses, workshops, attendance at conferences, publications, and guides to resources. These professional development opportunities should be rigorous and continually evaluated and updated to be consistent with the guidelines offered by the ethical principles and "best practices" identified by the discipline. (Messenger et al. 1999)

In response to these recommendations, the SAA has sponsored professional development workshops at its annual meetings in recent years, but these opportunities are limited in scope and in the number of persons able to attend. Many more opportunities for professional development exist through local and regional workshops provided at various organizational meetings, as well as through university-based, agency-provided, or even privately offered classes and workshops. However, there is still no process that provides credit for completing this type of training. Development of a means of providing credit for training and deciding which opportunities to provide credit for would give the Register a strong tool for meeting several of its goals and for convincing review agencies that RPA certification is meaningful and worth using as a measure of professional competency. By using opportunities already offered by a host of organizations, the Register would not have to create its own classes and workshops but would have only to consider those submitted by either the providing organization or participants to determine whether they provided the claimed training. Initially, even this would be a large task, but after a short period, a list of approved opportunities would be developed and could be advertised to those seeking continued education. The continuing development of electronic means of communication and distance learning will make this process easier because participants will be able to take classes held at distant locations and the Register will be able to evaluate opportunities for inclusion in the program without having to send representatives to each location. I encourage the Register, working with the SAA and other interested organizations, to make development of a continuing education program a priority in the near future.

The Value of Archaeological Research

If the larger society is to see CRM archaeology as having value, it is important to ensure that such research truly adds to people's understanding of the past. Canouts (1977) argued that archaeological surveys should be progressive, in that each work stage should be based on the results of earlier stages. She highlighted the importance of keeping the work of other researchers in mind when developing strategies and of cooperation between archaeologists to ensure that work conducted provides as much research data as possible. Although Canouts was considering large-scale Section 106 projects, the same concerns must be applied to the CRM field as a whole, including small projects in which only one or two sites may be identified. These sites are still part of the greater regional story, and work conducted on them becomes part of the whole on which a regional understanding can be developed. Research provides the cumulative basis for all subsequent projects, and this concept must be kept in mind at all times. It is essential that research be done in a way that truly adds to regional understanding, that research become part of a larger effort to understand the past, and that scopes of research and hypotheses not be so narrowly defined that they fail to provide useful data beyond the current study. Ortman, Varien, and Gripp (2007), in their consideration of the populations of Mesa Verde, provided a recent example of the way information from small projects can be combined to look at larger regional questions.

One problem CRM archaeologists face is that much of the data they generate is unpublished and difficult to access. Ortman and colleagues had the advantage of working in an area that has seen much publication, but in many other areas, the generated data are located in unpublished technical reports and are more difficult to access. King (chapter 7, this volume) discusses this issue in detail and offers some suggestions on how the electronic age may bring new solutions to this long-standing problem.

Archaeological research and data can also be seen as having significant value when they are connected to non-archaeological applications. More than 30 years ago, in the early days of CRM archaeology, Dixson (1977) discussed a variety of non-archaeological applications of archaeological data: long-range planning for the fishing industry; marine mammal studies; examination of climate change and weather history; studies of floodplain origin and development; studies of soil genesis and management; studies of disease, agricultural productivity, pollution, and geological phenomena; and medicine. As identified in the principles developed by the SAA Committee on Curriculum Reform (Bender and Smith 1998; Davis et al. 1999), archaeologists need to be aware of the diverse interest groups that have claims to archaeological knowledge, identify how archaeology is socially relevant, and effectively articulate the ways in which it benefits society.

Providing data applicable to other fields has reciprocal benefits for archaeology as well. Developing links to other fields is essential for building interdisciplinary research teams and creating new ways to examine archaeological questions. Further, increased awareness of archaeology and its research value helps to establish greater support for future research. Dixson argued that by making such connections, we could increase support for archaeological resource conservation. She hoped to illustrate potential ways to foster a consensus in the general public for the conservation of archaeological sites.

Although archaeological data have been used in interdisciplinary studies during the years since Dixson's article, the need to foster a better understanding outside the profession of the role of archaeological research and the need to conserve sites have remained constant. As a profession, we have not been very successful at communicating this. We still consistently face the questions of why archaeological research is important and what the value of archaeology is.

We are also asked why tax money or a developer's private funds should be spent on work that has no value to the rest of society. Minnis (2006) considered this question in a recent volume of the *SAA Archaeological Record*, in which he related that the question often stumped his graduate students. Clearly, we have not done as good a job at making the connections to the larger world as Dixson called for in 1977. Minnis, hoping to start a conversation about this topic, put the question to a number of his colleagues in the Society for American Archaeology. As he expected, respondents offered different reasons for the importance of archaeological research. They mentioned archaeology's ability to provide a perspective on history, as well as opportunities and information for tourism, the importance of heritage to modern societies, the importance of the science addressed by archaeologists, and the discipline's ability to help people understand systems that have developed independently in many places, such as urbanism, states, religion, literacy, and agriculture, and even to understand universal concepts of humanity.

Another answer referenced the recognition by the US Congress, in passing the NHPA, of the cultural, educational, aesthetic, and inspirational benefits of the study of the past. Still another focused on the ability of archaeology to provide a better understanding of contemporary ecosystems and to identify sustainable subsistence practices. The unique ability of archaeology to provide a temporal component to such studies was also seen as an important factor.

Van der Leeuw and Redman (2002) considered the importance of archaeology in "socio-natural" studies and argued that the future of archaeology was to work with the other natural and ecological sciences toward a better understanding of how humans have affected Earth's ecology in the past and how they might in the future. They identified this "transdisciplinary approach" as necessary for archaeology to be successful.

It seems that archaeology has gone full circle over the course of 30 years. Although the specific issues seen as illustrating the worth of archaeology to the general public may have changed, the need for interdisciplinary or transdisciplinary studies remains crucial. Many such interdisciplinary studies have been undertaken by our academic colleagues, but aside from large-scale projects, CRM work is less likely to incorporate interdisciplinary research. In part, this is because of the limited budgets and time frames of CRM research; it is impossible to expect every project to incorporate a wide range of interdisciplinary specialties. But we should encourage their use whenever possible and look for opportunities to incorporate a wider range of research in innovative ways. Chandler (chapter 6, this volume) considers the question of alternative mitigation approaches. As she points out, opportunities arise to develop mitigation measures beyond the typical large-scale excavations we are used to seeing. The incorporation of appropriate interdisciplinary studies that might add more to our understanding of history than a standard large-scale excavation is one possibility. It is difficult to provide specific guidance on this approach because each project and its research potential needs to be evaluated independently, but we should be aware that this approach is available as an alternative and has tremendous potential for examining new types of data as we gain a greater understanding of the past.

Most CRM studies concentrate only on what can be found within the area of potential effects (APE) for a particular project. Research is restricted to whatever can be done while keeping project costs minimal. Frequently, research is focused on issues that a particular archaeological consultant can address in-house, instead of considering what additional research potentials a site might have and reaching out to researchers or subconsultants with experience or interest in those topics. The approach of directing most work toward limited internal resources and minimizing or restricting possible partnerships with outside professionals has been a hindrance rather than a help to the advancement of CRM archaeology.

If we are to successfully redress the perception of CRM archaeology as a second-class science, we must ensure that our research is useful to a broad spectrum of interest groups and has broad value. Although it is easy to identify the advantages of broadening our research goals, the reality of the CRM world is that all too often we have insufficient time and money to address such goals. Unlike our academic-oriented colleagues, CRM archaeologists must be able to develop and implement research goals based on the sites available for investigation at the moment. A form of alternative mitigation that might address this issue is to look for opportunities to examine how a site or series of sites fits into a regional history. This scenario would see less emphasis on new excavation and more on developing contexts for a site or series of sites that make use of the mountains of data already collected elsewhere—perhaps using new excavations to test the conclusions. This approach should be familiar to archaeologists because it represents an application of the scientific method and is in line with traditional academic-based archaeology. In CRM archaeology, this approach has seldom been used, in large part because many projects are small and focused only on what can be found in a particular project area. It will take a shift in our understanding of the best way to use the extensive funds available through CRM research to provide the best overall data for the efforts expended.

What are some strategies we can employ to attain broader research goals? First, each of us must be as current as possible regarding other research being conducted by both CRM and academically oriented researchers. By being alert to research projects already in process, we can link to that research, both by providing additional data for those projects and by incorporating their results as part of our own analyses. When this approach is taken, it is often possible to subcontract with researchers who are already involved in such projects, expanding the level of expertise on the CRM project.

Second, we must ensure that any research undertaken is useful and that the analyses consist of more than simple descriptions of the material recovered. Every project must strive to add something of importance to the record. This should not be considered a difficult goal to accomplish. In order for any site to be considered National Register eligible and subject to data recovery or mitigation work, the site must have the potential to add to our understanding of the past (Little et al. 2000). By identifying and addressing substantive research goals, every project should be able to provide some research outcome of significance. If examination of a site cannot produce such research, then most likely that site should not have been identified as National Register eligible, and the expense of the investigation should not have been incurred.

Third, we need to make a concerted effort, whenever possible, to build upon prior work and to ensure that new research is synthesized with previous work. Tremendous amounts of data have been and are being collected, but under our current direction, they are unlikely ever to be synthesized. No single project or individual is capable of synthesizing the existing information without a tremendous input of resources. However, local and regional synthesis as part of individual CRM projects is a first and important step toward more comprehensive syntheses. A goal of any CRM project should be to add something to this process.

To accomplish any of these strategies, researchers must keep current on the work of their colleagues. There are several ways to accomplish this, including attending regional meetings, regularly reviewing journals, developing connections with CRM and academic colleagues, and reading the CRM reports of other firms. Firms should be encouraged to make it a regular practice to share their work with regional colleagues. The technology available today makes this a relatively effortless and inexpensive goal to achieve. Using the portable document file (PDF) format, anyone can create multiple electronic copies of reports of any size for the cost of the blank CDs. By distributing our work to our colleagues, all of us can keep abreast of ongoing research and the development and implementation of new technological advances and laboratory methods. Such sharing of information has the added benefit of increasing communication between researchers and can serve as an informal type of peer review.

Being successful at each of these strategies will help to raise awareness of and respect for the field of archaeology and to create a feedback loop. Better work leads to better outreach, which leads to better understanding and awareness, which leads to greater support for archaeological investigation.

SCIENCE VERSUS MANAGEMENT: EAST VERSUS WEST?

During our seminar discussions at the School for Advanced Research, participants continually noted that many aspects of the way archaeology is practiced vary between the western states and the eastern states. Differences exist in survey methods, levels of support, and facilities available for curation, among other things. At first look, this seemed to be an East–West split, but as the discussion continued, we came to an understanding that the differences were actually attributable to the way federal agencies were involved in archaeological research. Some agencies, such as the Bureau of Land Management and the National Park Service, are primarily land management agencies, responsible for extensive tracts of federal land and the large inventories of historic resources on that land. Other agencies, such as the Natural Resources Conservation Service, the Army Corps of Engineers, and the Environmental Protection Agency, are more likely to be permitting projects on private land and less likely to need to manage historic resources on their own land. This dichotomy can be seen as an East–West divide because federal land holdings are so large in the West and much smaller in the East.

This dichotomy can also lead to differences in perceptions of the goals of archaeological research. Among land management agencies, primary goals for archaeology are to identify and manage sites, determine how they can be protected over the long term, design projects to give significant sites a wide berth, and develop long-term plans to enhance site preservation. Under this model, a primary goal of any work is long-term management of *West* the resources, keeping them available for scientific study sometime down the road. This model seems to fit the concept of cultural resource management very well. Unfortunately, the same model of archaeological research cannot be used by non–land management agencies. In areas where the majority of work is done under federal permits for actions on private land, *East* it is impossible to develop long-range planning goals or programs of resource protection or to guarantee that sites will be available for future research. Although agencies in these situations still need to make good-faith efforts to identify sites and minimize adverse effects to them, the projects under consideration often cannot be modified to avoid damage altogether, and after the current project is completed, there is no way to ensure that the site will not be damaged later by nonpermitted actions. Therefore, archaeological work in these areas must focus more on accessing the site information now, not planning for possible future research.

Some people suggest that even in these areas, CRM archaeologists should do no more than gather the data—to pull the material from the ground and count artifacts—leaving the real scientific investigation to someone else to come later. I believe that this is not management of the resource in accordance with the regulations, but rather an approach that simply ends up creating large collections of questionable value. The need to develop and address significant research questions must be integral to any advanced study. Focusing on research questions helps to determine one's field methods, what will be collected, how it will be collected, and how it will be examined. Without a detailed research goal, archaeologists would simply be collecting everything possible, putting it on a shelf, and hoping that someone, someday, will make use of it. By focusing only on low-level data analysis and synthesis, it is unlikely that CRM archaeologists would ever make any significant finds, ultimately validating the lamented dichotomy between academic and CRM archaeology that is so often used to suggest that CRM archaeology is a lower form of the profession.

A CALL FOR INCREASED PEER REVIEW

Although some peer review is possible through the Section 106 process, in practice it does not always occur. Many federal land-managing agencies, such as the Bureau of Land Management and the National Park Service, have staff archaeologists who review draft work scopes and reports before sending them on to the SHPO for comment. However, most federal non–land managing or permitting agencies, such as the Department of Health, the Environmental Protection Agency, and the Army Corps of Engineers, do not employ archaeological staff and handle a tremendous volume of projects, making serious peer review unlikely. Typically, reports on undertakings associated with these agencies arrive at the state historic preservation office as initial drafts, and although SHPO staff attempt to review them closely, in reality the overwhelming project volume makes it difficult to review every report in detail. Additionally, many areas have state or local equivalents to the National Historic Preservation Act and the National Environmental Policy Act that provide no mechanism for peer review. As a result, true peer review within the context of the project review process is infeasible for a large portion of CRM-related work. Despite this limitation, most researchers seem to agree that peer review is an excellent idea and a helpful tool for improving the quality of archaeological research (Keel et al. 2007).

I would encourage voluntary peer review outside the compliance process. Such efforts would be helpful in identifying and establishing regional research issues, developing contacts between practitioners, and fostering ongoing communication. The distribution of electronic copies of reports to colleagues could be a first step in this process, although it would not guarantee that peer responses would be provided. To attain the goals I have outlined, it would be helpful to formalize a system of voluntary peer review to ensure that responses are developed and returned to each author. Only through such feedback will the goals of increasing communication and developing more detailed research questions be met. Efforts to encourage peer review and establish voluntary systems should be made through state and regional professional organizations. By developing these systems, the organizations would be doing a great service to both their members and the future of archaeological research.

THE BUSINESS OF PROFESSIONAL CRM ARCHAEOLOGY

Perhaps one of the largest stumbling blocks to changing the public's perception of CRM archaeology and increasing the value of our research is the perceived lack of a "culture of professionalism" across the discipline. Although this perception may not exist within the profession, it is often met when dealing with the public and project applicants. Elements that contribute to this perception range from poor understanding of the complexities of relevant legislation to the physical appearance of field crews and widely varying fee schedules, which suggest that nearly anyone with a trowel can go into business as an archaeologist.

Although the underlying causes of such elements may seem wide ranging, many of them can actually be attributed to relatively few root problems. These include a lack of training in how to be a successful CRM archaeologist, a lack of understanding of basic business principles among most archaeologists, poor communication skills, and the perception that a master's degree adequately prepares a person for doing any type of archaeology. Many of these problems can be traced back to the long-standing questions, should there be more focus on CRM archaeology in graduate programs, and if so, how should the topic be addressed? I leave these questions for others to consider; they are too large to address adequately here. However, another training consideration is the need to understand how to operate a successful business. Just as it is important to create a fully developed and realistic research plan before beginning any project, so it is important to develop a sound business plan before offering services to others. Unfortunately, all too often archaeologists do not receive the proper training or guidance to be successful at business ventures. Many currently existing firms have sought the knowledge necessary to run a successful business and have prospered despite a lack of initial training; many others, which did not find the proper help, have failed.

In the early days of CRM, the world was a different place, and many archaeologists, even without good backgrounds in business, were able to succeed because there was little competition, little regulation, and a wide open market for our services. Today there are many more archaeologists vying for work, many more regulations to consider, and a growing sense that we need to be seen as serious professionals, equivalent in all ways to our licensed counterparts.

A Business Model for Consulting CRM Archaeology

The following business model is presented as a suggestion for creating a successful archaeological venture and for helping to raise the professional standards of the field. The model is designed to be flexible and applicable to firms of all sizes. It was developed on the basis of my years of personal experience in a wide range of firms, both successful and unsuccessful, as well as discussions with the founders of several successful and long-established firms, including a past president of the American Cultural Resources Association (ACRA). I am grateful to these people for their input, but ultimately the following model represents my own thoughts about how to develop a successful business. Many of today's successful CRM archaeologists have already developed similar models through experience. Although this type of discussion is rarely presented in archaeological literature, it is extremely relevant to the CRM archaeologist of today.

Establish Goals

Each firm has its goals or direction. Some provide a wide range of services to a wide range of clients. Others are specific in the types of projects they undertake (for example, underwater and urban settings) or the products they wish to produce (for example, field studies, curriculum development, laboratory analyses, and historic records searches). Whatever a company's goals are, they should be well defined and consistently maintained.

Develop the Right Team

No single person has the ability or expertise in all areas to be successful alone. It is imperative to assemble a team that is capable of addressing any potential issue, whether field, laboratory, or business related (fig. 9.1). First and foremost, the team needs to include people with the necessary expertise to carry out the research goals identified. For example, if historic sites are to be a focus of research, then the team must include someone who is well versed in sites of that time period. Although this person might also have training in basic archaeological techniques that can be applied to early prehistoric sites, it would be inappropriate for the historic specialist to be in charge of research on a Paleoindian site.

This model does not suggest that every firm employ full-time specialists in every aspect of archaeological research, but rather that a firm have the ability to add pieces to address specific issues as they arise. It is not unusual for firms to hire subconsultants to address specific laboratory analyses such as faunal and botanical studies. It is less common for a firm to employ subconsultants to address specific field research issues, but field

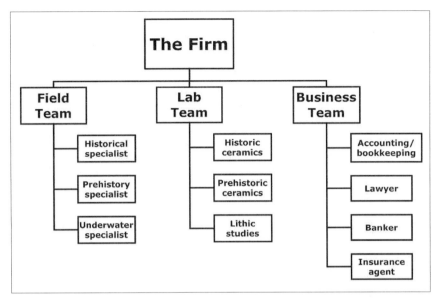

FIGURE 9.1

Sample organization for CRM firms. Not all the positions shown need be in-house employees.
Depending on the size of the firm, various positions can be contracted on a fee-for-services basis.

programs must include provisions for adding subconsultants when their expertise would be an advantage.

Although most archaeologists would agree with this in concept, the reality is that firms are often in direct competition with one another and unwilling to seek such subconsulting arrangements. Yet, an increase in this type of joint research would be a positive outcome for everyone involved. The data collected can be better used, the understanding of the past may be enhanced, and, by collaborating, all the archaeologists involved will gain experience both on topics that might not be their specialty and in developing connections that might prove useful for future projects.

A stumbling block to this model of developing networks for enhancing research is likely to be the difficulty of keeping staff members updated on the research interests and experience of other archaeologists when each is deeply involved in his or her own work. This obstacle can easily be overcome. Cooperative research can be supported by the development of regional databases that supply information on colleagues, their areas of expertise, and their research interests. I encourage state and regional organizations to develop these databases, and I encourage each archaeologist to become involved. In 2001 the New York Archaeological Council attempted to create such a "resource list" with the goals of facilitating cooperative research and helping to identify public speakers for various topics and locations. Unfortunately, only 11 members of the organization (fewer than 10 percent) responded, and the effort was not followed up. We must all take the responsibility not only to encourage the sharing of our expertise but also to ensure that in preparing our own research designs, we look for opportunities to include the specialties of others where they are appropriate. By combining the appropriate resources for a particular job, we can create an outcome that is beneficial to all parties involved and that results in a more professional image of the field in the public's eye.

Even a wide range of archaeological specialists, however, makes up only a portion of the team needed for a successful business. The team also needs to include lawyers, accountants, attorneys, bookkeeping staff, bankers, and even an insurance agent. Again, it is unnecessary to have each of these other types of persons on staff, but a firm must have solid relationships with specialists who can be called upon as needed. All too often, a failure to address these non-archaeological aspects of business creates problems even for a firm well set up for archaeological issues. By developing a team that includes people knowledgeable in these other areas, the archaeologists are free to focus on research and analysis of archaeological data.

Easily accessible national, state, and regional resources exist that are designed to help small businesses identify and address a variety of concerns. For example, the United States Small Business Administration (USSBA) helps small businesses through a network of state and regional organizations. Details about and contact information for these organizations can be found at the USSBA Web site, www.sba.gov. Additional information and links to useful Web sites can be found through the ACRA Web site, at www.acra-crm.org. (Click on ACRA Business Toolkit.) Also, ACRA offers training in business management and other business topics to both members and nonmembers, and it has undertaken other studies that can help CRM practitioners consider important topics such as salary levels, overhead, and profit margins and how they vary across the country.

Invest in the Team

Good team members are the most valuable assets of any organization. In order to remain successful in the long term, it is important to invest in and support the team in a variety of ways. Although some forms of support are readily apparent—for example, good pay rates and benefits such as health insurance, sick leave, paid vacation time, and retirement programs

—other forms of support can be just as important in assembling and maintaining a good team. Support for continued education and other professional development can have a cumulative positive effect. Not only will team members feel supported, but also the increased knowledge and expertise they bring back to the team will improve the firm's ability to succeed. Supporting conference presentations and publications on research in local, regional, and national venues can go a long way toward encouraging team members to be active in the larger archaeological community and thereby increase the firm's visibility and standing in the community.

Be a Useful Resource for the Client

It is imperative that a firm's personnel be knowledgeable about pertinent cultural resource legislation, agency review procedures, and potential issues involved with any project. Be prepared to give clients the soundest advice possible, even if it is not what they want to hear. By advocating strongly for resource preservation and significant research efforts in discussions with clients, a firm prepares clients for the sometimes difficult decisions that must be made. Failure to prepare a client in this way ultimately leads to anger on the client's part when a review agency recommends more work than the firm initially represented. It is in clients' best interest in the long run to know the potential scope of archaeological work so that they can adequately schedule their projects and budget for expenses.

A successful firm should also be ready to lose a client if good advice is not heeded or if the client is making requests that put the archaeologist in an ethical bind. Although it is not the job of an archaeological consultant to save every site, it is an ethical obligation to provide sound advice based on scientific observations and full knowledge of the applicable regulations.

Develop Professional Contacts Outside Archaeology

It is important to identify ways in which a firm and its members can become part of the larger corporate community. These can include sponsoring events, taking leadership roles in relevant organizations, and attending events that will help develop contacts beyond the archaeological community. Becoming involved in the larger community has several advantages. Increased interaction will make a team more visible and provide opportunities to connect with potential clients and maintain relations with prior clients. Additionally, by networking with community, business, and preservation organizations, a firm's personnel gain a greater understanding of the wide range of interested communities and their concerns. This knowledge can ultimately better prepare the firm to develop solutions that are acceptable to multiple parties. Finally, networking is the best way to gain new clients who will respect your work as a professional.

Numerous opportunities to develop these types of business networks exist in almost every community. Local chapters of national and international service organizations such as the Kiwanis Club, the Rotary Club, the Benevolent and Protective Order of Elks, and the Lions Club provide significant opportunities to network. Other organizations, such as business improvement districts (BIDs), business trade groups, and chambers of commerce, provide opportunities to develop potential clients and to raise the awareness of a firm in the community. At a broader level, organizations such as the American Cultural Resources Association provide materials, information, and workshops for their members on a variety of business-related topics, including networking. Using some combination of these resources can be an important factor in raising the status of an archaeological firm in the community.

Be Media Aware

Become adept at using media outlets, Web sites, and other venues to educate the public and increase enthusiasm for archaeological issues. Be aware of changing technologies and how the public is using them to access news and recreational information. Be sure that at least one team member has knowledge about how to use such outlets. Crass (chapter 11, this volume) discusses this topic in greater detail and suggests a number of approaches that all CRM archaeologists should take into consideration.

Let Your Business Make a Profit

When developing cost estimates and contracts, be aware of market conditions. It is important to understand issues such as what constitutes a fair price for the work proposed, including reasonable markups for overhead and profit. The latter costs are part of doing business and are accepted as a given in all other industries. However, many archaeologists and the people who hire them seem to expect archaeologists to work for no profit. As a result, many CRM firms find themselves always on the verge of needing the next job to stay in business. To be successful, any business needs to consider whether the proposed work can realistically be completed with the resources and time provided and whether the work produced will be of acceptable quality. CRM firms that leave little profit margin need to take on too many jobs at once to make ends meet. Consequently, quality suffers and the firm's business reputation and credibility decline. The use of good business sense in preparing cost estimates allows intelligent growth of a firm, the retention of qualified and knowledgeable staff, and the completion of projects in a timely fashion.

CONCLUSION

Using good business sense, conducting research useful to a wide range of audiences, and truly increasing knowledge of the past through the development of more detailed historical contexts can only result in a more professional image of CRM archaeology as a whole and increased support from the general public for archaeological research. The field has grown rapidly over the past 30 years and has faced some trying periods. As we look forward to the next 30 years, we have the opportunity to mature into a true profession and to take our place among the well-recognized professions with which we interact. In order to realize our full potential, it will be necessary to look beyond our day-to-day dealings and consider how we are perceived by the outside world. We have the ability to mature successfully, and we should eagerly anticipate discovering what the future holds with regard to study of the past.

APPENDIX

NCSHPO/NASA Questionnaire

A short questionnaire was sent to all members of the National Council of State Historic Preservation Offices (NCSHPO) and the National Association of State Archaeologists (NASA) via e-mail in order to stimulate written responses. The questions were meant not as a poll but rather as a starting point for any thoughts respondents might have on the issues. The goal of the inquiry was to consider the concept of "How do we move beyond doing the same old thing?" The questionnaire asked:

1. Are you happy with the general quality of work you see—is it really contributing to the field of archaeology, or does it seem to be aimed at meeting a minimalist standard? What do you think needs to change?
2. Have you seen the use of innovative approaches? If yes, how and when are they applied? If not, why not?
3. Have you been successful in encouraging (or even tried to encourage) new approaches/understandings?
4. As a central review place, our office sees the full spectrum of approaches being utilized. We try to disseminate this information to other firms in the state—with mixed results. Do you take a similar approach, and what kind of success have you had in this vein?

5. Are you aware of any other studies that have looked at this question?
6. What would you like to see change?
7. Any other thoughts?

State University of New York Programs

Archaeology professors with CRM experience at the four State University of New York University Centers (Albany, Binghamton, Buffalo, and Stony Brook) were asked a series of questions to gather information on the relationship between CRM and more traditional academic archaeology at their institutions.

1. Describe what kind of support you receive from other staff.
2. Are your more academic-focused colleagues interested in having their students learn about CRM?
3. What kinds of courses are available that are focused on CRM topics?
4. Do you have any thoughts on what could be done to alleviate the apparent split between academic and CRM archaeology in your setting?

Acknowledgments

In preparing this chapter, I sought the comments of many archaeologists and agency personnel. All interpretations presented here are my own, but I thank everyone who provided input into the preceding discussion. All views presented in the chapter are mine and do not represent the opinion of the New York State Office of Parks, Recreation, and Historic Preservation.

10

Archaeology and Ethics

Is There a Shared Vision for the Future?

Sarah T. Bridges

Today archaeology is practiced in an array of venues, many of them without the traditional ties to academia or government. During the past 30 years, the profession's expansion into new, applied arenas has been accompanied by an increasing range of ethical standards, principles, and values. These codes and statements are the products of national, regional, and state archaeological professional and membership organizations, academic institutions, environmental and trade organizations, research institutions, and government agencies, to name just a few. The majority of American archaeologists are most familiar with the ethical principles reviewed, updated, approved, and published by the Society for American Archaeology, or SAA (2007).

In this chapter, I review a range of the dominant national ethical standards and principles and recent interpretive literature on archaeological ethics, and I suggest that certain basic values crosscut our diverse profession and the publics we serve. The results may not be revolutionary, but I look at the current collaboration and coalescence that may help strengthen public archaeology and cultural resource management (CRM). Recognition of these shared values should benefit not only the archaeological resource base but also the interests of professional practitioners and concerned communities and publics. Additionally, a few serious questions emerge: Does archaeology have a shared vision of ethical thought and behavior that is relevant for practitioners in the future? If not, are we able to achieve a shared vision that is both rigorous and flexible? Is this vision moving toward a "virtue ethic," as Chip Colwell-Chanthaphonh and T. J. Ferguson (2004) have termed it, grounded in a collaborative environment of civic responsibility (Little and Shackel 2007)?

BACKGROUND

In 1977 the editors of *The Management of Archeological Resources: The Airlie House Report* (McGimsey and Davis 1977) predicted that cultural resource management would change the nature and practice of professional archaeology in certain expected and other unexpected ways. The Airlie House report noted a past and then-current crisis in American archaeology (Davis 1972), precipitated by massive, publicly funded, urban and rural development programs during the 30 years before the Airlie House seminar.[1] These landscape-altering programs created a sense of urgency in the profession and its supportive public to preserve and shelter archaeological resources and the information they contained from accelerating attrition and outright destruction. Protective strategies, enabled by federal and state laws and regulations, focused on preemptive excavation (salvage) or exploitation of the resource base.

Soon the archaeological profession recognized that this salvage strategy, coupled with large-scale and incremental landscape destruction and infrastructure development, threatened the entire archaeological resource base. As William Lipe (1974) observed, a broader conservation ethic emerged. This more comprehensive view reflected archaeologists' growing concern for the total nonrenewable resource base and incorporated society's concern for the broader human environment, including the cultural environment, as expressed in the National Historic Preservation Act (NHPA) of 1966, in the National Environmental Protection Act (NEPA) of 1969, and by other authorities (see Sebastian, chapter 1, this volume). Lipe (1974:214) wrote at the time that "a focus on resource conservation leads us to a position of responsibility for the whole resource base. We must actively begin to take steps to ensure that this resource base lasts as long as possible. Only if we are successful in slowing down the rate of site loss can the field of archaeology continue to evolve over many generations and thereby realize its potential contributions to science, the humanities, and society."

Cultural resource management emerged, adapted, and grew to be an affirmative collaboration among archaeological scientists, governmental entities, others who owned or controlled the land containing the resource base, and the benefiting public. Charles McGimsey and Hester Davis (1977:41) wrote that the field of CRM recognized increasingly diversified sponsor–archaeologist–public relationships and "opened up whole new dimensions of inquiry and responsibility for archaeologists." They wrote, "For the first time archaeologists have begun unifying their efforts to develop systematic regional plans [to meet] present and future scientific needs" and in doing so are "also [meeting] legal requirements under existing legislation" (1977:41). CRM archaeology had responsibilities for expanding scholarly research, making wise recommendations to management and sponsors regarding resource protection and treatment, and protecting the cultural environment for the benefit of contemporary and future generations.

During the 1960s and early 1970s, as archaeologists deliberated over these diversifying responsibilities, the SAA and other national organizations explored strategies for strengthening professional standards and accreditation. As Davis noted (1982:158), the SAA Executive Committee worked for years to provide archaeologists with guidance on ethics, but "the time was not right...and the matter lay dormant" until 1974. In that year, the SAA's Committee on Certification recommended the formation of a National Register of Professional Archaeologists (NRPA) and drafted a proposed set of by-law changes for the SAA that outlined types of membership and recommended the use of extant SAA standards of conduct (Davis 1982:158–159; Lipe and Lindsay 1974; McGimsey and Davis 1977:101–105).

Between 1974 and 1976, SAA committee deliberations focused on the nature, structure, and operation of the NRPA and concerns about the effects of the register's formation on the tax status of the SAA (McGimsey and Davis 1977:100–101). In 1976 the SAA Interim Committee on Standards (with representation from six national archaeological organizations) determined a need for action and formed the Society of Professional Archaeologists (SOPA), an independent, stand-alone organization to serve as an association of professional practitioners in North America (Brose 1983:817; Davis 1982:159; Lipe, personal communication, 2008). SOPA defined standards and professional qualifications and established two categories of affiliation: certified members and certification without membership. The purpose of SOPA was to define professionalism, develop standards to be used to measure acceptable performance, and provide a forum for discussing standards and performance. All certified archaeologists, members and nonmembers, agreed to adhere to SOPA's Code of Ethics,

Standards of Research Performance, Institutional Standards, and Basic Professional Characteristics as Promulgated by the Society of Professional Archeologists, which addressed individual and institutional responsibilities (see McGimsey and Davis 1977:97–105, 119–124). Both the NRPA concept and SOPA established a foundation for today's Register of Professional Archaeologists (RPA, "the Register"), founded in 1998; SOPA turned over its records and membership list to the Register.

The Register of Professional Archaeologists was not founded as a membership organization. It was designed to maintain and encourage standards of professional conduct in archaeology and provide for the registration of qualified archaeologists. It remains

> a listing of archaeologists who have agreed to abide by an explicit code of conduct and standards of research performance, who hold a graduate degree in archaeology, anthropology, art history, classics, history, or another germane discipline and who have substantial practical experience. Registration is a voluntary act that recognizes an individual's personal responsibility to be held accountable for [his or her] professional behavior. By formally acknowledging this relationship between personal actions and the wider discipline of archaeology, the act of registration is truly what sets the professional archaeologist apart from all others who are involved with or interested in archaeology. (RPA 2007)

The Register maintains a registry and a directory (available on its Web site, www.rpanet.org) that serve as tools for identifying and locating registered professional archaeologists (RPAs). The organization is distinguished by its education and outreach programs and its carefully controlled and formal grievance procedures. The latter employ investigation and pursue resolution through mediation of alleged violations of the code of conduct or standards of professional research. If these strategies do not work, then the Register's grievance committee follows up with formal review and possible expulsion of RPAs who have violated the code or standards (RPA 2007).

During the past 30 years, archaeologists, through their professional and membership organizations, have produced or participated in the production of, monitored, and updated institutional codes, standards of practice, laws, and international agreements and treaties designed to establish and promote modern ethical behavior. Over this period, such statements have changed to reflect responsibilities to an ever-expanding and diverse set of stakeholders. Simultaneously, there has been no dearth of analytical discourse on the complexity of the ethical issues archaeologists face. Most of the published works participating in this discourse, including the selection I discuss here, are timely and represent a balanced view of current and developing professional standards. Most analysts readily acknowledge a range of diverse ethical issues and principles that archaeologists must consider in their daily practice.

A quick review of a selection of these standards, the majority of which have been produced for archaeologists and anthropologists, reveals certain commonalities and basic responsibilities: attention to stewardship, accountability to one's specific professional reference group, accountability to various publics and clients, appropriate treatment and protection of archaeological sites and collections, and responsibility to use and share data with colleagues, community, and individual sources. A short list of some of the standards and principles and their Web locations is presented as an appendix to this chapter.

However, a review of selected literature produced during this period indicates quite diverse interpretations of and perspectives on these standards and a complexity of conflicting issues (see King 2008 for a thorough review of some of the most ubiquitous and difficult issues). This recalls the questions asked at the beginning of this chapter—Do archaeologists have a shared vision of ethical standards, and if not, can we achieve one?—and raises several others—Is self-regulation sufficient? Are there certain key principles shared by a majority of practitioners? How are these key principles ranked?

At present, a broad, shared view of ethical practice is developing that reflects a sense of civic responsibility to archaeological sites, data, and intellectual property. Increasingly, archaeologists recognize that they do not own the cultures they study or have exclusive rights to interpreting research data (see, among many others, Brown et al. 2006; Colwell-Chanthaphonh and Ferguson 2004; Scarre and Scarre 2006; Zimmerman, Vitelli, and Hollowell-Zimmer 2003). CRM archaeologists must often navigate, simultaneously, within several venues or communities of practice and reference; this shared view of civic responsibility should facilitate understanding and accommodation of differing perspectives.

Short histories of the Society for American Archaeology's standards and ethics statements by Charles McGimsey (2000), Alison Wylie (1995), and Mark Lynott (2000) clearly describe how perspectives have changed, dramatically, in less than 50 years. The SAA's first standards, published in 1961, focused on the definition of archaeology, adherence to appropriate archaeological methods, appropriate training for those entering careers in archaeology, and several ethical issues, including the need to serve and protect professional colleagues' and students' research, make records and data available to other scholars, and reject the marketing of artifacts and willful destruction of sites. Wylie suggested that the ethical standards even appeared to sanction hoarding of data and restricting access by anyone not involved in the original research and recovery. These were standards for a small and homogeneous community of practice.

Since then, archaeological membership organizations, nongovernmental and trade organizations, research institutes, and governmental agencies (federal, tribal, state, and local) have tried to keep pace with legal, societal, and resource concerns and have revised and updated their ethical and professional standards to reflect contemporary needs.[2]

Today and for the foreseeable future, archaeologists serve a much broader set of communities of practice and interaction. We are seeing considerable contemporary discourse about archaeologists' ethical responsibilities to engage stakeholder communities and to collaborate and even participate in the complex issues and programs of civic renewal or community action (Colwell-Chanthaphonh and Ferguson 2004:5–24; Ferguson, chapter 8, this volume; Little, 2007b:159–163). As Colwell-Chanthaphonh and Ferguson commented (2004:13–14), the line between the observers and the observed is blurring, perhaps disappearing.

WHAT DO CURRENT NATIONAL STANDARDS AND PRINCIPLES TELL US?

Many current ethical standards in archaeology and related fields are prescriptive or normative statements about what constitutes appropriate behavior and performance. Others are sets of suggestions that guide decision-making when one is faced with critical or complex questions. Most are voluntary, though some carry penalties, generally expulsion from the membership organization (for RPAs, removal from the registry) for certain unacceptable behaviors.

The American Anthropological Association's (AAA's) Code of Ethics (1998) provides members and other anthropologists with tools to make sound choices in an atmosphere of multiple responsibilities, involvements, and obligations within several venues of practice. In basic or clinical research, anthropological practitioners have responsibilities to people and animals with which they work, to people whose lives and cultures they study, to scholarship and science, and to the public. In teaching, anthropologists have ethical responsibilities to students and trainees and to their host institutions. In applied research, anthropologists are responsible to funders, colleagues, subjects, employers, staff, and the public. Applied anthropologists, who often work for public or business institutions outside the traditional venues, must also exercise caution in shaping or interpreting public policy and understand the consequences of doing so. The AAA also has the Statement of the Confidentiality of Field Notes.

The American Cultural Resources Association's (ACRA's) Code of Professional Conduct (1995) is designed as a guide to members and a vehicle to inform the public of the principles followed by members. The code acknowledges that members must follow proper legal and business practices. Members' behavior should adhere to principles of ethical conduct on behalf of the public, clients, employees, and professional colleagues. Members are to remain aware of the consequences of their work, present results of research to the public in an accurate manner, and support conservation for public benefit. An ACRA member is to serve the client honestly and accurately, understand the client's objectives and adhere to them if they are legal and in the public interest, fulfill contractual agreements, acknowledge the breadths and limits of professional competences, protect confidential information, and avoid conflicts of interest and disclosure of information for personal gain.

The Archaeological Institute of America's (AIA's) Code of Ethics (1997a) and Code of Professional Standards (1997b) call on members to ensure that exploration of sites employs the highest professional standards and is supervised by professionally qualified scholars who are dedicated to disseminating the results of the research. Members should refuse to participate in the trade of documented and undocumented antiquities and refrain from activities that enhance their value. Undocumented antiquities are those without documentation as part of a public or private collection before 1970, when the AIA endorsed the UNESCO Convention on Cultural Property. Members should also notify authorities of threats to or plunder of archaeological sites and the illegal import or export of archaeological materials.

The Register of Professional Archaeologists' Code of Conduct and Standards of Research Performance (1998) require people accepted to the registry to perform professionally, morally, honestly, and competently in behalf of the public, colleagues, employees and students, and employers and clients. The Code of Conduct addresses public benefits and explicitly lists performance expectations and prohibitions regarding professional commitment, conservation, respect for stakeholder communities, and trafficking of cultural property. Responsibilities to colleagues, employees, and students include appropriate attribution for work, dissemination of research results, sharing of data with colleagues, adherence to federal, state, and local laws, and adherence to the Register's Disciplinary Procedures. The code prohibits maligning colleagues and plagiarism. Responsibilities to employers and clients include respecting their interests as long as these do not conflict with the Register's code or the law, advising them of competency limits and recommending appropriate expertise, protecting confidential information, and refusing compensation for recommending additional experts.

The Register's Standards of Research Performance specify adequate preparation for any research project, adherence to scientific research plans, adherence to minimum field survey and excavation performance standards, employment of standard practices for making records, and protection of field data for future use by colleagues. Registered archaeologists must ensure that field and laboratory records correlate so that provenience information is protected as these materials are deposited in permanent curatorial facilities. They must ensure that collections and research records are appropriately curated, as permitted by law, and that research data and results are made accessible for future research.

The SAA's Principles of Archaeological Ethics (2007), first written and adopted in 1996, recognize the need for principles that archaeologists can use in "negotiating the complex responsibilities they have to archaeological resources and to all who have an interest in these resources or are other-wise affected by archaeological practice" (Lynott and Wylie 2000:8). The principles encourage the stewardship of sites and of the archaeological record for the benefit of all peoples; accountability to the public and all stakeholders (including proactive consultation); and rejection of commercialization of archaeological objects and avoidance of activities that enhance the value of such objects in the marketplace. They also encourage public education and outreach, protection of intellectual property derived from scholarly research (considered part of the record), ultimate accessibility of the primary record to other scholars, public reporting and publication, and preservation of collections and provision for long-term access to collections, records, and reports. Finally, in recognition that archaeological investigations may necessarily disturb some or all of a site's original context, archaeologists must ensure that all participants have appropriate professional training and experience to produce accurate and reproducible records. Participants must also have access to facilities and financial support so that they may conform to contemporary standards of practice.

The Society for Historical Archaeology's (SHA's) Ethical Principles

(2003) recognize professional responsibility when conducting research, teaching, disseminating results of research, and interacting with the public. They encourage efforts to support long-term site preservation, dissemination of research results to other scholars, careful data collection and recording, curation of site materials and accompanying records, respect for human rights, rejection of commercial trade or sale of archaeological items, public education, and appropriate inclusion of community members in the research process. All members and associated scholars are expected to support these principles.

ARE SANCTIONS AND ENFORCEMENT PROCEDURES NEEDED?

Jeffrey Altschul (2007) has noted that the Register's standards are voluntary and, like those of most national anthropological and archaeological membership organizations, cannot truly be enforced. Expulsion from archaeological membership organizations is rarely used as a sanction in the United States because few organizational by-laws give the officers or board the authority to oust members and because, presumably, members do not like to police their peers. Altschul explains that the Register was formed to support ethical oversight not only for applied archaeological practitioners but also for those in academia and research institutions. Additionally, the Register has a clear grievance process, detailed investigation procedures, and disciplinary procedures (including an extensive recordkeeping system). In 2008 the Register purchased liability insurance (Lynne Sebastian, personal communication, 2008).[3]

Altschul observes that only a small proportion of the archaeologists in colleges and universities—those who train the applied practitioners—are registered. Additionally, less than a majority of archaeologists employed by governmental agencies are RPAs. Altschul calls for universal acceptance of research standards such as those of the Register and for sincere management of practitioners' behavior within the profession. This will occur only if the Register achieves sufficient critical mass to be perceived from both inside and outside the profession as effective in pursuing violations of its Code of Ethics and Standards of Research Performance.[4] Altschul and Willem J. H. Willems (2006), drawing on Willems's experience in the Netherlands, have argued convincingly that if the profession does not police itself on a national scale, then others, such as governmental agencies in the United States and abroad, will do so.

Without the force of law and licensure supporting ethical standards (the way licenses are required for professional engineers and geologists in some states), sanctions for archaeologists are generally limited to responses to improper business practices such as misrepresenting credentials or billing for services not delivered. These infractions are pursued under non-archaeological rules of practice. Archaeologists who do poor or poorly reported science, who fail to ensure adequate curation or to disseminate the results of research, or who even falsify or misrepresent their credentials (an increasing problem in public service archaeology) may be sanctioned only within research and academic arenas—by denial of tenure or grants or loss of access to publication in juried journals. Public service archaeologists may be denied contracts or permits by agencies or foundations that receive public funds or by commercial clients who have had their projects delayed, but these archaeologists may move elsewhere and continue to practice.

If locally led self-monitoring is the goal of the archaeological profession, then we might look to two other complex fields, engineering and geology. Both professional groups struggled internally for decades before they took the initiative to work with state lawmakers and establish their own rules. Engineers now have state and national exams for state licensing, and states that accept the national exam and code of ethics administer state exams and codes for specialties such as civil and hydrological engineering. Professional geologists have worked with some state legislatures to establish registration and codes of ethics, and their goal is to establish registers in every state (Jerry Bernard, senior geologist, USDA NRCS, personal communication, 2007). In both engineering and geology and their subdisciplines, sanctions are enforced and licenses or registrations are lost on the basis of investigations by state boards. Removal of licenses and denial of registration occur in cases of poor scientific practice, falsification or misrepresentation of credentials (education, experience, or licensure), and dishonest business practices.

The questions posed by Altschul remain. Are we willing and able to police ourselves without statutes and government oversight? Some states have permitting processes for archaeology on state land and even on non-public land.[5] Is self-regulation sufficient for public accountability and protection of the archaeological record? Should we pursue state-based and even national testing, monitoring, and registration or licensing for archaeological research, fieldwork, and even reports? Does the multifaceted practice of archaeology outside the academy (including expert testimony in land tenure, crime scene investigation, and environmental protection cases) lend itself to controls beyond those already in place for business—protecting clients, including government agencies, communities, and academic and research institutions, from theft or fraud? The current answer to each of these questions seems to be a resounding "maybe." The profession needs to seriously consider Altschul's call for universal acceptance of a code and standards. The Register, with a 10-year track record of careful investigation and documentation of the few grievances filed, provides a ready-made tool. It needs to be used (see Mackey, chapter 9, this volume).

HOW HAVE ETHICAL CODES AND STANDARDS OF CONDUCT BEEN USED, AND WHAT ARE THE IMPLICATIONS?

Hester A. Davis, a retired Arkansas state archaeologist, an internationally recognized historic preservation scholar, and a two-term Register grievance coordinator, has written that standards of research performance and disciplinary procedures, once defined and established by archaeologists, may work if *others* accept them (Davis 2003). That is, professionalism and ethical codes and behavior must be recognized not only by members and practitioners but also by people who are employing them and evaluating their work. If the internal and external credibility of the profession—in academia, research, and business, among other venues—is established by the self-imposed controls on peer performance, then the system will work (Davis 2003:256–259).

Charles R. McGimsey, one of the recognized founders of conservation archaeology in the United States, in his brief but valuable history of ethics in archaeology (2000), reminds us that our principal purposes in establishing such codes in the past were to support traditional academic canons of behavior coupled with concerns about public archaeological practice and performance. The profession focused on issues regarding which academic degrees and experience constituted adequate credentials for academic or research positions, the intellectual property of research scientists, publication of research articles that used looted materials as their data (see also Vitelli 1996), and the ethical treatment of museum collections, students, and research assistants. As early as 1977, however, McGimsey presaged the need to evaluate the effectiveness of legislation in establishing ethical principles and positions. He observed that the Archaeological and Historic Preservation Act of 1974 (AHPA, PL 93–291, Moss-Bennett) had far-reaching effects on the archaeological profession:

> This legislation has been instrumental in causing a major restructuring of the entire profession. Archeology has changed from a profession made up largely of academics to one of academics,

full or nearly full time researchers and full or nearly full time administrators. Legislation has forced the profession to set standards of training and research performance, [and] to institute methods of quality control on research....Abuses are always possible and in a time of change and heavy funding the profession must be doubly on its guard.... [It must] establish and maintain mechanisms to recognize and reduce any such abuses which might develop or the profession will lose credibility....A profession which is not prepared to make whatever adjustments prove to be necessary to maintain and justify this credibility, and do so rapidly, would be ill advised to take the legislative route. Legislation is not for the timid, the unimaginative or those who cannot accept or face change. It is the best way for the profession to achieve its rightful level of public fiscal support, to enable it to develop an adequate level of public acceptance, and enable it to provide an appropriate input to the rest of the world....Without that public recognition and direction no discipline can make its optimum contribution. (McGimsey 1977:122)

Others hold that the combination of the NHPA, NEPA, Executive Order 11593 (1971, and its inclusion into the NHPA in 1984), and AHPA redirected the archaeological profession from a reactionary response to land development emphasizing data recovery and salvage to participation in the planning for large, landscape-altering projects (see Lipe, chapter 3, and Sebastian, chapter 1, this volume). This shift ultimately brought changes to the core curricula for historic preservation, anthropology, and archaeology in universities. Anthropology and archaeology were incorporated into historic preservation programs, and cultural resource management, public archaeology, and historic preservation were introduced into traditional anthropology programs (National Council for Preservation Education 2007; Woodcock 1996:103–105).[6]

Historian David Lowenthal (2005), an expert on landscape conservation and landscape history, has addressed the issue of intentional site destruction for financial or personal gain. He believes that sanctions seldom work in protecting cultural property from intentional destruction and trade. Indeed, Lowenthal argued that we are naive to believe that national and even international laws, ethical codes, and prohibitive statements do anything to quell such intentionally destructive actions (such as attacks on religious or national icons), because these depredations are political and economic statements and have nothing to do with science or scholarly study.

Neil Brodie and David Gill (2003) cited numerous cases of intentional destruction and looting to demonstrate the historical, ubiquitous, and growing political and commercial motives for such actions. They argued that international codes and sanctions that appeal to scientific, humanitarian, and even jingoistic values have little or no effect (Brodie and Gill 2003:40–42). If anything, well-meaning statements from organizations such as UNESCO and state or national governments may be perceived as sanctimonious and taken as challenges by those who believe it their right, as the producers, owners, or conquerors of the heritage resources, to sell such items and even to flaunt their depredation. Lowenthal and others also believe that sanctions and statements that all cultural property must be preserved in situ and in toto serve as impetuses to drive potential cooperators or partners in protecting cultural properties away or underground (Lowenthal 2005:393–424).

Some US archaeologists have long held that it is essential and beneficial to reach accommodation with nonprofessionals, including history buffs, collectors, avocational archaeologists, and commercial treasure salvagers, in order to protect cultural property, archaeological sites, and their data (Bense 1991; Davis 1991; King 1991). This is in part the philosophy behind many currently successful education and volunteer programs within state and local archaeology membership organizations. These programs encourage participation by interested persons in cooperative archaeological research, public education, and outreach.

George Bass (2003), although taking exception to the notion that underwater sites are scientifically or substantially distinct from sites on dry land, acknowledged that in the United States, submerged sites, including shipwreck sites, receive somewhat disparate legal protection.[7] This may be partly because portions of the public believe that these sites should be available to treasure salvagers and that cooperation with collectors involved with these sites is both sound recreation and the only reliable way to extract cultural information from the sites for scientific analysis. This belief finds its way into formal law in that the Abandoned Shipwreck Act of 1988 removes "abandoned" or downed ships from the laws of salvage and passes ownership of these wrecks to individual states. Each state may decide what type of law it wants to govern access to the property in these sites, but each also provides some version of public access to the sites. Thus, some accommodation is made with collectors, salvage and artifact dealers (even major auction houses), and commercial tourism ventures.

Bass also observed that the UNESCO Convention on the Protection of the Underwater Cultural Heritage makes certain basic ethical statements about removing underwater cultural heritage in international waters from trade or barter and prohibits the transfer of illicitly exported artifacts or remains into signatory ports. In November 2007, the Register's board of directors amended its code of conduct and disciplinary procedures to be consistent with the UNESCO convention, specifically regarding the ethics of professional archaeologists who cooperate with shipwreck salvagers. The code and procedures explicitly support the best practices rules of the US National Committee of the International Congress on Monuments and Sites (US/ICOMOS) and thereby comport with statements and principles of the Register's sponsoring organizations, the AAA, SHA, SAA, and AIA, as well as US/ICOMOS (Altschul 2007:10).

Thomas F. King (2008:1152) has argued that "one sees much articulation of ethical standards in the archaeological literature but little serious debate about such standards and their implications." Archaeological organizations and their members tend to agree that certain behaviors are correct and ethical and others are not, without examining the logical underpinnings or outcomes of these beliefs. We support the protection of archaeological resources and their data in appropriate museums and curatorial facilities, abhor the destruction of any site during development without scientifically sound research and recovery, and reject deaccessioning or returning portions of or complete collections to communities for local educational use, yet we sincerely and simultaneously bemoan the overcrowding or closure of museum storage facilities and consequent risk to the collections and related records (see Childs 1995, 2007; Childs, ed. 2004, on today's continuing "curation crisis," including ethical responsibilities for appropriate care of material remains and associated field and analytical records).[8]

King holds that it may be correct to employ nontraditional solutions to a few of these archaeological conundrums. For example, it might be possible to achieve cooperation between archaeologists and some groups classified as looters, traffickers, pot hunters, amateurs, or hacks. These relationships would permit "selected recovered objects [to] remain in private hands or enter the stream of commerce rather than go to museums and research institutions" if they were excavated using scientific archaeological methods (King 2008:1151). Yet, King observes that archaeologists who participate in these relationships or go to work with treasure recovery organizations, even under agreements that protect the provenience information and condition of the objects, are at best shunned in the profession. "This is an unresolved issue that will probably gain more exposure...particularly as treasure recovery companies gain expanded access to...extreme [underwater] environments using expensive high technology unavailable to ordinary archaeology researchers" (2008:1151). Some archaeologists, including Ferguson (chapter 8, this volume), Colwell-Chanthaphonh and Ferguson (2008:14–19), Smith and Jackson (2008), and King (2008:1151, 1153), have encouraged others to consider, whenever possible, less rigid adherence to professional principles and to include other participants, such as concerned indigenous, descendant, and "protective" communities, in the design, execution, and dissemination of the results of research and environmental compliance studies.[9] King (2008: 1151–1153) writes: "Descendent communities typically want to exercise a considerable amount of control over their ancestors' bones, artifacts, and places of residence, worship, and burial, and their interests may differ considerably from the information-driven interests of archaeologists." He warns that some archaeologists' science-based focus on descendant communities may risk ignoring the concerns of some protective communities regarding safeguarding the remains and sites of all past communities. These cultural concerns should be considered and accommodated. Indeed, according to King, early, active, and sincere accountability to and collaboration with contemporary indigenous and protective communities are becoming necessary guiding ethical principles for many archaeologists today.

Joe Watkins and colleagues (1995) present this "accountability" principle (the SAA's second ethical principle) as much more than paying lip service to non-archaeological interest groups—the funding public, clients, and, most important, affected cultural groups. Watkins and his coauthors discuss the need to seek collaborative and cooperative relationships with the people we study and their descendants. They encourage consultation early and often, if possible, before starting research or compliance studies. This strategy is not paternalistic and not merely "a reasonable and good faith effort" that documents attempts to permit others to express an opinion. Rather, these writers urge archaeologists to make an affirmative effort to accommodate the concerns of the affected communities and community members and, whenever feasible, make them part of the research and compliance study design and decision-making. They present a set of examples, not all of which they consider outstanding successes, that demonstrate the complexity of decisions that must be made by archaeologists today. For example, archaeologists must ensure access to data, including records and collections, for present and future scientific research and determine the ultimate disposition of collected materials and associated field and analytical records in ways that accommodate the concerns of the consulting parties.

CHARACTERISTICS OF RECENT ETHICS CASES

In 2004, in response to and reflecting increasing professional concern about a range of ethical issues, the SAA Committee on Ethics and board of directors began sponsoring intercollegiate "Ethics Bowls" at the organization's annual meeting. These popular events present hypothetical cases, most of them based on actual ethical cases, for review and debate. Concurrently, the committee started providing semiannual reviews of recent news in archaeological ethics.[10]

Ethics Bowl cases are diverse and demonstrate the increasing complexity of issues related to the commercialization of collections and research support, the integrity of collections, responsibilities under the Native American Graves Protection and Repatriation Act (NAGPRA) and the UNESCO Convention, intellectual property and access to collections, the rights of private property owners, and responsibility to the archaeological record. Several cases reflect increasing professional (domestic and international) concerns regarding the protection and commercialization of underwater archaeological resources and the appropriateness of cooperating with salvage businesses in order to retrieve some of the scientific data.[11]

Very few of the cases involve simple misconduct, such as plagiarism, on the part of one or several individuals. A few reflect ambivalence about the risks of open public or nonprofessional involvement in site destruction and fear of site destruction due to future looting. More often the examples demonstrate conflicting ethical positions and the need to balance valid responsibilities to two or more communities. Questions of intellectual property and who owns the past prevail.

As an example, one case reviewed by both the Ethics Bowl and the "Recent News" reports was that of the *USS Arizona* National Memorial. In 2006 the shell of this national historic landmark, an important World War II maritime history site revered by descendants of the ship's entombed naval personnel, was found to be deteriorating and spilling gradually increasing quantities of oil into the ocean at Pearl Harbor, along the shore of Oahu west of Honolulu. Repairing the monument would disturb the graves and destroy the monument's historical fabric. Taking no action might irreversibly damage the harbor and outlying ocean waters and the habitats of numerous marine plants and animals. Archaeologists, historians, marine biologists, and ecologists working for the National Park Service and the US Navy will have to work with the families of the war dead to reach an accommodation and appropriately protect the human remains, more recent burials at the memorial, and the other historical, archaeological, and natural resources in question. Studies are ongoing.

All the Ethics Bowl cases and news reports emphasize archaeologists' increasing recognition of their responsibilities and accountability to others, including their communities of reference and practice—their colleagues, employers, clients, indigenous people, cultural institutions, state and federal governments, and foreign nations. Increasingly, some also clearly recognize responsibilities to indigenous, descendant, and protective communities.

S. Terry Childs (2007), citing several cases and drawing on knowledge of countless others, reminds archaeologists that they also have ethical responsibilities to future generations of students, researchers, indigenous and descendant communities, and the public. These responsibilities involve careful and thoughtful planning for the management, conservation, curation, and control of archaeological collections, including material remains and associated field and analytical records, generated during research and CRM projects. She also reminds the professional membership organizations, registers, and their ethics committees that they have a role to play in ensuring that these collections and records are not lost or rendered inaccessible for current and future research, interpretation, and repatriation.

DO WE HAVE CORE ETHICAL PRINCIPLES THAT GO BEYOND ACCOUNTABILITY TO OTHERS?

It appears that many archaeologists who work with communities affected by their basic and applied research projects, including compliance projects, have already followed or are currently following principles that go beyond basic and static accountability, achieving active collaboration. This is particularly true, regardless of venue or research interests, if the archaeologist believes that the descendants and protectors of the indigenous producers of heritage resources have ownership rights to use and interpret those resources as they see best (see Ferguson, chapter 8, this volume).

Colwell-Chanthaphonh and Ferguson (2006) term this strategy a "framework of virtue ethics." They explain that the roots of virtue ethics reside in both Western and non-Western moral philosophies that turn away from simple and utilitarian obligations, rules, and consequences and embrace flexible and multitracked social relationships and spheres of interaction. Whereas some have argued that virtue ethics do not permit codification and oversight, others have held that such an approach is less culture bound and more flexible, lending itself to internal or contextual norms and controls.

Virtue ethics encompass many features, but Colwell-Chanthaphonh and Ferguson focus on the notion of trust as a basis for ethical behavior. They note that a discussion of virtue ethics and trust is frequently absent from the discourse on archaeological ethics, even though trust is essential to effectively collaborate with indigenous (and protective) communities. Collaboration, often practiced by social anthropologists and ethnographers, is manifested in a number of forms, "from informal dialogue among partners to elaborate associations that last throughout the entire enterprise of research" and life-long partnerships that benefit all participants (Colwell-Chanthaphonh and Ferguson 2004:6, 2008; Ferguson 1996). Colwell-Chanthaphonh and Ferguson note that although each partner in the collaborative process may derive benefits, they are not necessarily the same benefits. However, collaboration may work best when the interests of each party—the community, individual community members, and archaeologists—are viewed as "mutual concerns" (Colwell-Chanthaphonh and Ferguson 2004:7).

Colwell-Chanthaphonh and Ferguson explore the nature of contemporary collaborative research for archaeologists, how it is practiced, how establishing true trust relationships makes such collaboration possible, and how it may define virtue ethics and enrich the practice of virtue archaeology now and in the future. In contemplating a framework of virtue ethics, the authors outline five contemporary categories of trust relationships for archaeologists; these may be perceived as spheres of interaction that influence the practice of archaeology. The categories are professional trust, public trust, descendant trust, governmental trust, and generational trust (Colwell-Chanthaphonh and Ferguson 2006:122–129):

> These five categories generally describe the archaeologist's trust with other archaeologists (in academic and contract settings), the general public (avocational archaeologists, the lay public...), peoples whose culture is under examination (typically, but not necessarily, Native Americans in the United States), the government (which is responsible for overseeing many archaeological projects), and past and future generations who are associated with archaeological sites or who may (or may not) have an interest in archaeological knowledge and materials....There is a complex web of trust existing between all of these different groups that indubitably affects the relationship archaeologists have with others. (Colwell-Chanthaphonh and Ferguson 2006:123)

Colwell-Chanthaphonh and Ferguson acknowledge that trust relationships for archaeologists involve more than interpersonal relationships; they also involve relationships with institutions, objects, and knowledge—that is, who owns and controls the material remains and knowledge and interpretations of the past. They do not discount the need for codes and rules, but they argue convincingly that because archaeology must focus on cultural property and things, archaeologists need

> a professional ethics that provides the right kind of vocabulary and questions to guide their understanding of social interactions. More than a rule-based system...or a compilation of ideal principles, archaeologists will need to contemplate...the very nature of their relationships with colleagues, publics, descendent communities, governments, and past and future generations. While we do not disregard the value of codes of ethics and utilitarian philosophies...we have attempted to provide an alternative perspective to rigid notions of moral action by beginning with a question about cultivating trust. (Colwell-Chanthaphonh and Ferguson 2006:129–130).

In a system in which archaeologists are obliged to establish and maintain collaborative trust relationships, it seems that sanctions must necessarily be derived internally or systemically and most likely will involve rejection of the archaeologists' work by the collaborating community or its members. If archaeologists fail to achieve or maintain an open and mutually beneficial trust relationship, if they try to rush or coerce the relationship or manipulate the materials and associated cultural knowledge under study, they may be turned away or ignored.

Chris Scarre and Geoffrey Scarre (2006:1–12), in the introduction to their volume on the ethics of archaeology, challenge archaeological practitioners to balance their myriad professional and institutional obligations against the rights and obligations of a diverse array of other interest groups, including collaborators. They encourage all of us to become more than conversant with the philosophical roots of and recognized conflicts within ethical analysis. Indeed, they hold that it is essential to understand the philosophical history that informs contemporary perspectives. They note that ethics in general is "concerned with the critical appraisal of human conducts and characters. Moral judgments are sharply distinct in kind from factual ones" (2006:2). Behavior may be observed as what is being done (descriptive) or as whether it is appropriate and credible (evaluative). Scarre and Scarre state that too often, ethical analyses of archaeological or any other professional behavior focus only on principles and are presented prescriptively, as limitations or prohibitions on action: as "do's, don'ts, rules, limits, and constraints" (2006:3). Rather, ethics should also be "about positive and attractive springs of action: values, goals, and ideals, aspirations and personal and social fulfillment.... For Aristotle [in *Nicomachean Ethics*] ethics is about locating and attaining the highest goods available to us (...excellences of mind and character)....those who follow a more inspiring view of the ethical life not merely avoid the bad [behavior] but energetically pursue the good" (2006:3).

Scarre and Scarre warn that when these ideals move into the realm of professional ethics, one must proceed with caution. Archaeologists must determine not only what the "highest goods" of their profession are but also how they may be achieved in the multifaceted world of practice. Colwell-Chanthaphonh and Ferguson's five trust relationships may all need attention, and each interest group may believe that it holds the preferred perspective.

This "highest goods" approach may be a particularly difficult course of action if one works within the prescriptive and litigious venue of environmental and historic preservation compliance studies (that is, with Colwell-Chanthaphonh and Ferguson's government trust relationship). But simply because the highest goods for the scientific, data-focused profession of archaeology are not always compatible with those of other interest groups or communities, it does not follow that archaeologists should not collaboratively seek mutually beneficial goals and outcomes with all partners. We may not achieve a perfect fit in every situation, but we may achieve mutual respect and support for the most important "highest goods" for each participant. This may be perceived as an ethic of civic responsibility in archaeological practice.

Barbara J. Little (2002:3) convincingly presented the concept that archaeology has the capacity for providing a shared vision of the past for multiple publics and stakeholders: "We do archaeology—and spend public money on it—because archaeology provides benefits not only for professional archaeological research but also for the many participants and publics who use and value it." She reported that recent Harris Poll surveys had recorded public support for the protection of archaeological sites and continued research because many people believe that there is value in learning from the past; such knowledge guides decisions about the present and informs those about the future. Quoting Lipe (1984:2), Little expressed agreement with others that the public value of archaeological sites derives in part from the "universal role that the material culture environment plays in providing cultural continuity and perspective and hence in linking the past, present and future within the experience of any given human generation." However, she also referred to relatively recent works on archaeological ethics (Green 1984; Keel 1995) that presented the concepts of a shared and public trust for heritage resources and common ownership of the past, noting that these perceptions are not universal and may be partial causes for conflict between archaeologists and descendant communities, particularly American Indian tribes.

The question remains, How can archaeologists and other stakeholders achieve a common or shared vision of the past? Little proposed a number of strategies to present and promote the benefits: ordinances (local, state, and tribal) developed by all stakeholders and representing all their visions; presentation of interpretive exhibits; public service announcements; Web pages that remain current, interactive, and responsive to various public interests; newspaper articles; and school presentations, to mention just a few. Most important to Little was retaining humanity, sensitivity to all participants and stakeholders, and honesty. Archaeology should be used to convey dynamic and therefore shared visions of the past that represent multiple and diverse public and participant views, including successes, struggles, failures, conflicts, and inequities (Little 2002:13–16).

Lipe (2002) has warned that in bringing the public into our research, we need to avoid the traps of oversimplifying and reducing the results of archaeological research to basic problems solved and mysteries unsolved; we will lose credibility if we ignore the complexities and uncertainties in our interpretation to the public. It is essential to present and explain the complexities of understanding the past in public presentations. This will keep the involved publics, including descendant and protective communities and individuals, engaged at the levels they prefer and aware of the multivariate tools employed in understanding the past. If archaeologists succumb to pressures to simplify presentations on their research methodologies and findings, then participating partners and publics are not served and the profession is misrepresented. Our collaborators and partners will have little interest in continuing cooperative relationships. Oversimplifying will also "inhibit intellectual reflection on complex historical processes—both those that took place in the past and those even less well understood ones that are affecting our lives today.... The temporal scale and physical reality of the archaeological record forces us to recognize that our current lives are linked with the lives of others both past and present, as part of a deep and wide river of human experience moving through time" (Lipe 2002:28).

Today it seems that many archaeologists are seeking honest collaborative relationships with participant communities as equal partners while retaining professionally and publicly credible presentation of scientific archaeological research. Barbara Little and Paul Shackel (2007) proposed that in certain situations, affirmative action may be needed to achieve these ends. They suggested that moving archaeology into the arena of civic engagement might provide a useful venue for using sound scientific research, collaborative inquiry, and community participation to support dynamic social or community action and change.[12] Thus, civic engagement moves beyond collaborating and long-term coalition-building with communities of interest or indigenous stakeholders in order to investigate and interpret community history; it moves toward using archaeological and historical data for active participation in community action and change. Archaeological research—in certain settings, when welcomed by non-archaeologist participants, and when fully understood by all participants—may be used as an applied analytical tool for investigating and enacting social, political, or other community changes, including achieving social and economic justice (Shackel 2007:243–259; see also Colwell-Chanthaphonh and Ferguson 2004 and Fluehr-Lobban 2003 on the topic of seeking mutual benefits and learning different ways to understand and use the past).

Such anthropological or political science civic engagement tools clearly are not appropriate for all archaeological research. Some communities will not welcome archaeologists' participation in their community action. Nevertheless, this does not discount the value of an ethic of civic engagement in situations in which it can work and can be sought by all communities of interest. Additionally, civic engagement does not discount the value of the special scientific and analytical skills of archaeologists. Lipe (2000a) and Wylie (2000) have reminded archaeologists not to lose sight, in either their basic or their applied research, of their special responsibilities to a broader public, responsibilities to study and interpret the past for present and future generations.

A more basic ethic of collaboration appears to be an additional guiding principle today and for the foreseeable future. This "ethic of collaboration involves no simple rule or moral equation; it entails the cultivation of sincere relationships guided by virtuous ideals—civility, cooperativeness, tactfulness, patience, trust, honesty, thoughtfulness, tolerance, and respect" (Colwell-Chanthaphonh and Ferguson 2004:23). These ideals apply to all communities or spheres of interaction, including non-archaeological stakeholders, descendant and protective communities, and of course archaeological colleagues employed in academic, research, business, environmental compliance, public, and private venues.

SUMMARY

A selective review of current national ethical principles and related literature confirms that there are shared standards of archaeological practice that largely have to do with data-sharing and other research relationships within the profession and accountability to colleagues, clients, employers, funders, and communities of interest. These rules of behavior are strikingly similar to those of other scientific professions with both applied and basic research interests. The archaeological rules are prescriptive and normative, appear to be static and prohibitive, and seem to reveal limited concern for full participation by non-archaeologists in teaching, research, interpretation, and environmental protection. Recent literature recognizes broader responsibilities to communities of interest and to descendant and protective communities, as well as their equal status as owners of historical and cultural knowledge that is of great value to practicing archaeologists.

Some archaeologists (for example, Altschul, Davis, and McGimsey) look to these standards and stronger enforcement procedures or sanctions as means to establish and maintain credibility for the profession, particularly as it is observed from the outside by clients, partners, and administrators. Laws, sanctions, rules, and codes are sound professional and business controls for practitioners who are also members of professional oversight organizations; they also function in presenting a sound, respectable, and credible image to the public, lawmakers, and funders, especially those who fund archaeological activities with taxpayers' and other public money.

If the need for definition of sound professional practice, sanctions, and enforcement is compelling within the profession, then members must take affirmative action to support the extant national registration organization, the Register of Professional Archaeologists. The Register is not tied directly to any specific national membership organization, yet it has the potential for sufficient critical mass to be effective in protecting the integrity of the profession if practitioners truly want it. Because the Register is not tied to state or federal statutes or regulations, it has established its code of conduct, standards of performance, sanctions, and expulsion procedures without pressure or influence from other interested parties. Additionally, the Register is able to respond quickly to current or critical issues and concerns, if the directors and RPAs concur. Of course, when controversy arises, the board and attorneys do debate, consult, and deliberate, as is appropriate.[13]

Today, although most archaeologists believe that extant codes and ethical principles serve a useful purpose, an increasing number also recognizes broader professional responsibilities to communities of interest, to descendant and protective communities, and to others with special knowledge about their history and claims to their heritage resources. Randall H. McGuire (2003) and Alan Simmons (1999) both have reminded archaeologists that issues of archaeological ethics are "real archaeology" and are far more complex than once believed. Neither of them claims that the complexities of relationships between archaeological practitioners and living communities did not exist in the past; issues of ownership and valid knowledge of the past were simply unrecognized by the profession or were not central to its conduct of scientific research. This caused deep-seated conflict between archaeologists and indigenous communities, which some contemporary archaeologists argue is rooted in 500 years of power struggles between native and colonial populations (Colwell-Chanthaphonh and Ferguson 2004:22; Thomas 2000).

In order to correct for these oversights and establish more productive and accommodating working relationships with indigenous stakeholders, archaeologists are employing new strategies that extend beyond simple accountability, some of which are adapted from applied anthropology. Archaeologists are using true consultation, collaboration, and even civic engagement to ensure that the concerns, knowledge (intellectual property), and perspectives of contemporary indigenous, descendant, protective, and other participant communities are integrated into the design, execution, reporting, and dissemination of archaeological research. Such people include Colwell-Chanthaphonh and Ferguson, King, Little, Shackel, Scarre and Scarre, Lipe, and, back in 1977, McGimsey. Active collaboration is a new ethic that will continue to enhance archaeological research and practice in future decades and will prove to benefit and hold the interest of multiple concerned stakeholders and publics. Appropriate dissemination of the results of such enhanced basic and applied archaeological research to more general audiences will clearly realize a public benefit of enriched, broad-based understanding of the past. Additionally, such public education efforts will encourage an increased appreciation of the need to conserve a broad range of fragile, culturally significant, and nonrenewable archaeological heritage sites (Lipe 2000a:117).

CONCLUSION

It is clear that archaeologists in the United States and abroad want a strong and collaborative ethical framework and are personally and corporately committed to maintaining and supporting such a structure. Workshops and networks prevail at annual conferences and on listserves, within and among most of the professional organizations. Graduate and undergraduate syllabi for professional ethics and environmental ethics courses in departments of anthropology and interdisciplinary programs reflect an increasing concern that future practitioners have a broad-based understanding of ethical issues and behavior. The next steps, yet to be realized, should involve creation of mentoring and internship programs in private, public, governmental, and nongovernmental organizations, probably best organized by the Register of Professional Archaeologists.

Rules and principles of ethical conduct define normative responsibilities to professional colleagues, clients, employees, students, and multiple publics. They serve as useful guides to decision-making when archaeologists face possible conflicts or ambiguities. Associated national registers and their broadly framed sanctions, together with state-based professional registers with more narrowly devised sanctions and expulsion procedures, give the profession a means to establish and maintain credibility in the eyes of outsiders such as businesses, government personnel, academic administrators, and multiple publics and stakeholders. Such professional performance controls, particularly those with a national or international focus like the Register's, are needed and must be supported by the profession, or other controls may be placed upon us by outside interests.

These normative rules of conduct and oversight controls established by professional self-regulatory registers, however, should not be the core defining principles behind contemporary ethical thinking, behavior, and archaeological practice. A contemporary ethic of collaboration, somewhat akin to a more traditional ethic of accountability, is acknowledged by a number of archaeological practitioners. True collaboration is generally achieved through a sense of civic responsibility to multiple publics and communities, including the indigenous and protective communities, clients, consulting parties, and professional peers in an array of disciplines. Building collaborative partnerships at the local level by establishing trust relationships and heightening and promoting the shared benefits of meaningful and protracted archaeological research and historical interpretation is the civic responsibility of archaeologists as individuals and as members of and guests in various communities. Such ethical thinking and behavior will serve all participants well into the future.

As most of the national codes and those of the World Archaeological Congress (n.d.) acknowledge, these civic responsibilities must extend beyond national boundaries. Although not explicitly discussed in this chapter, the outcomes sought through archaeological collaboration recall those defined almost 60 years ago in the United Nations' Universal Declaration on Human Rights, adopted in December 1948. The Universal Declaration was proclaimed as the "common standard of achievement for all peoples and all nations" in terms of respect for human rights. It lists numerous rights—civil, political, economic, social, and cultural—to which people everywhere are entitled. The Universal Declaration was conceived as a statement of objectives and not as part of binding international law. Nonetheless, it may serve as a reminder to those concerned with ethical behavior and research and as a potent instrument to apply moral and diplomatic pressure on states that violate its principles. Of particular importance is Article 27, which advances the rights of all to participate fully in their own cultural life "and to share in scientific advancement and its benefits." Thus, collaborative archaeological endeavors, simultaneously representing different cultural traditions, will be both scientifically and culturally valid if the efforts are designed with common visions and aspirations in an atmosphere of mutual respect and shared values.[14]

APPENDIX

Additional Selected Standards, Principles, Statements, Agreements, and Other Resources Not Referenced in This Chapter

American Association for the Advancement of Science (AAAS)
2007 *Professional Ethics Report.* Washington, DC: Scientific Freedom, Responsibility, and Law Program of the AAAS, in collaboration with the Committee on Scientific Freedom and Responsibility, vol. 20, no. 3 (www.aaas.org/spp/sfrl/per/per50.pdf).

American Association of University Professors
1987 *Statement of Professional Ethics,* 1966, Updated 1987. Washington, DC: American Association of University Professors (www.aaup.org/AAUP/pubsres/policydocs/contents/statementonprofessionalethics.htm).

National Council on Public History (NCPH)
2007 *Code of Ethics and Professional Conduct.* Washington, DC: NCPH (www.ncph.org/AbouttheCouncil/BylawsandEthics/tabid/291/Default.aspx).

Acknowledgments

I thank Lynne Sebastian for inviting me to participate in the School for Advanced Research advanced seminar, and I express my appreciation to both Lynne and Bill Lipe for their patience with my choice of paper topic and for their insightful reviews and editorial commentaries. I am also grateful to several colleagues who generously shared their thoughts, ideas, manuscripts, and publications. These include T. J.

Ferguson and S. Terry Childs, who e-mailed me their publications, and Thomas F. King, who shared his prepublication manuscript (published in February 2008). Barbara Little not only shared her thoughts but also offered encouragement and suggested readings, as did Frank McManamon, Laura Dean, and Tom McCulloch. My colleagues in the US Department of Agriculture, Jerry Bernard, Don Williams, and Mark Locke, provided insights into the history and development of professional registration and licensing in geology and civil engineering. All the other seminar participants generously provided invaluable guidance; I hope that the final chapter adequately incorporates their thoughts and suggestions.

Although I work for the United States Department of Agriculture's Natural Resources Conservation Service, the ideas and opinions in this chapter are mine alone and do not reflect those of the USDA, the NRCS, or any other agency or institution.

Notes

1. See also White 1967, in which Lynn Townsend White Jr. argued, among other things, that World War II technology, when applied during the postwar era, was consuming the Earth's resources at an alarming rate.

2. See Lipe 2006b for an important and timely discussion of the effects of federal law on professional and ethical standards and the effect on one nongovernmental organization's code.

3. See the Register's description of its grievance procedures under the Governance dropdown screen at www.rpnet.org. Lipe (personal communication, 2008) has noted that the responsibilities of the grievance coordinator and Standards Board and the case of the city of Blaine, Washington (detailed on the same Web page) present a clearly enforceable and painstakingly recorded and archived procedure for investigating and adjudicating a complaint against an RPA.

4. In 2007 there were approximately 2,200 registered professional archaeologists (Davis, personal communication, 2007), drawn from the full range of archaeologists who work in the United States and abroad. Therefore, comparison with other membership organizations' numbers is not meaningful.

5. See Washington State's Revised Code, Chapter 27.53. Among other provisions, this statute requires private landowners to obtain permits and complete professional archaeological site documentation if they must affect a known archaeological site or a known human burial on their land. If landowners fail to follow these requirements, they may be charged with a misdemeanor for affecting a known site and a felony for affecting a human burial.

6. The National Council on Preservation Education (NCPE) was founded in 1978 to assist in the development of preservation programs and set basic standards for

preservation programs that include instruction in archaeology (see Woodcock 1996:103 and the NCPE Web page at www.uvm.edu.histpres/ncpe).

7. Traditionally, the United States has maintained a three-mile territorial sea. In 1988 President Reagan signed the Abandoned Shipwreck Act (ASA, PL 100-298, 43 USC 2101-2106), which extended the US territorial sea to 12 miles for national security purposes, but the proclamation did not affect existing laws. Therefore, the ASA still covers only the 3-mile territorial sea. In 1999 President Clinton extended the contiguous zone (previously extending to 12 miles) out to 24 miles. Beyond the contiguous zone, the United States declared jurisdiction over the continental shelf and an Exclusive Economic Zone (EEZ) to protect fisheries, extending out 200 miles from the coast. The United States has done little to protect cultural resources beyond the territorial sea, and treasure salvage occurs regularly. A few national marine sanctuaries, including one that protects the *USS Monitor*, are designated; these are subject to federal control. Also, areas leased for mining by the Minerals Management Service are subject to national laws such as the National Historic Preservation Act. The purpose of the ASA of 1988 is to vest title to certain abandoned historic shipwrecks that are buried in land of the respective states and to clarify the management authority of the states over these shipwrecks. The heart of the law is the simultaneous declaration of federal title to historic shipwrecks and the transfer of that title to individual states, which are then called upon to develop management programs for dealing with the shipwrecks. The effect is to remove the sites from the purview of federal admiralty court, where they would be subject to claims by treasure hunters. The law envisions the diverse groups that have interests in underwater shipwrecks, including preservationists and treasure salvagers, cooperating in their use and management. The law also allows the commercial salvage of shipwrecks.

8. See also the National Park Service Archeology Program's Web page, Managing Archaeological Collections (www.cr.nps.gov/archeology/collections/index.htm), for a thorough review of the conflicting issues related to archaeological collections and suggested guidance for resolving some of these issues.

9. Protective communities are those that take responsibility for safeguarding the cultural and human remains of their own ancestors or remains for which direct descent cannot be traced. This concept is similar to the extended family (*ohana*) in Hawaii, which takes responsibility for ancestors when contemporary descendants cannot take action (Ruby McDonald, Office of Hawaiian Affairs, personal communication, 2008; Carol Kawachi, Natural Resources Conservation Service, Honolulu, personal communication, 2008). Smith and Jackson (2008:175), writing about their research in Australia, refer to individuals who take responsibility for protecting ancestors (descendant or not) as "custodians."

10. For summaries of the cases, see www.saa.org/aboutSAA/committees/ethics/ebowl.html. For the semiannual reviews, see www.saa.org/aboutSAA/committees/ethics/Resources.html.

11. See Altschul 2007 for the Register's response to this problem.

12. Civic engagement, generally perceived as an educational strategy, involves community-based individual and collective actions designed to identify and address issues of public concern. As used in the Little and Shackel (2007) volume, civic engagement involves reacting to the expressed needs of one's various communities or interaction spheres, at local, national, and global scales. As good citizens of these communities, archaeologists may use their research and take action to achieve positive social change. Such a strategy presumes participating in community organizations and service, recognizing human and cultural diversity, and seeking commonalities (Working Definition of Civic Engagement, University of Maryland Coalition for Civic Engagement and Leadership, University of Maryland Office of Community Service-Learning, May 2007, www.apa.org/ed/slce/civicengagement.html#definition).

13. If state-based professional organizations want to establish their own procedures, then the archaeologists need to take action, write the ethical standards and codes, and identify sanctions and expulsion procedures, not merely express their interest. Otherwise, it will be done for them by well-meaning elected officials representing additional interests beyond archaeology (see McGimsey 1977:122). See also the Register's Web page on its grievance procedures. Its grievance coordinator and committee members play critical roles in negotiating the Register through the complex grievance process, which is designed to keep deliberations as objective as possible..

14. The full text of the 1948 Universal Declaration may be found at www.unhchr.ch/udhr/ (accessed Oct. 29, 2007). See also the outcomes of a one-day meeting of experts on human rights and the environment in 2001, including explicit statements on the essential need for sustaining the natural and man-made environment (www.unhchr.ch/environment/ [accessed Oct. 29, 2007]).

11

The Crisis in Communication

Still with Us?

David Colin Crass

Theodore Roosevelt, newly president of the United States and at the time president of the American Historical Association, addressed the organization's annual meeting in Boston on December 27, 1912. He delivered an address that, although flowery by today's standards, stands as a powerful statement of the importance of history, in which he included archaeology. Roosevelt, no mean historian himself, sketched out his ideal historian-archaeologist:

> The greatest of future archaeologists will be the great historian who instead of being a mere antiquarian delver in dust-heaps has the genius to reconstruct for us the immense panorama of the past....What he brings from the charnel-house he must use with such potent wizardry that we shall see the life that was and not the death that is....The great historian must be able to paint for us the life of the plain people, the ordinary men and women, of the time of which he writes. He can do this only if he possesses the highest kind of imagination. (Roosevelt 1913:480)

Fifty-four years later, Section 1 of the National Historic Preservation Act (NHPA) of 1966 reiterated Roosevelt's rationale in language that was equally direct, if more restrained: "The Congress finds that the historical and cultural foundations of the Nation should be preserved as a living part of our community life...in order to give a sense of orientation to the American people."

The American people apparently agree with both Roosevelt and the authors of the NHPA. In a recent Harris Interactive poll commissioned by a consortium of archaeological organizations, 99 percent of respondents said that archaeological sites had educational and scientific value. Respondents felt that archaeology was important to understanding the modern world and to forming societal values, an opinion borne out by recent findings that the ability to remember past events seems to correlate strongly with the ability to envision and plan for the future (News Staff 2007; Ramos and Duganne 2000).

These figures, and many more like them, point to widespread support for public archaeology among voters. Simultaneously, considerable confusion exists outside the profession about the very nature of archaeology. For instance, about 8 in 10 respondents in the Harris Interactive poll thought that archaeology included the study of dinosaurs. Although this should not cause us as a profession to lose sleep at night, it is a wake-up call, signaling that the central messages of archaeology are rather blurry in most people's minds.

In short, public support for archaeology is a mile wide—but its depth is currently unknown. I believe that we ignore the depth of public support for public archaeology at our peril, and critical to building greater public support are communications strategies and tactics. I begin this chapter with a review of the Airlie House discussions on communications and an evaluation of the discipline's current status relative to the objectives set in 1974. Next follows a discussion focused on enhancing archaeological communications and then a brief primer on media relations, which consists of a series of tactical considerations that virtually any archaeologist can use to enhance his or her communications. I end with more strategic recommendations and a concluding statement.

THE 1974 AIRLIE HOUSE DISCUSSIONS

In 1971, at the dawn of cultural resource management (CRM) under Section 106 of the NHPA, Charles McGimsey (1971) noted that the lack of public support for archaeology could be tied directly to the reticence of many in the profession to get involved in the necessary legislative and outreach efforts. So it is no surprise that a substantial effort at Airlie House was devoted to examining the audiences for archaeological knowledge and suggesting how to reach those audiences.

By way of background, in 1974 the forerunner of the Internet, ARPANET, was in its initial, defense-related testing stages. Outside of the Pentagon and its contractors, no one had heard of packet theory, the underlying data construct that would transform electronic communications. Vaudevillian Jack Benny died in 1974, and *Love, American Style* was wrapping up a successful run on TV. Eight-track audiotape was the format of choice for car stereos. It was in this pre-Internet, predigital world that the discussion of archaeological communications took place at Airlie House. Interestingly, the conference was titled "The Crisis in Communication." The following review is summarized from Charles McGimsey and Hester Davis's report on the conference (1977:78–89).

The Airlie House discussants rightly (and wryly) noted that although archaeology was traditionally the most action oriented of the anthropological disciplines, it was also the "most intellectually introverted." The discussants focused most of their attention on communications with a "wider" (non-archaeological) audience, noting that the public's right to know was exceeded only by the archaeologist's need to know what is going on among his colleagues. Implicit in the discussion was the assumption that existing professional organs served communications among archaeologists reasonably well (archaeologists themselves were referred to as "Active Participants"; hereafter I refer to this audience simply as "other archaeologists"). The "crisis" referenced in the title was that "widespread understanding of archeology, as distinguished from simple popular interest, [was] still lacking" (McGimsey and Davis 1977:79).

In addition to archaeologists themselves, the discussants defined two external audiences: "the more passively involved general public" and "landowners or those with administrative responsibilities" over land-management decisions affecting archaeological resources (McGimsey and Davis 1977:79). Among archaeologists, the then current approaches—monographs, conferences, newsletters, training programs, and the like—were seen as necessary but insufficient for the future growth of the field. Critical to that growth was a recommendation for a "central office," described as a base for "rapid communications within the profession" that would also serve as a media liaison, center for school curricula, legislative monitoring system, and general resource for practicing archaeologists (1977:80–84).

The Airlie House discussants devoted the bulk of their deliberations to communication with the "General Public." Interestingly, in light of the Harris Interactive poll cited earlier, the discussants shared a sense that "a large majority of the American public seems to be of the opinion that archeology is a 'good thing'...[but that] a vast number of that same public knows precious little about archeology or its results, much less how it might have some applicability to their own lives" (McGimsey and Davis 1977:84). The discussants concluded that most of the general public could be broken into two subgroups: those who took an active interest and sought out archaeological information and those who did not but who might include people who could be helpful to archaeology—for example, those in professions such as teaching or the media. This group also included pothunters, who might be educated to give up their activities.

A range of approaches including both strategies and tactics was suggested for reaching the general public. A key strategic concept involved graduate school education. There, "equal training in the ability to express ideas to nonarchaeologists" was advocated because "the profession cannot expect the public to develop and maintain on their own attitudes favorable to archeology" (McGimsey and Davis 1977:84). Other important strategic concepts involved the written word (tactics included popular books, magazine articles, newspapers, and curricula development), visual presentations including museum displays, and, most intriguing, a strategy referred to as "the organizational approach." The contributors noted that "the profession is becoming aware of an organized approach to communication, but has yet to provide adequate support for this mechanism" (1977:87). Today we would refer to this as a communications strategy.

The final audience identified, "Those Who Control the Land," consisted largely of public officials, especially at the county level. Implicit but critical to this portion of the discussion was a recognition that in the United States, the vast majority of private land-use decisions affecting archaeological resources were made at the level of the county commission or zoning board. Advice for reaching this audience was not as robust as that offered for the general public, possibly because this was such a new audience for archaeologists to consider. The critical recommendations included development of what is often called an "elevator speech"—a quick, to-the-point overview of an issue—and a solid working knowledge of the local land-use planning process.

The Airlie House discussants closed with prescient observations and a warning. It is, they wrote, "no longer appropriate for archeologists to operate totally within an ivory tower....While it will always be true that archeologists need to communicate effectively among themselves, it now is abundantly clear that unless they also communicate effectively with the general public, and with those making decisions affecting the cultural resource base, all else will be wasted effort" (McGimsey and Davis 1977:89).

There seems little doubt that the evaluation of the Airlie House discussants—that archaeology communications was, broadly speaking, in a state of crisis—was true in the 1970s. Communication with other archaeologists in the mid-1970s was increasingly sophisticated, but communication with the general public was nearly nonexistent, with the exception of catch-as-catch-can local efforts. Almost no one in the profession had any knowledge of local land-use planning, public agency land-use practices, or the politics that attend local zoning ordinances.

Indeed, just a year after publication of the Airlie House report, McGimsey gave an invited paper titled "Archeology, Anthropology, and the Public" in which he called for a demonstration that "the scientific output does indeed have a meaning and relevance to the public" and that archaeologists could communicate that relevance to a variety of audiences (McGimsey 2004:124). It is unsurprising that archaeology needed such calls to action. From the founding of the Society for American Archaeology (SAA) in 1935 through the 1950s, the discipline focused on establishing chronologies and began to tackle questions of function. One author has noted that during this period, archaeology was in a classic Kuhnian "normal science" phase, with all that this implies (Dunnell 1986:29). The development of first the Smithsonian's River Basin Surveys program in the 1940s and later the demands of gearing up to address the new responsibilities of Section 106 had left archaeologists little time to ponder how they might build public support—and in any case, they were ill-prepared by training to do so. This is not to say that even at that early date, no progress was being made. Indeed, it is to the everlasting credit of the profession that archaeologists such as McGimsey and Fred Wendorf learned to play the communications game so quickly and that their efforts, and the efforts of others like them, were so broadly supported by the profession, even if most members of the time were not active participants in these efforts.

COMMUNICATION AMONG ARCHAEOLOGISTS: THE PRESENT

By implication, the Airlie House discussants' evaluation of communication among archaeologists was positive, and it has mostly improved since the issuance of their original report. Monographs, journals, newsletters, reviews, meetings, and training programs—all these mechanisms for professional communication are even better developed now than they were in 1974. The two principal American archaeological professional organizations, the SAA and the Society for Historical Archaeology (SHA), are at all-time highs in membership and ranges of activities. The American Cultural Resources Association (ACRA) supports the cultural resource management industry and has been extremely active (and successful) in communicating information about the legislative scene to and between archaeologists.

The success in communications on the national level is to some extent mirrored on the state level. Many states now have active professional councils that are involved in developing guidelines for survey and excavation, legislative monitoring and action, preservation efforts, and other activities. Most have some form of professional newsletter, whether in hard copy or by e-mail.

Some of the "Possibilities for the Future" envisioned by the Airlie House discussants have been fulfilled. The SAA to a large extent now fulfills the role of the "central office" that, it was hoped, would monitor legislation and maintain liaisons with other, kindred organizations. This, combined with the rapid integration of Web-based technology in archaeology, has resulted in a small, archaeological version of the "flat world" that *New York Times* columnist Thomas Friedman (2005) has written about so eloquently. Information of certain kinds (for instance, professional news, new discoveries, and conference papers) circulates nearly instantaneously.

In one area of communications within the profession addressed by the Airlie House discussants, however, archaeologists have little to cheer about. The distribution of CRM-derived archaeological data was identified in 1974 as a critical concern. It is a credit to the participants of the time that they foresaw the rapid accumulation of information that would result from the growth of CRM and attempted to wrestle with how to distribute those data. In the pre-Internet world, a system of microfiche reports seemed to be an efficient solution to the upcoming onslaught of data.

Unfortunately, more than three decades after archaeology data distribution was identified as an area requiring attention, the problem has become worse, not better (King, chapter 7, this volume). Although the National Archaeological Database (NADB) provides a partial listing of titles in the gray literature, no single source exists through which to access even the abstracts of the great majority of archaeological reports published today (National Park Service 2008). Meanwhile, the volume of information available through the so-called gray literature has grown many times over what it was in 1974.

COMMUNICATION WITH THE GENERAL PUBLIC: THE PRESENT

It is in the area of communication with the "general public" (about which, more later) that archaeology as a profession has made the most significant strides since 1974—somewhat paradoxically, because some of the most important recommendations of the Airlie House discussants have never been meaningfully addressed. Because public support of archaeology is so critical today, it is worth dissecting some of the issues identified in 1974 in some detail.

The 1974 discussants recognized that graduate-level education in public communication was a critical first step: "There needs to be equal training [in graduate school] in the ability to express ideas to nonarcheologists" (McGimsey and Davis 1977:84). Unfortunately, this is still the case. No graduate school anthropology or archaeology programs include a basic course in public communication as a requirement. This failure to develop professional communications skills in graduate school hobbles graduates who go on to practice in the public sphere. The skill set needed to present an academic argument in, for instance, a dissertation defense is quite different from that needed to communicate effectively to a local policy maker. This lack has negative effects on both careers and the resource base itself.

Archaeologists have come a long way since 1974 in writing for popular audiences. For instance, many archaeologists now have a good command of the written word for nonprofessional audiences. One of the most popular books at recent SAA and SHA conferences has been a volume by Brian Fagan, one of the premier authors in the field, titled *Writing Archaeology: Telling Stories about the Past* (2005). Fagan sets out, in his typically comfortable style, the basics of learning to write, writing for newspapers and magazines, dealing with agents, and all the other issues that serious writers must address in order to be successful. Workshops at conferences on both the national and regional levels now address writing, and they usually fill up early during registration. Volumes such as William Kelso's *Jamestown: The Buried Truth* (2006) do well in the market (and can capture the attention of the queen of England), as do titles ranging from *I Can Be an Archaeologist* (Pickering 1987) to *Archaeology and You* (Stuart and McManamon 1996). Archaeologists are also deeply involved in curriculum development—witness the SAA's Web page, Archaeology for the Public, and its detailed lesson plans (www.saa.org/publicftp/PUBLIC/home/home.html). And each year, more than 1,100 students participate in archaeology at Fort Frederica National Monument in Georgia, where archaeology has been formally adopted into the framework of the fourth-grade curriculum. Teachers are trained to instruct students in the history of the eighteenth-century fort and town of Frederica and in the methods of historical archaeology (Strojan 2003). This approach—"teaching the teachers"—is an effective way of reaching young people because it leverages a preexisting edu-cational system and puts it to work in the service of archaeological site conservation.

The spoken word has also seen dramatic improvement as a communications tool. For instance, the SHA regularly features archaeology in public lectures as part of its annual conference; in 2007 the featured speaker was Ivor Noel Hume, one of the founders of historical archaeology in the United States and one of the best public speakers (and writers) in the field. State archaeological societies regularly feature speakers for "Archaeology Week" (or month) who discuss high-profile projects, and many have speakers bureaus.

Visual presentation—by which the Airlie House discussants meant videotapes, museum displays, and archaeological kits (teaching trunks)— seem to have experienced a somewhat more checkered developmental history, although, again, hard information is difficult to come by. Videotapes have been supplanted by various Web- and cable-based programs, which seem to be popular. A recent Georgia Public Broadcasting show on current archaeological research in Georgia was the second most-watched episode in an outdoor series, shown 12 times over a year and reaching 83,000 households. Shows such as *History's Mysteries* have steady viewerships in the remunerative "male, 25–54" demographic (History Channel Web site, www.aetninternational.com/build_history.jsp, May 15, 2007), although their content is sometimes open to criticism. The Archaeology Channel provides a mix of both print and video presentations on topics that appeal to a wide range of audiences. Some recent offerings included presentations on Ur, Amelia Earhart, and forensic anthropology (Pettigrew 2002). The National Park Service's Southeast Archeological Center (www.nps.gov /seac/) serves as a portal to many other Web-based resources and carries much original content as well.

Museum displays may not be faring as well. This may be largely because of an ongoing phenomenon in the museum world: many museums seem to be experiencing declines in visitorship. In part, this may be self-inflicted. Museum displays are expensive to mount, and archaeological displays are among the most expensive because of the environmental conditions that have to be maintained. The decline in visitorship is also attributable, however, to the increasing segmentation of the museum market and, just as important, to visitor expectations, which are being driven by the Internet, computer-generated graphics, podcasts, and all the other near-simultaneous and interactive media that are available to the modern consumer.

COMMUNICATION WITH THOSE WHO CONTROL THE LAND: THE PRESENT

The Airlie House discussants acknowledged the strong private property ethic in the United States, but they also recognized that an educated landowner could be a valuable stewardship partner (McGimsey and Davis 1977:88). Similar education efforts were urged to reach out to public officials. Perhaps one of the most insightful recommendations of the 1974 discussants, however, was that the profession acquaint itself with local land-use regulations and establish a relationship with the National Association of Counties, or NACo (www.naco.org). In many states, especially in the intermountain West, the Southwest, and the Southeast, state constitutions contain strong "home rule" components. Home rule implies that governmental decisions are best made at the lowest possible level, and in most cases, this means that land-use planning takes place at the county level.

From a resource management perspective, this approach carries significant downsides. Archaeological cultures are not distributed along modern jurisdictional lines, and the plethora of sometimes competing, sometimes cooperating local governments makes the management of cultural, as well as natural, resources at a regional level extremely challenging. Nonetheless, this is the governmental system we as a profession must work with, and the panel's suggestion relative to the establishment of relationships with county officials has much merit, even if it has been acted on only locally and sporadically. In many of the western states, such as Nevada, much if not most of the public land is managed by federal agencies, such as the Bureau of Land Management. Although the sheer size of this bureaucracy might be daunting, this type of land-use planning context is actually much easier to work in, because one agency controls vast acreage and is relatively easy to communicate with. However, the importance of personal relationships is still critical because trust and credibility can be invaluable in negotiating the federal bureaucracy.

A Context for Communication in Public Archaeology

Where, then, does the state of archaeological communications stand today? First, it is worth noting that at a basic but meaningful level, there is no such thing as "archaeological" communication. There is only communication—the ability to get ideas and concepts across to an audience. The content is in a certain sense irrelevant. Indeed, although unarticulated, this was implicit in the Airlie House discussions. Most of the panel's report dealt not with archaeological content, but with strategies and tactics for communicating that content to specified audiences.

It should be acknowledged that the term *general public* is, at least in today's world, an oversimplification. The general public consists of multiple audiences of differing educational levels, social statuses, economic statuses, and interests. The loss of viewers experienced by what used to be called the "major networks" (ABC, CBS, NBC), as well as the decline of major metropolitan daily newspapers, many of which are losing readership precipitously, points to an all-important fact of the modern media market: increasing segmentation. This is not to say that more traditional media such as books, newspapers, and television are not effective tools that archaeologists should use. It *is* to say that in an age of "narrowcasting" (the term speaks for itself), archaeologists must have at least a rudimentary understanding of the communications world and need a sophisticated tool kit if they are to effectively speak to the public(s).

Even more intimidating for archaeologists (who, like historians, thrive on written records), reading habits seem to be changing as well. Nearly all major newspapers now have Web editions by which they hope to offset their loss of paper edition readers. Although there are no published hard data on the subject, informal discussions with reporters for several major daily newspapers that have instituted Web editions indicate that Web readers tend to jump from article to article, and from Web page to Web page, in a way that is fundamentally different from sitting at the kitchen table and slowly reading the news. The implications of these types of changes are just beginning to be felt in the news industry, but one thing is for sure: they will affect—indeed already are affecting—the way the public absorbs archaeological or any other kind of scientific news. Bit by bit, the major newspapers are cutting coverage of the sciences; many no longer have a science box at all, even in their signature Sunday editions. Instead, stories revolving around popular culture, sports, and entertainment—what used to be in the "Living" section of most major dailies—are gradually moving to the front sections. The bottom line for archaeologists: the media world has changed in significant ways since 1974. New technologies have led to increased market segmentation and shorter attention spans.

Edelman, the world's largest independent public relations firm, produces a window into this rapidly evolving world of media and information. Each year, it conducts a global trust and credibility survey, the "Trust Barometer," of opinion leaders, who are defined for the purposes of the study as college educated, between 35 and 64 years of age, reporting a household income in the top quartile of their country, and interested in or engaged with the media and policy affairs. Edelman's survey ignores significant sectors of the population in the United States that archaeologists are interested in reaching, such as high school and college students and minorities. However, if a significant goal of archaeological communication is to build support for further conservation and research, the opinion leaders Edelman surveys certainly constitute an important constituency.

A key finding of the Edelman Trust Barometer for 2007 was that in the developed world, "a person like yourself" ranked with doctors and academics as the most trusted sources of information (58–59 percent of respondents). In the United States, "a person like yourself" was trusted by 68 percent of respondents (Edelman 2007). The bad news for public archaeology is that only 39 percent of respondents counted a "government official or regulator" as a credible source of information (results varied only slightly by country). But who is this semi-mythical "person like yourself?" The definition is based not on shared gender, religion, or race, but on shared interests, professions, and political beliefs (2007:3–7). The rise of social media has driven much of this, in the opinion of the Edelman analysts: "We can find people in all parts of the world with kindred interests, even in the most specialized fields. So instead of putting our trust in a few people we know well, we tend to have webs of acquaintances" (2007:8). The lack of trust in established institutions and figures of authority has motivated people to trust their peers as the best sources of information, prompting many companies to shift from top-down communication with elites to a peer-to-peer model of communication. Importantly, the report emphasized the role of passion in effective communications (2007:2).

RECOMMENDATIONS: COMMUNICATION WITH OTHER ARCHAEOLOGISTS

Although no single database or library is available to access the gray literature nationwide (and it seems increasingly unlikely that such a mechanism will be developed), individual states have made substantial progress in systematizing their archaeological data collections. Often this is in conjunction with a Web-based geographical information systems (GIS) application that allows users to access archaeological site file data remotely. In Georgia, for instance, the development of NAHRGIS (Natural, Archaeological, and Historical Resources GIS) allows archaeological users to search the state for sites (point locations), plot those on 1:24,000 scale topographic maps, and then access PDF files of the site forms and reports. Shape files of all surveyed areas are currently being processed. Arizona and South Carolina have similar efforts under way, and Wyoming and New Mexico have relatively advanced systems.

Rather than attempt to impose a one-size-fits-all solution for access to the gray literature (the intent of the NADB), it seems wiser to convene a task force under the leadership of ACRA that would include members from both the SAA and the SHA (see also King, chapter 7, this volume). The charge to the task force would be to survey the status of gray literature collections nationwide, focusing on states that have made or are in the process of making the literature widely available. These examples might then encourage states that have not yet done so to explore various models for platforms, funding sources, access, and the like. The report of the task force could be posted on the ACRA Web site, with links from the Web sites of the SAA, the SHA, the National Association of State Archaeologists, and the National Conference of State Historic Preservation Officers. Starting with large-area surveys and big mitigation projects would maximize the return quickly. Ultimately, it might be possible to develop a portal that allows users to access any state that has Web-based reports and site files. In this connection, it is worth noting that the Colorado Council of Professional Archaeologists, with funding from the state, has produced regional-level contexts that could serve as useful models (see Colorado Council of Professional Archaeologists 2008).

RECOMMENDATIONS: COMMUNICATION WITH THE GENERAL PUBLIC

The single most important long-term recommendation regarding communications in archaeology in the 1977 Airlie House report still, unfortunately, stands. It is not enough for graduate schools to teach students the technical skills necessary to become competent archaeologists. If the profession of archaeology is serious about developing a more robust communications program, then graduate schools simply must step up to the plate and provide the basic training necessary to communicate in the world outside academe. Consider the case of a hypothetical, newly minted PhD. He or she may be interested in an academic career or may seek a job in a consulting firm or a state or federal agency. In the former case, the expertise necessary to communicate outside campus will enhance the new hire's public service bona fides, an important part of many tenure evaluations. It will also help the new professor connect with students, especially those who may be reticent. And of course such skills will increase public knowledge of archaeological resources and their values.

For the archaeologist in the public sector, where our hypothetical PhD will most likely find employment, such skills may well prove critical to career advancement. Let us consider the hypothetical new PhD a bit more. He or she has found employment in a state historic preservation office, and a good thing too, because divers have been looting publicly owned shipwrecks that are, theoretically at least, protected under state law. The arrests of several perpetrators lead to a series of legislative hearings. The legislators are mostly business people from more rural parts of the state, where hunting artifacts in farm fields is an old tradition, and they are shocked to learn that there is a state law protecting shipwrecks. After all, doesn't *National Geographic* cover treasure hunters? And aren't the divers, as they claim, "saving history"? If no one from "the state" is going to "save" these shipwrecks, why *shouldn't* average citizens step in? Why *should* the state have a law keeping them from doing so?

Thrust into such a situation, which is commoner than some people probably realize, if you were the new PhD, which would you rather have— the ability to apply practice theory and the work of Bourdieu to postcolonial archaeology in Turkmenistan or the ability to put together a cogent argument for resource protection in language that could be used in a local news broadcast?

A similar argument could be made for new PhDs who go to work for cultural resource firms and find themselves having to present complex (and relatively expensive) research designs for mitigation projects to developers who consider Section 106 just one more environmental regulatory hoop to jump through. And even if a new PhD is never faced with such a situation, it is likely that he or she will be a member of a state professional society, which will periodically have to address public policy concerns.

My new PhD may be hypothetical, but these scenarios are not. All of them occur with regularity and likely will result in one of two outcomes: increased public resource awareness and protection, or less. None of this is to argue that students should not have the technical skills they require to be productive archaeologists. It *is* to argue that in today's world, even more than in 1974, such skills are in and of themselves insufficient. In short, we need more tools in our tool kit.

At a minimum, graduate-level training in communications for archaeologists should include a selection from the following components:

- Basic Public Speaking à la Toastmasters. This is critical. The skills of argumentation that are necessary to successfully defend a thesis or dissertation only partially overlap with those needed to reach a nontechnical audience. Such audiences will at some point likely include elected policy makers, whose chief interests often revolve around budgetary concerns and value to the taxpayer rather than the intrinsic (and to practitioners, self-evident) importance of the past.
- Print Journalism 101. With few exceptions (and those, likely at the

major metro dailies), most reporters are trained as generalists. This will become more the case in the future as the metro newspapers come under increasing pressure to cut staff, a movement that has already severely affected the depth and breadth of their reportage. Therefore, it will become more, not less, important that students understand and be comfortable with the "who, what, where, when, why" mode used by most print journalists, which virtually every journalist learns in undergraduate school.

- Broadcast Media 101. The local print media are often willing to work with a combination of e-mail exchanges and telephone interviews. This gives the archaeologist an opportunity to refine or correct misperceptions before they reach print. The broadcast media offer an entirely different environment—rich with increased possibilities but also full of potential pitfalls. For instance, although so-called ambush interviews are relatively rare, they can be tremendously damaging to a legislative agenda—whether that agenda consists of defending current laws and budgets or advocating for new ones. However, most local television stations are interested in the visual and auditory aspects of archaeology, so linking one's legislative or policy concerns to an actual project can be immensely helpful.

- Web Design 101. At this point, almost any graduate-level archaeology student is going to be savvier about the latest innovations in Web page design, social networking, and the like, than his or her professors. A proseminar environment is an excellent way to bring these areas of expertise forward so that the entire class has the opportunity to benefit.

- Policy 101. For students expecting any kind of role in public archaeology—whether as university-based advocate or agency-based practitioner—understanding the basics of public policy is a bedrock principle. Certain principles will apply whether one works with federal, state, or local agencies. However, the political cultures of state governments vary widely (so, indeed, do the political cultures of federal agencies). Even a basic understanding of these commonalities and differences would be immensely useful as we advocate for archaeological resources and their wise management.

This proposal may seem radical, but it is less so than it might appear at first glance. The SAA recently published the Recommended Model Curriculum: Master's in Applied Anthropology, which includes several components I have noted. Undergraduate archaeology course materials from the SAA initiative Making Archaeology Teaching Relevant in the XXIst Century (MATRIX) are also available online (www.saa.org/aboutSAA/committees/curriculum/index.html), and the organization promotes the teaching of archaeology through an annual awards program. Just as important, several universities are taking concrete steps to make such content available. The University of Arizona already offers a class in professional skills that presents basic tips on many topics typically thought of as ancillary. East Carolina University in tidewater North Carolina requires its maritime history (underwater archaeology) graduate students to keep online journals as a component of their field school requirements. Currently, three virtual exhibits and seven project journals are posted on the Web site of the Museum of Underwater Archaeology (www.uri.edu/artsci/his/mua/MUA.htm), a Web site built and maintained by Kurt Knoerl and hosted by the University of Rhode Island.

The larger point is that this process can begin with small steps and each department can incorporate the type and level of communications instruction the faculty thinks appropriate. Graduating archaeologists who understand the power and pitfalls of modern media and who know how to use those media to enhance the central messages of the field would lead over time to a culture shift in the discipline. The key is understanding that archaeologists usually are the providers of information and perspectives to writers, journalists, television producers, and the like. We need to understand something about how these professions function and how we can help them produce stories that are accurate and make at least some of the points we are concerned about. This in turn would put archaeology in a much stronger position to advance resource conservation and research, which, regardless of one's employment sector, should be the primary goal. Critical to the successful execution of such a strategy is calibrating both the medium itself and the way the story is presented to the target audience.

The preceding topics could be couched comfortably in a cultural anthropology course—call it "The Anthropology of the Media and Public Archaeology." The point is not to make every archaeologist a media maven; it is to give students a broad overview that will enable them to fully develop their communications skills throughout their careers. An SAA-sponsored committee to keep tabs on new media developments and their applicability to archaeology could also present periodic updates and best management practices on the Web or develop training symposia for those of us who are farther along in our careers.

The SAA Student Affairs Committee could make a substantial contribution in this area immediately. The committee has proved that it is serious about collegial assistance through its ongoing education efforts at the
annual conference. It could engage practicing archaeologists with track
records in public affairs and media personnel with experience in archaeological stories to present periodic symposia that would provide a real and
solid basis for new graduates.

State Archaeological Societies and Site Steward Programs

State archaeological societies should not be neglected as we think
about communications tactics. For example, the Arkansas Archaeological
Society, the South Carolina Archaeological Society, and the Archaeological
Society of New Mexico provide opportunities to communicate both to and
through educated laypeople. Although annual conferences, displays, and
the like, spring to mind as commonly used communication methods, it is
worth remembering that in general, state archaeological society members
are "people like yourself" to their own circle of friends and acquaintances.
It bears remembering that when we as professionals give papers or poster
sessions at state society meetings, we are communicating not just with the
people in attendance but perhaps indirectly with some of their friends and
acquaintances also.

Although every state archaeological society is different, the existence
of an institutional base of some kind, often a university or museum, is critical to the long-term success of such efforts. Kiwanis clubs, Elks chapters,
and similar fraternal organizations, though often moribund in large urban
centers, are still viable forces in more rural areas. Speaking at their lunches
is time intensive but can yield big results because often the local "movers
and shakers" (including local policy makers) are in attendance. Communicating about what archaeologists have learned about the past is a value in
and of itself, and it helps give society some return on its investment in what
we do. Making the link between this sort of thing and the importance of
stewarding the archaeological record can be much more difficult. It is easy
even for experienced speakers among us to slip into a "preachy mode that
privileges our somewhat arcane knowledge above other perspectives"
(Holtorf 2007; see also Lees and King 2007).

The Texas Site Steward program is a wonderful example of how a relatively small group of dedicated citizens can make a real difference in
resource conservation and education. The Edelman study makes it clear
why this small group has been so successful: the group consists of the "people like yourself" the study identified as so important when it comes to

credibility. Arkansas, Nevada, and Arizona offer three additional examples of robust stewardship programs (see Arizona Archaeological Society, http:/// azarchsoc.org; Arkansas Archaeological Survey, www.uark.edu/cam pus-resources/archinfo; Nevada Archaeological Association, www.nvarch .org). The Bureau of Land Management offers a good example of a federal agency stewardship program (see www.blm.gov/education/Learning Landscapes/teachers/archaeology.html), as does the US Forest Service's Passport in Time program (www.passportintime.com).

Site stewardship programs bring people together with archaeological resources and also promote camaraderie, which is an important component of any successful statewide program. Several offer certification or other types of training. However, such programs do not run themselves or even run with a part-time coordinator. It is better not to have such a program than to have one in which the volunteers can never get the coordinator on the phone and end up feeling used. Never attempt to undertake a site stewardship program without a full-time coordinator.

SAA Public Affairs Officer

It is absolutely critical for the Society for American Archaeology to fund a public affairs position. The holder of such a position could start by determining how the profession as a whole is engaging the media. For instance, what could the profession do to serve as a collective resource for the media? Is there a place for an annual resource guide? Such an approach could leverage the considerable latent communications talent in the field of archaeology to engage important media sectors. The key would be to identify and focus on those media sectors that are most critical and then tailor our communications tactics to reach them effectively. Such an approach does not always involve large expenditures of money; it simply requires us to think imaginatively with a trained public affairs specialist.

Media Relations

It seems clear that archaeology has advanced significantly in some of the areas identified by the original Airlie House panelists. Archaeologists are becoming increasingly adept at writing about their discoveries in books and magazine articles, and numerous examples and prescriptive models are now available for how to do that. An excellent primer on working with print media was published in *American Antiquity* (DeCicco 1988; see also Harding 2007; Joffe 2006; Scherzler 2007). Similarly, good examples exist of both sophisticated electronic media presentations (especially using the Web) and newspaper, TV, and radio coverage of projects. However, these examples are individual in scope. In large part, that is because writing a book (or even a magazine article) or developing a Web site takes money and time—neither of which are abundant for most archaeological projects, either under Section 106 or otherwise.

In the absence of such resources, how can we as a profession reach our general public audiences? A relatively straightforward recommendation is for archaeologists to develop, individually, good relationships with local news media. Local freelance writers and producers can provide a valuable entrée into small newspapers and other niche vehicles (DeCicco 1988:855–856) Media coverage of our projects is timely and, most important, free. Furthermore, outside the major media markets, people still count on their local newspapers and radio and TV stations for the bulk of their news. Why? Because local news organs employ local reporters—the "people like yourself" identified by the Edelman study. A good first step to increase the efficiency of communications in archaeology, then, is through local media. Some basic principles of media relations follow.

Although the media are often referred to as the "fourth estate" because of their watchdog role over government, most electronic and print media outlets are constantly scouting for new stories that have human interest. Archaeologists are well positioned to take advantage of this interest because we have great stories to tell. Even in this day of "narrowcasting," a well-told story has near universal appeal, especially if it involves science. Series such as *History Detectives* and *Myth Busters* would not be aired unless they were highly successful. The key is to focus on the story told by the archaeology and on the process of putting the pieces together that make the story. Archaeology has an inherent romance because of its association in most people's minds with discovery. We should not be defensive about that any more than early environmentalists were defensive about the appeal of the bald eagle in introducing a discussion of DDT. We can use archaeology's innate appeal as a hook and *then* move into a discussion of the realities of the archaeological process.

The media market is a business, and like all businesses, the bottom line is earnings. Earnings in the electronic media are determined by ratings, whereas the goal of print media is increased circulation. Most larger cities have a daily newspaper that is regional in scope. Smaller towns more often have a local paper that is issued once or twice a week, often by a small staff. Although some large metro papers have a science reporter, this is increasingly rare. Reporters themselves are often young (especially at local media outlets) and relatively inexperienced. Often, in larger markets, they have college degrees (usually in English or journalism), but in small markets, that is not necessarily the case. Newspaper reporters often conduct their interviews by telephone, but if you are conducting ongoing fieldwork, you should never hesitate to invite local reporters out to your site. Never assume that a reporter has more than a passing familiarity with archaeology, and accept that their ideas have likely been formed by other news accounts and popular culture.

Television stations are located primarily in larger cities. TV stations with newscasts are often associated with one of the networks and can pull down stories of regional or national interest from satellites. They also have local reporters, who are assigned to stories by the news director, usually the day the story is scheduled to air. If a story is especially important (for instance, a press conference), the reporter may bring a satellite truck and crew in order to send the story directly to the station for a live remote broadcast. More often, the reporter brings a cameraman. Issues that are highly visual and interactive get more coverage on the newscast. Remember, television reporters usually work on very short deadlines so that they can get their interviews done and the tape back to the station for editing. They are looking for quick facts, so you should have some key points memorized and ready to go (about which, more later).

Radio stations vary widely in format and staff size. Larger radio stations are often associated with a TV station, but almost universally reporters work by telephone rather than in the field. An exception may be the local public broadcasting station. PBS stations often like to do a "soundscape" type of interview if the audio is interesting. Such broadcasts might involve the sounds of shovels scraping, trowels troweling, or, for an underwater archaeology story, boat engines and bubbles. Do not forget, although these sounds are a routine part of the job for us, most listeners have never heard them, and using them to illustrate a verbal description or interview of the action adds immediacy that is invaluable.

Magazines offer another written venue for reaching an interested audience. Today, with publications like *American Archaeology* and *Archaeology*, as well as the more traditional *National Geographic*, there are a number of national venues to make your projects known. Do not forget magazines that are not traditional venues for archaeology, however. For instance, many larger cities have magazines that cover the local cultural or business scene and new trends in development. Airline in-flight magazines are constantly looking for content. These are excellent venues to reach audiences that might have never thought about archaeological resources except as potential sources of trouble. Using Section 106 projects to demonstrate otherwise is a critical strategy for reaching these audiences, a point I return to later.

Several common tools of the trade are available to the media-savvy archaeologist. *Press releases* are used to provide a general overview of an issue or a project and usually involve quotes from key people (like you) about the significance of the announcement. E-mail has made distribution of press releases much easier than it used to be, and most state media associations publish a contacts list so that you can develop an e-mail group. Such groups can be tailored for specific types of projects; for instance, coastal media might be targeted for shipwreck stories. *Public service announcements* (PSAs) are similar to advertisements but are aired free of charge. Most TV and radio stations use PSAs to fill in between programming; most PSAs last between 30 seconds and a minute. *Media advisories* direct quick attention to an event or issue and are usually issued in advance of a press conference or media event. They provide the who, what, where, when, and why. *Press conferences* are formal announcements of information to the media. These last two tools are used less often than the preceding two, although for public agencies such as state historic preservation offices, they may be helpful. Field days, or *media events*, are less formal than press conferences and, as the names indicate, provide the media with an opportunity to get out into the field. If your state has an Archaeology Week or Month, this is a good time to host a field day. *Press packets* present in-depth information about a media campaign or an event. They often include press releases, background information, fact sheets, photographs, and the like. Press packets are best distributed at a press conference or field day.

When a reporter calls about a project or when you call a reporter, it is best to take charge of the process as much as possible. The basic questions you should ask before the interview starts include the following:

- What is the deadline for the reporter's story? Be sure to understand the time frame.
- What logistical support will be needed, if it is not just a telephone interview?
- What is the angle of the story? Is it a feature story or hard news? Will you be one of a panel of experts or the only one with knowledge of the subject?
- Are you familiar with the reporter's work? Some reporters, especially investigative journalists, specialize in the "ambush interview," in which the point is to put you on the defensive and lead you to make a statement that can then be spun into a conflict-oriented story. This is

something to be especially aware of if you work with NAGPRA issues or sensitive Section 106 undertakings in which consultation, negotiation, or both are called for.

- Who is the audience?
- Topics—what is the nature of the story?

Preparing for an interview, like preparing to present a professional paper, involves careful thought. Be sure you know the topic of discussion well so that you have clear objectives in mind for the interview. Organize your thinking, and most important, eliminate extraneous information. Nothing will kill reader or viewer interest faster than droning on about the finer points of ceramic typology or the difference between a 4 mHz and a 15 mHz antenna on a GPR unit. Do not "dumb down" your information, but learn to present it in short, straightforward sentences.

Before the interview, write down the main points you want to make about the project. Put them in priority order. If the reporter does not ask questions that bring out these points, take charge and do that at the end of the interview. Most seasoned reporters will ask you toward the end, "Is there anything else you would like to say about this project?" This is your chance to advocate not just for your project but also for the discipline of archaeology and its importance. Think ahead of time about what the toughest questions are likely to be. A simple way to develop this ability is to watch some of the more confrontational TV interview shows and then think about what types of questions the interviewer would ask if you were the subject. Sometimes questions that we as archaeologists think have self-evident answers—such as "Why is Section 106 necessary?"—can leave us tongue-tied in front of a camera. One of the commonest mistakes archaeologists make is to fall back into "graduate student at a beer bust" mode. In this scenario, the graduate student (you) is under the misimpression that when someone asks you about your dissertation, he or she wants to know about every jot and tittle. Unless this person is your significant other, he or she does not. Neither do reporters. Give them the top three reasons your project is important, and stay, as the politicians say, "on message." Always have a strong final statement to make to the reporter. Remember, the reporter cannot read your mind, so be explicit in making your points. An interview wrap-up is a great time to hand a reporter a fact sheet or press packet that reinforces the topic of the interview.

The media approach for archaeologists involved in the public sector and those working in the academic sector may vary, because public agencies normally come in for more scrutiny than do academic institutions.

However, it is always good to remember that there is no such thing as "off the record"—if you say it, the reporter can use it. Always correct inaccuracies on the spot—insufficient or erroneous information propagates very quickly now, partly because of the Internet. Take a deep breath before answering the hard questions. If you work in the public sector, you can expect to be asked questions such as "Why should the citizens of the state spend their hard-earned money digging up broken pottery?" and "Why shouldn't artifact hunters be allowed to metal-detect on land before it is developed?" When a reporter calls, always write down his or her name, publication or station, and telephone number and the information being requested. Keep your media contacts in a separate file or database; they will come in handy repeatedly during your career. Ask reporters how they would like to handle the interview—would they rather ask questions first or get an overview from you first? Remember, repetition of your critical points is critical. Never assume that you will see a story before it airs or runs in print. A reporter may offer this as a courtesy, but it is by no means normal operating procedure.

Most of us in archaeology have a well-deserved reputation for scruffiness. Although it is unlikely that we as a profession will suddenly adopt upscale safari wear for our interviews, some basics of professionalism will go a long way toward increasing our credibility. The most important thing to remember is something that we as anthropologists should know well—body language speaks volumes. Facial expressions are critical. It is unnecessary to project a Suzy Sunshine image (unless that is your normal demeanor), but frowning puts the viewer off. *Do not* wear sunglasses. They may look cool, but they give your audience the impression that you have something to hide, because people cannot see your eyes. Hats, although necessary for those of us who are hair challenged, shade your face as well. Lean forward slightly if you are being filmed or are appearing live, and look the reporter directly in the eye. Try to appear attentive.

The best way to ensure good media coverage of your projects is to build relationships at the local level. Most local media are hungry for stories. Getting a chance to interview a real archaeologist is a treat for them; most of the time, they will jump at the chance to take you up on an offer of a field day. Developing a trust relationship with a local reporter is often critical to long-term success. On small-town newspapers and electronic media outlets, these relationships will require constant tending because the staff reporters are often young and looking for opportunities to move up to larger markets. Turnover is likely to be high, which means that we must be prepared to "train" our media contacts almost continually. Such efforts can pay off, however, especially when dealing with a potentially controversial project.

For instance, if you are wrapping up a mitigation project, contact the local media (after clearing it with your client, of course). Talk to them about the National Historic Preservation Act and mention the federal agencies and project sponsors. Most people are unaware of the NHPA; this is a golden chance to get the word out at the grass roots and demonstrate to your client that archaeology is not just one more regulatory hoop to jump through.

To sum up:

- Approach the media in the way you want others to treat you. If you are distant or hostile, those attitudes will be returned.

- Do not assume that reporters know anything about you, your project, or archaeology. If they did, they would not be interviewing you.

- Speak in 30-second quotes. An interview is not a dissertation defense or a panel discussion; it is an opportunity for you to put archaeology front and center.

- Avoid technical jargon. Even commonly used terms such as *stratigraphy* can be off-putting.

- Keep in mind that all stories consist of two equal parts—the writer (or interviewer) and the interviewee. If you do not tell your part of the story well, neither will the reporter.

- Listen carefully to the questions. If you need clarification, ask for it.

- Provide supporting material, such as a press packet.

- Be yourself. If you try to change your normal presentation too much, you will appear stilted.

- Do not make the media search for facts. If you do, expect mistakes.

- Enjoy the experience. We were all trained as anthropologists first, so think of yourself as an anthropologist when engaging the media.

Section 106

Speaking broadly, federal agencies are well integrated into the archaeological communications network. There are exceptions, of course, and to some extent the degree of integration changes over time according to current politics—but politics will always be a part of public archaeology, for better or for ill. There is, however, one vital step that federal agencies could take that would vastly improve archaeological communication, and that is to be more imaginative about using what are often (and wrongly) referred to as "alternative" mitigative measures in the Section 106 Memoranda of

Agreements (MOA) and Programmatic Agreements. A recent informal survey of state historic preservation officers over the National Council of State Historic Preservation Officers listserve indicated wide variance in the extent to which outreach is considered as a mitigation strategy. However, it can serve several important purposes (see Chandler, chapter 6, this volume). A recent case study from Georgia provides an example (there are others from other states, but this is one with which I am personally familiar).

When the Georgia Ports Authority (GPA) decided to build a new container ship docking facility in Savannah harbor, the US Army Corps of Engineers archaeologist and the state historic preservation office, working through the Section 106 process, reviewed the Phase I survey design and the resulting report. Interestingly, although it had been known that a late-eighteenth-century plantation existed on the site (which was physically located during the survey), early-eighteenth-century artifacts hinted at a previously unknown occupant. Further research and National Register eligibility testing conducted by Southeastern Archaeological Services determined that the occupant was a woman named Mary Musgrove, a half-Creek, half-Scots deerskin trader who was critical to the early English colonization of the coast. Little is known of Musgrove, whose Creek name was Coosaponakeesa, but she clearly was skilled at negotiating and served as an intermediary for the colonial leaders (for better or worse).

Phase III excavations, coupled with intensive documentary research, uncovered Musgrove's house and trading post and artifacts associated with both her everyday existence and the trade. To their credit, both the Army Corps of Engineers and the GPA recognized the educational value of the find and wrote measures into the MOA that maximized not just the research but also the educational value of the site. As I write, development of the technical report is proceeding in tandem with development of a museum display at the Georgia Coastal Heritage Society, accompanying lesson plans, a re-creation of Musgrove's trading post and house based on archaeological and archival data, and a popular book that will be offered for sale in the museum store. Meanwhile, the project has generated broad media coverage emphasizing both the importance of the find and the GPA's recognition of the educational benefits it could yield.

Such projects—and there are more than one might suspect—can truly fulfill the NHPA's intent that the past should "live" in the present. They also can redound to the credit of the project sponsor, whether or not that sponsor is a public agency like the GPA. For another example, at the southern tip of Georgia's coast, the St. Mary's River forms the boundary with Florida. A high-end development outside the town of St. Mary's, at Point

Peter, resulted in the discovery of a War of 1812 fort associated with the final battle of the war. As part of the mitigation plan, Brockington and Associates developed an extensive education program, including lesson plans, an educational trunk, a Web site, and a Web game. The goal of the educational program was to present the events and effects of one of the most forgotten wars in US history, the War of 1812. Programs were designed for middle school students and met Georgia Department of Education curricular standards. Lessons focused on the lives of soldiers, the effects of the war on national and foreign policy, the lives of enslaved Africans living in Georgia during the war, and archaeological method and theory.

In addition to the educational program, the story of the last invasion and last battle of the War of 1812 is told in a multimedia exhibit titled Forgotten Invasion at the National Park Service's Cumberland Island National Seashore Museum in St. Mary's. The exhibit uses history and archaeology to reveal the story of the Battery at Point Peter. Twelve interpretive panels, a video, sound recordings, artifacts, and replica uniforms illustrate the period up to and including the War of 1812 at this coastal Georgia fortification. Panels about the archaeology describe how science is used to supplement our knowledge about and understanding of written history, often revealing forgotten or lost information. The exhibit even includes a replica of a ship's interior, complete with a telescope for viewing the enemy on the high seas. Children's-size replica uniforms are available for dressing up. An interpretive panel in this section shows a cutaway of a British ship of the line and an American gunboat.

Projects such as Point Peter and dozens of others prove that mitigation not only yields good scientific data but also redounds to the project sponsor's credit. Although one has to be careful with this strategy, with responsible oversight by the federal and state office and a willing project sponsor, such mitigation projects can be enormously helpful in building an identity for public archaeology and the resources it addresses. Such approaches have recently been explicitly endorsed by the Advisory Council on Historic Preservation's Archeology Task Force (ACHP 2007b; see also Lees and King 2007). An excellent resource in this regard is the volume *Archaeologists and Local Communities: Partners in Exploring the Past* (Derry and Malloy 2003).

RECOMMENDATIONS: COMMUNICATIONS WITH THOSE WHO MANAGE THE LAND

Outreach to county governments should start with the National Association of Counties (NACo), the only national association for county governance. NACo has a wide range of task forces, caucuses, and committees, the members of which are appointed by the president of the association. Outreach to NACo should start with a coordinated approach by the SAA and SHA because these two organizations are not industry based, as ACRA is, and are therefore more likely to be seen as advocating for the resource base free of commercial interest. The SAA and SHA should examine the education initiatives already available through NACo, with an eye toward developing a module that addresses basic land-use issues and their effects on archaeological resources. The module should include components addressing why local political leaders should care about the resource base, including the benefits that can be derived through heritage tourism, preservation of green space, watershed protection, and the like. All these environmental values can positively affect archaeological site protection.

In many states, the best protection for archaeological sites on the county level is through a combination of ordinances and landowner education. Although model ordinances exist (for instance, in Alexandria, Virginia), they are few and far between. This is because the political culture of each state, and sometimes within states, can vary greatly and new land-use ordinances can be contentious issues. Therefore, outreach to those who manage the land should also include development of a basic landowner education tool kit by the joint SAA-SHA committee. This might be modeled after SAA's public education Web page, but it would be tailored toward land-use issues and their effects on archaeological sites, heritage, and environmental values.

At the state agency level, consideration of archaeological sites varies widely both from state to state and from agency to agency. Lack of opportunity for improvement is definitely *not* an issue here. However, the single most critical communication effort that can be made at the state level may well be through law enforcement. Archaeologists have worked closely with law enforcement agencies for decades, but in most states, local and state law enforcement officers receive little education, if any, in the state code sections (and related federal laws) that protect cultural resources (including, for the purposes of this discussion, burials). In particular, conservation rangers and marine patrol officers often have wide-ranging powers to enter property and enforce state codes. Moreover, like many archaeologists, conservation rangers and marine patrol officers often enjoy being in the field and respect those (such as archaeologists) who are able to function under difficult environmental circumstances. A state-specific education module that could be presented to cadets during their peace officer training would be invaluable in sensitizing them to archaeological resources. Many states have a central police academy through which most peace officers, if not all of them, receive their training before taking their first posting—this is the best time to reach out to them.

Once law enforcement officers are sensitized to archaeological sites, archaeologists should use their communications skills to maintain contact with them. Personal relationships are important in the law enforcement world, and we would do well to cultivate such relationships. Again, this is where our training in cultural anthropology is invaluable. Law enforcement personnel consider themselves a subculture apart from the rest of society. Learning how to win their respect and communicate about archaeological resource protection using our basic cultural anthropologist skills can yield large dividends. This emphasis on personal relationships holds true for private landowners as well. It can take months, even years, to develop the trust needed to gain access to collections or sites on private land. Take your time, be yourself, and approach this challenge just as you would developing a relationship in any other setting.

CONCLUSION

Archaeologists have made substantial progress in many of the areas identified by the original Airlie House participants. In large part, this progress has been the result of leadership exercised by individuals, often through the SAA and later the SHA. In particular, communication with secondary school students and communication through the written word (and increasingly the World Wide Web) have been areas in which archaeology has made great progress, partly because of the appearance of new technologies (see, for instance, Chisholm, Leone, and Bentley 2007; Clarke 2004; Corbin and Smith 2008; Hall 2008; Robinson 2005; van Dyke 2006). Similarly, communication within the discipline has increased dramatically and with wholly beneficial results. Communications with the public could be enhanced relatively easily by implementing some of the suggestions I have offered regarding media relations.

Nevertheless, several of the core programmatic recommendations of the Airlie House panelists have not been meaningfully addressed. Foremost among these is the importance of graduate school training in communications. The world of communications has changed radically since 1977. More and more information is available to the average citizen, and the trend of new technologies to deliver that information shows no sign of slowing down—quite the contrary. These developments have driven the formation of communities of interest in which, as the Edelman Trust Barometer indicates, people gain information important to them from "people like yourself." If true, this observation has multiscalar societal implications that are somewhat intimidating to consider. However, if the observation is accurate—and on the basis of current information, it seems to be—then archaeological communication must change with it, or we risk becoming ever more marginalized. In large part, this means shifting from a top-down model of communication to one that includes a substantial horizontal element. Archaeologists must become more adept at negotiating this complex new communications world, and the best place to accomplish that over the long term is through graduate school education.

What would the ideal world of American archaeology communications look like several decades from now? Effective communication, especially to public officials and the world outside the profession, would be recognized as a critical component of a successful career. The intellectual and operations-side infrastructure would exist to make it possible—indeed, expected—for a broad corpus of MA- and PhD-level practitioners to translate the most important findings of our field to the increasingly segmented audiences of the modern media world. Current federal protections for cultural resources would continue, but support and advocacy from the SAA, SHA, and ACRA would be enhanced at the agency level. More important, policy makers, especially at the state and local levels, would become more aware of the importance of such resources to their constituents, even if they did not always personally agree that such resources were important.

How would we measure success? Because communication is a process, it is never "successful," if being successful means that we as a profession can stop factoring it into our planning. In that sense, the crisis in communications identified by the Airlie House panelists has passed—or perhaps *evolved* would be a better term. Archaeology in the United States is now at the stage that we are wrestling with how to communicate most effectively (often on a shoestring budget), building on vehicles that have existed since 1977 and on emergent technologies.

If the profession, in partnership with Congress, can maintain current federal protections into the future, then I believe that much of our effort should be devoted to reaching state and local audiences, including policy makers. Because state political cultures vary widely, there is no one-size-fits-all definition of success, but there are basic helpful indicators. If, for instance, we could survey the national scene several decades from now and see significant increases in the number of states with recognizable and substantial mechanisms for promoting an archaeology conservation ethic in their citizens, that would count toward our success. Such mechanisms might be housed in universities (as in the case of the Arkansas

Archaeological Survey), in state historic preservation offices, or even in nongovernmental organizations (NGOs), but they would be ongoing, with a steady funding stream, whether state, private, federal, or, in the most likely scenario, all three. An increase in the number of counties that incorporate archaeological resources at some level in their planning process could be counted as a success, as would more recognition by development interests that archaeological resources can help establish the sense of place so many people are increasingly searching for.

All of the preceding point back to the importance of effective communication with state and local policy makers. It is important to remember that at the state and local governmental levels, we are working with people who in many cases are our neighbors. They come from local communities and feel a strong sense of responsibility to provide maximum return for the public dollars with which they are entrusted. If we are perceived as hectoring from the sidelines or if in our efforts to educate policy makers, we fall back on one of the many variants of George Santayana's aphorism about those who do not know their past, then we are doomed, just as he wrote, to repeat our mistakes. Instead, we need to focus on concrete results at the local level. Whether these results take the form of educational materials for the local school system that are spun off from a Section 106 undertaking, or increased participation by local (voting) citizen scientists in stewardship of state-owned resources, or increased visitorship at a local park because of better programming featuring archaeology is unimportant. What is important is that we show definable results that count to local and state taxpayers.

None of this is easy, as many archaeologists already know. We should take heart, however. As a discipline, we have several things going for us that, if used effectively, can vastly extend our communications reach. First, we have authentic stories about people. In a world where authenticity is increasingly valued because it seems all too rare, this is an ace that we would do well to play early and often. Further, authenticity appeals to all of our potential audiences. And people still enjoy a good story if it is told well, as Brian Fagan's book title attests. As Theodore Roosevelt so elegantly stated, we have to show our audiences "the life that was and not the death that is."

Second, we are, above all, anthropologists. We know, because we are trained to know, how to analyze and understand cultural phenomena through observation and communication. We should adopt the strategies and tactics of successful communicators and put these to work on behalf of archaeology. In short, it is time that we got over the "intellectual introspection" so perceptively noted by the first Airlie House discussants and applied some of our basic anthropological skills to the betterment of the resources we research and manage.

Acknowledgments

Many of the recommendations in the media relations portion of this chapter were born out of conversations with my public affairs colleagues in the Georgia Department of Natural Resources, especially Beth Brown and Robin Hill. Mike Toner, formerly of the *Atlanta Journal Constitution* and a Society for American Archaeology Gene S. Stuart (and Pulitzer) Prize winner, has offered invaluable advice over the years on print media relations. Ryan Kennedy assisted in editing the chapter.

12

Perspectives from the Advanced Seminar

William D. Lipe and Lynne Sebastian

Cultural resource management (CRM) archaeology emerged in the mid-1970s in response to laws and public policies focused on resource management and planning, rather than on the "salvage" of sites that were "in the way of progress." As Davis (chapter 2) discusses, the ability of the archaeological community to win passage of the Moss-Bennett legislation in 1974 was a major turning point. In that same year, the Advisory Council on Historic Preservation issued its initial Procedures for the Protection of Historic and Cultural Properties (36 CFR Part 800), and the Cultural Resource Management Conference in Denver (Lipe and Lindsay 1974) marked the appearance of "CRM" as a label for a new and more comprehensive approach to public archaeology. The mid-1970s also saw the development of CRM archaeology as a professional specialty distinct from employment in universities and museums (McGimsey 1974).

To those of us old enough to have been in the trenches long before 1974, CRM archaeology today is a huge success in comparison with the reactive, often poorly funded salvage archaeology that came before it. In most if not all parts of the United States, the great majority of the currently known archaeological sites has been recorded since the mid-1970s, and well-funded, multidisciplinary survey and excavation projects designed to "mitigate the adverse effects" of economic development have become commonplace. CRM archaeology has produced great increases in our understanding of this nation's archaeological past and preserved tens of thousands of sites that might otherwise have been destroyed by development or looting. And the passage of NAGPRA and amendments to the National Historic Preservation Act has required CRM archaeologists and federal agencies to respond more systematically to the interests of Native Americans in ways that are still evolving but that increasingly show promise of mutually beneficial results, as T. J. Ferguson discusses (chapter 8). It is easy to imagine alternative scenarios for the past several decades that would have produced outcomes far worse for preservation and management of the archaeological record and for the delivery of public benefits from the expenditure of public funds on archaeology.

As all the chapters in this volume attest, however, CRM archaeology has its problems. Our goal in this book is to put forward a vision of what the field of CRM archaeology might become—how it might more nearly achieve its great promise. In the advanced seminar, we challenged ourselves not only to delineate aspects of that vision but also to describe some of the impediments to achieving it and what might be done to resolve or reduce those impediments. The contributors to the volume see it not as a cookbook filled with recipes for improving CRM archaeology, but as a way of encouraging those concerned about the future of American public archaeology to envision that future and to work toward making the vision a reality.

ELEMENTS OF A VISION FOR THE FUTURE

What follows is an attempt to capture the flavor of our discussions of several major issues, rather than recap the individual chapters—they speak for themselves. The main message of this chapter, and of this book, is that improving CRM archaeology is more a matter of changing the expectations of its practitioners—of changing the field's culture—than of tinkering with laws or federal regulations, although that may eventually be needed as well.

Public Benefits

Sebastian, in her introductory summary of the federal historic preservation laws that provide explicit statements about congressional intent (chapter 1), notes that in every case, the intent was to ensure that the nation could benefit, over the long-term future, from the active preservation and management of the country's heritage of archaeological and historical properties. Everything else in these laws and their implementing regulations is instrumental, designed to spell out what is to be done to provide those benefits. This perspective became a dominant theme during the advanced seminar: how can CRM archaeology do a better job of delivering public benefits, in both the short and the long term?

Numerous works have focused on archaeology's contributions to society (for example, Clarke 1957; Colwell-Chanthaphonh and Ferguson 2008; Little 2002; McGimsey 1972; Petrie 1904; Sabloff 2008; Trigger 1986), but this topic is so basic that it needs to be continually revisited. Lipe (chapter 3) recognizes six kinds of archaeological resource values—preservation, research, heritage, educational, aesthetic, and economic—from which various segments of society can benefit and that provide the rationale for CRM archaeology.

The advanced seminar discussions called for an attitude shift on the part of all participants in "the CRM system"—public agency resource managers, state historic preservation officers (SHPOs), CRM consultants, and the private-sector clients who often pay much of the cost of CRM work. Of course, there often are many steps between an on-the-ground CRM project and the production of something that will be seen as a benefit by some segment of society. The main point is that CRM practitioners, including resource managers, consulting archaeologists, and those from other fields, must think from the outset about how CRM projects might contribute—either directly or indirectly, short-term or long-term—to eventual public benefits. And they must design their work to promote, or at least not obstruct, the delivery of those benefits.

CRM archaeology is most often justified as ensuring that sites are preserved for research, educational, or heritage uses over the long-term future. This is well and good, if steps are taken to ensure that long-term preservation will actually take place and that appropriately justified uses are not arbitrarily prohibited. Much of the public seems comfortable with seeing preservation as a benefit either for its own sake or because heritage, aesthetic, or other values can be realized without affecting the sites themselves. But there are also public benefits that may involve some physical effects on sites from research, stabilization, increased visitation, and so forth. It is appropriate to consider when and how preserved sites might be made available for uses of these sorts. In other words, a concern for public benefits implies that in situ preservation will be coupled with a continuing management concern for the sites thus preserved.

CRM archaeology projects, whether they lead to in situ preservation of sites or to "data recovery," involve studies and activities that can and should contribute to societal benefits. These might include a published scholarly article, a museum exhibit or media treatment featuring archaeology, a state site database with both research and planning potential, enhanced collaboration between archaeologists and descendant groups, an educational unit for a school—the list is limited only by our imagination. Individual, small CRM projects may not directly produce such benefits, but collectively they may show large-scale, long-term regional trends and patterns (as in the population estimates based largely on multiple CRM surveys in Varien et al. 2007). The CRM field must take responsibility for seeing that CRM archaeological activities, collectively and over the long run, lead to judicious realization of archaeological values.

Multiple Publics

There are of course multiple publics for public archaeology (McManamon 1991), including researchers, educators, descendant communities, federal and state agencies, developers, and the large but diffusely defined "general public." CRM programs and projects should be designed from the outset to take into account the various publics that might benefit and the ways they might benefit. One of the benefits sought by a wide segment of the general public is more and better insight into archaeological findings and the process of archaeology itself. CRM archaeologists may be able to satisfy this interest themselves, through popular articles, lectures, and the like, but also numerous specialists in print, digital, and visual media are constantly looking for content about archaeological results that they can communicate to the general public (see Crass, chapter 11, about interfacing with the media).

The relationship between CRM practitioners and the various publics that have stakeholder interests in archaeology is not entirely a one-way street, with CRM specialists producing "products" such as reports, publications, and educational programs, which are then "consumed" by the public. Rather, CRM programs and projects of all sorts often receive input, implicitly and explicitly, from various stakeholders. Certainly the views, practices, and interests of the research, historic preservation, and regional planning communities have substantial influence on the way CRM projects are designed and conducted. And Smith (2006) reminds us that "the public" plays an active role in defining public benefits, because individuals and groups find their own ways to incorporate and make sense of archaeological sites and artifacts, the information put forth by archaeologists, and the treatments of archaeology that they encounter in the media, in parks and monuments, and in museum exhibits.

The view that archaeologists should be in charge of defining the benefits that various engaged publics should receive has been challenged most effectively in the field's relationship with descendant communities, especially Native Americans. These communities usually have their own views about what archaeological work is appropriate at ancestral sites and what kinds of research will meet their interests. Swidler and colleagues (1997), Watkins (2000), and Colwell-Chanthaphonh and Ferguson (2008) have discussed ways in which archaeologists and descendant communities may avoid confrontation and seek common ground. Ferguson (chapter 8) discusses in detail how members of Native American communities are increasingly becoming collaborators with CRM archaeologists in the shaping and execution of archaeological CRM projects.

As noted earlier, in situ preservation of sites is often the direct objective of CRM archaeology, under the presumption that preservation will in some way make these sites available for new or continuing public benefits in the future. For this reason, archaeology's multiple stakeholder groups have an interest in ensuring that sites thus preserved continue to be protected and that future uses are well justified and have conservative effects.

Linking Means and Ends

CRM archaeology has lofty, abstract goals, starting with the stated purposes of the laws that support it. The practice of CRM archaeology, however, consists of detailed technical procedures, usually based on federal or state regulations and policies. The challenge for CRM archaeologists and resource managers is to avoid reifying these procedures so that the process becomes the goal rather than the means to one or more beneficial ends. Although laws and regulations do constrain CRM procedures, they offer more flexibility than is typically assumed.

Chandler (chapter 6) gives some examples of innovative approaches to the mitigation of adverse effects to archaeological sites. In some cases, a portion of the funds allocated to mitigation were expended on producing regional data syntheses as alternatives to redundant excavations of types of small sites that were already well understood. In other words, the judgment was made that synthesizing the results of previous projects would be of greater public benefit than producing additional site-specific descriptive reports.

In chapter 7, King discusses the low visibility of CRM archaeology in both scholarly and public discussions of regional culture and history. She points out the benefits of allocating some portion of the funds spent on CRM archaeology to producing regional syntheses and problem-oriented studies that incorporate and make generally available the vast amount of information generated by CRM work. Mackey (chapter 9) also comments on the negative effects on CRM practice and on the reputation of CRM archaeology that result from the lack of syntheses and wide dissemination of results.

Quality Counts

The seminar participants agreed that much of the best archaeology done in the United States in recent years has been done in a CRM context. There was also agreement that some CRM projects and practitioners are to be found at the lowest end of the performance scale. Substandard or "barely get by" work puts at a competitive disadvantage the individuals and firms who maintain high standards. It tarnishes the image of CRM archaeology generally, represents an abdication of responsibility by the public agencies presumably in charge, and seldom produces results that lead to public benefits. In chapters 9 and 10, Mackey and Bridges, respectively, address aspects of strengthening ethical and professional behavior in the field of CRM archaeology.

Cost-Effectiveness

Cultural resource managers and CRM archaeologists in public agencies and in consulting firms are responsible for the long-term fate of the nation's irreplaceable archaeological resources. Increasingly, CRM work determines most of what we know and can find out about the past as it is represented in the archaeological record. At the same time, agency cultural resource managers, and to some extent CRM consultants, also help to provide the interface between the archaeological record and the heritage concerns of descendant communities, particularly Native Americans.

Given the size and seriousness of their responsibilities, there is no reason for CRM archaeologists to apologize for the cost of what they do, provided that those costs are well justified. In the aggregate, the money spent on CRM represents a tiny proportion of federal and state budgets, let alone of development expenditures in the private sector. However, noble aims do not provide a license for inefficiency or unnecessary costs. Seminar participants thought that cost-ineffective work often resulted from rigid adherence to process for its own sake, to the detriment of outcome-based project design. And a clearer focus on actually generating public benefits would make it easier to justify CRM archaeology costs and fend off the field's detractors, nationally and for particular projects.

IMPEDIMENTS (AND SOLUTIONS)

In our discussions of how new visions for the future of CRM archaeology might be implemented, seminar participants examined features of current CRM practice that pose common, though not universal, impediments to productive change. We discussed ways such impediments might be removed or circumvented. Because our ideas about solutions were linked to what we saw as problems, impediments and possible solutions are considered together in what follows.

Process Rigor Mortis

Barker and Sebastian, in chapters 4 and 5, respectively, discuss some of the problems with procedures that often seem to work against cost-effective, outcome-oriented project design and execution. One class of problems comprises multiple small, overlapping projects in areas of heavy development. In some cases, this leads to dealing repeatedly with the same sites, to uncoordinated, redundant treatment of common types of sites, and to "missing the forest for the trees." For example, Wilshusen (1995) discussed an area of heavy development in New Mexico where large-scale patterns such as Pueblo villages with scattered habitation units had been poorly documented despite numerous small surveys.

Barker argues that regional predictive models can avoid some of the limitations of site-by-site, project-by-project evaluations, reduce compliance costs, and lead to more effective recognition of large-scale archaeological patterns. This of course requires the public agency in charge to come up with the funds to implement a large-scale, regional-planning approach or to convince multiple development proponents that it is in their interest to support regional planning for an area larger than any of their individual development projects. Barker's example shows that this can be done.

Sebastian explores some alternatives to site-by-site evaluations based on the very general National Register criteria. In many cases, the standard approach may be a poor fit for the characteristics of archaeological sites, the way archaeologists assign value to them, and their potential for eventually supporting public benefits through research or education. Sebastian suggests some alternatives to the standard Section 106 process that she thinks might produce better results more cost-effectively. She would base decisions about site significance on a set of "generally useful attributes" distilled from what archaeologists actually rely on when they do research or archaeological education.

In general, it seems to us that the process-related problems identified by Sebastian, Barker, and others at the advanced seminar stem from the application of one-size-fits-all procedures to a huge diversity of archaeological distributions and characteristics. Also, since the 1960s, archaeological research has typically focused less on the study of distinctive sites or even "type sites." Rather, research commonly depends on studying variation within and among regional populations of sites. Procedures commonly used to implement Section 106 seem, however, to represent typological rather than population thinking (see Binford 1964; Mayr 2000). That does not mean that we cannot think of ways to use Section 106 to more appropriately address an archaeological record viewed as populations of features, sites, and settlement patterns. Chapters 4, 5, and 6 by Barker, Sebastian, and Chandler, respectively, lead us in this direction.

Self-Limiting Views of "the System's" Potential

Among the impediments to making the CRM "system" work more effectively to deliver public benefits is a long list of "can't do's" that seems rooted more in CRM traditions than in law or regulation or even policy. Although provisions for educational products and activities are increasingly appearing in archaeological scopes of work, especially for large mitigation projects, it still is generally off-limits for CRM archaeologists to get paid to produce publishable articles reporting what their work has contributed to the sum total of knowledge about the human past. This despite the fact that such publications would take advantage of the well-established system of journal and book publishing through which archaeological results are disseminated among scholars. These are the very sources upon which journalists, other media specialists, museum exhibitors, and educators also depend when they develop treatments of archaeology for larger public audiences.

This particular "can't do" seems to us to be a holdover from the early days of CRM archaeology, when agencies and consultants timidly approached development proponents with offers of archaeological "clearances" for their projects. This term implied of course that archaeological sites were nuisances standing in the way of progress—attractive nuisances perhaps, but nuisances nonetheless that needed to be "cleared" so that the more serious interests of society could forge ahead.

Out of this same formative period came a reluctance to label as "research" anything that CRM archaeologists did (Lipe 1985), despite the fact that they were excavating sites precisely because they met the National Register criterion of being "likely to yield information important in American history or prehistory." This reluctance was perhaps inherited from the salvage era, when analysis and reporting were often left unfunded under the presumption that these activities would be accomplished as a matter of course by the academicians who were at the time the ones usually in charge of salvage projects.

In the post-salvage era, funding for the production of long, highly detailed excavation and testing reports has become routine, but the work is curiously referred to as "data recovery," as if "data" are somehow discovered in the ground rather than being created from observations and measurements made by archaeologists through a process indistinguishable from other types of archaeological research. We are not complaining here about the production of technical "descriptive" reports, many of which are excellent and will serve as important data sources long into the future, provided that researchers and educators can discover their existence (see King, chapter 7, and Mackey, chapter 9). Rather, the point is that the culture and history of CRM archaeology may be keeping it from delivering some of the societal benefits that provide the justification for doing the work in the first place.

People who work in the CRM field can offer additional examples of "can't do" notions that keep us from developing products or carrying out activities that would increase societal benefits from the expenditure of public funds. But we can also cite examples in which "pushing the system" has resulted in improvements. The Fruitland Coal Gas project described by Chandler (chapter 6), for example, required that competing energy companies and competing CRM firms work together to create a unified archaeological approach to what would otherwise have been hundreds, perhaps thousands, of separate Section 106 undertakings. Although this created great gnashing of teeth at first, all the participants came to see the benefits of the approach, and soon attitudes shifted from "We've never done it this way" to "Why can't we do other projects this way?"

Ferguson (chapter 8) discusses relationships between CRM archaeologists and Native American tribes and communities in terms of a "resistance" mode versus a "participation" mode. Many CRM archaeologists and tribes remain stuck in the resistance mode and seem to assume that this is simply the nature of the relationship. Ferguson provides examples, however, of a transition from resistance to mutual participation, leading to collaboration on the design and conduct of CRM archaeological projects. Furthermore, he argues that such collaborative efforts are considerably more likely to produce innovative and informative research results than are projects done in a resistance mode.

As yet another example, in the 1990s the Society for American Archaeology's (SAA's) Public Education Committee launched an effective drive to make archaeology more accessible to the public, helping to break down the prevailing expectations that archaeologists avoid "popularization" and communicate primarily with professional peers. In addition to helping develop public events focused on archaeology, as well as school curricula that incorporate archaeological information, the committee's work led some agencies to require selected CRM archaeological projects to produce public educational materials, as well as technical reports.

A problem more difficult to solve is the need for regional and topical syntheses, including those that depend on data from many small and large CRM projects (as discussed by King, chapter 7). This is an "overhead" cost that may be difficult to charge back to individual development projects. Yet, such syntheses are extremely valuable, both for making the results of CRM work more widely accessible to scholars, interpretive specialists, and the general public and for orienting CRM practitioners as they design and implement individual projects. Chandler and King (chapters 6 and 7, respectively) each discuss several success stories in the production of archaeological reports that synthesize regional CRM literature, but they also note the lack of consistent sources of funding for these efforts. Still, an increased awareness of the importance of regional and topical syntheses, as well as the sharing of information about what has worked in various states and regions, will perhaps result in additions to King's list of successes.

Given that, in some cases, project scopes of work now include the production of public education materials such as brochures, exhibits, videos, and presentations, why can't scopes of work for major projects also specify the production of article-length synthetic and analytical research reports that can receive wide dissemination and thus be available to media and educational "interpreters," as well as to scholars? In the concluding section of this chapter, we discuss some ways of making existing major CRM reports and syntheses more available.

Preservation as Wishful Thinking

Much CRM archaeology has as its goal the in situ preservation of portions of the archaeological record. The preserved sites can thus continue to be available to meet various public interests now and in the future. This makes sense only if the sites will, in fact, remain intact over the long term and if there are ways in which these sites can be accessed for societal benefits in the future. In situ preservation is, however, often treated as a one-shot, passive solution, as if maintaining site protection and ensuring beneficial future uses will somehow take care of themselves.

Two kinds of concern were expressed at the advanced seminar. First, in areas where moderate to intense development is taking place in small increments, experience has shown that avoidance of sites on a site-by-site, project-by-project basis may not result in preservation. Instead, the cumulative direct and indirect effects of multiple small and often overlapping development projects may result in loss of integrity for many or even most of the sites in an affected region. Barker and Chandler (chapters 4 and 6, respectively) each discuss aspects of this problem. In such cases, agency managers need to consider the big picture and propose mitigation measures ranging from "hardening" a sample of sites, to studies that will produce information about the past from sites that will be lost. Some agencies are also attempting to increase both the temporal and spatial scales of planning for developments such as drilling for oil and gas. For example, the Bureau of Land Management now has the option of requiring drilling proponents to work with the agency to produce Geographic Area Development Plans (BLM 2003), which promise to help avoid the cumulative effects of "one small project at a time" development.

The other concern is whether a passive approach to preservation will ensure that some future public benefits can be gained from at least some of the sites thus preserved. It is pointless to say that sites are being saved for research at some future time when information recovery methods will have improved, without providing some guidelines about how the arrival of that future will be recognized. That is, the possibility always exists that archaeological methods will be better in the future. If this possibility is always used to deny permission for investigator-initiated archaeological research projects or to recommend avoidance even when long-term preservation is far from assured, this will guarantee that the public benefits that could be attained through intrusive research will always be postponed into an indefinite future (Lipe 2000a). The same kinds of questions can often be raised if in-place preservation is justified because of a site's educational, heritage, or other value. The questions are, What are the criteria for permitting access for such uses? Will they have direct or indirect impacts on site characteristics? And if there are use-related impacts, can these be tolerated or adequately managed while still permitting the public interest to be served?

Public agency planning documents often do not address these questions effectively, even though they are supposed to provide guidance for future agency actions. The agencies responsible for preserved cultural resources need to develop policies to guide site protection, as well as policies that will permit beneficial uses in ways that balance public good against potential damage to preserved resources.

Toleration of Low Standards

Bridges, in chapter 10, reviews the professional and ethical standards of societies and associations relevant to the practice of CRM archaeology.

Seminar participants thought that most CRM practitioners attempt to conform to such standards, but they agreed that those who do not conform cause problems for the credibility and effectiveness of the CRM field. Mackey (chapter 9) reviews some of the negative effects of the "race to the bottom," cost-cutting, and professional disengagement.

Solutions discussed by seminar participants include the following:

- Efforts to increase enrollment in the Register of Professional Archaeologists and much greater publicity about its grievance process. The Register does not have enforcement capacity per se, but persons who become registered professionals agree to uphold its Code of Ethics and Standards of Research Performance. Furthermore, they agree that if there is a credible complaint about their ethics or performance, they will participate in the grievance process. As Bridges discusses, this can result in loss of registration and the Register's grievance coordinator's publication of a report on the violations.

- Increased opportunities and incentives for continuing professional education. Professional societies such as the SAA and the Society for Historical Archaeology (SHA), state and regional professional groups, and the public agencies that have cultural resource responsibilities need to develop and promote opportunities for continuing education. CRM consulting firms should also provide time and incentives for their employees to engage in professional education.

- Awards and other types of public recognition. Such awards can serve as incentives and produce role models for improving ethical and professional behavior. Although this is being done in some cases, the public recognition of "good actors" needs to be further developed by professional societies and groups at the national, regional, and state levels, as well as by public agencies.

- Improved graduate education in CRM archaeology. Although education for CRM careers was one of the topics not taken up during the advanced seminar, because of time and space limits (see chapter 1), this clearly is an area that needs improvement if the level of professional performance in CRM archaeology is to be raised (see Society for American Archaeology 2006). Mackey (chapter 9) reports that in his experience, graduate programs that treat CRM employment as a worthwhile and fully professional career are much more likely to produce graduates who adhere to professional and ethical standards when employed. Our perspective is that academic programs that fail to value employment in the CRM field need to wake up to reality. More than half the professional archaeologists in the United States are employed in CRM. Most other disciplines recognize and prepare their students for both "applied" and academic jobs—think of psychology and economics, for example. A number of US university graduate programs in archaeology do an excellent job of preparing students for CRM careers, and the situation is much better than it was 20 years ago, but much more progress needs to be made.

CONCLUSION: WHAT'S NEXT?

In chapter 2, Davis quotes a comment by Frank McManamon that "it probably isn't necessary to spend a lot of time redefining what the needs are; more energy should be devoted to coming up with ideas for addressing them." If this book had an epigraph, that would be a good choice. Our instructions to the seminar participants were to deemphasize long discussions of "what's wrong about the way we do things now" and focus on how we ought to be doing things and how we might go about getting there—visions for the future.

As McGimsey points out in the foreword, many of the same issues that were worrying people at Airlie House in 1974 are still perplexing and worrying us in this volume. In part, this is because of the scale at which we tend to view these problems and their solutions. The most recent attempt to address some of these issues at a national scale—the "Renewing American Archaeology" conferences of the mid-1990s (Davis, chapter 2; Lipe 1997; Lipe and Redman 1996)—focused on high-level or large-scale solutions. There were, for example, calls for new archaeological guidance from the Advisory Council on Historic Preservation and for requiring that all federal agency archaeologists meet the secretary of the interior's standards for historic preservation professionals. Some of these higher-level solutions have been implemented, at least to some extent, but these institutional kinds of responses are too far removed from the daily experiences of most archaeologists. For this reason, the Renewing conferences and some of their predecessors (for example, Irwin-Williams and Fowler 1986) failed to engage the general archaeological population in activities or debates or in the search for other solutions.

The good news is to be found in one of the lessons derived from Davis's chapter 2: again and again in the history of public archaeology, we see that individuals or small groups of determined people have succeeded in bringing about extraordinary changes. McGimsey, Chapman, and Corbett looked about one day in 1968 and said, with breathtaking naivety, "Well, couldn't we just get a law passed?" And amazingly enough, they did. Many other people helped, but it took only three determined persons to start up that change engine.

Nothing that any of us propose in this book would require anything as extreme as a change in the law or regulations. Even our most ambitious proposals would require only changes in guidance. Much of what we propose could be implemented tomorrow or next month or this year, given an advocate or advocates and sufficient determination. As part of a recently initiated project at Fort Benning, Georgia, for example, Sebastian and several colleagues are developing a significance-based site evaluation process of the type discussed in chapter 5 and will assist the cultural resource staff at Fort Benning as this approach is incorporated into planning and management.

Every archaeologist has unique talents, interests, passions. Some of us cringe at the very thought of congressional visits and lobbying; others relish the "inside the beltway" experience. Some devote endless hours to public education and outreach; others would rather be beaten thoroughly with a large stick than be locked in a room with 30 first-graders.

But each of us has something we care passionately about, something we think needs to be changed. Each of us has an area of current archaeological practice that we think is the perfect candidate for the SDSS[2] (stop doing stupid stuff, start doing smart stuff) approach to improving CRM archaeology. Figure out what your issue is, where you can contribute, and then go for it. Are you worried about shoddy excavation or substandard surveys? Become an RPA yourself and work with other RPAs in your area to convince clients and land-managing agencies to require registration as a condition of receiving contracts or permits.

Are you sick of churning out endless, repetitive, negative survey reports that cost your clients time and money and do nothing to advance archaeological knowledge or improve site management? Find a few like-minded colleagues and design a streamlined, programmatic approach that still makes needed information available but frees up agency, SHPO, and consultant time and money to be spent on things that actually make a difference for archaeology and yield a public benefit. Does it seem impossible to find new hires with the needed skills and knowledge? Work with local firms and agencies to develop a mentoring group for students at the local university who want to go into CRM. Are you disheartened by the constant loss of archaeological sites to uncontrolled local development? Find or create a champion on your city council and start working toward development of a local archaeological ordinance.

The possibilities are endless. For example, during our seminar discussions, we were struggling with how to get syntheses of local or regional archaeology done, make them available, and keep them updated and current. Someone said, "Contract reports for large projects often have wonderful syntheses, but the reports have such limited distribution." Someone else noted that MA theses and PhD dissertations also have excellent, very current syntheses in them but that these documents have even *more* limited distributions. The ideal would be for authors to turn those report or thesis chapters into articles for publication, but this takes time and energy that many of us just do not have.

"Well," someone said, "what about the low-energy solution? Have a Web site where people can post their synthesis chapters as PDFs in an 'as is' format." The Web site could be hosted by the state archaeologist or the state professional council or one of the university anthropology departments, and all this great information could be readily available without the authors' having to put in much additional work. Also, universities are increasingly permitting or requiring theses and dissertations to be submitted digitally, and they often post these on the university library website. Some universities are cooperating in a program called "The Research Exchange," in which research-related documents can be posted and the links be kept up-to-date by university library staff. For example, Lipe recently helped set up a Research Exchange "community" focused on theses and other reports relating to the Cedar Mesa Project in southeastern Utah (see https://research.wsulibs.wsu.edu:8443/dspace/handle/2376/735).

Think about the problem; think of as many creative solutions as possible—high-tech, low-tech, high-energy input or low-energy. There is not an issue raised in this book that cannot be addressed, at least in part, through individual or small group efforts. The history of American CRM archaeology has been formed in this way; its future can be as well.

References

ACHP (Advisory Council on Historic Preservation)

1979   Report to the Advisory Council on Historic Preservation from the Task Force
        on Archeology Policy. Version adopted by full council, May 9, 1979.
        Photocopy.

2007a   Section 106 Archaeology Guidance. Electronic document,
        www.achp.gov/archguide, accessed Oct. 28, 2007.

2007b   ACHP's Archaeology Task Force. Electronic document, www.achp.gov
        /atfupdate.html#strategies, accessed Jan. 4, 2009.

2008   National Register Evaluation Criteria. Electronic document,
        www.achp.gov/nrcriteria.html, accessed November 19, 2009.

Adler, Michael, and Susan Bruning

2008   Navigating the Fluidity of Social Identity: Collaborative Research into
        Cultural Affiliation in the American Southwest. *In* Collaboration in
        Archaeological Practice: Engaging Descendant Communities, edited by Chip
        Colwell-Chanthaphonh and T. J. Ferguson, pp. 35–54. Walnut Creek, CA:
        AltaMira.

Ahlstrom, Richard V. N., Malcolm Adair, R. Thomas Euler, and Robert C. Euler

1992   Pothunting in Central Arizona: The Perry Mesa Archaeological Vandalism
        Study. Cultural Resources Management Reports 13. Phoenix: Bureau of Land
        Management, Arizona State Office.

Aikens, C. Melvin

1986   Current Status of CRM Archaeology in the Great Basin. Cultural Resource
        Series 9. Reno: Bureau of Land Management, Nevada.

Altschul, Jeffrey H.

2005   Significance in American Cultural Resource Management. *In* Heritage of
        Value, Archaeology of Renown: Reshaping Archaeological Assessment and
        Significance, edited by Clay Mathers, Timothy Darvill, and Barbara J. Little,
        pp. 192–210. Gainesville: University Press of Florida.

2007   The Issue of Commercialism: Proposed Changes to the Register's Code of
        Conduct. Archaeological Record 7(4):10.

References

Altschul, Jeffrey H., L. Sebastian, C. M. Rohe, W. E. Hayden, and S. Hall
2005   Results and Discussion: The Loco Hills Study Area. *In* Adaptive
         Management and Planning Models for Cultural Resources in Oil and Gas
         Fields in New Mexico and Wyoming: Final Technical Report (DE-FC26-
         02NT15445), by E. Ingbar et al. Department of Energy Technical Report.
         Electronic document, www.gnomon.com.

Altschul, Jeffrey H., and Willem J. Willems
2006   The Register of Professional Archaeologists' Standards Are Voluntary.
         Anthropology News 47(5):24–25.

American Anthropological Association
1998   Code of Ethics of the American Anthropological Association. Electronic
         document, www.aaanet.org/committees/ethics/ethcode.htm, accessed Oct.
         29, 2007.

American Cultural Resources Association
1995   Code of Ethics and Professional Conduct. Electronic document,
         http://acra-crm.org/displaycommon.cfm?an=1&subarticlenbr=20, accessed
         Nov. 17, 2008.

American Philological Association
2007   APA/AIA Task Force on Electronic Publications: Final Report. Electronic
         document, www.webfiles.berkeley.edu/%7Epinax/APAAIATaskForce.html.

Anderson, David G., and J. W. Joseph
1988   Prehistory and History along the Upper Savannah River: Technical Synthesis
         of Cultural Resource Investigations, Richard B. Russell Multiple Resource
         Area. 2 vols. Atlanta, GA: National Park Service, Interagency Archeological
         Services Division.

Anyon, Roger, T. J. Ferguson, and John Welch
2000   Heritage Management by American Indian Tribes in the Southwestern
         United States. *In* Cultural Resource Management in Contemporary Society,
         edited by Francis McManamon and Alf Hatton, pp. 120–141. London:
         Routledge.

Archaeological Institute of America
1997a   Code of Ethics (adopted 1990, amended 1997). Electronic document,
         www.archaeological.org/pdfs/AIA_Code_of_EthicsA5S.pdf.
1997b   Code of Professional Standards (adopted 1994, amended 1997). Electronic
         document,
         www.archaeological.org/pdfs/AIA_Code_of_Professional_StandardsA5S.pdf.
2006   Joint Statement on Digital Publication. Electronic document, www.archaeo-
         logical.org/pdfs/estatement.pdf, accessed Mar. 30, 2008.

Atwood, Roger
2004   Stealing History: Tomb Raiders, Smugglers, and the Looting of the Ancient
         World. New York: St. Martin's.

Aultman, Jennifer, Kate Grillo, Nick Bon-Harper, and Jillian Galle
2007   DAACS Cataloging Manual: Ceramics. Updated September 4, 2007.

Electronic document, www.daacs.org/aboutDatabase/pdf/cataloging/
Ceramics.pdf.

Bass, George F.

2003   The Ethics of Shipwreck Archaeology. *In* Ethical Issues in Archaeology, edited by Larry J. Zimmerman, Karen D. Vitelli, and Julie Hollowell-Zimmer, pp. 57–70. Walnut Creek, CA: AltaMira.

Becker, Alice M.

1986   Nevada. *In* Current Status of CRM Archaeology in the Great Basin, edited by C. Melvin Aikens, pp. 7–39. Cultural Resource Series 9. Reno: Bureau of Land Management, Nevada (www.blm.gov/nv).

Beckerman, Ira

2006   Tribal Consultation in Pennsylvania: A Personal View from within the Pennsylvania Department of Transportation. *In* Cross-Cultural Collaboration: Native Peoples and Archaeology in the Northeastern United States, edited by Jordan E. Kerber, pp. 183–196. Lincoln: University of Nebraska Press.

Begay, Richard M.

1997   The Role of Archaeology on Indian Lands. *In* Native Americans and Archaeologists: Stepping Stones to Common Ground, edited by Nina Swidler, Kurt E. Dongoske, Roger Anyon, and Alan S. Downer, pp. 161–166. Walnut Creek, CA: AltaMira.

Bender, Susan J., and George S. Smith

1998   SAA's Workshop on Teaching Archaeology in the Twenty-first Century: Promoting a National Dialogue on Curricula Reform. Society for American Archaeology Bulletin 16(5):11. Electronic document, www.saa.org/Publications/SAAbulletin/16–5/SAA10.html.

Bender, Susan J., and George S. Smith, eds.

2000   Teaching Archaeology in the Twenty-first Century. Washington, DC: Society for American Archaeology.

Bense, Judith A.

1991   Archaeology at Home: A Partnership in Pensacola, Florida. *In* Protecting the Past, edited by George S. Smith and John E. Ehrenhard. Boca Raton, FL: CRC Press. Out of print; available at www.nps.gov/seac/protectg.htm, in chapter 2, "Protecting Archaeological Sites through Education."

Berkin, Jon

2008   Moving Forward from Tucson. ACRA Edition 14-6:17–18.

Bettinger, R. L.

1991   Hunter-Gatherers: Archaeological and Evolutionary Theory. New York: Plenum.

Binford, Lewis R.

1964   A Consideration of Archaeological Research Design. American Antiquity 29(4):425–441.

1972   Contemporary Model Building: Paradigms and the Current State of Paleolithic Research. *In* Models in Archaeology, edited by D. L. Clark, pp. 109–166. London: Methuen.

Blair, Lynda M., and Diane L. Winslow

2003   Prehistoric Turquoise Mining in the Mojave Desert: Data from the Dr. Albert Mohr Collections. Report prepared by HRC, Las Vegas, NV, for Kern River Gas Transmission Company, Salt Lake City, Utah.

Blanton, Dennis B., and Julia A. King, eds.

2004   Indian and European Contact in Context: The Mid-Atlantic Region. Gainesville: University Press of Florida.

BLM (Bureau of Land Management)

2003   Instruction Memorandum no. 2003–152: Application for Permit to Drill (APD)—Process Improvement no. 1—Comprehensive Strategies. Washington, DC: US Department of the Interior, Bureau of Land Management.

2004   BLM Manual 8110: Identifying and Evaluating Cultural Resources. Washington, DC: US Department of the Interior, Bureau of Land Management.

2005   BLM Handbook H-1601-1: Land Use Planning. Washington, DC: US Department of the Interior, Bureau of Land Management.

2007a   Protecting America's "Outdoor Museum": The Site Steward Program. Electronic document, www.blm.gov/heritage/adventures/want_2_help/site_steward.html, accessed Dec. 23, 2007.

2007b   Canyons of the Ancients National Monument Draft Resource Management Plan and Draft Environmental Impact Statement. Lakewood, CO: Bureau of Land Management, Colorado State Office.

Blume, Cara Lee

2006   Working Together: Developing Partnerships with American Indians in New Jersey and Delaware. In Cross-Cultural Collaboration: Native Peoples and Archaeology in the Northeastern United States, edited by Jordan E. Kerber, pp. 197–212. Lincoln: University of Nebraska Press.

Borgstede, Greg

2002   Defining the Descendant Community in a Non-Western Context: The Maya of Highland Guatemala. Teaching Anthropology: Society for Anthropology in Community Colleges Notes 9(1):27–29, 38.

Brew, J. O.

1962   Introduction. In A Guide for Salvage Archaeology, by Fred Wendorf, pp. 7–25. Santa Fe: Museum of New Mexico Press.

Briuer, Frederick I., and Clay Mathers

1996   Trends and Patterns in Cultural Resource Significance: An Historical Perspective and Annotated Bibliography. IWR Report 96-EL-1. Vicksburg, MS: US Army Corps of Engineers, Waterways Experiment Station, Center for Cultural Site Preservation Technology (www.iwr.usace.army.mil/inside/products/pub/iwrreports/96–EL-1.pdf).

Brodie, Neil, and David Gill

2003   Looting: An International View. In Ethical Issues in Archaeology, edited by

Larry J. Zimmerman, Karen D. Vitelli, and Julie Hollowell-Zimmer, pp. 31–42. Walnut Creek, CA: AltaMira.

Brodie, Neil, Morag Kersel, Christina Luke, and Katheryn Walker Tubb, eds.
2006   Archaeology, Cultural Heritage, and the Antiquities Trade. Gainesville: University Press of Florida.

Brose, David S.
1983   Professionalism and Performance in Archaeological Organizations: A Disputation of the Incoming Presidential Remarks of Richard E. W. Adams. American Antiquity 48(4):817–819.

Brown, Gregory A., Julia A. King, Catherine L. Alston, Edward E. Chaney, C. Jane Cox, David F. Muraca, and Dennis J. Pogue
2006   A Comparative Archaeological Study of Colonial Chesapeake Culture. Prepared for the National Endowment for the Humanities and the Virginia Department of Historic Resources. Electronic document, www.chesa-peakearchaeology.org.

Brown, Michael
2006   Who Owns Native Culture? Cambridge, MA: Harvard University Press.

Bryne, Stephen
2005   Legislative Liaison Report: NHPA Amendments Alert. Society for California Archaeology Newsletter 39(2):4.

Burke, Heather, Claire Smith, Dorothy Lippert, Joe Watkins, and Larry Zimmerman, eds.
2008   Kennewick Man: Perspectives on the Ancient One. Walnut Creek, CA: Left Coast Press.

Cajete, Gregory
2000   Native Science: Natural Laws of Interdependence. Santa Fe, NM: Clear Light Publishers.

California State Parks
2007   Collections for Research. Electronic document, www.parks.ca.gov/?page_id=22205, accessed Nov. 25, 2007.

Cameron, Fiona, and Sarah Kenderdine, eds.
2007   Theorizing Digital Cultural Heritage: A Critical Discourse. Cambridge, MA: MIT Press.

Canouts, Veletta
1977   Management Strategies for Effective Research. In Conservation Archaeology: A Guide for Cultural Resource Management Studies, edited by Michael B. Schiffer and George J. Gumerman, pp. 121–127. New York: Academic Press.

Cantwell, Anne-Marie, and Diana diZerega Wall
2001   Unearthing Gotham: The Archaeology of New York City. New Haven, CT: Yale University Press.

Cary, Amy C.
1999   Reconsidering Marion: Feminization and the Library Profession. Working Papers Series 53(2). Ann Arbor: University of Michigan, Institute for Research on Women and Gender.

REFERENCES

Center for Desert Archaeology
2008   Coalescent Communities in the Southern Southwest. Electronic document,
        www.cdarc.org/pages/heritage/coalescent.php.
Champe, John L., Douglas S. Byers, Clifford Evans, A. K. Guthe, Henry W. Hamilton,
Edward D. Jelks, Clement W. Meighan, Sigfus Olafson, George I. Quimby,
Watson Smith, and Fred Wendorf
1961   Four Statements for Archaeology. American Antiquity 27(2):137–138.
Childs, S. Terry
1995   The Curation Crisis: What Is Being Done? Federal Archaeology 7(4):11–15.
2006   Managing Archeological Collections. Electronic document,
        www.cr.nps.gov/archeology/collections.
2007   Other Pieces for the Big Picture Are the Collections and Associated
        Records: Current Problems and Potentials in the United States. Paper pre-
        sented at the annual meeting of the Society for American Archaeology,
        Austin, TX.
n.d.   Notes from the Forum: The Archaeological Gray Literature. Unpublished
        manuscript.
Childs, S. Terry, ed.
2004   Our Collective Responsibility: The Ethics and Practice of Archaeological
        Collections Stewardship. Washington, DC: Society for American
        Archaeology.
Childs, S. Terry, org.
2005   Forum: The Archaeological Gray Literature. Forum presented at the annual
        meeting of the Society for American Archaeology, Salt Lake City, Utah.
Childs, S. Terry, and Karolyn Kinsey
2004   A Survey of SHPO Archeological Report Bibliographic Systems, 2002.
        Studies in Archeology and Ethnography 5. Washington, DC: National Park
        Service. Electronic document,
        www.nps.gov/archeology/PUBS/studies/STUDY05A.htm.
Chisholm, Amelia G., Mark P. Leone, and Brett T. Bentley
2007   Archaeology in the Classroom: Using a Dig Box to Understand the Past.
        Social Education 71(5):272–277.
Church, Minette C., Steven G. Baker, Bonnie J. Clark, Richard F. Carillo,
Jonathon C. Horn, Carl D. Späth, David R. Guilfoyle, and E. Steve Cassells
2007   Colorado History: A Context for Historical Archaeology. Denver: Colorado
        Council of Professional Archaeologists.
Clarke, Catherine
2004   The Politics of Storytelling: Electronic Media in Archaeological
        Interpretation and Education. World Archaeology 36(2):275–286.
Clarke, Grahame
1957   Archaeology and Society. 3rd ed. London: Methuen.
Clay, Berle R.
2006   The Day-to-Day Duties of the Grievance Coordinator. SAA Archaeological
        Record 6(2):5, 31.

Colorado Council of Professional Archaeologists

2008   Colorado History: A Context for Historical Archaeology. Electronic document, www.coloradoarchaeologists.org.

Colwell-Chanthaphonh, Chip

2004   Those Obscure Objects of Desire: Collecting Cultures of the Archaeological Landscape in the San Pedro Valley of Arizona. Journal of Contemporary Ethnography 33(5):571–601.

Colwell-Chanthaphonh, Chip, and T. J. Ferguson

2004   Virtue Ethics and the Practice of History: Native Americans and Archaeologists along the San Pedro Valley of Arizona. Journal of Social Archaeology 4(1):5–27.

2006   Trust and Archaeological Practice: Towards a Framework of Virtue Ethics. *In* The Ethics of Archaeology: Philosophical Perspectives on Archaeological Practice, edited by Chris Scarre and Geoffrey Scarre, pp. 115–130. Cambridge: Cambridge University Press.

2008   Introduction: The Collaborative Continuum. *In* Collaboration in Archaeological Practice: Engaging Descendant Communities, edited by Chip Colwell-Chanthaphonh and T. J. Ferguson, pp. 1–32. Lanham, MD: AltaMira.

Colwell-Chanthaphonh, Chip, and T. J. Ferguson, eds.

2008   Collaboration in Archaeological Practice: Engaging Descendant Communities. Lanham, MD: AltaMira.

Condori, Carlos M.

1989   History and Prehistory in Bolivia: What about the Indians? *In* Conflict in the Archaeology of Living Traditions, edited by Robert Layton, pp. 46–59. London: Unwin Hyman.

Copeland, James M., and David Simons

1995   The Fruitland Coal Gas Data Recovery Project. Paper presented at the annual meeting of the Society for American Archaeology, Minneapolis.

Corbett, John M., ed.

1961   Symposium on Salvage Archaeology. Washington, DC: US Department of the Interior, National Park Service. Mimeographed.

Corbin, Annalies, and Sheli Smith

2008   After the Fanfare: Education, the Lasting Legacy. International Journal of Historical Archaeology 12(2):157–180.

Corbyn, Ronald C.

1980   HCRS Cultural Programs. American Society for Conservation Archaeology Newsletter 7(2):17.

Cuddy, Thomas W., and Mark P. Leone

2008   New Africa: Understanding the Americanization of African Descent Groups through Archaeology. *In* Collaboration in Archaeological Practice: Engaging Descendant Communities, edited by Chip Colwell-Chanthaphonh and T. J. Ferguson, pp. 203–223. Lanham, MD: AltaMira.

Cushman, David W., and Lynne Sebastian
2008   Integrating Archaeological Models: Management and Compliance on
         Military Installations. SRI Foundation Preservation Research Series 7.
         Electronic document, www.srifoundation.org/library.html.

Darvill, Timothy
2005   "Sorted for East and Whiz"? Approaching Value and Importance in
         Archaeological Resource Management. *In* Heritage of Value, Archaeology of
         Renown, edited by Clay Mathers, Timothy Darvill, and Barbara J. Little, pp.
         21–42. Gainesville: University Press of Florida.

Davis, Hester A.
1971   Is There a Future for the Past? Archaeology 24(4):300–306.
1972   The Crisis in American Archaeology. Science 175(4019):267–272.
1982   Forum: Professionalism in Archaeology. American Antiquity 47(1):158–163.
1991   Avocational Archaeology Groups: A Secret Weapon for Site Protection. *In*
         Protecting the Past, edited by George S. Smith and John E. Ehrenhard. Boca
         Raton, FL: CRC Press. Out of print; available at www.nps.gov/seac/
         protectg.htm, in chapter 2, "Protecting Archaeological Sites through
         Education."
2003   Creating and Implementing a Code and Standards. *In* Ethical Issues in
         Archaeology, edited by Larry J. Zimmerman, Karen D. Vitelli, and Julie
         Hollowell-Zimmer, pp. 252–260. Walnut Creek, CA: AltaMira.

**Davis, Hester A., Jeffrey H. Altschul, Judith Bense, Elizabeth M. Brumfiel,
Shereen Lerner, James J. Miller, Vincas P. Steponaitis, and Joe Watkins**
1999   Teaching Archaeology in the Twenty-first Century: Thoughts on
         Undergraduate Education. Society for American Archaeology Bulletin
         17(1):18–20.

Davis, M. Elaine, and Marjorie R. Connolly, eds.
2000   Windows into the Past: Crow Canyon Archaeological Center's Guide for
         Teachers. Dubuque, IA: Kendall-Hunt.

Davis, Margo Muhl
2001   Archaeology in the Classroom: A Resource Guide by State for Teachers and
         Parents. 2nd ed. Dubuque, IA: Kendall-Hunt.

Dean, Robert L., and Douglas J. Perrelli
2006   Highway Archaeology in Western New York: Archaeologists' Views of
         Cooperation between State and Tribal Review Agencies. *In* Cross-Cultural
         Collaboration: Native Peoples and Archaeology in the Northeastern United
         States, edited by Jordan E. Kerber, pp. 131–149. Lincoln: University of
         Nebraska Press.

DeCicco, Gabriel
1988   A Public Relations Primer. American Antiquity 53(4):840–856.

De Cunzo, Lu Ann
2004   A Historical Archaeology of Delaware: People, Contexts, and the Cultures of
         Agriculture. Knoxville: University of Tennessee Press.

De la Torre, Marta, ed.
2002   Assessing the Values of Cultural Heritage: Research Report. The Getty
Conservation Institute, Los Angeles. Electronic document,
www.getty.edu/conservation/publications/pdf_publications/assessing.pdf.

Derry, Linda, and Maureen Malloy, eds.
2003   Archaeologists and Local Communities: Partners in Exploring the Past.
Washington, DC: Society for American Archaeology.

Diamond, Jared
1997   Guns, Germs, and Steel: The Fates of Human Societies. New York:
W. W. Norton.
2005   Collapse: How Societies Choose to Fail or Succeed. New York: Penguin
Group, Viking.

Dixson, Keith
1977   Applications of Archaeological Resources: Broadening the Basis of
Significance. In Conservation Archaeology: A Guide for Cultural Resource
Management Studies, edited by Michael B. Schiffer and George J.
Gumerman, pp. 277–290. New York: Academic Press.

Doelle, William H., and David A. Phillips Jr.
2005   From the Academy to the Private Sector: CRM's Rapid Transformation within
the Archaeological Professions. In Southwest Archaeology in the Twentieth
Century, edited by Linda S. Cordell and Don D. Fowler, pp. 97–108. Salt
Lake City: University of Utah Press.

Dongoske, Kurt E., Mark Alderderfer, and Karen Doehner, eds.
2000   Working Together: Native Americans and Archaeologists. Washington, DC:
Society for American Archaeology.

Dowdall, Katherine M., and Otis O. Parrish
2003   A Meaningful Disturbance of the Earth. Journal of Social Archaeology
3(1):99–133.

Drews, Michael, Eric Ingbar, and Alyce Branigan
2004   Great Basin Restoration Initiative: Cultural Resource Landscape Level
Planning Model. Cultural Resources Series 14. Reno: Bureau of Land
Management, Nevada (www.blm.gov/nv).

Drews, Michael, Eric Ingbar, David Zeanah, and William Eckerle
2004   A Cultural Resources Model for Pine Valley, Nevada. Cultural Resources
Series 13. Reno: Bureau of Land Management, Nevada (www.blm.gov/nv).

Dunnell, Robert C.
1986   Five Decades of American Archaeology. In American Archaeology Past and
Future: A Celebration of the Society for American Archaeology 1935–1985,
edited by David J. Meltzer, Donald D. Fowler, and Jeremy A. Sabloff, pp.
23–49. Washington, DC: Smithsonian Institution Press.

Ebert, James, I.
2001   Distributional Archaeology. Salt Lake City: University of Utah Press.

Echo-Hawk, Roger C.
2000   Ancient History in the New World: Integrating Oral Traditions and the
          Archaeological Record. American Antiquity 65(2):267–290.
Edelman
2007   Edelman Trust Barometer 2007. Atlanta, GA: Edelman.
Eiteljorg, Harrison, II
2005   Archiving Archaeological Data: Is There a Viable Business Model for a U.S.
          Repository? CSA Newsletter 17(3). Electronic document,
          www.csanet.org/newsletter/winter05/nlw0501.html.
2007   Center for the Study of Architecture home page,
          www.csanet.org/index.html#info, accessed Nov. 25, 2007.
Evans, Thomas
2005   Digital Archaeology: Bridging Method and Theory. New York: Routledge.
Fagan, Brian
2005   Writing Archaeology: Telling Stories about the Past. Walnut Creek, CA: Left
          Coast Press.
Fagette, Paul
1996   Digging for Dollars: American Archaeology and the New Deal.
          Albuquerque: University of New Mexico Press.
Ferguson, T. J.
1996   Native Americans and the Practice of Archaeology. Annual Review of
          Anthropology 25:63–79.
1998   Öngtupka niqw Pisisvayu (Salt, Salt Canyon, and the Colorado River): The
          Hopi People and the Grand Canyon. Final ethnohistoric report for Hopi
          Glen Canyon Environmental Studies. Kykotsmovi, AZ: Hopi Cultural
          Preservation Office.
2000   NHPA: Changing the Role of Native Americans in the Archaeological Study
          of the Past. *In* Working Together: Native Americans and Archaeologists,
          edited by Kurt E. Dongoske, Mark Alderderfer, and Karen Doehner, pp.
          25–36. Washington, DC: Society for American Archaeology.
Fluehr-Lobban, C., ed.
2003   Ethics and the Profession of Anthropology: Dialogue for Ethically Conscious
          Practice. Walnut Creek, CA: AltaMira.
Fowler, Don D., and Barbara Malinky
2005   The Origins of ARPA: Crafting the Archaeological Resources Protection Act
          of 1979. *In* Presenting Archaeology in Court: Legal Strategies for Protecting
          Cultural Resources, edited by Sherry Hutt, Marion P. Forsyth, and David
          Tarler, pp. 1–23. Lanham, MD: AltaMira.
Friedman, Thomas
2005   The World Is Flat: A Brief History of the Twenty-first Century. New York:
          Farrar, Straus and Giroux.
General Accounting Office (GAO)
1981   Are Agencies Doing Enough or Too Much for Archeological Preservation?
          Guidance Needed. Washington, DC: Government Printing Office.

1985 Cultural Resources: Results of Questionnaire on Federal Agency History Preservation Activities. Washington, DC: Government Printing Office.

1987 Cultural Resources: Problems Protecting and Preserving Federal Archeological Resources. Washington, DC: Government Printing Office.

Gibb, James G.

2000 Imaginary, but by No Means Unimaginable: Storytelling, Science, and Historical Archaeology. Historical Archaeology 34(2):1–6.

Gibbons, Michael, Camille Limoges, Helga Nowotny, Simon Schwartzman, Peter Scott, and Martin Trow

1994 The New Production of Knowledge: The Dynamics of Science and Research in Contemporary Societies. London: Sage.

Gifford, Carol A., and Elizabeth A. Morris

1985 Digging for Credit: Early Archaeological Field Schools in the American Southwest. American Antiquity 50(2):395–411.

Gilmore, Kevin P., Marcia Tate, Mark L. Chenault, Bonnie Clark, Terri McBride, and Margaret Wood

2004 Colorado Prehistory: A Context for the Platte River Basin. Salt Lake City: University of Utah Press.

Glass, James A.

1990 The Beginnings of a New National Historic Preservation Program, 1957 to 1969. Nashville, TN: American Association for State and Local History.

Goddard, Jennifer

2007 Pot-Hunting as an Ontological Mechanism in Southeastern Utah, USA. Paper presented at the annual meeting of the Theoretical Archaeology Group, York, UK.

2008a Understanding Motivations for Artefact-Hunting in the USA Southwest. Paper presented at the Sixth World Archaeological Congress, Dublin, Ireland.

2008b Our Legacies in Saving the Past. In Archaeological Histories, edited by Monique Boddington and Naomi Farrington, pp. 25–40. Archaeological Review from Cambridge 23(1) (25th anniversary edition). Cambridge, UK.

Goodby, Robert G.

2006 Working with the Abenaki in New Hampshire: The Education of an Archaeologist. In Cross-Cultural Collaboration: Native Peoples and Archaeology in the Northeastern United States, edited by Jordan E. Kerber, pp. 94–111. Lincoln: University of Nebraska Press.

Graham, Willie, Carter L. Hugins, Carl R. Lounsbury, Fraser D. Neiman, and James P. Whittenburg

2007 Adaptation and Innovation: Archaeological and Architectural Perspectives on the Seventeenth-Century Chesapeake. William and Mary Quarterly, third series, 64(3):451–522.

Green, Ernestene I., ed.

1984 Ethics and Values in Archaeology. New York: Free Press.

Griffin, James B.

1985   The Formation of the Society for American Archaeology. American Antiquity 50(2):261–271.

Guthe, Carl E.

1939   The Basic Needs of American Archeology. Science 90(2345):528–530.

1967   Reflections on the Founding of the Society for American Archaeology. American Antiquity 32(4):433–440.

Haag, William G.

1985   Federal Aid to Archaeology in the Southeast, 1933–1942. American Antiquity 50(2):272–280.

Hall, Andrew

2008   Looking over the Archaeologists' Shoulders: Web-Based Public Outreach in the Deep Wrecks Project. International Journal of Historical Archaeology 12(2):146–156.

Hardesty, Donald L., and Barbara J. Little

2000   Assessing Site Significance: A Guide for Archaeologists and Historians. Walnut Creek, CA: AltaMira.

Harding, Anthony

2007   Communication in Archaeology. European Journal of Archaeology 10(2–3):119–133.

Harman, David, Francis P. McManamon, and Dwight T. Pitcaithley

2006   The Antiquities Act: A Century of American Archaeology, Historic Preservation, and Nature Conservation. Tucson: University of Arizona Press.

Heckenberger, Michael

2004   Archaeology as Indigenous Advocacy in Amazonia. Practicing Anthropology 26(3):35–39.

Hill, J. Brett, Jeffrey J. Clark, William H. Doelle, and Patrick D. Lyons

2004   Prehistoric Demography in the Southwest: Migration, Coalescence, and Hohokam Population Decline. American Antiquity 69(4):689–716.

Hodder, Ian

1999   The Archaeological Process. Oxford: Blackwell.

Hollowell, Julie

2006   Moral Arguments on Subsistence Digging. In The Ethics of Archaeology: Philosophical Perspectives on Archaeological Practice, edited by Chris Scarre and Geoffrey Scarre, pp. 69–93. Cambridge: Cambridge University Press.

Hollowell, Julie, and Richard Wilk

1995   Are Practices of Archaeological Field Projects Related to Positive Relationships with Local Communities? A Quantitative Analysis of 84 Cases. Paper presented at the annual meeting of the Society for American Archaeology, Chicago.

Holtorf, Cornelius

2007   Can You Hear Me at the Back? Archaeology, Communication and Society. European Journal of Archaeology 10(2–3):149–165.

Hoopes, John W.
1998   The Online Lab Manual: Reference Collections on the Web. Society for American Archaeology Bulletin 16(5):17–19, 39.

Hovezak, Tim D., and Leslie M. Sesler
2002   Fruitland Data Recovery Project. La Plata Archaeological Consultants Research Paper 4. Dolores, CO.

Hughes, Richard B., and Dixie L. Henry
2006   Forging New Partnerships: Archaeologists and the Native People of Maryland. *In* Cross-Cultural Collaboration: Native Peoples and Archaeology in the Northeastern United States, edited by Jordan E. Kerber, pp. 112–128. Lincoln: University of Nebraska Press.

Hutt, Sherry, and Jamie Lavallee
2005   Tribal Consultation: Best Practices in Historic Preservation. Washington, DC: National Association of Tribal Historic Preservation Officers.

Ingbar, Eric, Pat Barker, David Zeanah, Steve Wells, and John Snow
2001   Expediting Permitting of Oil and Gas Exploration through Archaeological Modeling. Proceedings of the Eighth Annual International Petroleum Environmental Conference, 2001. Electronic document, http://ipec.utulsa.edu/conferences.

Ingbar, Eric, L. Sebastian, J. Altschul, M. Hopkins, W. Eckerle, P. Robinson, J. Finley, S. Hall, W. Hayden, C. Rohe, T. Seaman, S. Taddie, and S. Thompson
2005   Adaptive Management and Planning Models for Cultural Resources in Oil and Gas Fields in New Mexico and Wyoming: Final Technical Report (DE-FC26-02NT15445). Department of Energy Technical Report. Electronic document, www.gnomon.com.

Irwin-Williams, Cynthia and Don D. Fowler
1984   An Open Letter to the Professional Archaeological Community. Reno, Nevada: University of Nevada, Historic Preservation Program. Mimeographed, 4 pages.

Irwin-Williams, Cynthia, and Don D. Fowler, eds.
1986   Regional Conferences Summary Report. Washington, DC: Society for American Archaeology.

Jameson, John H., ed.
1997   Presenting Archaeology to the Public: Digging for Truths. Walnut Creek, CA: AltaMira.

Jennings, Jesse D.
1986   American Archaeology, 1930–1985. *In* American Archaeology Past and Future: A Celebration of the Society for American Archaeology, 1935–1985, edited by David J. Meltzer, Don D. Fowler, and Jeremy A. Sabloff, pp. 53–62. Washington, DC: Smithsonian Institution Press.

Joffe, Alexander H.
2006   Social Science and Modern Society. Society 43(6):71–76.

REFERENCES

Johnson, Frederick
1961   Opening Remarks on Behalf of the Committee for the Recovery of
        Archaeological Remains. *In* Symposium on Salvage Archaeology, edited by
        John M. Corbett, pp. 1–4. Washington, DC: US Department of the Interior,
        National Park Service. Mimeographed.
Joyce, Rosemary
2002   The Languages of Archaeology: Dialogue, Narrative, and Writing. New York:
        Blackwell.
Judge, W. James
2006   Conservation Archaeology and the Southwestern Anthropological Research
        Group. *In* Tracking Ancient Footsteps: William D. Lipe's Contributions to
        Southwestern Prehistory and Public Archaeology, edited by R. G. Matson
        and Timothy A. Kohler, pp. 97–108. Pullman: Washington State University
        Press.
Kane, Sharyn, and Richard Keeton
1993   Beneath These Waters: Archaeological and Historical Studies of 11,500 Years
        along the Savannah River. Atlanta, GA: National Park Service.
1994   In Those Days: African American Life near the Savannah River. Atlanta, GA:
        National Park Service.
Katz, Gregory, and Daniel N. Bailey
2003   Archaeological and Geological Study of Shriver Chert in Snyder and Union
        Counties, Pennsylvania: Alternative Mitigation for the Troxell Site (36SN91)
        S.R. 0522, Section 043, Bridge Replacement Project, Franklin Township,
        Snyder County, Pennsylvania E.R. no. 97–6002–109. Report prepared by A.
        D. Marble and Company, Conshohocken, PA, for the Pennsylvania
        Department of Transportation, Montoursville, PA.
Keel, Bennie C.
1995   The Public Trust. *In* The Public Trust and the First Americans, edited by
        Ruthann Knudson and Bennie C. Keel, pp. 7–8. Corvallis: Oregon State
        University Press.
Keel, Bennie, Barbara J. Little, Martha Graham, Mary Carroll, and Francis P.
McManamon
2007   Peer Review of Federal Archeological Projects and Programs. Technical
        Brief 21. Washington, DC: US Department of the Interior, National Park
        Service, Archeology Program.
Kelly, Robert L.
1995   The Foraging Spectrum: Diversity in Hunter-Gatherer Lifeways. Washington,
        DC: Smithsonian Institution Press.
2000   Native Americans and Archaeology: A Vital Partnership. *In* Working
        Together: Native Americans and Archaeologists, edited by Kurt E.
        Dongoske, Mark Alderderfer, and Karen Doehner, pp. 97–101. Washington,
        DC: Society for American Archaeology.
Kelso, William M.
2006   Jamestown: The Buried Truth. Charlottesville: University of Virginia Press.

Kemp, Brian M., Ripan S. Malhi, John McDonough, Deborah A. Bolnick,
Jason A. Eshleman, Olga Rickards, Christina Martinez-Labarga, John R. Johnson,
Joseph G. Lorenz, E. James Dixon, Terrence E. Fifield, Timothy H. Heaton,
Rosita Worl, and David Glenn Smith
2007   Genetic Analysis of Early Holocene Skeletal Remains from Alaska and Its
        Implications for the Settlement of the Americas. American Journal of
        Physical Anthropology 132:605–621.

Kerber, Jordan E., ed.
2006   Cross-Cultural Collaboration: Native Peoples and Archaeology in the
        Northeastern United States. Lincoln: University of Nebraska Press.

Killion, Thomas W., ed.
2008   Opening Archaeology: Repatriation's Impact on Contemporary Research
        and Practice. Santa Fe, NM: School for Advanced Research Press.

Killion, Thomas W., and Paula Molloy
2000   Repatriation's Silver Lining. In Working Together: Native Americans and
        Archaeologists, edited by Kurt E. Dongoske, Mark Alderderfer, and Karen
        Doehner, pp. 111–117. Washington, DC: Society for American Archaeology.

King, Julia A.
2006   Issues in Plow Zone Archaeology: A Forum Held at the 2006 Middle Atlantic
        Archaeological Conference. Journal of Middle Atlantic Archaeology
        22:111–133.

King, Thomas F.
1977   The Archeological Survey: Methods and Uses. Washington, DC: Interagency
        Archeological Services Division, National Park Service.
1982   Preservation and Rescue. Journal of Field Archaeology 9(2):389–395.
1991   Some Dimensions of the Pothunting Problem. In Protecting the Past, edited
        by George S. Smith and John E. Ehrenhard. Boca Raton, FL: CRC Press. Out
        of print; available at www.nps.gov/seac/protectg.htm, in chapter 2,
        "Archaeological Site Destruction."
1998   Cultural Resource Laws and Practice: An Introductory Guide. Walnut Creek,
        CA: AltaMira.
2002   Thinking about Cultural Resource Management: Essays from the Edge.
        Walnut Creek, CA: AltaMira.
2003   Places That Count: Traditional Cultural Properties in Cultural Resource
        Management. Walnut Creek, CA: AltaMira.
2004   Cultural Resource Laws and Practice: An Introductory Guide. 3rd ed. Walnut
        Creek, CA: AltaMira.
2008   Ethical Issues in the Practice of Archaeology. In Elsevier's Encyclopedia of
        Archaeology, vol. 2, edited by Barbara Pearsall, pp. 1149–1155. San Diego:
        Academic Press.

King, Thomas F., Patricia Parker Hickman, and Gary Berg
1977   Anthropology in Historic Preservation: Caring for Culture's Clutter. New
        York: Academic Press.

Kintigh, Keith
2006   The Promise and Challenge of Archaeological Data Integration. American
        Antiquity 71(3):567–578.
Kipfer, Barbara Ann
2007   Synthesis. Archaeology Wordsmith. Electronic document, www.reference-
        wordsmith.com/cgi-bin/lookup.cgi?exact=1&terms=synthesis, accessed Nov.
        25, 2007.
Klein, Joel I.
1994   Alternatives to Archaeological Data Recovery. Northeast Historical
        Archaeology (Council of Northeast Historic Archaeologists, Buffalo, NY)
        21–22(1992–1993):173–182.
Klesert, Anthony L., and Alan S. Downer, eds.
1990   Preservation on the Reservation: Native Americans, Native American Lands,
        and Archaeology. Navajo Nation Papers in Anthropology 26. Window Rock,
        AZ: Navajo Nation Archaeology Department/Navajo Nation Historic
        Preservation Department.
Knudson, Ruthann
1991   The Archaeological Public Trust in Context. In Protecting the Past, edited
        by George S. Smith and John E. Ehrenhard, pp. 3–8. Boca Raton, FL: CRC
        Press.
Kohler, Timothy A.
1988   Predictive Locational Modeling: History and Current Practice. In
        Quantifying the Present and Predicting the Past: Theory, Method, and
        Application of Archaeological Predictive Modeling, edited by W. J. Judge
        and L. Sebastian, pp. 19–60. Denver, CO: Bureau of Land Management.
Kula, Christine
2007   Alternative Mitigation Strategies for Archaeological Sites Affected by
        Transportation Projects. Paper presented at the annual meeting of the
        Society for American Archaeology, Austin, TX.
Kula, Christine, and Ira Beckerman
2004   Archaeology in the 21st Century: Recent Successes, New Challenges. Paper
        presented at the 2004 Pennsylvania Archaeological Council Symposium,
        Clarion, PA.
Kuwanwisiwma, Leigh J.
2002   Hopi Understanding of the Past: A Collaborative Approach. In Public
        Benefits of Archaeology, edited by Barbara J. Little, pp. 46–50. Gainesville:
        University Press of Florida.
2008   Collaboration Means Equality, Respect, and Reciprocity: A Conversation
        about Archaeology and the Hopi Tribe. In Collaboration in Archaeological
        Practice: Engaging Descendant Communities, edited by Chip Colwell-
        Chanthaphonh and T. J. Ferguson, pp. 151–169. Walnut Creek, CA:
        AltaMira.
Lange, A. G., ed.
2004   Reference Collections: Foundation for Future Archaeology. Amersfoort,
        Netherlands: Rijksdienst voor het Ouheidkundig Bodemunderzoek.

Lawrence, John W., and David L. Weinberg

2003   Alternative Mitigation to the Interstate Fairgrounds Site (36BR210) S.R. 1056, Section 001, Athens Bridge Replacement Project, Athens Township, Bradford County, Pennsylvania E.R. no. 00–8029–015. Report prepared by A. D. Marble and Company, Conshohocken, PA, for Dewberry-Goodkind, Inc., Carlisle, PA, and the Pennsylvania Department of Transportation, Montoursville, PA.

Lees, William B., and Julia A. King

2007   What Are We Really Learning through Publicly Funded Historical Archaeology (and Is It Worth the Considerable Expense?). Historical Archaeology 41(2):54–61.

Lenihan, D. J., T. L. Carrell, S. Fosberg, S. L. Rayl, and J. A. Ware

1981   The Final Report of the National Reservoir Inundation Study. 2 vols. Santa Fe, NM: National Park Service, Southwest Regional Office.

Leone, Mark P.

2005   The Archaeology of Liberty in an American Capital: Excavations in Annapolis. Berkeley: University of California Press.

Lightfoot, Kent G.

2004   Indians, Missionaries, and Merchants: The Legacy of Colonial Encounters on the California Frontiers. Berkeley: University of California Press.

Lipe, William D.

1974   A Conservation Model for American Archaeology. The Kiva 39(3–4):213–245.

1978   Contracts, Bureaucrats, and Research: Some Emerging Problems of Conservation Archaeology in the United States. In Archaeological Essays in Honor of Irving B. Rouse, edited by Robert C. Dunnell and Edwin S. Hall, pp. 121–147. The Hague: Mouton.

1984   Value and Meaning in Cultural Resources. In Approaches to the Archaeological Heritage, edited by Henry Cleere, pp. 1–11. Cambridge: Cambridge University Press.

1985   Conservation for What? Proceedings of the American Society for Conservation Archaeology, pp. 1–11.

1994   Strategies for Resource Protection: Results from Save the Past for the Future. Society for American Archaeology Bulletin 12(5):4–7.

1997   Report of the Second Conference on Renewing Our National Archaeological Program, February 9–11, 1997. Submitted to the board of directors, Society for American Archaeology.

2000a   In Defense of Digging: Archaeological Preservation as a Means, Not an End. In Ethics in American Archaeology, 2nd ed., edited by Mark Lynott and Alison Wylie, pp. 113–117. Washington, DC: Society for American Archaeology.

2000b   A View from the Lake: The Dolores Archaeological Program in the McPhee Reservoir Area, SW Colorado. CRM 23(1):21–24.

2001   Threat to Knowledge: Research and the Future of Archeology in the National Parks [interview format]. Common Ground, Summer–Fall:24–33.

2002 Public Benefits of Archaeological Research. *In* Public Benefits of Archaeology, edited by Barbara J. Little, pp. 20–28. Gainesville: University Press of Florida.

2006a Confessions of an Archaeological Tour Bus Driver. Keynote address, Heritage Tourism Workshop, Santa Fe, NM. Electronic document, www.blm.gov/ heritage/adventures/tourism_2006_presentations.html.

2006b Archaeological Ethics and the Law. Cortez, CO: Crow Canyon Archaeological Center. Electronic document, www.crowcanyon.org/education/ethics _law.asp.

Lipe, William D., and Alexander J. Lindsay Jr., eds.

1974 Proceedings of the 1974 Cultural Resource Management Conference, Federal Center, Denver, Colorado. Technical Series 14. Flagstaff: Museum of Northern Arizona.

Lipe, William D., and Charles Redman

1996 Conference on "Renewing Our National Archaeological Program." Society for American Archaeology Bulletin 14(4):14–20.

Lipe, William D., Mark D. Varien, and R. H. Wilshusen

1999 Colorado Prehistory: A Context for the Southern Colorado River Basin. Denver: Colorado Council of Professional Archaeologists.

Little, Barbara J.

2000 Compelling Images through Storytelling: Comment on "Imaginary, but by No Means Unimaginable: Storytelling, Science, and Historical Archaeology." Historical Archaeology 34(2):10–13.

2007a What Are We Learning? Who Are We Serving? Publicly Funded Historical Archaeology and Public Scholarship. Historical Archaeology 41(2):72–79.

Little, Barbara J., ed.

2002 Public Benefits of Archaeology. Gainesville: University Press of Florida.

2007b Historical Archaeology: Why the Past Matters. Walnut Creek, CA: Left Coast Press.

Little, Barbara J., Erika Martin Seibert, Jan Townsend, John H. Sprinkle Jr., and John Knoerl

2000 Guidelines for Evaluating and Registering Archaeological Properties. National Register Bulletin. Washington, DC: US Department of the Interior, National Park Service.

Little, Barbara J., and Paul A. Shackel, eds.

2007 Archaeology as a Tool of Civic Engagement. Walnut Creek, CA: AltaMira.

Lock, Gary

2003 Using Computers in Archaeology: Towards Virtual Pasts. New York: Routledge.

Lowenthal, David

1996 The Heritage Crusade and the Spoils of History. New York: Free Press.

2005 Why Sanctions Seldom Work: Reflections on Cultural Property Internationalism. International Journal of Cultural Property 12(3):393–424.

Lynott, Mark E.

1997 Archaeological Principles and Archaeological Practice: Development of an Ethics Policy. American Antiquity 62(4):589–599.

2000 Ethical Principles and Archaeological Practice: Development of an Ethics Policy. In Ethics in American Archaeology, 2nd ed., edited by Mark J. Lynott and Alison Wylie, pp. 26–34. Washington, DC: Society for American Archaeology.

Lynott, Mark E., and Alison Wylie, eds.

1995 Ethics in American Archaeology: Challenges for the 1990s. Washington, DC: Society for American Archaeology.

2000 Ethics in American Archaeology. 2nd ed. Washington, DC: Society for American Archaeology.

Lyon, Edwin A.

1996 A New Deal for Southeastern Archaeology. Tuscaloosa: University of Alabama Press.

Lyons, Patrick D.

2003 Hopi Ethnoarchaeology in Relation to the Hohokam. In Yep Hisat Hoopoq'yaqam Yeesiwa (Hopi Ancestors Were Once Here): Hopi-Hohokam Cultural Affiliation Study, compiled by T. J. Ferguson, pp. 123–164. Kykotsmovi, AZ: Hopi Cultural Preservation Office.

Madsen, Torsten

2004 Classification and Archaeological Knowledge Bases. In Reference Collections: Foundation for Future Archaeology, edited by A. G. Lange, pp. 35–42. Amersfoort, Netherlands: Rijksdienst voor het Ouheidkundig Bodemunderzoek.

Marquardt, William H., ed.

1977 Regional Centers in Archaeology: Prospects and Problems. Columbia: Missouri Archaeological Society.

Martorano, Marilyn A., Ted Hoefer III, Margaret A. Jodry, Vince Spero, and Melissa L. Taylor

1999 Colorado Prehistory: A Context for the Rio Grande Basin. Denver: Colorado Council of Professional Archaeologists.

Mathers, Clay, Timothy Darvill, and Barbara J. Little, eds.

2005 Heritage of Value, Archaeology of Renown: Reshaping Archaeological Assessment and Significance. Gainesville: University Press of Florida.

Matson, R. G., and Timothy A. Kohler, eds.

2006 Tracking Ancient Footsteps: William D. Lipe's Contributions to Southwestern Prehistory and Public Archaeology. Pullman: Washington State University Press.

Mayer-Oakes, William J., and Alice W. Portnoy

1979 Scholars and Contractors. Washington, DC: Heritage Conservation and Recreation Service, Interagency Archeological Services Division.

Mayr, Ernst

2000 Darwin's Influence on Modern Thought. Scientific American, July:79–83.

McDavid, Carol

2002   Archaeologies That Hurt, Descendants That Matter: A Pragmatic Approach to Collaboration in the Public Interpretation of African-American Archaeology. World Archaeology 34(2):303–314.

McGimsey, Charles R., III

1971   Archeology and the Law. American Antiquity 36(2):121–126.

1972   Public Archeology. New York: Seminar Press.

1973   Archeology and Archeological Resources: A Guide for Those Planning to Use, Affect, or Alter the Land's Surface. Washington, DC: Society for American Archaeology.

1974   The Restructuring of a Profession. *In* Proceedings of the 1974 Cultural Resource Management Conference, Federal Center, Denver, Colorado, edited by William D. Lipe and Alexander J. Lindsay Jr., pp. 171–179. Technical Series 14. Flagstaff: Museum of Northern Arizona.

1977   Good Legislation Beats a Better Mousetrap: The Archeological Experience. Paper presented at the annual meeting of the Society of Applied Archaeology, San Diego, CA. Published in CRM on CRM: One Person's Perspective on the Birth and Early Development of Cultural Resource Management, by Charles R. McGimsey III, pp. 119–122. Fayetteville: Arkansas Archeological Survey, 2004.

2000   Standards, Ethics, and Archaeology: A Brief History. *In* Ethics in Archaeology, 2nd ed., edited by Mark J. Lynott and Alison Wylie, pp. 16–18. Washington, DC: Society for American Archaeology.

2004   CRM on CRM: One Person's Perspective on the Birth and Early Development of Cultural Resource Management. Fayetteville: Arkansas Archeological Survey.

McGimsey, Charles R., III, Carl H. Chapman, and Hester A. Davis

1970   Stewards of the Past. Columbia: University of Missouri Press.

McGimsey, Charles R., III, and Hester A. Davis, eds.

1977   The Management of Archeological Resources: The Airlie House Report. Washington, DC: Society for American Archaeology.

McGimsey, Chip, Leslie E. Eisenberg, and John D. Doershunk

2003   Register of Professional Archaeologists Standards Board Decision Regarding the Complains against Dr. Gordon C. Tucker Jr., RPA. Finding of the Registry of Professional Archaeologists Standards Board. Electronic document, http://rpanet.org/associations/8360/files/resources/members_ tucker_report.html.

McGuire, Randall H.

2003   Foreword. *In* Ethical Issues in Archaeology, edited by Larry J. Zimmerman, Karen D. Vitelli, and Julie Hollowell-Zimmer, pp. vii–ix. Walnut Creek, CA: AltaMira.

McKeown, C. Timothy

1997a   The Meaning of Consultation. Common Ground 2(3–4). Electronic document, www.nps.gov/archeology/Cg/vol2_num3-4/meaning.htm.

1997b   Good Faith. Common Ground 2(3–4). Electronic document, www.nps.gov/archeology/Cg/vol2_num3-4/faith.htm.

McManamon, Francis P.

1991   The Many Publics for Archaeology. American Antiquity 56(1):121–130.

1997   Why Consult? Common Ground 2(3–4). Electronic document, www.nps.gov/archeology/Cg/vol2_num3-4/why.htm.

Medford, Edna Greene

2006   The New York African Burial Ground: History Final Report. Prepared by Howard University, Washington, DC, for US General Services Administration, Northeastern and Caribbean Region, Washington, DC.

Mehrer, Mark, and Konnie Wescott

2006   GIS and Archaeological Site Location Modeling. Boca Raton, FL: CRC Press.

Messenger, Phyllis E., Dennis B. Blanton, Tobi A. Brimsek, Noel Broadbent, Pamela Cressey, Nancy DeGrummond, John E. Ehrenhard, Dorothy S. Krass, Charles R. McGimsey III, and Nancy M. White

1999   Teaching Archaeology in the Twenty-first Century: Thoughts on Postgraduate Education/Professional Development. Society for American Archaeology Bulletin 17(2). Electronic document, www.saa.org/publications /SAAbulletin/17–2/SAA11.html.

Minnis, Paul E.

2006   Call-Answer: Answering the Skeptic's Question. Answers provided by Barbara Little, Robert Kelly, Scott E. Ingram, Dean Snow, Lynne Sebastian, and Katherine A. Spielmann. SAA Archaeological Record 6(5):17–20.

Mulloy, Elizabeth D.

1976   The History of the National Trust for Historic Preservation, 1963–1973. Washington, DC: Preservation Press.

Murtagh, William J.

2006   Keeping Time: The History and Theory of Preservation in America. 3rd ed. Hoboken, NJ: John Wiley.

Naranjo, Tessie

1995   Thoughts on Migration by Santa Clara Pueblo. Journal of Anthropological Archaeology 14(2):247–250.

Naranjo, Tito

1999   Orality vs. Literacy. In Colorado Prehistory: A Context for the Southern Colorado River Basin, edited by William D. Lipe, Mark D. Varien, and Richard H. Wilshusen, pp. 397–404. Denver: Colorado Council of Professional Archaeologists.

National Council on Preservation Education

2007   Education Standards for Preservation Degree Granting Graduate and Undergraduate Programs. Electronic document, www.uvm.edu/histpres /ncpe/, accessed Nov. 17, 2008.

National Park Service

1990   How to Apply the National Register Criteria for Evaluation. National Register Bulletin 15, finalized by Patrick Andrus and edited by Rebecca Shrimpton. Washington, DC: US Department of the Interior, National Park Service.

2000   Guidelines for Evaluating and Registering Archeological Properties. National Register Bulletin by Barbara J. Little, Erika Martin Seibert, Jan Townsend, John H. Sprinkle Jr., and John Knoerl. Washington, DC: US Department of the Interior, National Park Service.

2002   Federal Historic Preservation Laws. Department of Transportation Act. National Center for Cultural Resources. Washington, DC: National Park Service.

2008   NADB-Reports: National Archeological Database. Washington, DC: National Park Service Archeology Program. Electronic document, www.cast.uark .edu/other/nps/nadb/, accessed Jan. 4, 2009.

2009   National NAGPRA OnLine Databases. Electronic document, www.nps.gov /history/nagpra/ONLINEDB/INDEX.HTM, accessed July 5, 2009.

National Register of Historic Places

2007   Teaching with Historic Places. Electronic document, www.nps.gov/history/nr/twhp/, accessed Dec. 28, 2007.

Navrud, Ståle, and Richard Ready

2002   Valuing Cultural Heritage: Applying Environmental Valuation Techniques to Historic Buildings, Monuments, and Artifacts. London: Edward Elgar.

Neumann, Thomas W., and Robert M. Sanford

2001   Cultural Resources Archaeology: An Introduction. Walnut Creek, CA: AltaMira.

News Staff

2007   Back to the Future. *In* Breakthrough of the Year: Runners-Up. Science 318(5858):1844–1849.

Nickens, Paul R., Signa L. Larralde, and Gordon C. Tucker Jr.

1981   A Survey of Vandalism to Archaeological Resources in Southwestern Colorado. Cultural Resources Series 11. Denver: Bureau of Land Management, Colorado State Office.

Nicolar, Joseph

2007   The Life and Traditions of the Red Man. Edited, annotated, and with a history of the Penobscot Nation and an introduction by Annette Kolodny. Durham, NC: Duke University Press.

Nowotny, Helga, Peter Scott, and Michael Gibbons

2001   Re-thinking Science, Knowledge and the Public in an Age of Uncertainty. Cambridge: Polity.

O'Brien, Michael J. and R. Lee Lyman, eds.

2001   Setting the Agenda for American Archaeology. The National Research Council Archaeological Conferences of 1929, 1932, and 1935. Tuscaloosa, Alabama: University of Alabama Press.

Ortman, Scott G., Mark D. Varien, and T. Lee Gripp

2007   Empirical Bayesian Methods for Archaeological Survey Data: An Application from the Mesa Verde Region. American Antiquity 72(2):241–272.

Owsley, Douglas W., and Richard L. Jantz

2001   Archaeological Politics and Public Interest in Paleoamerican Studies:

Lessons from Gordon Creek Woman and Kennewick Man. *American Antiquity* 66(4):565–575.

Parker, Patricia L., and Thomas F. King
1990   Guidelines for Evaluating and Documenting Traditional Cultural Properties. National Register Bulletin 38. Washington, DC: US Department of the Interior, National Park Service.

Pauketat, Timothy R., and Thomas E. Emerson
1997   *Cahokia: Domination and Ideology in the Mississippian World.* Lincoln: University of Nebraska Press.

Paulett, Robert
2007   The Monster at the End of the Book: The Limits of the Frontier as a Narrative Construct. Paper presented at the biennial meeting of the Society for Early Americanists, Williamsburg, VA. Electronic document, http://oieahc.wm.edu/conferences/13thannual/thur.html.

Perry, Warren R., Jean Howson, and Barbara A. Bianco, eds.
2006   *The New York African Burial Ground: Archaeology Final Report.* 4 vols. Prepared by Howard University, Washington, DC, for US General Services Administration, Northeastern and Caribbean Region, Washington, DC.

Petrie, W. M. Flinders
1904   *Methods and Aims in Archaeology.* London: Macmillan. Reprint, 1972. New York: Benjamin Blom.

Pettigrew, Richard
2002   Archaeological Legacy Institute. Archaeology Channel. Electronic document, www.archaeologychannel.org, accessed Jan. 4, 2009.

Pickering, Robert B.
1987   *I Can Be an Archaeologist.* Baltimore, MD: Pro Quo Books.

Plog, Fred T., and James N. Hill
1971   Explaining Variability in the Distribution of Sites. *In* The Distribution of Prehistoric Population Aggregates, edited by George J. Gumerman, pp. 7–36. Prescott College Anthropological Reports 1. Prescott, AZ.

Plog, Stephen E., Richard M. Leventhal, Worthy N. Martin, Julia A. King, and Fraser D. Neiman
2007   The Need for a Center for Digital Archaeology. Manuscript on file, Department of Anthropology, University of Virginia, Charlottesville.

Portnoy, Alice W., ed.
1978   Scholars as Managers or How Can Managers Do It Better. Cultural Resource Management Studies, Stock No. 024-016-00098-6. Washington, DC: US Department of the Interior, Heritage Conservation and Recreation Service, Office of Archeology and Historic Preservation, Interagency Archeological Services Division.

Professional Archaeologists of Kansas
2007   Getting the Archaeological Green Light for Your Projects: A Basic Guide to Complying with Laws Regarding Archaeological Sites. Brochure. Copies available from the Kansas State Historical Society, Topeka.

Project Archaeology

2007   Project Archaeology Web site. Electronic document, http://projectarchae ology.org/, accessed Dec. 23, 2007.

Raab, L. Mark

1984   Achieving Professionalism through Ethical Fragmentation: Warnings from Client-Oriented Archaeology. *In* Ethics and Values in Archaeology, edited by Ernestene L. Green, pp. 51–61. New York: Free Press.

Ramos, Marie, and David Duganne

2000   Exploring Public Attitudes and Perceptions about Archaeology. Rochester, NY: Harris Interactive.

Reed, Alan D., and Michael D. Metcalf

1999   Colorado Prehistory: A Context for the Northern Colorado River Basin. Denver: Colorado Council of Professional Archaeologists.

Reed, Alan D., Matthew Seddon, and Heather Stettler, eds.

2005   Kern River 2003 Expansion Project, Utah, vols. 1–7. Report prepared by Alpine Archaeological Consultants, Inc., Montrose, CO, and SWCA, Inc., Salt Lake City, Utah, for Kern River Gas Transmission Company, Salt Lake City. Submitted to Bureau of Land Management, Salt Lake City.

Reinhart, Theodore R., ed.

1996   The Archaeology of Eighteenth-Century Virginia. Special Publication 35. Richmond: Archeological Society of Virginia.

Reinhart, Theodore R., and Mary Ellen N. Hodges, eds.

1990   Early and Middle Archaic Research in Virginia: A Synthesis. Special Publication 22. Richmond: Archeological Society of Virginia.

1991   Late Archaic and Early Woodland Research in Virginia: A Synthesis. Special Publication 23. Richmond: Archeological Society of Virginia.

1992   Middle and Late Woodland Research in Virginia: A Synthesis. Special Publication 29. Richmond: Archeological Society of Virginia.

Reinhart, Theodore R., and Dennis J. Pogue, eds.

1993   The Archaeology of Seventeenth-Century Virginia. Special Publication 30. Richmond: Archeological Society of Virginia.

Renfrew, Colin

2000   Loot, Legitimacy, and Ownership: The Ethical Crisis in Archaeology. London: Gerald Duckworth.

Ritchey, Thomas

1991   Analysis and Synthesis: On Scientific Method—Based on a Study by Bernhard Riemann. Systems Research 8(4):21–41.

Roberts, Frank H. H.

1961   Status of the Salvage Program in the Missouri Basin. *In* Symposium on Salvage Archaeology, edited by John M. Corbett, pp. 4–10. Washington, DC: US Department of the Interior, National Park Service. Mimeographed.

Roberts, Heidi, Richard V. N. Ahlstrom, and Barbara Roth

2004   From Campus to Corporation: The Emergence of Contract Archaeology in the Southwestern United States. Washington, DC: Society for American Archaeology.

Robinson, Alice
2005   Can You Dig It? School Library Journal 51(3):33.

Roosevelt, Theodore
1913   History as Literature. American Historical Review 18(3):473–489.

Rose, J. C., Thomas J. Green, and Victoria D. Green
1996   NAGPRA Is Forever: Osteology and the Repatriation of Skeletons. Annual Review of Anthropology 25:81–103.

Rountree, Helen C., and E. Randolph Turner
2002   Before and after Jamestown: Virginia's Powhatans and Their Predecessors. Gainesville: University Press of Florida.

Rowan, Yorke, and Uzi Baram, eds.
2004   Marketing Heritage: Archaeology and the Consumption of the Past. Walnut Creek, CA: AltaMira.

RPA (Register of Professional Archaeologists)
1998   Code of Conduct and Standards of Research Performance. Electronic document, www.rpanet.org, accessed date?.
2007   About the Register of Professional Archaeologists. Electronic document, www.rpanet.org/, accessed Nov. 17, 2008.

Ruppert, Dave
1997   New Language for a New Partnership. Common Ground 2(3–4). Electronic document, www.nps.gov/archeology/Cg/vol2_num3-4/language.htm.

Sabloff, Jeremy A.
2008   Archaeology Matters: Action Archaeology in the Modern World. Walnut Creek, CA: Left Coast Press.

Scarre, Chris, and Geoffrey Scarre, eds.
2006   The Ethics of Archaeology: Philosophical Perspectives on Archaeological Practice. Cambridge: Cambridge University Press.

Scherzler, Diane
2007   Journalists and Archaeologists: Notes on Dealing Constructively with the Mass Media. European Journal of Archaeology 10(2–3):185–206.

Schiffer, Michael B.
1985   Is There a "Pompeii Premise" in Archaeology? Journal of Anthropological Research 41:18–41.
1987   Formation Processes of the Archaeological Record. Albuquerque: University of New Mexico Press.

Schiffer, Michael B., and George J. Gumerman
1977   Conservation Archaeology: A Guide for Cultural Resource Management Studies. New York: Academic Press.

Schneider, Joan S., and Jeffrey H. Altschul, eds.
2000   Of Stones and Spirits: Pursuing the Past of Antelope Hill. Technical Series 76. Tucson, AZ: Statistical Research.

Sealaska Heritage Institute
2005   Kuwóot yas.éin, His Spirit Is Looking Out from the Cave. DVD. Juneau, AK: Sealaska Heritage Institute.

Sebastian, Lynne
2006   The Conservation Model Today and Historic Preservation. *In* Tracking Ancient Footsteps: William D. Lipe's Contributions to Southwestern Prehistory, edited by R. G. Matson and Timothy A. Kohler, pp. 109–125. Pullman: Washington State University Press.

Sebastian, L., J. H. Altschul, C. M. Rohe, S. Thompson, and W. E. Hayden
2005   Adaptive Management and Planning Models for Cultural Resources in Oil and Gas Fields: New Mexico PUMP III Project. *In* Adaptive Management and Planning Models for Cultural Resources in Oil and Gas Fields in New Mexico and Wyoming: Final Technical Report (DE-FC26-02NT15445), by E. Ingbar et al. Department of Energy Technical Report. Electronic document, www.gnomon.com.

Sebastian, L., E. Ingbar, and D. W. Cushman
2005   Adaptive Management and Planning Models for Cultural Resources in Oil and Gas Fields: New Mexico PUMP III Project—Conclusions and Management Recommendations. *In* Adaptive Management and Planning Models for Cultural Resources in Oil and Gas Fields in New Mexico and Wyoming: Final Technical Report (DE-FC26-02NT15445), by E. Ingbar et al. Department of Energy Technical Report. Electronic document, www.gnomon.com.

Sebastian, L., C. Van West, and J. H. Altschul
2005   Adaptive Management and Planning Models for Cultural Resources in Oil and Gas Fields: New Mexico PUMP III Project—Experimental: The New Mexico Modeling Project. *In* Adaptive Management and Planning Models for Cultural Resources in Oil and Gas Fields in New Mexico and Wyoming: Final Technical Report (DE-FC26-02NT15445), by E. Ingbar et al. Department of Energy Technical Report. Electronic document, www.gno mon.com.

Seddon, Matt
2007   Personal communication.

Shackel, Paul A.
2007   Civic Engagement and Social Justice: Race on the Illinois Frontier. *In* Archaeology as a Tool of Civic Engagement, edited by Barbara J. Little and Paul A. Shackel, pp. 243–262. Lanham, MD: AltaMira.

Shackel, Paul A., and David A. Gadsby
2008   "I Wish for Paradise": Memory and Class in Hampden, Baltimore. *In* Collaboration in Archaeological Practice: Engaging Descendant Communities, edited by Chip Colwell-Chanthaphonh and T. J. Ferguson, pp. 225–242. Lanham, MD: AltaMira.

Shields, David
2005   Review of "The Atlantic World and Virginia, 1550–1624," Omohundro

Institute of Early American History and Culture Conference. Early American Literature 40(1):220–223.

Silliman, Stephen, ed.

2008   Collaborating at the Trowel's Edge: Teaching and Learning in Indigenous Archaeology. Tucson: University of Arizona Press.

Simmons, Alan H.

1999   Review of Archaeological Ethics, edited by Karen Vitelli. Journal of Field Archaeology 26(1):99–100.

Simon, Brona G.

2006   Collaboration between Archaeologists and Native Americans in Massachusetts: Preservation, Archaeology, and Native American Concerns in Balance. *In* Cross-Cultural Collaboration: Native Peoples and Archaeology in the Northeastern United States, edited by Jordan E. Kerber, pp. 44–58. Lincoln: University of Nebraska Press.

Singleton, Theresa A., and Charles H. Orser

2003   Descendant Communities: Linking People in the Present to the Past. *In* Ethical Issues in Archaeology, edited by Larry J. Zimmerman, Karen D. Vitelli, and Julie Hollowell-Zimmer, pp. 143–152. Walnut Creek, CA: AltaMira.

Skeates, Robin

2000   Debating the Archaeological Heritage. London: Gerald Duckworth.

Slotkin, Richard

1985   The Fatal Environment: The Myth of the Frontier in the Age of Industrialization, 1800–1890. New York: Atheneum.

Smardz, Karolyn, and Shelley Smith, eds.

2000   The Archaeology Education Handbook: Sharing the Past with Kids. Walnut Creek, CA: AltaMira.

Smith, Claire, and Gary Jackson

2008   The Ethics of Collaboration: Whose Culture? Whose Intellectual Property? Whose Benefits? *In* Collaboration in Archaeological Practice: Engaging Descendant Communities, edited by Chip Colwell-Chanthaphonh and T. J. Ferguson, pp. 171–199. Lanham, MD: AltaMira.

Smith, Laurajane

2004   Archaeological Theory and the Politics of Cultural Heritage. New York: Routledge.

2006   Uses of Heritage. New York: Routledge.

Smith, Linda Tuhiwai

1999   Decolonizing Methodologies: Research and Indigenous Peoples. London: Zed Books.

Smith, Maurice

2007   Finding Aid: The Steamship Conestoga and the Schooner Lillie Parsons. Marine Museum of the Great Lakes at Kingston, Kingston, Ontario. Electronic document, www.marmuseum.ca/findingaids/Finding%20Aid%20Conestoga%20&%20Parsons.htm, accessed Nov. 25, 2007.

Snow, Dean R., Mark Gahegan, C. Lee Giles, Kenneth G. Hirth, George R. Milner, Prasenjit Mitra, and James Z. Wang
2006   Cybertools and Archaeology. Science 311(5763):958–959.

Society for American Archaeology (SAA)
1990   Save the Past for the Future: Actions for the '90s. Final Report, Taos Working Conference on Preventing Archaeological Looting and Vandalism. Washington, DC: Society for American Archaeology.
2007   Special Section: Revisiting the Graduate Curriculum. SAA Archaeological Record 6(5):23–35.
2009   Committee on Museums, Collections, and Curation. Electronic document, https://ecommerce.saa.org/saa/staticcontent/staticpages/adminDir/committeeDisplay.cfm?Committee=COMMITTEE%2FCURA; accessed November 25, 2009.

Society for Historical Archaeology (SHA)
2003   Ethical Principles of the Society for Historical Archaeology. Electronic document, www.sha.org/about/ethics.htm, accessed Nov. 18, 2008.

Spaulding, W. Geoffrey
1994a   Kern River Pipeline Cultural Resources Data Recovery Report: Utah, vol. 1, Research Context and Data Analysis. Report prepared by Dames and Moore, Las Vegas, NV, for Kern River Gas Transmission Company, Salt Lake City, Utah. Submitted to Federal Energy Regulatory Commission, Washington, DC.
1994b   Kern River Pipeline Cultural Resources Data Recovery Report: Utah, vol. 2, Archaeological Sites along the Kern River Pipeline Corridor in Utah. Report prepared by Dames and Moore, Las Vegas, NV, for Kern River Gas Transmission Company, Salt Lake City, Utah. Submitted to Federal Energy Regulatory Commission, Washington, DC.
1994c   Kern River Pipeline Cultural Resources Data Recovery Report: Utah, vol. 3, Syntheses and Conclusions. Report prepared by Dames and Moore, Las Vegas, NV, for Kern River Gas Transmission Company, Salt Lake City, Utah. Submitted to Federal Energy Regulatory Commission, Washington, DC.

Spender, Dale
1995   Nattering on the Net: Women, Power and Cyberspace. North Melbourne, Australia: Spinifex.

Sprinkle, John H., and Theodore R. Reinhart, eds.
1999   The Archaeology of Nineteenth-Century Virginia. Special Publication 36. Richmond: Archeological Society of Virginia.

Stapp, Darby C., and Michael S. Burney
2002   Tribal Cultural Resource Management: The Full Circle of Stewardship. Walnut Creek, CA: AltaMira.

Stapp, Darby, and J. G. Longenecker
1999   The Times, They Are A-Changin': Can Archaeologists and Native Americans Change with the Times? SAA Bulletin 18(2):18–20, 27.

Stettler, Heather K., and Mathew T. Seddon, eds.
2005   From Hunters to Homesteaders: Recent Encounters with Past Communities

in Utah's West Desert. Report prepared by SWCA, Inc., Salt Lake City, UT, and Alpine Archaeological Consultants, Inc., Montrose, CO, for Kern River Gas Transmission Company, Salt Lake City.

Steward, Julian

1938   Basin-Plateau Aboriginal Socio-political Groups. Bureau of American Ethnology Bulletin 120. Washington, DC.

Stewart Millar, Melanie

1998   Cracking the Gender Code: Who Rules the Wired World? Toronto, Canada: Second Story Press.

Strojan, Ellen

2003   A Colonial Classroom: Fort Frederica National Monument. Washington, DC: National Park Service. Electronic document, www.cr.nps.gov/seac/fofr.

Stuart, George E., and Frank P. McManamon

1996   Archaeology and You. Washington, DC: National Park Service.

Sullivan, Alan P., III

2001   Surface Archaeology. Albuquerque: University of New Mexico Press.

2008   Archaeological Concepts for the Study of the Past. Albuquerque: University of New Mexico Press.

Sullivan, Lynne P., and S. Terry Childs, eds.

2003   Curating Archaeological Collections: From the Field to the Repository. Walnut Creek, CA: AltaMira.

Swidler, Nina, and Janet Cohen

1997   Issues in Intertribal Consultation. *In* Native Americans and Archaeologists: Stepping Stones to Common Ground, edited by Nina Swidler, Kurt E. Dongoske, Roger Anyon, and Alan S. Downer, pp. 197–206. Walnut Creek, CA: AltaMira.

Swidler, Nina, Kurt E. Dongoske, Roger Anyon, and Alan S. Downer, eds.

1997   Native Americans and Archaeologists: Stepping Stones to Common Ground. Walnut Creek, CA: AltaMira.

Swidler, Nina, David C. Eck, T. J. Ferguson, Leigh J. Kuwanwisiwma, Roger Anyon, Loren Panteah, Klara Kelley, and Harris Francis

2000   Multiple Views of the Past: Integrating Archaeology and Ethnography in the Jeddito Valley. CRM 9:49–53.

Thomas, David H.

1988   The Archaeology of Monitor Valley, vol. 3, Survey and Additional Excavations. Anthropological Papers of the American Museum of Natural History 66(2). New York.

2000   Skull Wars: Kennewick Man, Archaeology, and the Battle for Native American Identity. New York: Basic Books.

Thomas, Roger, and Timothy Darvill

2007   Small Pieces: Big Picture—Making Results from Contract Archaeology Illuminate the Past. Symposium organized for the annual meeting of the Society for American Archaeology, Austin, TX.

Thompson, Raymond H.
2000   An Old and Reliable Authority: An Act for the Preservation of American Antiquities. Journal of the Southwest 42(2) (whole issue).

Towse, Ruth, ed.
2003   A Handbook of Cultural Economics. London: Edward Elgar.

Travers, Ann
1999   Writing the Public in Cyberspace: Redefining Inclusion on the Net. New York: Routledge.

Trigger, Bruce G.
1986   Prehistoric Archaeology and American Society. In American Archaeology Past and Future, edited by David J. Meltzer, Don D. Fowler, and Jeremy A. Sabloff, pp. 187–215. Washington, DC: Smithsonian Institution Press.
1989   A History of Archaeological Thought. Cambridge: Cambridge University Press.

US Department of the Interior
1983   Archeology and Historic Preservation: The Secretary of the Interior's Standards and Guidelines. Federal Register 48:44716–44740.

US General Services Administration
2006   Strategies for Successful Tribal Consultation. Electronic document, www.gsa.gov/Portal/gsa/ep/contentView.do?programId=11282&channelId=17662&ooid=19506&contentId=19508&pageTypeId=8195&contentType=GSA_BASIC&programPage=%2Fep%2Fprogram%2FgsaBasic.jsp&P=PMHP.

van der Leeuw, Sander, and Charles Redman
2002   Placing Archaeology at the Center of Socio-natural Studies. American Antiquity 67(4):597–605.

van Dyke, Ruth M.
2006   Seeing the Past: Visual Media in Archaeology. American Anthropologist 108(2):370–375.

Varien, Mark D., Scott G. Ortman, Timothy A. Kohler, Donna M. Glowacki, and C. David Johnson
2007   Historical Ecology in the Mesa Verde Region: Results from the Village Ecodynamics Project. American Antiquity 72(2):273–299.

Versaggi, Nina M.
2006   NAGPRA Consultations with the Iroquois Confederacy of Sovereign Nations of New York. In Cross-Cultural Collaboration: Native Peoples and Archaeology in the Northeastern United States, edited by Jordan E. Kerber, pp. 18–31. Lincoln: University of Nebraska Press.

Vitelli, Karen D., ed.
1996   Archaeological Ethics. Walnut Creek, CA: AltaMira.

Washington State Department of Transportation
2003   Executive Order 1025, Tribal Consultation. Electronic document, www.wsdot.wa.gov/NR/rdonlyres/847C3EC9–3373–41A7–ADBE-AC4D8E3F6ED6/0/ConsultationPolicy.pdf.

Watkins, Joe

1999   Conflicting Codes: Professional, Ethical, and Legal Obligations in
        Archaeology. Science and Engineering Ethics 5(3):337–345.

2000   Indigenous Archaeology: American Indian Values and Scientific Practice.
        Walnut Creek, CA: AltaMira.

2004   Becoming American or Becoming Indian? NAGPRA, Kennewick, and
        Cultural Affiliation. Journal of Social Archaeology 4(1):60–80.

2005   The Politics of American Archaeology: Cultural Resources, Cultural
        Affiliation, and Kennewick. *In* Indigenous Archaeologies: Decolonizing
        Theory and Practice, edited by Claire Smith and H. Martin Wobst, pp.
        189–203. New York: Routledge.

Watkins, Joe, and T. J. Ferguson

2005   Working with and Working for Indigenous Communities. *In* Handbook of
        Archaeological Methods, edited by Herbert D. G. Maschner and Christopher
        Chippindale, pp. 1371–1405. Walnut Creek, CA: AltaMira.

Watkins, Joe, Lynne Goldstein, Karen Vitelli, and Leigh Jenkins

1995   Accountability: Responsibilities of Archaeologists to Other Interest Groups.
        In Ethics in American Archaeology: Challenges for the 1990s, edited by Mark
        J. Lynott and Alison Wylie, pp. 33–37. Washington, DC: Society for American
        Archaeology.

Webster, Laurie D., and Micah Loma'omvaya

2004   Textiles, Baskets, and Hopi Cultural Identity. *In* Identity, Feasting, and the
        Archaeology of the Greater Southwest, edited by Barbara J. Mills, pp. 74–82.
        Boulder: University Press of Colorado.

Welch, John R.

2000   The White Mountain Apache Tribe Heritage Program: Origins, Operations,
        and Challenges. *In* Working Together: Native Americans and Archaeologists,
        edited by Kurt E. Dongoske, Mark Aldenderfer, and Karen Doehner, pp.
        67–83. Washington, DC: Society for American Archaeology.

Welch, John R., and T. J. Ferguson

2007   Putting Patria into Repatriation: Assessing Cultural Affiliation on White
        Mountain Apache Tribal Lands. Journal of Social Archaeology 7(2):171–198.

Wendorf, Fred

1957   The New Mexico Program in Highway Archaeological Salvage. American
        Antiquity 23(1):74–78.

1962   A Guide for Salvage Archaeology. Santa Fe: Museum of New Mexico Press.

Wendorf, Fred, and Raymond H. Thompson

2002   The Committee for the Recovery of Archaeological Remains: Three Decades
        of Service to the Archaeological Profession. American Antiquity
        67(2):317–330.

White, Lynn Townsend, Jr.

1967   The Historical Roots of Our Ecological Crisis. Science 155(3767):1203–1207.

Whiteley, Peter M.

2002   Archaeology and Oral Tradition: The Scientific Importance of Dialogue.
        American Antiquity 67(3):405–415.

Whitson, Brian

2004   Omohundro Conference Redefines Field of Historical Significance. William and Mary News, March 12, 2004. Electronic document, http://web.wm.edu/news/archive/index .php?id=3467.

Wildesen, Leslie E.

1984   The Search for an Ethic in Archaeology: An Historic Perspective. *In* Ethics and Values in Archaeology, edited by Ernestene L. Green, pp. 3–12. New York: Free Press.

Wilkins, David E., and K. Tsianina Lomawaima

2001   Uneven Ground: American Indian Sovereignty and Federal Law. Norman: University of Oklahoma Press.

Wilshusen, Richard H.

1995   Conclusions, Management Suggestions, and Directions for Future Research. *In* The Cedar Hill Special Treatment Project, compiled by Richard H. Wilshusen, pp. 117–120. Research Papers 1. Dolores, CO: La Plata Archaeological Consultants.

Wilshusen, Richard H., comp.

1995   The Cedar Hill Special Treatment Project: Late Pueblo I, Early Navajo, and Historic Occupations in Northwestern New Mexico. Research Papers 1. Dolores, CO: La Plata Archaeological Consultants.

Wilshusen, Richard H., Leslie M. Sesler, and Timothy D. Hovezak

2000   Pueblo I Sites across the San Juan Region. *In* Frances Mesa Alternative Treatment Project, compiled by R. H. Wilshusen, T. D. Hovezak, and L. M. Sesler, pp. 111–157. Research Paper 3. Dolores, CO: La Plata Archaeological Consultants.

Winter, Joseph C.

1984   The Way to Somewhere: Ethics in American Archaeology. *In* Ethics and Values in Archaeology, edited by Ernestene L. Green, pp. 36–47. New York: Free Press.

Wittkofski, J. Mark, and Theodore R. Reinhart, eds.

1989   Paleoindian Research in Virginia: A Synthesis. Special Publications 19. Richmond: Archeological Society of Virginia.

Woodall, J. Ned, ed.

1990   Predicaments, Pragmatics, and Professionalism: Ethical Conduct in Archeology. Oklahoma City: Society of Professional Archeologists.

Woodcock, David G.

1996   Professional Certification for Preservation and Rehabilitation. *In* Standards for Preservation and Rehabilitation, edited by Steven J. Kelley, pp. 100–108. West Conshohocken, PA: ASTM (American Society for Testing Materials) International.

World Archaeological Congress

n.d.   World Archaeological Congress Codes of Ethics, including the First Code of Ethics (adopted 1990), the Vermillion Accord on Human Remains (adopted

1989), and the Tamaki Makau-rau Accord on the Display of Human Remains and Sacred Objects (adopted 2006). Electronic document, www.worldarchae ologicalcongress.org/site/about_ethi.php, accessed Nov. 17, 2008.

Wylie, Alison

1995   Archaeology and the Antiquities Market: The Use of Looted Data. *In* Ethics in American Archaeology: Challenges for the 1990s, edited by Mark J. Lynott and Alison Wylie, pp. 17–21. Washington, DC: Society for American Archaeology.

1999   Science, Conservation, and Stewardship: Evolving Codes of Conduct in Archaeology. Science and Engineering Ethics 5(3):319–336.

2000   Ethical Dilemmas in Archaeological Practice: Looting, Repatriation, Stewardship, and the (Trans)Formation of Disciplinary Identity. *In* Ethics in American Archaeology, 2nd ed., edited by Mark J. Lynott and Alison Wylie, pp. 138–157. Washington, DC: Society for American Archaeology.

Yamin, Rebecca

1997   New York's Mythic Slum: Digging Lower Manhattan's Infamous Five Points. Archaeology 50(2):44–53.

Yamin, Rebecca, ed.

2000   Tales of Five Points: Working-Class Life in Nineteenth-Century New York. Westchester, PA: John Milner Associates.

Zeanah, David W., Eric Ingbar, Robert Elston, and Charles Zeier

2004   Archaeological Predictive Model, Management Plan, and Treatment Plans for Northern Railroad Valley, Nevada. Cultural Resources Series 15. Reno: Bureau of Land Management, Nevada (www.blm.gov/nv).

Zier, Christian J., and Stephen M. Kalasz

1999   Colorado Prehistory: A Context for the Arkansas River Basin. Denver: Colorado Council of Professional Archaeologists.

Zimmerman, Larry J.

2000   Remythologizing the Relationship between Indians and Archaeologists. *In* Native Americans and Archaeologists: Stepping Stones to Common Ground, edited by Nina Swidler, Kurt E. Dongoske, Roger Anyon, and Alan S. Downer, pp. 44–56. Walnut Creek, CA: AltaMira.

Zimmerman, Larry J., Karen D. Vitelli, and Julie Hollowell-Zimmer, eds.

2003   Ethical Issues in Archaeology. Walnut Creek, CA: AltaMira.

Index

land-use planning, 83–85, 87, 89
law enforcement: and public education,
278–79; and site protection, 47
Lawrence, John, 125–26
Lees, William, 4, 144, 147
legislation: and history of CRM archae-
ology, 39; and public perceptions of
cultural resource laws and policies,
60; and public policy on CRM archae-
ology, 7–11
Lemley, Harry J., 21
Leone, Mark, 156, 157
Leventhal, Richard M., 163
Life and Traditions of the Red Man, The
(Nicolar 2007), 158
Lightfoot, Kent G., 156
Lillie Parsons (schooner), 150
Lipe, William D., 3, 14, 16, 30, 36, 38, 92,
117, 132, 157, 184, 224, 242, 243, 244,
249n2–3, 285, 297
Little, Barbara J., 242–43, 244, 251n12
locational predictive modeling, 73, 106
Loco Hills (New Mexico), 80–83
looting: and Great Depression, 22–23;
protection of sites from, 47, 57–58.
See also treasury recovery companies
Lowenthal, David, 54, 234
Lynott, Mark E., 227, 230

Mackey, Douglas, 15, 287–88, 294–95
magazines, and communication with public, 271–72
Maine, Penobscots and history of, 158
Making Archaeology Teaching Relevant
in the XXIst Century (MATRIX), 267
Malloy, Maureen, 61
*Management of Archeological Resources: The
Airlie House Report, The* (McGimsey
and Davis 1977), 224
Managing Archaeological Collections
program (National Park Service),
250n8
marine sanctuaries, 250n7
Maryland: collections management and
historic preservation in, 146; and
synthetic studies, 155, 156
Maryland Archaeological Conservation

Laboratory (MAC Lab), 145–47, 150,
167n3
MATRIX (Making Archaeology Teaching
Relevant in the XXI Century), 36
McGimsey, Charles R., III, 28, 29, 70, 120,
225, 227, 233–34, 254, 255, 257, 295,
296
McGuire, Randall H., 246
McManamon, Francis P., 38, 176, 295
media: and business model for contract
archaeology, 220; and communication
with public about archaeology, 262–
63, 265–66, 269–75. *See also* newspapers; television
memorandum of agreement (MOA), 127,
275–76
Mesa Verde archaeological region, 154
Metcalf Archaeological Consultants, Inc.,
134
middle-range theory, 73
military installations, and significance-
based management, 109
Minnis, Paul E., 209
mitigation: alternative or creative
approaches to, 121–22; and current
compliance with NHPA, 117–20,
275–77; ethics of creative approaches
to, 160; and examples of innovative
projects, 122–35; and future of CRM
archaeology, 293; obstacles to innovative approaches for, 135–36; public
perception of, 115–16; and significance-based management, 107–108;
and standard methods of archaeological data recovery, 116–17; strategies
for moving forward with innovative
approaches to, 136–39; and treatment
phase of Section 106 process, 71
Montana State University, 134
Moss, Frank, 28
multiyear preservation easements, 119
Museum of Underwater Archaeology, 267
museums: and communication with general public, 260; and implementation
of NAGPRA, 172. *See also* collections
management
Mythbusters (television), 270

perception of archaeologists, 198
Programmatic Agreements, 276
Project Archaeology (BLM), 134–35
protective communities, 250n9
public archaeology: context for communication in, 261–63; growth of interest
in, 166; multiple publics for, 286–87;
and politics, 275; public support for,
254; and university courses in CRM
archaeology, 166, 201, 202
Public Archeology (McGimsey 1972), 28
publications: and archaeological resource
values, 50–51; and archaeological
writing for popular audiences, 259;
and future of CRM archaeology, 297;
and innovative approaches to mitigation, 138; and value of archaeological
research, 212. *See also* communication;
dissemination; gray literature
public benefits: and future of CRM
archaeology, 63, 284–86; as goal of
archaeological resource management,
46; and investigator-initiated research,
51–52; and research values of archaeological sites, 50
public education: and archaeological
mitigation projects, 134–35; and
archaeological resource values, 58–60;
and civic engagement, 251n12; and
dissemination of data and interpretations, 161; and future of CRM archaeology, 291–92; and Native American
interests in archaeology and historic
preservation, 186; for private landowners and public officials, 261, 278;
and proposed amendments to
National Historic Preservation Act in
2005–2006, 39
public history, 40
public opinion: importance of, 196; on
mitigation, 115–16; on protection of
archaeological sites, 242; on value of
archaeological sites and historic
preservation, 254
public policy: and graduate education,
266; and legislative basis of CRM
archaeology, 7–11; and public percep-

tions of cultural resources laws, 60;
and significance-based management,
114
public service announcements (PSAs),
272
Pueblo peoples, and study of historical
ecology, 154. *See also* Zuni, Pueblo of

Radio, and communication with public,
270, 271, 272
Railroad Valley (Nevada), 74–80
rationality, and NHPA Section 106
process, 73–83
Reagan, Ronald, 32, 250n7
Redman, Charles, 38, 210
regional approaches: focus on in CRM
archaeology, 66–67; and NHPA
Section 106 process, 86–89
"Regional Centers in Archaeology: Prospects and Problems" (May 1976), 31
regional databases, cooperative research
and development of, 217–18
regional planning models, 85
Register of Professional Archaeologists,
181–82, 205–208, 226, 229–30, 231,
245, 249n3, 251n13, 294
"Renewing American Archaeology" conferences, 37–38, 39, 295
"Renewing Our National Archaeological
Program" (conferences), 12
research, and archaeological resource
values, 48–53
"Research Exchange, The," 297
reserves, Section 110 of NHPA and establishment of, 108–109
Reservoir Salvage Act of 1960, 8, 11, 26
resistance, and historical modes of interaction with descendant communities,
188, 189, 291
resource management plans, 104
resource sensitivity maps, 86–87, 103–104
Richard B. Russell Dam and Lake (South
Carolina/Georgia), 155
Ritchey, Thomas, 156–57
River Basin Surveys (SI-RBS), 25, 26, 257
Rockies Express Pipeline (Colorado), 134
Roosevelt, Theodore, 20, 253–54, 281

School for Advanced Research Advanced Seminar Series

PUBLISHED BY SAR PRESS

CHACO & HOHOKAM: PREHISTORIC
REGIONAL SYSTEMS IN THE AMERICAN
SOUTHWEST
Patricia L. Crown & W. James Judge, eds.

RECAPTURING ANTHROPOLOGY: WORKING IN
THE PRESENT
Richard G. Fox, ed.

WAR IN THE TRIBAL ZONE: EXPANDING
STATES AND INDIGENOUS WARFARE
R. Brian Ferguson &
Neil L. Whitehead, eds.

IDEOLOGY AND PRE-COLUMBIAN
CIVILIZATIONS
Arthur A. Demarest &
Geoffrey W. Conrad, eds.

DREAMING: ANTHROPOLOGICAL AND
PSYCHOLOGICAL INTERPRETATIONS
Barbara Tedlock, ed.

HISTORICAL ECOLOGY: CULTURAL
KNOWLEDGE AND CHANGING LANDSCAPES
Carole L. Crumley, ed.

THEMES IN SOUTHWEST PREHISTORY
George J. Gumerman, ed.

MEMORY, HISTORY, AND OPPOSITION UNDER
STATE SOCIALISM
Rubie S. Watson, ed.

OTHER INTENTIONS: CULTURAL CONTEXTS
AND THE ATTRIBUTION OF INNER STATES
Lawrence Rosen, ed.

LAST HUNTERS–FIRST FARMERS: NEW
PERSPECTIVES ON THE PREHISTORIC
TRANSITION TO AGRICULTURE
T. Douglas Price &
Anne Birgitte Gebauer, eds.

MAKING ALTERNATIVE HISTORIES:
THE PRACTICE OF ARCHAEOLOGY AND
HISTORY IN NON-WESTERN SETTINGS
Peter R. Schmidt & Thomas C. Patterson, eds.

SENSES OF PLACE
Steven Feld & Keith H. Basso, eds.

CYBORGS & CITADELS: ANTHROPOLOGICAL
INTERVENTIONS IN EMERGING SCIENCES AND
TECHNOLOGIES
Gary Lee Downey & Joseph Dumit, eds.

THE ORIGINS OF LANGUAGE: WHAT
NONHUMAN PRIMATES CAN TELL US
Barbara J. King, ed.

CRITICAL ANTHROPOLOGY NOW:
UNEXPECTED CONTEXTS, SHIFTING
CONSTITUENCIES, CHANGING AGENDAS
George E. Marcus, ed.

ARCHAIC STATES
Gary M. Feinman & Joyce Marcus, eds.

REGIMES OF LANGUAGE: IDEOLOGIES,
POLITIES, AND IDENTITIES
Paul V. Kroskrity, ed.

BIOLOGY, BRAINS, AND BEHAVIOR: THE
EVOLUTION OF HUMAN DEVELOPMENT
Sue Taylor Parker, Jonas Langer, &
Michael L. McKinney, eds.

WOMEN & MEN IN THE PREHISPANIC
SOUTHWEST: LABOR, POWER, & PRESTIGE
Patricia L. Crown, ed.

HISTORY IN PERSON: ENDURING STRUGGLES,
CONTENTIOUS PRACTICE, INTIMATE
IDENTITIES
Dorothy Holland & Jean Lave, eds.

THE EMPIRE OF THINGS: REGIMES OF VALUE
AND MATERIAL CULTURE
Fred R. Myers, ed.

CATASTROPHE & CULTURE: THE
ANTHROPOLOGY OF DISASTER
Susanna M. Hoffman &
Anthony Oliver-Smith, eds.

URUK MESOPOTAMIA & ITS NEIGHBORS:
CROSS-CULTURAL INTERACTIONS IN THE ERA
OF STATE FORMATION
Mitchell S. Rothman, ed.

REMAKING LIFE & DEATH: TOWARD AN
ANTHROPOLOGY OF THE BIOSCIENCES
Sarah Franklin & Margaret Lock, eds.

TIKAL: DYNASTIES, FOREIGNERS,
& AFFAIRS OF STATE: ADVANCING
MAYA ARCHAEOLOGY
Jeremy A. Sabloff, ed.

GRAY AREAS: ETHNOGRAPHIC ENCOUNTERS
WITH NURSING HOME CULTURE
Philip B. Stafford, ed.

PLURALIZING ETHNOGRAPHY: COMPARISON
AND REPRESENTATION IN MAYA CULTURES,
HISTORIES, AND IDENTITIES
John M. Watanabe & Edward F. Fischer, eds.

AMERICAN ARRIVALS: ANTHROPOLOGY
ENGAGES THE NEW IMMIGRATION
Nancy Foner, ed.

PUBLISHED BY CAMBRIDGE UNIVERSITY PRESS

Participants in the School for Advanced Research advanced seminar
"Archaeology and Public Policy: A New Vision for the Future," Santa
Fe, New Mexico, July 15–19, 2007. Left to right: William D. Lipe,
Sarah T. Bridges, Pat Barker, Lynne Sebastian, David Colin Crass,
Hester A. Davis, T. J. Ferguson, Susan M. Chandler, Douglas P. Mackey, Jr.,
and Douglas Schwartz.